Highway Users Federation
FOR SAFETY AND MOBILITY

A R C O

Bus Driver's
Guide To Commercial
Driver Licensing

Contains the
QUESTIONS
& ANSWERS
you need to pass
the test

CDL

What You Need To Know To Become Licensed!

BUS DRIVER'S GUIDE TO COMMERCIAL DRIVER LICENSING

by
**HIGHWAY USERS FEDERATION
FOR SAFETY and MOBILITY
and
ROBERT M. CALVIN**

FROM NOW ON,

ONLY THE BEST WILL DRIVE

ARCO
New York

Senior Editor: Marilyn M. Martin
Assistant Editor: Valerie L. Gervin
Graphic Designer: Mark Harris
Technical Support: Don Harris
Desktop Publishing: Alan Borie/Hector Arvizu
Artwork: Jim Koehler

Apple is a trademark of Apple Computer, Inc.
LaserWriter II NTX is a trademark of Apple Computer, Inc.
Macintosh is a trademark of Apple Computer, Inc.
PageMaker is a trademark of Aldus Corporation
Freehand is a trademark of Aldus Corporation
Word is a trademarek of Microsoft Corp.

95% of this guide was produced by Desktop Publishing techniques
using Microsoft Word, Aldus PageMaker and Aldus Freehand on
Macintosh Computers and output to a LaserWriter II NTX printer.

This publication is designed to provide accurate and authoritative information in regard to the subject matter covered. It is sold with the understanding that the publisher is not engaged in rendering legal, accounting or other professional service. If legal advice or other expert assistance is required, the service of a competent professional person should be sought.

Disclaimer: The information in this book has been obtained from sourcss believed to be reliable. However, because of the possibility of human or mechanical error, the Publisher does not guarantee its accuracy, adequacy, or completeness and is not responsible for any errors, omissions, misprintings, or ambiguities contained herein, or for the results obtained from use of such information. The book has not been examined for safety engineering, compliance with OSHA , consumer or workplace safety or similar or dissimilar laws or regulations. No responsibility is assumed for any injury and or/damage to persons or property as a matter of products liability, negligence or otherwise, or for any use or operation of any methods, products, instructions, or ideas contained herein.

For large quantity purchases for school use, contact:
    Career Publishing, Inc.
    910 N. Main Street, Orange. CA 92667
    1 (800) 854-4014
    *Order number CPB-177-X
Companies are invited to purchase large quantities for training use at attractive discounts. Contact:
    Simon & Schuster Special Sales Department
    15 Columbus Circle, New York, NY 10023
    (212) 373-8026

First Edition

 ARCO

Simon & Schuster, Inc.
15 Columbus Circle
New York, NY 10023

DISTRIBUTED BY PRENTICE HALL TRADE SALES

Manufactured in the United States of America

1 2 3 4 5 6 7 8 9 10

Library of Congress Cataloging-in-Publication Data

Bus driver's guide to commercial driver licensing / by Highway Users
    Federation for Safety and Mobility and Robert M. Calvin
        p. cm.
    ISBN 0-13-091885-7: $24.95
    1. Bus driving. 2. Bus drivers—Licenses—United States.
I. Calvin, Robert M. II. Highway Users Federation for Safety and
Mobility
TL232.3.B86 1990
629.28'333'0973—dc20

89-27172
CIP

Table of Contents

Bus Driver's Complete Guide to Commercial Driver Licensing with Reference Material

CHAPTER 3
THE LICENSING PROGRAM **79**

PART II

CHAPTER 4
WHAT EVERY COMMERCIAL DRIVER SHOULD KNOW 113

CHAPTER 5
CARRYING PASSENGERS SAFELY 239

Introduction

Although the author's goal is to keep the GUIDE simple and easy to read, yet it must be detailed enough to be useful. Because of this detail, the text is meant not so much to be read as to be used. As you read and study it, you will realize this manual is really a guidebook. That is why the title is the BUS DRIVER'S COMPLETE GUIDE TO COMMERCIAL DRIVER LICENSING.

If you wish to properly drive a bus, you will — at some point — have to acquire most of the material which is presented here. You may find using this GUIDE is the easiest and most painless way.

The BUS DRIVER'S COMPLETE GUIDE... is not a substitute for the manual your state issues, and it does not cover all federal, state, or local laws that pertain to driving a bus. As a bus driver, you will be expected to know and follow the Federal Motor Carrier Safety Regulations as well as state and local laws, so you will have to assume the responsibility of obtaining the materials which contain such information. This book will provide, however, all of the information that you need for obtaining your commercial driver's license.

The BUS DRIVER'S COMPLETE GUIDE... is in five parts. The first part introduces the bus driver's licensing system created by the Commercial Motor Vehicle Safety Act of 1986. It explains the national license, defines key terms, and illustrates the vehicles which bus drivers operate.

Part Two is a bus driver's manual in itself. There are four chapters. Chapter Four covers the "common core" of driving knowledge and safe practices which all commercial drivers should know and on which they may be tested. Chapter Five contains the material which should be studied by persons who will operate buses. The information in this chapter applies, in general, to operating all types of buses. Chapter Six is for drivers who intend to operate buses equipped with air brakes. Chapter Seven is about driving a tractor-trailer bus.

Part Three is devoted to bus driver's license tests. Chapters Eight through Eleven cover the various knowledge tests an applicant can be expected to take. Behind-the-wheel skill tests and road tests are explained in Chapters Twelve through Fourteen.

Part Four contains the behind-the-wheel skill tests and road tests. Test helpers are provided as well as practice exercises.

Part Five is the reference segment of the BUS DRIVER'S COMPLETE GUIDE... This Part offers fourteen sections of resource material. Each section provides specific, detailed information on subject areas which are important to commercial driver licensing.

About the Author

Robert M. Calvin is Manager of Highway Safety Programs for the Highway Users Federation and the Automotive Safety Foundation of Washington, D.C. He is a specialist in the field of driver and traffic safety education and training programs. In addition, he serves as a Technical Services Consultant for the Professional Truck Driver Institute of America (PTDIA).

Mr. Calvin has worked at the local, state, and national levels as a teacher, research associate, curriculum developer, evaluator, consultant, instructional technologist, and technical writer. He has developed numerous innovative instructional materials for use in traffic safety education and training programs that range from pre-school to adult education. He has authored many articles, books, and film programs that deal with traffic safety, highway user behavior, and driver education and training.

Mr. Calvin has broad experience in the evaluation of heavy vehicle driver training courses. He has served on numerous on-site evaluation teams including those of the PTDIA. He was instrumental in the development and pilot-test evaluation of the curricular and certification documents by which the PTDIA certifies the quality of truck driver training courses for organizations that voluntarily seek such certification.

The Highway Users Federation

The Highway Users Federation is a national coalition of corporations, associations, and individuals committed to securing better, safer highway transportation for the entire nation. Bringing together a membership of 400 major corporations, companies, and business associations from more than 20 different industry areas, it is the largest, most diverse private-sector highway transportation and traffic safety support organization in America.

The Federation has its headquarters in Washington, D.C. and maintains 14 regional offices around the country. These regional offices work with the affiliated highway user groups in every state and in 12 metropolitan areas.

For more than 50 years, the Federation and its predecessors have led the private sector movement to improve highway safety and efficiency. Its longstanding record as a major influence in the highway safety movement uniquely equips the Federation for its current leadership role in helping to shape the future of commercial carrier safety.

Preface

Material which covers licensing bus drivers is often hard to find. Usually, there is no one book to which you may turn. You have to go to several sources to get all the facts. This is a real handicap; one we hope the BUS DRIVER'S COMPLETE GUIDE... eliminates.

There is another problem. A national driver's license law for commercial vehicle drivers is now on the books. All states, including your own, are gearing up to comply with it. This law, the Commercial Motor Vehicle Safety Act of 1986, will be in full effect by 1993. This means that truck and bus drivers, including school bus drivers, are under a new set of licensing rules.

Your bus driver's license will still be issued by your state. You will still take a state test. Your license will still be from your state, but the state is now bound by law to follow federal regulations. That is why it is called a national license.

What you need to know and do to obtain a bus driver's license is the basis for this text. With all of the federal and state rules and laws, plus a national license, there is a lot to know and do. A quick review of what you will need to know to drive a bus follows. There are at least five levels of information or knowledge which apply.

Knowledge of Safe Driving

It is assumed that persons applying for a commercial driver's license are already licensed as automobile drivers. There is a body of facts and rules all drivers must possess. Reading and understanding road signs is one example. Knowing the basic rules of the road is another. This information is covered by your state's basic operator's license tests. Your state's Driver's Manual provides an up-to-date review of the basic knowledge you are expected to know. If you do not have a copy of this manual, get one. The BUS DRIVER'S COMPLETE GUIDE... provides "A General Knowledge Test On Safe Driving" for your use. This test, along with an explanation of answers, is found in Appendix A.

Knowledge of State and Local Laws

Bus drivers are subject to state and local laws as well as federal regulations. Each state has its own laws, procedures, and regulations covering bus operations. These rules may exceed federal requirements. The same may be true for local jurisdictions. It is beyond the scope and space limits of this book to cover the particular requirements of each state and local area. However, the BUS DRIVER'S COMPLETE GUIDE includes a Model Uniform Commercial Driver's License Act in Appendix B to give you an idea of what a "model" state law should say. Local school districts and others who transport school children have their own requirements in addition to those covered by federal and state law. You will need to become familiar with these rules if they apply to you.

Knowledge of Federal Regulations

The Commercial Motor Vehicle Safety Act of 1986 (CMVSA/86) requires all commercial drivers to have a working knowledge of Federal regulations. This knowledge pertains to the safe operation of commercial vehicles. It is found in Title 49 of the Code of Federal Regulations. Parts 390 through 399 of Title 49 are called the Federal Motor Carrier Safety Regulations (FMCSR). All commercial drivers, including bus drivers, should be familiar with them. As a condition of employment you may be tested on the FMCSR. The FMCSR are not reproduced in this book. You can and should obtain a copy of them. The FMCSR are available from the:

U.S. Government Printing Office, Washington, D.C. 20401

Ask for 49 CFR 200-399. A complete list of GPO Bookstores is provided in Appendix C. Handy small size editions are available from organizations such as the American Trucking Association, 2200 Mill Road, Alexandria, VA 22314. The BUS DRIVER'S COMPLETE GUIDE... does, however, include a summary of the FMCSR and includes the standard written test on federal regulations in Section D.

Knowledge of Personal Safety Principles

Most of the knowledge requirements for licensing are about protecting the safety of the public, but much information on protecting your own safety as a commercial driver and employee is also included. There are some actions involved in driving a truck or bus which do not present a crash hazard or danger to the highway-using public, but drivers should know. For example, a trucker should wear a hard hat while loading cargo. There is a correct way to exit a cab and a proper method of using a citizen's band radio and other types of equipment. You also need to know how to protect yourself during crimes of hijacking, theft, larceny, etc.

As you can see, many personal and general safety principles are not included in the licensing process, yet they are very important because they deal with your safety. Licensing manuals, tests, and guides such as this are designed to serve a licensing, not training, purpose. Remember, licensing and training programs have different goals. Both are important, but the BUS DRIVER'S COMPLETE GUIDE... focuses on the licensing process, so it may not cover all of the personal safety principles important to you.

Desirable Knowledge

The licensing process recognizes that there are bus driving knowledges and skills which do not present a public safety threat and may be acquired after licensing. Remember, the licensing process concentrates on items which pose a hazard or threat to public safety. The content of driver's licensing manuals and tests focuses on public safety priorities and essential information. As a result, there is a body of knowledge which may be desirable (good to know) but may not be essential (need to know) during the licensing process. What this means is that:

- Obtaining a license does not end the learning process.

- There are knowledges and skills to be acquired after licensing.

- The licensing process may not deal with knowledges and skills covered by other tests, procedures and programs.

- Certain types of knowledge that need to be learned for reasons other than licensing.

Chapters Four through Seven present the body of knowledge from which the written test questions are chosen. Again, these chapters deal only with the information necessary for licensing. For comparison purposes, we have included a list of the knowledge requirements for the commercial driver in Part Five — Section G. This will help you identify information a bus driver should know which goes beyond the licensing requirements.

Remember that licensing requirements focus on attitudes and behavior that are critical for safely operating a CMV and protecting the public safety. Yet, there are other attitudes and behavior which are critical to truck and bus driver success. These include such things as self-improvement, fuel economy, employer policies, public and employer relations, trip planning, map reading, record keeping, and vehicle specifications — to name a few.

In summary, the BUS DRIVER'S COMPLETE GUIDE... is about driver licensing, is not state-specific, assumes you already are licensed to drive a car, provides training material related to licensing requirements, and for the best results you should use, along with the GUIDE, any commercial driving material you can obtain, especially:

- Your state's rules of the road manual and commercial driver licensing material.
- The Federal Motor Carrier Safety Regulations.

Since the Guide discusses the national CDL in general and not the laws of any one state, you will do well to study, at the same time or later, your state's licensing rules.

Acknowledgements

The Highway Users Federation for Safety and Mobility is deeply grateful to Career Publishing Incorporated for making this publication possible. Particularly:

Harold A. Haase, Publisher, whose initiative, support, commitment, and overall management and supervision guided the publication from its inception to its successful completion.

Marilyn M. Martin, Senior Editor and Project Coordinator, for her detailed manuscript review, editing, and coordination of project activities.

In addition, appreciation and recognition is extended to the following people for their efforts: Valerie L. Gervin, Assistant Editor; Don Harris, Technical Support; Mark Harris, Graphic Designer; Alan Borie and Hector Arvizu, Desktop Publishing; and Jim Koehler, Artwork.

Special appreciation is also expressed to the Professional Truck Driver Institute of America for their cooperation, assistance, and guidance in the early stages of project planning. Information from which the Guide was prepared came from a variety of sources. However, particularly extensive use was made of information contained in the following publications:

* Wylie, C. Dennis and Schultz, Ted. *Model Driver's Manual for Commercial Vehicle Driver Licensing.* Essex Corporation, January, 1989.
* U. S. Department of Transportation. "Commercial Driver Testing and Licensing Standards; Final Rule." Federal Highway Administration. *Federal Register,* July 21, 1988.

PART ONE
BUS DRIVER'S GUIDE
TO COMMERCIAL DRIVER LICENSING

This section of the book explains the Commercial Motor Vehicle Safety Act of 1986 and the national commercial driver's licensing program as it impacts bus drivers. The three chapters that comprise it are listed below.

Chapter 1: A National License
This chapter presents the need for a national license by citing abuses to licensing that have occured in the past. Specific problems that have occurred because of drivers with multiple licenses are discussed, as well as requirements for drivers and federal disqualifications.

Chapter 2: Terms and Buses
Because many bus drivers, such as those for schools and churches, are not acquainted with the variety of buses available, this entire chapter has been devoted to descriptions and drawings of buses and definitions of bus terms.

Chapter 3: The Licensing Program
A definition of the drivers that are covered by the CDL program is given, along with the national rules for states, and what states may do in addition to the national rules. The CDL classifications and endorsements are given, and the necessary tests for each category are listed.

A NATIONAL LICENSE

CHAPTER

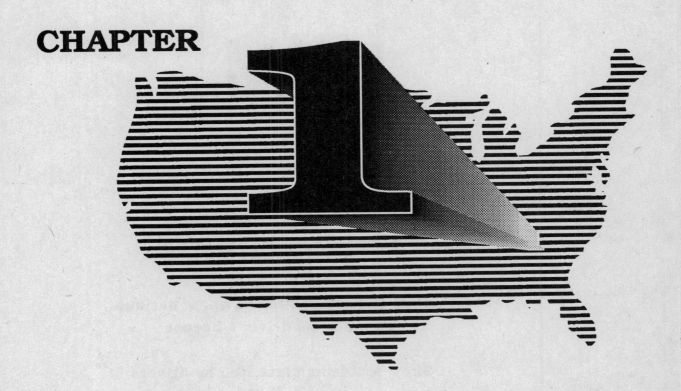

FROM NOW ON,

ONLY THE BEST WILL DRIVE

Chapter Objectives

Explain the reasons for having a national
commercial driver's license

Show problems presented by drivers
having many licenses

Describe the Commercial Motor Vehicle
Safety Act of 1986 and the commercial
driver's license

Explain licensing procedures and
violations which can disqualify a driver

CHAPTER ONE

A NATIONAL LICENSE

Who are the best drivers on the road? Who should be the best drivers? How good should they be?

In times past, people said truck and bus drivers should be the best drivers, and they were. In the public's mind, truck and bus drivers were true *professionals*. So good, in fact, that the third question did not even need an answer — but times have changed.

Today, the public, Congress and everyone else who cares are concerned only with this third question. There are a lot of good reasons for this concern.

Good Reasons

THE NATIONAL COMMERCIAL DRIVER LICENSE

FROM NOW ON,

ONLY THE BEST WILL DRIVE

IF YOU DRIVE A COMMERCIAL MOTOR VEHICLE YOU MAY NEED THE NATIONAL COMMERCIAL DRIVER LICENSE (CDL). "COMMERCIAL MOTOR VEHICLE" MEANS ANY SINGLE OR COMBINATION VEHICLE USED IN COMMERCE TO TRANSPORT PROPERTY OR PASSENGERS, INCLUDING:

- A VEHICLE WITH A GROSS VEHICLE WEIGHT RATING OF 26,001 POUNDS OR MORE.

- A TRAILER WITH A GROSS VEHICLE WEIGHT RATING OF 10,001 POUNDS OR MORE.

- ANY VEHICLE WHICH TRANSPORTS HAZARDOUS MATERIALS THAT REQUIRE PLACARDING.

- A BUS DESIGNED TO TRANSPORT MORE THAN 15 PASSENGERS INCLUDING THE DRIVER.

NOTE: THESE ARE MINIMUM REQUIREMENTS. YOUR STATE MAY HAVE STRICTER STANDARDS.

For one thing, there are more trucks and buses than ever. While these big vehicles are becoming longer, wider, higher and heavier, cars are getting smaller. The number of **vehicles** trying to "share" the road is growing faster than ever. In fact, for every mile of road, there are 45 vehicles trying to share it. Look at the numbers:

More Big Vehicles

Year	Registered Vehicles (millions)	Licensed Drivers (millions)	Miles of Streets and Roads (millions)	Vehicles per Mile of Road (average)
1960	74	87	3.5	21
1970	109	112	3.7	29
1980	157	145	3.9	40
1985	172	157	3.9	44
1988	177	160	3.9	45

Source: Federal Highway Administration

FIGURE 1-1

If you like numbers, here is one more. If all our motor vehicles were parked along every road and street in the country, there would be one car, truck, or bus every 117 feet! That is a large number of vehicles! This number is even more amazing because it includes all miles of all toll roads, **interstate** highways, city streets and unpaved country roads.

The public's big concern, of course, is the Nation's *commercial* vehicles. First, let's look at the total number of cars, buses, and trucks.

Year	Cars	Buses	Trucks	Total
1960	62,000,000	271,000	12,000,000	74,271,000
1970	89,000,000	380,000	19,000,000	108,380,000
1980	22,000,000	528,000	34,000,000	156,528,000
1985	132,000,000	593,000	39,000,000	171,593,000

Source: Federal Highway Administration

FIGURE 1-2

Now we will break down the number of buses. This should give you a better idea of the size and make up of the nation's bus fleet.

Year	Publicly Owned School Buses	Privately Owned School Buses*	Transit Buses and Intercity Buses	Federal Buses	Total Buses
1960	134,000	61,000	75,000	900	270,900
1970	193,000	95,000	90,000	2,000	380,000
1980	270,000	147,000	107,000	4,000	528,000
1985	320,000	159,000	110,000	4,500	593,500

* Includes church, industrial, and other private buses
Source: Federal Highway Administration

FIGURE 1-3

Of the buses on the road in 1985, four out of five were school buses:

	Number	Percent
School Buses*	479,000	81%
Transit Buses (city service)	55,000	9%
Intercity Buses	25,000	4%
Other Buses	34,500	6%
Total	593,500	100%

*Combines publicly and privately owned school buses
 Source: Federal Highway Administration
 National Research Council — Special Report 216. 1987

FIGURE 1-4

Here is an estimate of the miles that school, transit, and intercity buses travel each year:

	Miles Traveled
School Buses	3,400,000,000
Transit Buses	1,600,000,000
Intercity Buses	3,300,000,000

Based on 1985 travel

FIGURE 1-5

That's a lot of travel from a lot of buses.

Many Unqualified Drivers

The increase in bus and truck travel will continue. Mileage is expected to double by the end of the century. This means more drivers will be operating more vehicles. That is another reason the public wants bus and truck drivers to be *qualified* to drive the vehicles they operate.

There are more than 160 million licensed drivers in the United States today. Each driver deserves some promise that fellow motorists are properly qualified to drive their vehicles.

In 19 states, prior to 1986, any person licensed to drive a car could also legally operate a heavy duty truck. They could operate a tractor-trailer or big bus in traffic. No special license or training was required. Yet, we all know that certain types of big vehicles call for special skills, knowledge, and other qualifications. An ordinary automobile driver's license is not enough! Even today, too many drivers may be operating vehicles that they may not be qualified to drive.

We use the year 1986 because that is when our national licensing program for commercial drivers was started. Yet, the safety problems go back far beyond the 1980s.

By 1986, only 32 states issued some form of a classified driver's license. You will be reading a lot about this type of license. It is the license which shows the type of vehicles the holder may operate.

The other 18 states did not test drivers if the *applicant* met certain conditions, such as testing by the employer or proof of approved training. Some states and the District of Columbia did not make applicants prove they could drive the kinds of vehicles they were licensed to drive.

Drivers in these states who might have been qualified to drive only a passenger car could also drive an 18-wheeler or a three-axle intercity bus. Little wonder the public was edgy.

WHAT IS A COMMERCIAL MOTOR VEHICLE (CMV)?

- A vehicle with a gross vehicle weight rating of 26,001 or more pounds

- A vehicle designed to carry more than 15 passengers

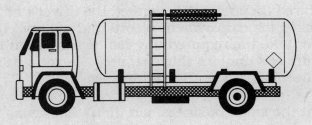

- Any vehicle, regardless of weight, transporting hazardous materials

FIGURE 1-6

Many Licenses

Another problem is presented by many driver's licenses. Some commercial drivers avoid possible license suspension by holding licenses in more than one state. By spreading their violations among several states, these drivers try to stay ahead of the law. And, unfortunately, they stay behind the wheel.

Holding more than one license is *illegal* today. Still, it occurs, and unsafe commercial drivers remain behind the wheel. On the other hand, there are men and women who drive millions of miles without *violations*, accidents, or tricky licenses. These are the drivers who work hard. They honor the public trust. They are true professionals because they care. These professionals work for the busing industry as well as the trucking industry. Those who oppose our national license program are not the pro's — the drivers who care — but the ones who abuse the state licensing program.

Here is a story about a bus company:

Once there was a small businessman who decided to go into the bus industry. Perhaps he was naive, but he wanted to be safe, legal, and comply with all the rules. He bought a bus and put $150,000 of his money on the table. He got his financing. He got his *authority* from the Interstate Commerce Commission. He filed for all the required licenses from his state and other states. He paid his seat mile taxes and got his fuel stamps and markers. Then he read the federal safety rules. He bought his log books and inspection forms. He set up a filing system and was ready to hire a driver.

He hired the driver. He verified the driver's ability to drive, checked his employment record and history. He had the driver take the required physical exam. Then he checked the driver's motor vehicle record. He got a printout from the licensing state. Everything was ready.

What the small businessman didn't know was that his driver had several licenses. It wasn't too long until the driver had a serious accident. This accident almost ruined the company. His history of unsafe driving was not known to the businessman who wanted to be legal and safe. The new company was almost put out of business because of an unsafe driver with a hidden driving record.

It is not unusual for a driver to have licenses from two, four, six, eight, or even nine different states. What is the purpose? More than likely, it is so that if one license is revoked, another one can be used. This driver is like a cat with nine lives. Of course, a driver like this will oppose a national licensing program.

This is not the way we want trucks and buses to be operated in our country. The situation is really an insult to the professional truck and bus drivers of the nation. The fact is, although there are a lot more good truck and bus drivers than bad, unfortunately, we notice the bad ones most.

Accidents

You can see that there is much concern about the growing number and size of commercial vehicles. This leads to the fear that the drivers of these vehicles may not always be qualified. We all know and understand the many problems of licensing drivers. These problems come to public attention, most often, when a serious crash occurs.

The accident situation is made worse when the public learns that the crash involved a commercial driver who held several licenses to hide a poor safety record.

How many accidents do commercial vehicle drivers have? They are involved in about 440,000 crashes a year.

ESTIMATE OF CRASHES ANNUALLY

Vehicle Type	Number of Crashes
Passenger Cars	5,157,000
Heavy Trucks	300,000
Medium Trucks	78,000
Buses*	63,500

*Buses include school, transit, charter, *suburban*, and *intercity* buses.
Source: National Highway Traffic Safety Administration
U.S. Department of Transportation, 1987

FIGURE 1-7

When trucks are involved in accidents, the people outside these trucks are at the greatest risk. This is due in part to the size and mass of trucks. This is also true of most buses; however, the people inside the bus are also at great risk in a crash.

The worst situation may be a truck-bus crash. Here is one reported by the National Transportation Safety Board (NTSB 1987):

> A tractor-trailer combination was making a U-turn at a highway crossover. The semitrailer was struck by a cross-country intercity bus. The truck driver and his co-driver were not injured. The bus driver and 27 passengers received injuries ranging from serious to minor. One passenger was not injured.
>
> The NTSB determined that the probable cause was the truck's illegal U-turn at a highway crossover. One reason for the severity of the crash was the speed of the intercity bus. The bus' speed did not give enough time and distance to slow or stop. These causes are but two of the more than 100 factors which may cause an accident. At the back of the book, we have a listing of factors which may lead to a commercial motor vehicle accident (Part Five — Section K). You may want to review the list now.

Operating trucks and buses places special demands on the driver—demands he or she may not always be able to meet. Long stopping distances, a vehicle which is less able to maneuver about, cargo shifts, a chance for brake fade on hills: these are only a few of the problems that the CMV driver must face all of the time, but which car drivers rarely have to face.

A report from a USDOT (United States Department of Transportation) task force said that the skills needed to drive large vehicles are much more complex than those needed to drive a car. Larger vehicles operate in traffic made up mainly of cars which can maneuver more quickly, so CMV drivers need to make up for the size of their vehicles. This means allowing greater distances for turning, passing, stopping and speeding up. This means the driver must think ahead about what can happen.

The Congress passed the Commercial Motor Vehicle Safety Act of 1986 *(CMVSA/86)* to address these problems. The Act directs the Secretary of Transportation to issue minimum testing standards. These standards are to make sure drivers of commercial motor vehicles are qualified to drive their particular machines. In general, the standards include written tests and driving tests. These tests are explained in detail in Chapters Nine through Fourteen.

The written tests cover what a bus driver must know for safe and proper operation of his or her vehicle. You will be tested on your knowledge of safe vehicle operations and the vehicle safety system. You will need to know safe operating procedures for various traffic and weather conditions. You will also have to know how to transport passengers safely and how to handle emergencies.

The road and skill tests must be taken in a vehicle like the bus you will drive or expect to drive. The standards make sure that persons are qualified to operate a commercial motor vehicle (CMV) according to federal regulations. The regulations are officially called the Federal Motor Carrier Safety Regulations. To save space we will refer to them as *FMCSR.*

Bus drivers must comply with the FMCSR to the extent that the rules apply to buses and their operation. For instance, some of the rules apply only to trucks or trucking. Others apply both to trucks and buses. In some cases, the federal rules deal only with interstate (between states) commerce.

The Safety Act makes it illegal for an *operator* of a commercial motor vehicle (truck or bus) to have more than one driver's license.

The basis of the Act of 1986 and our national commercial driver license (CDL) is the classified driver license. Driving certain kinds of vehicles calls for special skills, knowledge, and other *qualifications* beyond what is needed for driving a car. This means that for drivers of special types of vehicles, special and more strict tests are given.

With the national classification licensing system, there is only one license and one record. No matter how many different types or classes of vehicles a person has been qualified to drive in his or her home state, all types and classes are noted on one driver's license.

YOUR COMMERCIAL DRIVER'S LICENSE (CDL)

SINGLE LICENSE   You hold only one license. There is no need for more than one license. In the past, you may have held an operator's license for your car and a chauffeur license for bus. When our national CDL system is fully in place, you will not need two licenses.

CLASSIFIED LICENSE   Your CDL permits you to operate a class of commercial motor vehicles. It states the class of vehicle you are qualified to drive. To be issued a CDL, you must be tested in a vehicle like the one you intend to drive. If you are going to drive a transit bus, you cannot take the test in a passenger car. You must take the test in a bus.

NATIONAL LICENSE   Your CDL is based on one set of national standards. The standards are issued by the United States government. Your CDL is issued by a state. Each state may have their own test system, but each state must meet the U.S. standards. Since these standards are the same all over the nation, the CDL is a national license.

FIGURE 1-8

Instead of each state keeping records on the drivers they license, the Commercial Driver License Information System (CDLIS) will keep track of all of the records. Each driver will have one record, and no matter what state he or she is in when a traffic violation occurs, it will be entered on this record. States must check with the **CDLIS** before they can issue a license, and employers can find out what is on each record.

Information System

Take a look at the goals and purposes for the national license.

Briefly stated, the goals are to:

- Improve driver quality.

- Remove problem drivers from the road.

- Prevent operators of commercial motor vehicles, such as trucks and buses, from having more than one driver's license.

Some of the basic purposes of a national license are to:

- Ensure the same testing and qualifications for drivers among all the states.

- Help remove unqualified drivers by setting up minimum national **standards** for written tests and driving tests.

- Stop granting heavy vehicle licenses to persons who have taken a driving test in a car or vehicle not like the one they plan to operate as a commercial driver.

- Make sure the driving test will require them to prove they can drive the type of vehicle for which they seek a license.

- Set up a computer link among states. This link helps states to know if an applicant has another license. It also helps states send and receive driver record information. This will stop unsafe drivers from driving trucks and buses.

Goals and Purposes

Driver Requirements

As a commercial driver, it is important for you to know:

- You cannot have more than one driver's license. It is against the law.

- You must report **convictions** of traffic violations to your state and to your employer.

- You must notify your employer if your **CDL** has been **suspended**, **revoked** or **canceled** or if you have been **disqualified** from driving a commercial vehicle.

- When applying for a job, you must provide at least ten years of prior job history.

Your employer has requirements also. The Act of 1986 says that no employer shall knowingly employ you if:

- Your CDL has been suspended, revoked or canceled.

- You have been disqualified from driving a CMV.

- You have more than one driver's license.

Federal Disqualifications

You may lose your CDL through federal action. Here is a review of what the Act of 1986 says.

First Violation

The U.S. Secretary of Transportation shall disqualify you for a year if you have committed a first violation of:

- Driving your commercial motor vehicle (CMV) under the influence of alcohol or drugs (DWI).

- Leaving the scene of an accident in which you were driving your CMV.

- Operating your CMV while committing a **felony**.

- If any of these violations occur while you are carrying **hazardous materials,** the disqualification shall be for three years.

Second Violation

The Secretary of Transportation shall disqualify you for a period of not less than 10 years if you have committed a second violation of:

- Driving your CMV under the influence of alcohol or drugs.

- Leaving the scene of an accident in which you were driving your CMV.

- Using a CMV while committing a felony.

- Using a CMV while committing a felony involving making or giving out a controlled substance (such as drugs), or having them but intending to give them to someone else.

Serious Traffic Violations

The Secretary of Transportation shall disqualify you for a period of at least 60 days if you commit two serious traffic violations in a CMV within a three-year period. You will be disqualified for at least 120 days if you have three serious traffic violations in a three-year period.

Serious traffic violations are:

- Reckless driving (each state and city has their own laws).

- Violating a state or local traffic control law (other than a parking violation) and there is an accident in which someone dies.

- Excess speeding (the Secretary of Transportation decides what is speeding).

- Any violation of a state or local motor vehicle traffic law which the Secretary of Transportation decides is serious.

These are strict and serious United States *penalties*. Then again, driving a CMV is a strict and serious business. That is why there is now a national license, and you are using this book to learn how you can pass the tests and get your license.

FEDERAL DISQUALIFICATIONS WHILE DRIVING A COMMERCIAL VEHICLE

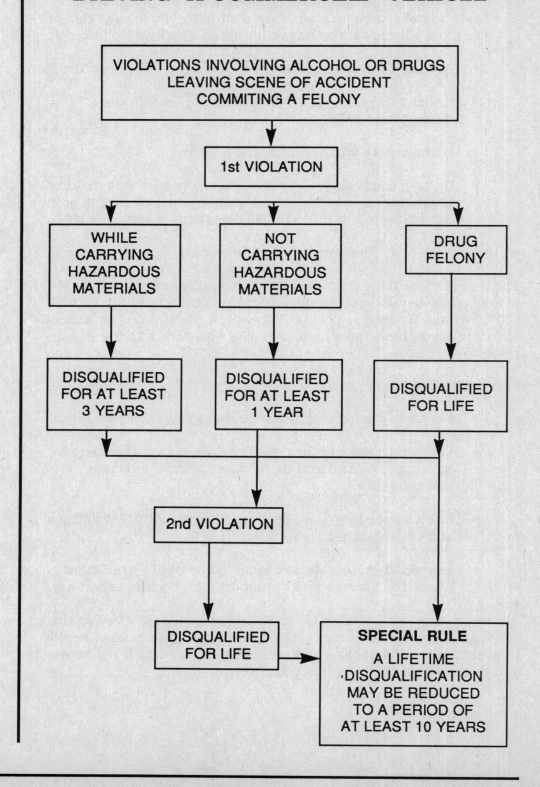

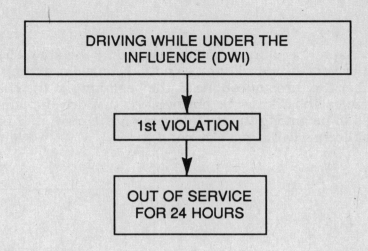

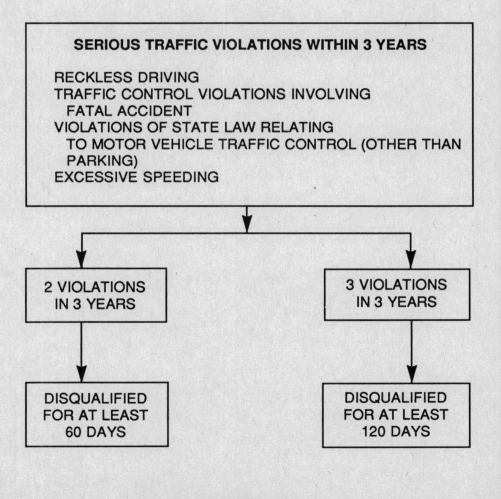

FIGURE 1-9

Summary

In this chapter, a national license, issued by the states for commercial drivers, was explained — not a license for driving a car. Remember the three questions at the beginning of the chapter? The answers should now be obvious. As bus drivers, you are expected to be among the best drivers on the road, and the national license will almost demand it.

Key Words

Applicant — A person who is trying to get something such as a job or CDL

Authority — Someone who has the lawful power and right to act in a certain way

Cancel — To make something no longer in effect

CDL — Commercial Driver's License

CDLIS — Commercial Driver License Information System

CMV — Commercial Motor Vehicle

CMVSA/86 — Commercial Motor Vehicle Safety Act of 1986. Also called the Act of 1986

Commercial Vehicles — Trucks or buses which carry people or goods from one place to another

Conviction — Being found guilty by the law

Disqualified Driver — A driver who has lost his or her commercial driving privilege

Felony — Breaking an important law such as burglary or murder

FMCSR — Federal Motor Carrier Safety Regulations

Hazardous Material — Dangerous material such as dynamite or gasoline

Illegal — Against the law

Intercity — Between two or more cities

Interstate — Between two or more states

Operator — A person driving a car, truck, or bus

Penalty — A punishment for breaking the law

Professional Driver — A driver who knows and obeys all rules and drives in the safest way possible

Qualified Driver — A driver who has passed all of the tests for his CDL

Revoke — To take away

Standards — Requirements of quality

Suburban — Areas outside of the main part of a city

Suspend — To stop for a certain amount of time

Vehicle — A means of transportation such as a car, bus or truck

Violation — Something that is done that is against the law, such as speeding or reckless driving

REVIEW QUESTIONS

Write your answers the space below each question.

1. Who should be the best drivers on the road? Why?

    _____

    _____

2. How many miles of streets and roads are there in the
    U.S.? For every mile of road, there are _____ vehicles
    trying to share it.

    _____

    _____

3. How many cars, buses, and trucks are there?

    _____

    _____

4. In 1985, how many buses were there? What types of
    buses were the most numerous?

    _____

    _____

5. About how many miles do buses travel each year?

    _____

    _____

6. How many licensed drivers are there in the United
    States?

    _____

    _____

7. What is a commercial motor vehicle (CMV)?

    _____

    _____

8. About how many crashes do commercial motor vehicle drivers have each year?

_____

_____

9. What may be the worst type of motor vehicle crash? Why?

_____

_____

10. What are some of the problems that face a commercial vehicle driver, but which car drivers experience rarely, if at all?

_____

_____

11. What law was enacted in 1986 to address the safety problems of commercial drivers?

_____

_____

12. How many driver's licenses can a bus or truck driver hold? What if you are qualified to drive three different commercial motor vehicles?

_____

_____

13. What is a classified driver's license?

_____

_____

14. What is a commercial driver's license (CDL)? Why is it called a national license?

_____

_____

15. What system helps states to identify the nation's commercial drivers?

_____

_____

16. What are some of the ways you can lose your CDL through federal action?

_____

_____

17. What traffic violations are considered the most serious?

_____

_____

18. How long can a commercial vehicle driver be disqualified for driving a CMV under the influence of alcohol or other drugs?

_____

_____

19. What are the three questions asked at the beginning of the chapter? Can you answer them?

_____

_____

TERMS AND BUSES

CHAPTER

Initials
Federal Agencies
Interstate Commerce
License Law
Endorsements
Restrictions
Disqualification Terms
Bus Types
Bus Terms
Equipment Terms
Bus Sizes
Seating Plans
Wheelbase Terms

Axle Terms
Intercity Buses
Transit Buses
Suburban Buses
School Buses
Tractor-Trailer Buses
Articulated Buses
Trolley Bus
Double-Deck Bus
Passenger Vans
Other Buses
Key Words
Review Questions

FROM NOW ON,

ONLY THE BEST WILL DRIVE

Chapter Objectives

**Present the words and terms important to
bus drivers**

**Explain terms and abbreviations commonly used in
the transportation industry**

**Define which license endorsements are required
to drive each type of vehicle**

Identify the different types of buses

CHAPTER TWO

TERMS AND BUSES

This chapter presents a review of the special words and terms important to bus drivers. There is also a look at the different kinds of buses in use today. For any activity, it is important to understand the special words and phrases of that subject — and so we begin this chapter.

What follows is a basic bus and licensing vocabulary. All through your career you will be using these special words and terms. In fact, some of them were already used in Chapter One.

Terms in this chapter will be described in brief remarks rather than in dictionary style. Some will be abbreviations or initials (letters). We will use initials because that is how they are often used in the bus industry.   In some cases, we use them to save space.

Initials

Most initials used in this book are a short way for writing government terms. Since most government wording is "long-winded," you'll understand why we want to save space with abbreviations. For example, "USDOT" or "DOT" is used in place of United States Department of Transportation.

Federal Agencies

Because your commercial driver's license (CDL) is based on federal regulations, it's a good idea to know about the agencies that make rules. The term "OMC," refers to the Office of Motor Carriers. The OMC is a part of the Federal Highway Administration (FHWA). The FHWA is a part of USDOT. The OMC replaced the Bureau of Motor Carrier Safety (BMCS) in the mid-1980s as the agency within USDOT that issues and enforces the Federal Motor Carrier Safety Regulations (FMCSR).

The FMCSR are very important to bus drivers. They are the federal rules that tell how trucks and buses must operate in commerce business among states. The FMCSR decides insurance requirements, driver qualifications, and how many hours they can work. They also deal with accident reports, inspection and repair of vehicles as well as parts and extras needed to operate vehicles safely. Drivers often refer to the FMCSR as the "DOT Rules."

Interstate Commerce

Another federal agency important to busing is the Interstate Commerce Commission or ICC. The ICC enforces Acts of Congress which affect interstate commerce.

INTER = BETWEEN OR AMONG

INTRA = WITHIN

Interstate means between states. Intrastate means operating only within one state.

Commerce is buying, selling, trading, and transporting goods and services. So, interstate commerce is the exchange of goods and services by two or more states. This also applies to people from one state to another.

If the starting place for the trip and the ending place are in the same state, but on the way the bus goes through another state, it is still interstate commerce. It also applies to commerce between a state and foreign country.

Intrastate commerce is transportation which from beginning to end is within one state. Intrastate commerce and drivers are usually regulated by the Public Utilities Commission (PUC). However, with the single national CDL (commercial driver license), there are federal rules to follow.

The Interstate Commerce Commission (ICC) was set up in 1887. In 1935, it began regulating interstate trucking and busing. Today, it issues operating permits to carriers and sets interstate rates. A carrier (motorcarrier) is a person or company in the business of hauling goods or people.

An intrastate carrier is a transportation company operating between points within one state. Remember, "intra" is the Latin word meaning "within." And "inter" means between or among. An interstate carrier is a company operating between two states or among many states.

License Law

We can shorten the Commercial Motor Vehicle Safety Act of 1986 to CMVSA/86. We will also refer to it as the Act of 1986.

The CMVSA/86 was passed by Congress on October 28, 1986. The Act of 1986 created a national driver's license. This license is for drivers of tractor-trailers, heavy trucks, transit buses, suburban buses, intercity buses, and school buses. The license is also for drivers of any vehicle carrying hazardous (dangerous) materials (HAZMAT).

The act of 1986 is the central point of a national effort to improve truck and bus safety. The national license established by this act is the Commercial Driver's License or CDL. The national CDL is the license issued by a state to a person which lets that person operate a class of commercial motor vehicles (CMV).

That is enough abbreviations for now. We will now define the terms which refer to licensing.

By now, you know that the CDL is a national license. It is issued by your state. It lets a person operate a certain class or classes of commercial motor vehicles (CMV). This means the CDL is a classified driver's license. This kind of license says the holder has been tested and knows how to drive vehicles of the classification for which he or she applied. What counts is that the person is qualified to operate the type of vehicle he or she is driving or expects to drive.

Endorsements

To operate some commercial motor vehicles (CMV) you may need an endorsement code added to a CDL (a letter of the alphabet). This means that there is an addition to your CDL which lets you operate certain types of CMVs. For example, drivers who intend to operate a tanker, double/triple trailers, vehicles carrying hazardous material, or buses designed to carry 16 or more persons must have an endorsement on their CDL. Here is how it works.

Under the CDL system there are three basic vehicle classes — A, B, and C. Class A includes all combination vehicles like tractor-trailer rigs. Class B vehicles are straight trucks and large buses including articulated (the body can bend) buses. Class C includes CMVs under 26,000 pounds, like small buses and smaller trucks pulling a trailer. A driver with a Class A license would need a passenger vehicle endorsement (P) to operate a tractor-trailer bus.

FIGURE 2-1: TRUCK-HAULED PASSENGER TRAILER
Class A License with a Passenger Endorsement (P)

The same driver would need a double and triple endorsement (T) to pull double or triple trailers.

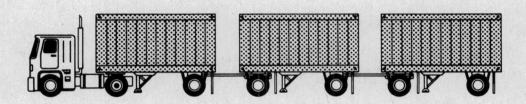

FIGURE 2-2: DOUBLE /TRIPLE TRAILERS
Class A License with a Double/Triple
Endorsement (T)

An operator must obtain a state-issued endorsement to his/her CDL to operate these vehicles:

1. Double/triple trailer (T)

2. Passenger Vehicles (Buses)(P)

3. Tank Vehicle (N)

4. Vehicle containing hazardous
    materials (H)

5. Combination of a tank vehicle and hazardous
    materials (X)

Quickly review these important factors. The groups or classes of CMVs that a driver needs a CDL to operate are:

A   Combination vehicles

B   Heavy straight vehicles

C   Small vehicles.

The endorsements which may be added to a CDL are:

T   Double/triple trailers

P   Passenger vehicles

N   Tank vehicles

H   Hazardous materials

X   A combination of the tank vehicle and hazardous materials endorsement

The Act of 1986 allows your state to add other endorsements, so there may be other codes on your state's CDL.

While we are reviewing, we will define the term "hazardous material." This is material such as gasoline or explosives that is a danger to health, safety, and property during transportation. The HAZMAT rules require diamond shaped warning signs with the term HAZMAT in the center to be placed on all four sides of a vehicle carrying dangerous products. These signs are called placards. If a bus is carrying such materials, the driver would need the "H" endorsement on the CDL. Of course, there would have to be the "P" endorsement because a bus is a passenger vehicle.

Restrictions

Like other driver's licenses, a CDL may be restricted (limited). The CDL has an air brake restriction. If you take your CDL test in a vehicle that does not have air brakes, a restriction is placed on your CDL showing that you are not qualified to operate a vehicle with air brakes.

Some states may restrict you to driving only vehicles with an automatic transmission. If you take your CDL driving test in a vehicle with an automatic transmission, this restriction would show that you are not permited to operate CMVs with manual transmission.

A restriction, therefore, is an addition to your CDL that shows what types of equipment you are not qualified to drive.

Disqualification Terms

Federal rules require that persons who operate CMVs shall have only one driver's license. What if you have more than one? You will be disqualified! Also, the rules will not let a state issue a CDL to a person whose license is suspended, revoked, or canceled. A person who has been disqualified from operating a CMV cannot be issued a CDL.

You can be disqualified if you recieve too many traffic violations. A violation means breaking a law. Speeding is one example. Chapter One lists the various ways you may lose your CDL through violations. For a review, see the "Federal Disqualification" section of Chapter One on page 16.

Since your state can take action against your license, you will want to review the rules the state set down for suspending, revoking, or canceling your privilege to drive.

The state must make sure you can meet CDL requirements. To do this, your state checks and considers information in your current driving record. The state can use the Commercial Driver License Information System (CDLIS) and National Driver Register to do this. Also, you must certify that you hold only one license and that you are not subject to any action against your driving privilege. If a lie is discovered either before or after your CDL is issued, your CDL may be suspended, revoked, or canceled.

Here are those three terms again. Find out how your state defines them. Your privilege to drive a CMV may be affected. You can become a "disqualified driver." To be disqualified means you cannot drive because you violated the rules. Your privilege to drive a CMV is taken away.

In most states, having a license revoked ends a person's licensing privilege. At the end of the revocation period, the person can reapply and obtain a new license. But only if he or she qualifies. This means being tested again.

If a license is suspended, usually it is a temporary loss of the driving privilege. The person cannot drive for a set period of time. In most cases, the person is reinstated as a driver (can be a driver again) at the end of the suspension period.

Cancellation means your license is null and void. It no longer exists. It has been canceled. It is no longer in effect. You must reapply.

Bus Types

General Categories

A bus is a self-propelled (contains its own engine) rubber-tired vehicle which is meant to carry large numbers of people. It operates on streets and roads. The Act of 1986 refers to a bus as a passenger vehicle. Under federal rules, a passenger vehicle is one that transports 16 or more passengers, including the driver.

The five general groups of buses are intercity buses, transit buses, suburban buses, school buses, and passenger vans.

Intercity Bus

An intercity bus is one intended for long distance travel. Some types of intercity buses are charter buses, tour buses, and buses providing service between cities.

Intercity buses usually have one passenger door. All seats face forward. There is underfloor space for luggage and cargo. The seating deck is above the wheels. This allows more underfloor storage.

Transit Bus

A transit bus provides service within a city or local area. It is built to carry many people who may be seated or standing. There are several entry and exit doors for quick loading and unloading.

Transit buses usually have low floors. The low floor removes cargo space but helps people enter or exit the bus.

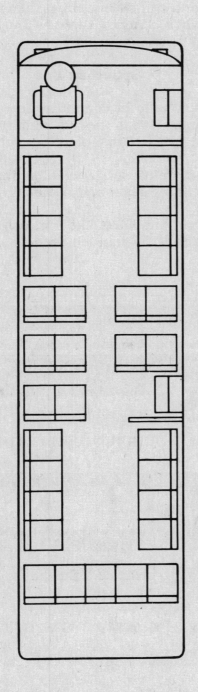

FIGURE 2-3: SEATING ARRANGEMENT

The seating plan for a transit bus must take into account the wheel wells. Usually a bench of three or four seats is placed over the wheels. It faces the center line.

Suburban Bus

The suburban bus is built for commuter travel. In other words, it is a commuter bus. This is the bus which takes people from a place near where they live to a place near their work.

This bus provides more passenger comfort than a transit bus. Often there are reclining seats and some overhead storage.

The typical suburban bus looks like a transit bus but all seats face forward. There are no standee windows and no rear passenger door.

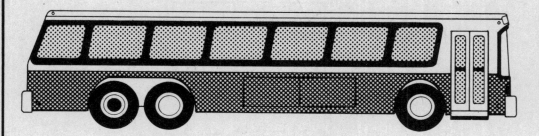

FIGURE 2-4: SUBURBAN BUS WITH ONE DOOR

FIGURE 2-5: TRANSIT BUS WITH TWO DOORS

FIGURE 2-6: SCHOOL BUS

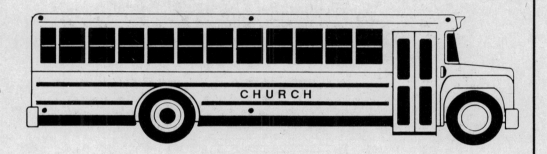

FIGURE 2-7: CHURCH BUS

School

The term "school bus" is misleading. The classic school bus is also used by churches, industry, camps and other groups. The term, as used here, refers to a vehicle group. "School bus" means a bus:

- Owned and operated by a public or governmental agency to transport students to and from school and school activities.

- That is privately owned and operated on a fee basis or is used to transport passengers who are customers, employees, or members.

In either case, a school-type bus has special features. There is a rear emergency door. There are large warning flasher lights and stop signals. There are "rub rails" on each side to strengthen the bus walls. And, of course, there is the school bus "look."

School buses must meet special safety design standards. Safety is the highest priority when transporting people. The warning signal system is a good safety example. There are two systems found on school buses:

- Four-light — flashing red only

- Eight-light — flashing amber and flashing red or both

The eight-light system has four amber and four red lights. They turn on when the driver brakes or the service door is opened.

FIGURE 2-8: FRONT OF CONVENTIONAL SCHOOL BUS

There are many types of school buses. Here are some examples.

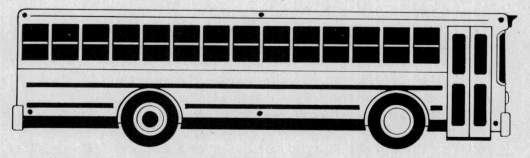

FIGURE 2-9: LARGE SCHOOL BUS — PUSHER TYPE
INTEGRAL CONSTRUCTION

FIGURE 2-10: SMALL CONVENTIONAL SCHOOL BUS
30 PASSENGERS

FIGURE 2-11: SCHOOL MINIBUS

In summary, we can say a school bus meets special safety design standards. It is built for school children. Yet, many school-type buses are used by other groups.

Usually a school-type bus is of light-duty construction with smaller space between seats to increase seating space. School bus seating plans allow for six across — three small children on each side (3-3 plan); or three small children on one side and two larger children on the other (3-2 plan). Adult seating usually allows for four across. With six across and very close seat spacing, 90 seats are possible in a 40-foot school bus. The most common school bus is the 66-seater — 11 rows of six across.

Many school buses are still built by installing a bus body on truck chassis. The result is the classic yellow bus with the front engine under the hood. Growing more popular are integral buses. Integral buses have a rear engine or an engine under the floor. This school bus looks a lot like a transit bus.

School buses have changed a lot over the years. Federal standards that went into effect in 1977 require new buses to meet stricter safety rules in these areas:

- Emergency exits

- Interior protection

- Floor systems

- Seating

- Crashworthiness

- Operating systems

- Windows

- Fuel systems

The greatest change is in seats. School bus seats have more padding and are taller than transit bus seats. Seat frames are energy absorbing. They are made to bend but not to break in a crash.

Passenger Van

A van is a small passenger vehicle built from a light-weight truck. As compared to a regular bus, vans are of light-duty construction and smaller in length, width, and passenger capacity.

There are several kinds of passenger vans. Small buses or vans built to serve elderly and handicapped people are called E and H Buses. They can be identified by their wheelchair lifts and doors.

Buses or vans that make back-and forth trips, usually over a short distance or between certain points are called shuttle buses. Examples are the vans that operate between an airport and the parking lot, rental car lot, motel, hotel, or downtown.

Passenger vans can carry between 16 and 40 people.

FIGURE 2-12: PASSENGER VAN

Bus Terms

Now we will define some of the other terms which describe the other types of buses you might drive.

Articulated Bus

A motor bus that can carry 50 percent more passengers than a traditional bus. The "Artic" is any bus which has a flexible joint in the middle which, allows the body of the bus to bend while turning. The bus consists of two rigid sections connected by a bending middle.

FIGURE 2-13: ARTICULATED BUS

Coach

This term indicates both a freight and passenger unit. Some buses have some of their passenger area converted into space for freight. This area is usually at the rear. Freight, of course, means the goods being shipped.

Double-Deck Bus

This is the bus with two passenger compartments, one on top of the other. A double-deck bus provides more passenger space without increasing road space.

FIGURE 2-14: DOUBLE-DECK BUS

Deck-and-a-Half Bus

The back rows of seats of this bus are higher than those in the front. This provides more underfloor luggage space.

Jitney

The term refers to a small passenger van which carries 6-15 persons. A jitney usually does not have a fixed schedule or fixed stops. They are usually privately-owned and operated. They compete with fixed-route, scheduled transit service.

Motorbus

A motorbus is a passenger vehicle which has rubber tires and operates on roadways and city streets. It contains an internal combustion engine.

Over-The-Road Bus

This bus is usually an intercity bus. "Parlor Car" or "Parlor Bus" also refers to intercity bus.

Pusher

"Pusher" generally refers to a bus with an engine in the rear. Figure 2-9 on page 38 shows a school bus which could be called a pusher.

Recliner

A "recliner" is a bus with reclining (tilt back) seats. Modern intercity buses and some suburban-type buses have reclining seats.

Sightseeing Bus

Any bus designed for sightseeing has extra windows in the roof and/or larger windows on the front and sides.

Trolley Bus

This is a transit bus which operates on electric current drawn from overhead lines. It is a rubber-tired electric bus which operates on city streets. It may be called a "trackless trolley," a streetcar with rubber tires, or a trolley coach. This bus is built to operate in mixed traffic, change lanes, and pick up passengers at the street curb.

FIGURE 2-15: TROLLEY BUS

Equipment Terms

Doors

Buses and vans have many types of doors. A sedan door, or single-piece door, is the type usually found on intercity buses. Some transit buses have push doors or treadle doors.

A push door is a rear exit door. It can be pushed open by the passenger after the driver unlocks it. The treadle door is another type of rear exit door. It opens when the person steps on a pad on the rear steps.

A door with two hinged panels on each side of the center parting line is called a bi-fold door.

A front door which has a single panel on each side of the parting line is called a slide-glide door.

A pantograph door opens by first moving away from the bus body and then parting in the middle. Each section of this door then slides either forward or backward along the outside of the bus. It is also known as a plug door. This type of door is used on transit buses.

Bus Body

There are two main types of bus bodies. The first is the one mounted onto a separate chassis. The standard school bus is an example of this construction. The other type is integral construction. Rather than use a separate chassis to carry the load, the body is built as a part of the chassis so that the sides of the bus serve as load-carrying members. This design, used by many bus manufacturers, makes the bus weigh less.

Bus Signs

A sign on the bus which identifies the bus route or destination is called the Designation Sign. A Head Sign is a destination sign on the front of the bus. A Side Sign is a destination sign on the side of the bus.

Lights

Lights mounted at the four corners of the roof are known as Clearance Lights. Side Marker Lights are mounted on the sides of the coach at the front, middle and rear. They tell other drivers who are approaching the bus from the side how long the bus is.

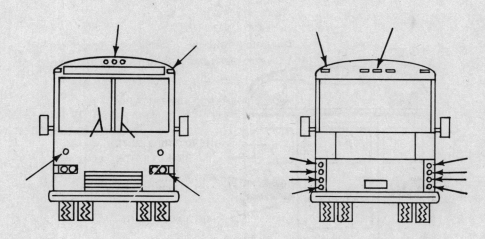

FIGURE 2-16: CLEARANCE LIGHTS

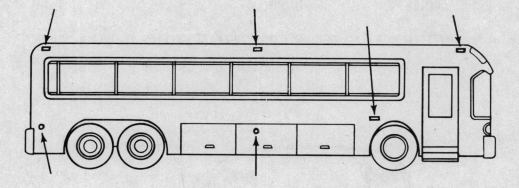

FIGURE 2-17: SIDE MARKER LIGHTS

A school bus is required to have other safety lights. The rear of a modern school bus has 12 signal lights plus three running lights. See Figures 2-18 and 2-19. Two of them are large brake lights. Two of them are small brake lights. There are two large red loading lights. There are also several sets of lights on the front of school buses.

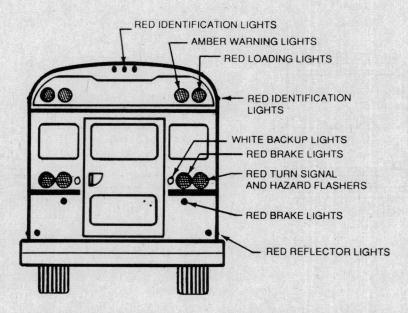

FIGURE 2-18: REAR LIGHTS ON SCHOOL BUS

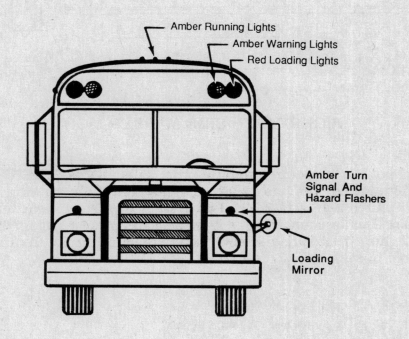

FIGURE 2-19: FRONT LIGHTS ON SCHOOL BUS

Intercity buses are usually 40 feet long. Before the federal rules changed in 1953, the standard length was 35 feet.

The standard transit bus is 40 feet long and 102 inches wide. Some cities, with many narrow streets, continue to use 96-inch-wide transit buses. The bus most often used by smaller cities is the 35-footer. Some 30-foot buses are in use. Whether buses are 30, 35, or 40 feet long, they can be either 96 or 102 inches wide. However, 30-foot buses are usually 96 inches wide.

Buses over 40 feet long usually are articulated. This means they have a middle joint which allows them to bend while turning. Most articulated buses are 60 feet in length, but some 55-foot models are in use.

Bus Sizes

FIGURE 2-20: THREE-AXLE ARTICULATED BUS

The standard school bus varies greatly in length because of the number of seats. A small bus, built to carry 16 adults and 20 children, could be 18 feet long and 84 inches wide. The conventional large school bus (the 66-passenger model), is 96 inches wide and 35 feet long. Except for those with short bodies, school buses are usually 96 inches wide.

Here's a quick review of the typical width and length of intercity and transit buses.

Width in inches: 96, 102

Length in feet
• Single chassis: 30, 35, 40
• Articulated: 55, 60

Seating Plans

The plans which follow should give you an idea of how seating is arranged on different buses.

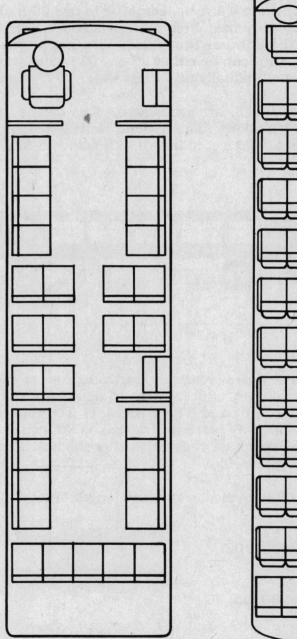

FIGURE 2-21:
2-DOOR TRANSIT BUS

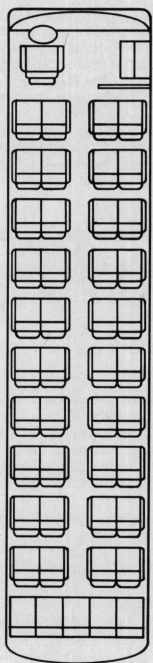

FIGURE 2-22:
SUBURBAN BUS
45 SEATS

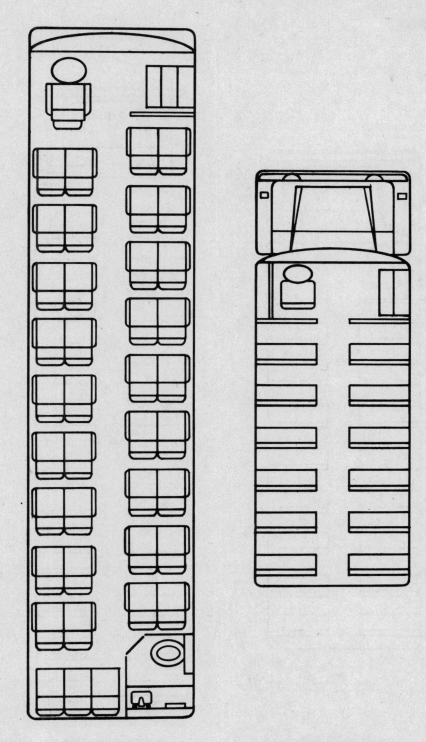

FIGURE 2-23:
INTERCITY BUS
39 SEATS WITH
LAVATORY

FIGURE 2-24:
SMALL SCHOOL BUS
36 SEATS (CHILDREN)
24 SEATS (ADULTS)

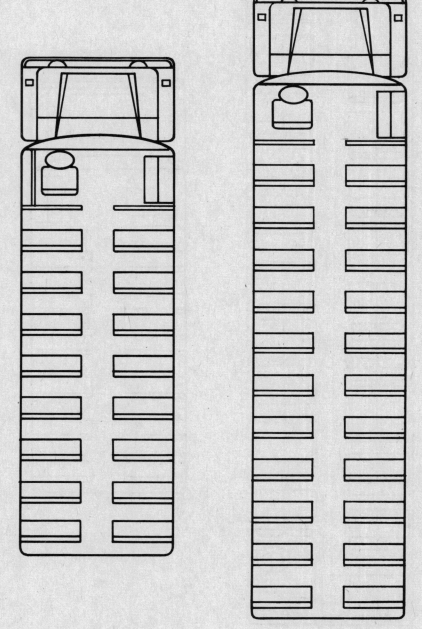

FIGURE 2-25:
SCHOOL BUS
48 SEATS (CHILDREN)
32 SEATS (ADULTS)

FIGURE 2-26:
SCHOOL BUS
66 SEATS (CHILDREN)
44 SEATS (ADULTS)

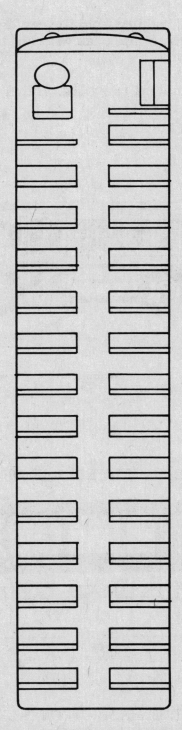

FIGURE 2-27: SCHOOL BUS (PUSHER)
84 SEATS (CHILDREN)
56 SEATS (ADULTS)

Wheelbase Terms

The wheelbase is the distance from the center hub of the front wheel to the center hub of the back wheel or the center of the space between tandems.

A tandem is an assembly of two axles. Either one or both of the axles may be powered.

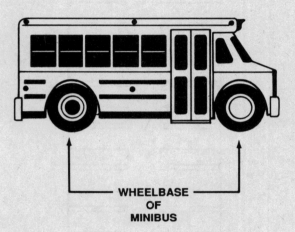

FIGURE 2-28: WHEELBASE OF MINIBUS

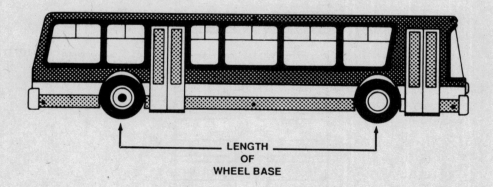

FIGURE 2-29: WHEELBASE OF TWO-AXLE TRANSIT BUS

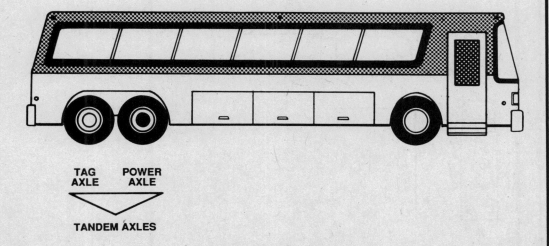

TAG
AXLE

POWER
AXLE

TANDEM AXLES

FIGURE 2-30: WHEELBASE OF TANDEM AXLE
INTERCITY BUS

Wheelbase length affects the turning radius of a bus. In a tight spot, such as a sharp right turn, turning space is critical. A bus with a short wheelbase can turn in a tighter area. A longer bus needs more room.

The expert driver knows the relationship between wheelbase length and path of the turn. The expert knows that the rear wheels follow a shorter path than the front wheels during turns. This is called "off-tracking" because the rear wheels are "off the track" of the front wheels.

Off-tracking is the term used to refer to the path taken by the rear end of a bus when turning. The path of the rear wheels is shorter than the path of the front. The greater the distance between front and rear wheels, the greater the off-tracking.

Take a moment to study Figure 2-31 which shows the turning radius and turning band of the bus. The "turning band" is the space over which any part of the bus passes.

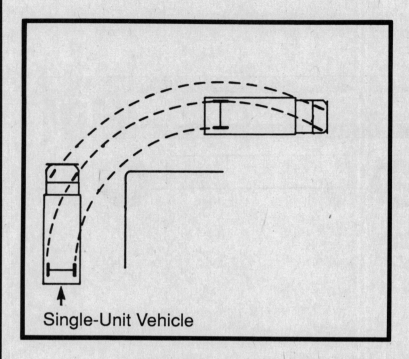

Single-Unit Vehicle

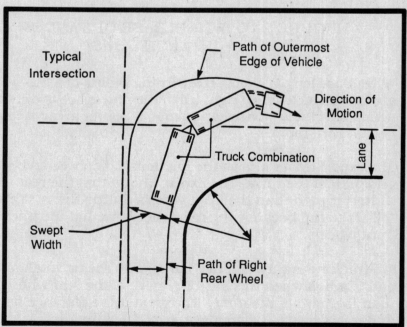

FIGURE 2-31: TURNING RADIUS AND
TURNING BAND OF A BUS

Axle Terms

Notice the path of the outermost corner of the bus. Compare it with the path of the inner rear wheel. The space between these tracking paths is the turning band. Now compare the path of the single-unit vehicle (bus) with the path of the longer tractor-trailer.

The tractor-trailer has more axles. A two-axle vehicle usually has a shorter wheelbase. This allows a turn to be made in a tighter area but it limits the amount of weight it can carry.

Most 40-foot, two-axle buses are near the axle-weight load limit set by most states. The buses which go over the load limit for two axles need a third axle. The third axle is usually a "tag" axle. The tag axle is added to carry the extra weight.

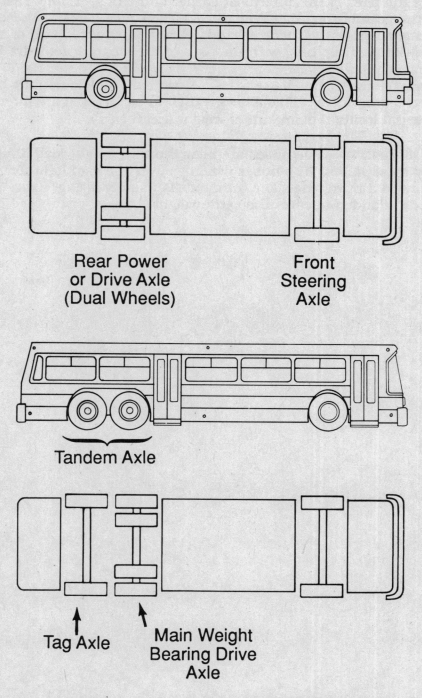

Rear Power
or Drive Axle
(Dual Wheels)

Front
Steering
Axle

Tandem Axle

Tag Axle

Main Weight
Bearing Drive
Axle

FIGURE 2-32: AXLE ARRANGEMENTS

The regular rear axle has two tires, called "duals," on each side. Tag axles usually have only one tire on each side. This single-tired axle carries only as much weight as needed to make the bus weight legal. For instance, a "tag" axle may support only 4,000 pounds while the main rear axle may carry as much as 18,000 pounds.

The usual location of the tag axle on a bus is behind the drive or power axle. The main power axle on a bus is the one with dual tires. You can identify it by its indented hub. The single-tired tag axle has a hub without the indent.

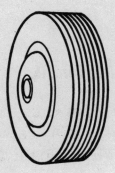 

FIGURE 2-33: POWER AXLE WITH INDENTED HUB
AND TAG AXLE WITHOUT INDENT

Sometimes, it may be desirable to raise the tag and axle wheels off the road. Most buses with tags have jacks and chains which will let them do that. Some intercity buses have a tag axle which can be raised off the road by an air system. The driver can flip a switch to do this, even while driving.

Some large buses are built with a complete tandem rear axle. When both axles on a tandem are powered, the combination is often called a "twin screw." This means that there are two rear axles, both powered, both with four tires each, and both carrying the weight equally.

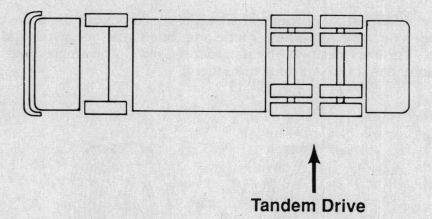

Tandem Drive

- Four Tires On Each Axle
- Both Axles Are Drive Axles
- Both Share Weight Equally

FIGURE 2-34: BUS WITH COMPLETE
TANDEM DRIVE AXLES

There are few four-axle buses in the world. The bus shown in Figure 2-35 is among the world's largest. This double-decker has two steerable front axles and tandem drive axles.

FIGURE 2-35: DOUBLE-DECK BUS WITH FOUR AXLES

This double-decker is a suburban service bus. To give you an idea of its size, here are some of its details:

Length:	40 feet
Width:	98 inches
Height:	13.25 feet
Wheelbase:	21.8 feet
Seating:	74 - 86

These details are part of this bus' specs or specifications. That is a fancy term. It also is the last term we'll define in this chapter. What does it mean? Well – "specs" are based on need; in other words, they describe in detail how the bus will be used and what equipment it will need to do the job.

A bus is "spec'ed out" (the specifications are decided upon) to match the job it will perform. A bus that will be used in city transit service will have different "specs" from a suburban service or intercity bus.

For instance, the transit bus will need a shorter wheelbase to handle the tight turns on narrow streets. It will need several doors while the intercity bus needs only one. At any rate, for every purpose there is a bus with its own specifications.

The rest of this chapter will show you examples of the buses on the road today. The buses shown represent typical buses of each class. They are only an identification guide. For some buses, specs such as height, weight, length, and number of seats are given. These figures may vary with actual buses, but they should give you a better idea about the various types of buses and how they may be identified and described.

To help you identify axle types, wheel drawings are coded. A drive axle is shown with a small circle inside the rim area. Steering and tag axles have a large circle.

**Intercity
Buses**

FIGURE 2-36: INTERCITY SHORT BUS WITH TWO AXLES

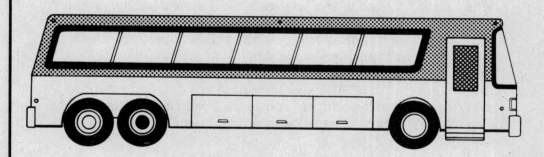

FIGURE 2-37: HIGH BODY INTERCITY
BUS WITH THREE AXLES

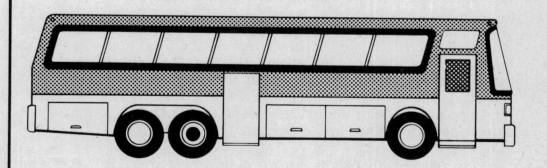

FIGURE 2-38: HIGH BODY INTERCITY BUS WITH
THREE AXLES AND A LOWER DECK

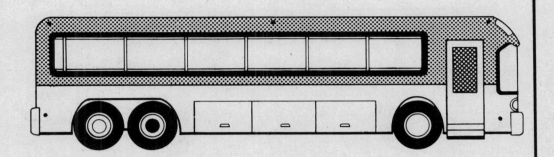

FIGURE 2-39: HIGH BODY INTERCITY BUS
WITH THREE AXLES AND SLOPING FRONT CAP

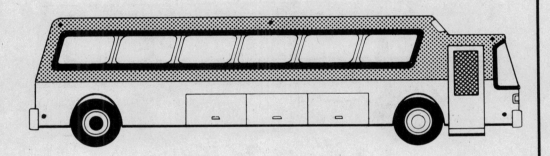

FIGURE 2-40: INTERCITY BUS WITH TWO AXLES
AND A HUMPED ROOF

Transit Buses

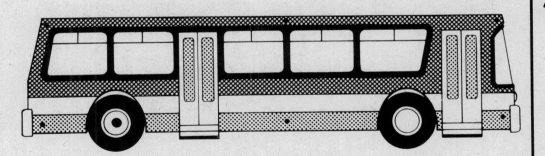

FIGURE 2-41: TRANSIT BUS WITH TWO AXLES
AND TWO DOORS

FIGURE 2-42: TRANSIT BUS WITH TWO AXLES AND
ONE DOOR

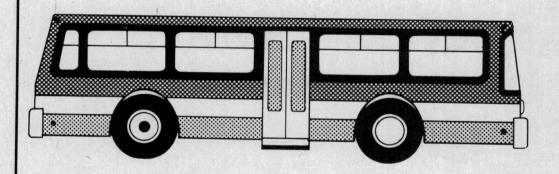

FIGURE 2-43: TRANSIT BUS WITH TWO AXLES
AND MIDDLE DOOR

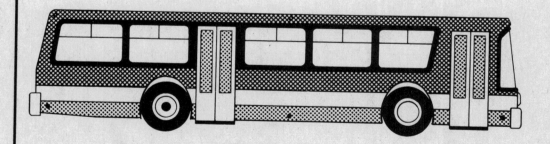

FIGURE 2-44: TRANSIT BUS WITH TWO AXLES AND
TWO DOORS (40 FOOTER)

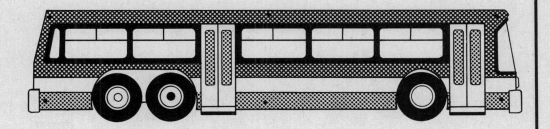

FIGURE 2-45: TRANSIT BUS WITH THREE AXLES
AND A LOW FLOOR

FIGURE 2-46: TRANSIT BUS WITH TWO AXLES,
TWO DOORS, AND BIG WINDOWS

FIGURE 2-47: SHORT TRANSIT BUS

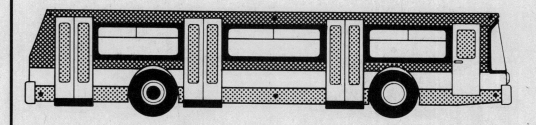

FIGURE 2-48: TRANSIT SHUTTLE BUS WITH THREE
PASSENGER DOORS

Suburban Buses

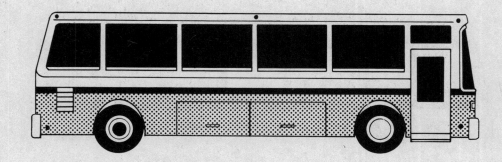

FIGURE 2-49: SUBURBAN BUS WITH A HIGH DECK

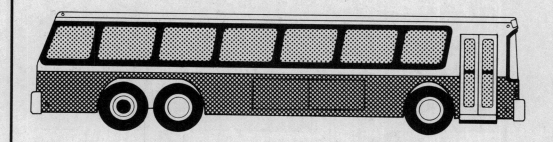

FIGURE 2-50: SUBURBAN COMMUTER BUS
WITH THREE AXLES

FIGURE 2-51: DOUBLE-DECK SUBURBAN BUS

School Buses

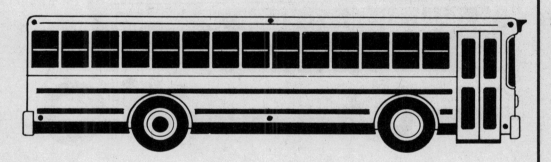

FIGURE 2-52: SCHOOL BUS
REAR ENGINE TRANSIT TYPE

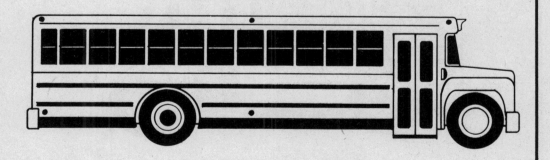

FIGURE 2-53: CONVENTIONAL FRONT ENGINE 35-FOOT
SCHOOL BUS

FIGURE 2-54: CONVENTIONAL 25-FOOT SCHOOL BUS

FIGURE 2-55: 30-FOOT SCHOOL BUS

FIGURE 2-56: SCHOOL MINIBUS

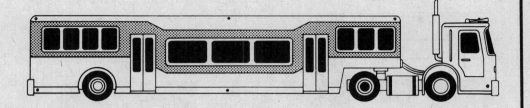

FIGURE 2-57: TRACTOR-TRAILER BUS
LONG TRAILER

FIGURE 2-58: TRACTOR-TRAILER BUS
SHORT TRAILER

FIGURE 2-59: ARTICULATED TRANSIT BUS
THREE-AXLES

Tractor-Trailer Buses

Articulated Buses

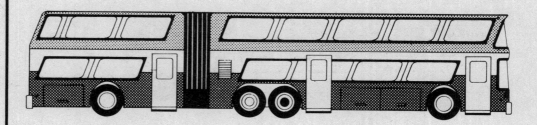

FIGURE 2-60: DOUBLE-DECK ARTICULATED INTERCITY
BUS — FOUR AXLES

FIGURE 2-61: ARTICULATED INTERCITY TOUR BUS
FIVE AXLES

Trolley Bus

FIGURE 2-62: TROLLEY BUS

FIGURE 2-63: DOUBLE-DECK BUS

Vans are used like buses. Yet, they are smaller than a bus in both length, width, height, and seating. The drawings show two types of passenger vans. List other types you have seen.

_____

_____

_____

_____

Remember, if you drive a van which carries 16 or more passengers, you will need a CDL with a "passenger endorsement."

FIGURE 2-64: VAN

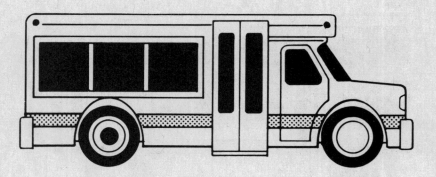

FIGURE 2-65: VAN WITH BI-FOLD DOORS

FIGURE 2-66: VAN
CARGO VAN CHASSIS

Other Bus Vehicles

Transit buses, intercity buses, and school buses do more than carry people. Sometimes they are converted into mobile offices, museums, or libraries. Under CDL rules, these converted vehicles are still classed as buses. List as many other ways you can think of that buses are used.

_____

_____

_____

_____

_____

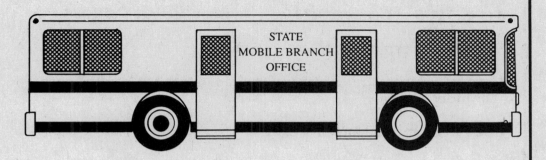

FIGURE 2-67: MOBILE BRANCH OFFICE

FIGURE 2-68: BOOKMOBILE

Key Words

Act of 1986 — Commercial Motor Vehicle Safety Act of 1986

BMCS — Bureau of Motor Carrier Safety

Carrier — A person or company in the business of hauling goods for other people

CDL — Commercial Driver's License

CDLIS — Commercial Driver License Information System

CMVSA/86 — Commercial Motor Vehicle Safety Act of 1986

DOT — United States Department of Transportation

Endorsement — A letter of the alphabet added to a CDL which means the driver is qualified to drive other types of vehicles

FHWA — Federal Highway Administration

FMCSR — Federal Motor Carrier Safety Regulations

HAZMAT — Hazardous material such as gasoline and explosives

Intra — Within

Inter — Between or among

OMC — Office of Motor Carriers

Restriction — A limit stated on a CDL which lets the driver drive only certain types of vehicles

USDOT — United States Department of Transportation

REVIEW QUESTIONS

Write your answers in the space below each question.

1. What do these initials (abbreviations) stand for?

    DOT _____

    USDOT _____

    CDL _____

    OMC _____

    FHW _____

    FMCSR _____

    ICC _____

    PUC _____

    CMVSA/86 _____

    HAZMAT _____

    CMV _____

    CDLIS _____

    T (endorsement) _____

    P (endorsement) _____

    N (endorsement) _____

    H (endorsement) _____

    X (endorsement) _____

2. Although we have a national CDL in the United
    States, who issues it — the Federal Government
    or your state?

    _____

3. What is a Classified Driver's License?

    _____

    _____

4. What are the five types of endorsements that may
    be added to your CDL?

    _____

    _____

    _____

    _____

    _____

5. What type of endorsement does a bus driver need?

    _____

6. Under the CDL system, there are three basic vehicle
    classes. What are they called?

    _____

    _____

    _____

7. What is a placard? What is a placarded vehicle?
    Is it possible for a bus to be placarded? (Explain).

    _____

    _____

    _____

    _____

    _____

8. Give five examples of hazardous material that may be hauled by commercial motor vehicles.

_____

_____

_____

9. Explain the term restriction as it relates to a CDL.

_____

_____

_____

10. Explain these terms:

Revocation _____

_____

Suspension _____

_____

Cancellation _____

_____

Disqualification _____

_____

11. What is a violation? Give several examples of traffic violations.

_____

_____

_____

12. Define or describe each of the following.

    A. Intercity Bus _____
       _____

    B. Transit Bus _____
       _____

    C. Suburban Bus _____
       _____

    D. School Bus _____
       _____

    E. Articulated Bus _____
       _____

    F. Tractor-Trailer Bus _____
       _____

    G. Passenger Van _____
       _____

    H. Double-Deck Bus _____
       _____

    I. Trolley Bus _____
       _____

13. List at least four kinds of doors found on buses.

    _____

    _____

14. What is meant by an integral construction or integral body bus?

    _____

    _____

    _____

15. What is a clearance light?

_____

_____

16. How long are most intercity buses?

_____

17. How wide are most buses?

_____

18. Which type of bus is the longest?

_____

19. Which type of bus is most likely to have bench seats?

_____

20. Explain these terms:

Wheelbase _____

_____

Turning radius _____

_____

Tandem _____

_____

Off-tracking _____

_____

21. What is the difference between a drive axle and a tag axle? What is the reason tag axles are used on buses?

_____

_____

_____

22. How can you tell the difference between a tag axle and power axle by looking at the wheel hub?

_____

_____

23. Explain the term specifications.

_____

_____

24. Describe one of the largest of all buses. Would it have 3, 4, or 5 axles?   Would it be articulated? How many decks would it have?

_____

_____

_____

_____

25. What is a trackless trolley? What kind of power (energy) does it need to run?

_____

_____

_____

26. Which kind of passenger vehicle is the smallest? How does it differ from a standard bus?

_____

_____

_____

27. A CDL is needed to operate a bus or van when it is designed to carry _____ or more passengers.

28. Which type of bus is this — transit or suburban?

     This bus usually has no rear passenger door. There are no standee windows. There is a raised floor. There are parcel racks. All seats are high-backed and face forward. Most models have two axles.

_____

THE LICENSING PROGRAM

CHAPTER

FROM NOW ON,

ONLY THE BEST WILL DRIVE

Chapter Objectives

Define national and state rules for commercial drivers

Identify classes of vehicles

Understand types of CDL endorsements

Explain restrictions to CDL classifications

Describe the CDL testing program

Explain exceptions to the national CDL rules

CHAPTER THREE

THE LICENSING PROGRAM

As a bus driver, you are under a national licensing program. This chapter will give you a general idea of the national commercial driver license program. As a bus driver, you fall under these rules. So does your state.

The CMVSA/86 sets licensing standards for all commercial drivers in the nation. This Safety Act also sets standards or rules for each state to follow. All of these rules are made by the USDOT.

These national CDL standards are minimum rules. This means that each state must meet all of the basic national requirements. This also means that each state is free to add other rules — and these rules may be stricter. For this reason, you should also study your state's *CDL Driver's Handbook* and other bus licensing materials along with this book.

National Rules For States

National standards require that you, as a bus driver, must pass certain tests. There are two main types of examinations: knowledge tests and performance tests. These tests cover commercial vehicle driving in general. They also cover safe bus operation.

CDL bus driver tests have an important purpose. They make sure drivers have the basic knowledge and skills for operating a bus safely.

Your state's bus driver license tests must meet minimum national CDL standards. But remember your state can set higher standards. In this chapter, we will be looking only at national requirements.

What States May Do

The national CDL program gives each state a lot of leeway. Each state may:

- Set its own CDL fee.

- Set age limits for CDL holders not covered by FMCSR.

- Set its own penalties for driver applicants who give false information.

- Require or omit tests for applicants who want to renew or transfer a CDL from another state.

- Do away with, or insist upon, driving skill tests for certain categories of first-time CDL applicants who are already CMV operators.

- Allow knowledge tests to be in written, oral, or machine form. This means a test can be given by a machine; or be a paper and pencil test; or test questions can be given by a reader or translator.

- Prepare its own knowledge test questions and procedures as long as the test includes the required information.

- Develop its own methods for skills (road) testing and scoring.

- Set the waiting period between tests for an applicant who needs to take a test that was failed again.

- Set the number of times a person may take and fail any test.

Each state may also add requirements or rules which are stricter than the national CDL standards.

A state may also allow local governments, industries or other groups to conduct the driving tests.

These various state options show why we keep reminding you to check your state's rules, methods, and materials.

Now we will go on to the national CDL program.

All drivers must have a CDL if they drive a single or combination vehicle which weighs more than 26,001 pounds. This applies to both interstate and intrastate drivers.

Any bus driver who operates a vehicle which can carry 16 or more passengers must also have a CDL. This number includes the driver.

The driver of any size vehicle carrying hazardous material in certain amounts set by law must have a CDL. The law requires that these vehicles display placards showing the kind of material being hauled. Drivers who haul amounts of hazardous material requiring placards must also have a HAZMAT endorsement on their CDL.

Drivers Covered By CDL Program

Here are some examples of the diamond-shaped placards:

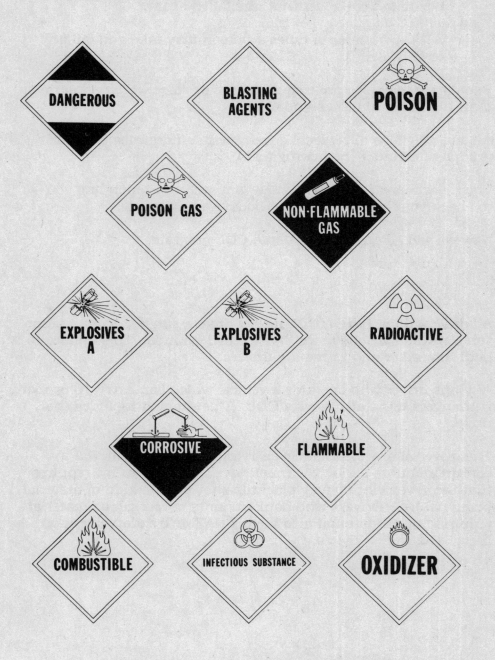

FIGURE 3-1: HAZMAT PLACARD EXAMPLES

What are the classes of vehicles which need a CDL to be driven? The CDL classification system, together with various endorsements and one restriction, is shown in Figure 3-2.

CDL Classifications

COMMERCIAL DRIVER LICENSE (CDL) CLASSIFICATION SYSTEM			
LICENSE CLASS	**VEHICLE DISCRIPTION**	**BUSES**	**TRUCKS**
A	Any combination vehicle: • Tractor-Semitrailer • Truck and Trailer • Double Trailers • Triple Trailers • Trailer Weighing 10,001 pounds or more	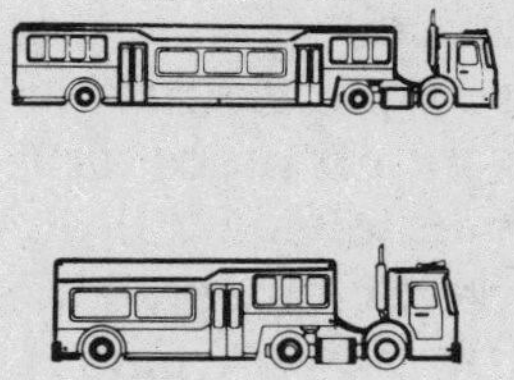	
B	Any vehicle weighing 26,001 pounds or more: • Straight Trucks • Large Buses • Trucks with Trailers weighing less than 10,000 pounds		
C	Any vehicle weighing less than 26,001 pounds that is: • Designed to carry 16 or more passengers in cluding the driver, or • Carrying hazardous materials that require placarding		

A special *endorsement* on your CDL is also required to drive a: bus (P); tank vehicle (N); double/triple trailers (T); and any vehicle carrying hazardous materials which require placards (H). If your vehicle has airbrakes, you must take the CDL Airbrakes Test. If you do not pass the test, your CDL will restrict you to driving only vehicles not equipped with airbrakes.

FIGURE 3-2: CDL CLASSIFICATION SYSTEM

There are three general vehicle classes in the CDL classification system. They are as follows:

CLASS A

Class A includes heavy combination vehicles (tractor-trailer or truck and trailer). Typically, these vehicles have Gross Combination Weight Ratings (**GCWR**) ranging from 45,000 to 80,000 pounds. Most Class A vehicles are trucks, although tractor-trailer buses are in operation in a few cities. Driving a Class A vehicle requires much more skill and knowledge than driving a Class B or Class C vehicle. Skills include those needed to drive Class B and Class C vehicles as well as some additional ones. Therefore, a driver who has a Class A license may also drive vehicles in Classes B and C.

CLASS B

Class B includes straight trucks and large buses (including articulated buses), with GVWR's greater than 26,000 pounds. A trailer weighing less than 10,000 pounds (GVWR) may be pulled. Safely driving these heavy vehicles requires more knowledge and skill than driving the small trucks and buses found in Class C. Skills include those needed to drive Class C vehicles. Therefore, drivers who have qualified for a Class B license may also drive a Class C vehicle.

CLASS C

Class C includes single or combination vehicles weighing not more than 26,000 pounds (GVWR). It also includes smaller buses with a designed capacity of more than 15 passengers including the driver, which do not exceed 26,000 pounds (GVWR). A great variety of vehicles will be found in Class C. A CDL Class C license is required for driving any of these vehicles if they are used to: (a) haul hazardous material; or (b) transport passengers.

Some rather large Class C vehicles require more skill and knowledge to operate than the smaller ones do. However, the licensing class is based mainly on the type of cargo carried. Because of the seriousness of an accident involving hazardous material or human passengers, a great variety of Class C vehicles are included under the CDL system.

There are four kinds of CDL endorsements. These depend on the type of equipment being driven or the type of cargo being hauled.

Endorsements

1. **Tankers (N)**

   Drivers of Class A or Class B vehicles that are used to haul liquids in bulk must have special knowledge and skills to drive safely. Liquids in bulk cause driving control problems because the cargo is heavy, it shifts, and it has a high center of gravity. These drivers must obtain an endorsement (the letter N) to their license showing they have passed a written examination on the special problems caused by large volume liquid cargoes.

2. **Hazardous Materials (H)**

   Any driver, regardless of the class of his or her vehicle (A, B or C), who wishes to haul hazardous material or waste must have a hazardous material endorsement (the letter H) to his or her CDL. He or she must also pass a written test on how to recognize, handle and transport hazardous materials.

3. **Double and triple trailers (T)**

   Many drivers who are qualified to drive Class A vehicles may wish to pull double or triple trailers. Much extra knowledge and skill is needed to safely drive double and triple trailers in certain traffic, road, and weather conditions. As a result, the CDL system requires an endorsement (the letter T) to be added to the license of a Class A driver showing that he or she has the required additional knowledge. A special written exam on multiple (double or triple) trailers must be passed.

4. Passengers (P)

Any driver who wishes to drive a motor vehicle built to carry 15 or more passengers, including the driver, must secure a Passenger endorsement (the letter P) to his CDL. He or she must pass a written exam on special safety factors when carrying passengers. The endorsement applies to applicants for a license to drive a bus in any category (A, B, or C).

The endorsement code "X" is used for those drivers qualified for both the hazardous material and tank vehicle endorsements.

Review of Codes

The group or groups of CMVs that a driver can be authorized to operate are coded as follows:

- A for combination vehicles;

- B for heavy straight vehicles; and

- C for small vehicles.

The endorsements are coded as follows:

- N for tank vehicles;

- T for double/triple trailers;

- P for passenger vehicles;

- H for hazardous materials; and

- X for both tank vehicle and hazardous materials.

A state may add other codes if it sees fit to do so.

There is one restriction in the CDL classification scheme. This is on the type of braking system on the vehicle the driver will be using.

Air Brake Restriction

Most drivers of heavy commercial vehicles will have trucks or buses with **air brakes**. These drivers must pass a written exam on the operation and parts of the air brake system. All Class A vehicles and most Class B vehicles have air brakes. A few Class C vehicles also have air brakes, but most do not. If you take a test in a commercial vehicle that does not have air brakes, a restriction must be placed on your CDL showing that you are not qualified to operate a vehicle with air brakes.

Some states may also require a manual transmission (you must shift gears) restriction. The reason for this is that driving a CMV with a manual transmission requires different knowledge and skill than driving a vehicle with an automatic transmission.

Most Class A and Class B vehicles have manual transmissions; yet some Class A and Class B and many Class C vehicles have automatic transmissions. If your state has a manual transmission restriction, and if you take a test in an automatic transmission vehicle, a restriction will be placed on your CDL. This restriction will show that you are not qualified to drive a CMV with a manual transmission. You will be able to drive only vehicles with automatic transmissions. So, again, check your state's rules.

Representative vehicle is a long-winded term. But that is the way it is stated. The Safety Act of 1986 requires each person who operates a CMV to pass certain tests. These tests include vehicle inspection, basic vehicle control skills, and on-road driving. Skill and road tests must be taken in a vehicle which is "representative" of the vehicle the license applicant intends to operate. This means it is like the type of vehicle the driver intends to operate.

Figures 3-3, 3-4, and 3-5 show examples of the various buses by their license classes. The classes of buses are set by their size, weight, and vehicle group. These figures are used to help you know which buses belong in each class. If you are not sure which class of bus you are to drive, check the bus' gross vehicle weight rating (**GVWR**).

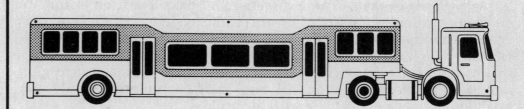

Tractor-Trailer Bus — Long Trailer

Tractor-Trailer Bus — Short Trailer

FIGURE 3-3: EXAMPLES OF CLASS A BUSES

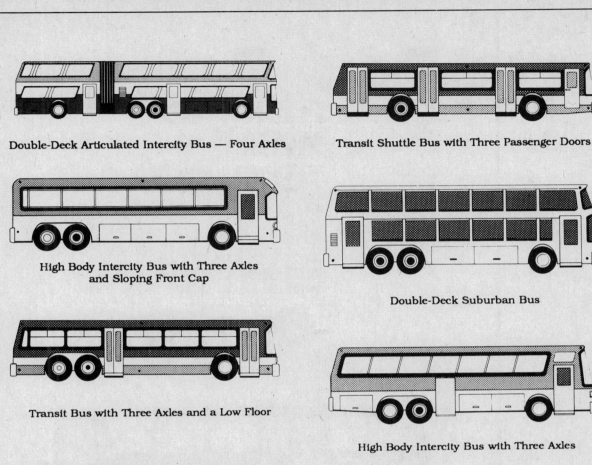

Double-Deck Articulated Intercity Bus — Four Axles

Transit Shuttle Bus with Three Passenger Doors

High Body Intercity Bus with Three Axles and Sloping Front Cap

Double-Deck Suburban Bus

Transit Bus with Three Axles and a Low Floor

High Body Intercity Bus with Three Axles

High Body Intercity Bus with Three Axles and a Lower Deck

Suburban Bus with a High Deck

Intercity Bus with Two Axles and a Humped Roof

Articulated Transit Bus — Three-Axles

FIGURE 3-4: EXAMPLES OF CLASS B BUSES

- These buses typify, but do not fully cover, the types of buses in this class.

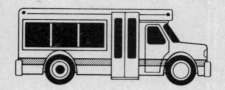

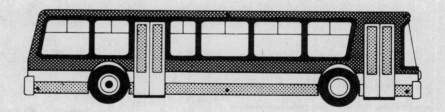

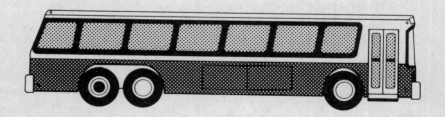

FIGURE 3-5: CLASS C BUSES

- Class C buses have a GVRW of less than 26,001 pounds and are designed to carry 16 or more passengers. Class C also applies to vehicles of this size which are placarded for hazardous materials.

Karla Belinda Martinez

nacio   09/18/79

          EN El SALVADOR C.A

There are several CDL tests. Which test you will take will depend on the vehicle class and endorsement you are trying to obtain. There are two kinds of CDL tests: knowledge tests and performance (driving) tests. Knowledge tests are usually written tests. However, some states may allow a person to read the questions to or translate them for an applicant.

Written tests are given to decide whether the person has the knowledge about safe driving necessary to operate a CMV. As you know, written tests are no guarantee that the person can drive the vehicle on a highway in traffic, so the CDL testing program also calls for several performance tests.

The **performance tests** cover on-road driving and other skills. A road test is required for all three CDL classes (A, B, and C). A basic control skill test (how well you can control the bus) is required for Class A and Class B vehicles. A pre-trip inspection is also required for Class A and Class B vehicles.

To help you understand the test requirements, see the chart of tests (Figure 3-6 on the following page). The chart shows what tests are to be taken for each vehicle class and endorsement. It also shows that all applicants for a CDL must take a written General Knowledge Test. This applies to all truck and bus drivers. All applicants driving air brake vehicles must take the air brakes written test, and all applicants for a Class A CDL must take the *Combination Vehicles* Test.

In addition to these three basic requirements, you may have to take other written tests. This depends upon which endorsement(s) you want. A bus driver will have to take the Passenger Vehicle or Bus Test (Endorsement P). If you wish to drive tankers (N), double or triple trailers (T), or haul hazardous *cargo* (H), you must take and pass special tests for each of these endorsements. These test requirements are explained in Part Three of this guide.

CDL Testing Program

CHART OF CDL TESTS AND ENDORSEMENTS

TESTS REQUIRED FOR EACH CLASS OF CDL

CLASSIFICATION TESTS	CLASS A	CLASS B	CLASS C
General Test	Required	Required	Required
Air Brakes Test or Questions	Required	Required*	Required*
Combination Vehicles Test	Required	—	—

TESTS AVAILABLE FOR CDL ENDORSEMENTS

ENDORSEMENT TESTS	CLASS A	CLASS B	CLASS C
Tanker (N) Test	Available	Available	—
Double/Triple Trailer (T) Test	Available	—	—
Passenger (P) Test	Available	Available	Available
Hazardous Materials (H) Test	Available	Available	Available

IF VEHICLE IS EQUIPPED WITH AIR BRAKES

FIGURE 3-6: CDL TESTS AND ENDORSMENTS

Knowledge Tests

Here are some key points to remember about CDL knowledge tests.

1. The CDL testing system includes seven written tests.

2. These tests measure what you must know to drive the CMVs included in each class.

3. The state's CDL Driver's Manual contains this information. It is also found in Chapters Nine through Twelve of this book.

4. The CDL tests make sure that each driver knows this information.

5. All of the knowledge tested is very important for safe driving.

6. Different drivers will take different written tests to receive a license.

7. The tests a driver takes will depend on the type of vehicle to be driven. A different test may be required for hauling certain types of cargoes.

8. There are also different forms of each test so that drivers who fail can be retested.

Now, we will take a look at the different tests. There are two basic types: A General written test and specialized tests. Here is what each type covers:

The General Knowledge Written Test

The purpose of the **General Knowledge Test** is to test the applicant's knowledge of information that all commercial drivers need to know.

This knowledge does not depend upon the type of vehicle to be driven or the cargo to be hauled. ALL drivers need to know how to handle emergencies. They should know how to choose a safe speed, and so on. This type of knowledge — which all drivers need to know — is what is measured by the General Test.

Every driver who wants a CDL — any type of CDL — must first pass the General Test. If a driver does not receive a passing score, he or she cannot take the performance tests. Chapter Nine provides samples of questions found on the General Test.

Specialized Tests

Specialized tests measure knowledge needed by only certain drivers. They differ from the General Test in that not all commercial drivers need to take each specialized test. The tests a driver needs to take depend on the type of vehicle to be driven and the cargo to be hauled.

In addition to the General Test, two of the *specialized tests* qualify drivers for the Class A or Class B license. The rest of the tests qualify drivers for CDL endorsements.

A description of each specialized test and the drivers who are to take it follows.

Air Brake Test: This test measures the knowledge that is required to drive trucks and buses equipped with air brakes. Every person who wants to drive a vehicle with air brakes must pass this test regardless of which class of license is appropriate for that vehicle.

Passenger Test: This test measures the knowledge required of bus drivers. Every person who wishes to drive a bus must pass this test to obtain a Passenger Vehicle or Bus Endorsement (P).

Tanker Test: This test measures the knowledge needed to drive tankers that haul liquid in bulk. Those who pass it receive a Tanker Endorsement (N) to their Class A or Class B CDL. Those with a Class C license cannot obtain this endorsement.

Combination Vehicle Test: This test measures what a person needs to know to drive a combination vehicle such as a tractor-trailer rig. The only drivers who take this test are those who want a Class A license.

Hazardous Materials Test: This test covers basic knowledge of regulations for hauling hazardous goods. Every driver who hauls material covered by HAZMAT regulations must pass it to receive a Hazardous Materials Endorsement (H). Hazardous material cannot be hauled without it.

Which Test To Take

By now you should be familiar with the classes of licenses and types of CDL endorsements. This is important because you should know for which test to prepare. Remember, the test you must take and pass will depend upon the type of vehicle you are to drive and the cargo you are to haul.

For review purposes, refer back to Figure 3-6 on page 94. The top part of the Chart shows the classification tests. These are the tests required for each license class. Only the General Test, Air Brakes Test, and Combination Vehicles Test qualify you for the different license classes. The lower part of the chart lists the four tests that qualify drivers for CDL endorsements. Each of these tests, when passed, leads to an endorsement of a person's CDL.

Remember, certain endorsements are available only to people in a certain license class. Look at Figure 3-6 on page 94 again. The term "available" means that the test and its endorsement are available to the license class. For instance, a person with a Class C license cannot receive a Tanker (N) Endorsement or Double/Triple Trailer (T) Endorsement.

List of CDL Tests

A CDL applicant will have to take one or more written tests. The number of tests depends on what class of license and what endorsement the applicant needs. The CDL knowledge tests include:

- The General Knowledge Test, taken by all applicants.

- The Passenger Test, taken by all bus driver applicants.

- The Air Brake Test, which you must take if your vehicle has air brakes.

- The Combination Vehicles Test, which is required if you want to drive combination vehicles.

- The Hazardous Materials Test, required if you want to haul hazardous material or waste.

- The Tanker Test, if you want to haul liquids in bulk.

- The Double/Triple Trailer Test, required if you want to pull double or triple trailers.

Tests for Bus Driver CDL

As a bus driver, here are the CDL knowledge tests you will have to pass:

- The General Knowledge Test

- The Passenger Test

If your bus is equipped with air brakes:

- The Air Brake Test

If you intend to drive a tractor-trailer bus:

- The Combination Vehicles Test

If you plan to drive a tractor-trailer bus which has air brakes, you will have to take all four of the tests. Practice tests are found in Chapters Eight through Eleven.

Besides these written tests, you may have to pass the CDL Performance Tests.

MAYBE YOU WILL NOT HAVE TO TAKE THE PERFORMANCE TESTS

BUT YOU WILL HAVE TO TAKE THE KNOWLEDGE TEST! ALL DRIVERS DO.

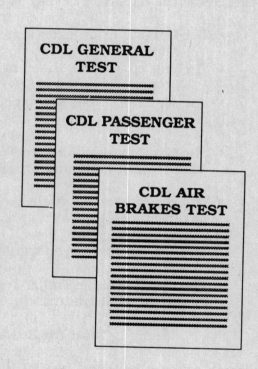

CDL GENERAL TEST

CDL PASSENGER TEST

CDL AIR BRAKES TEST

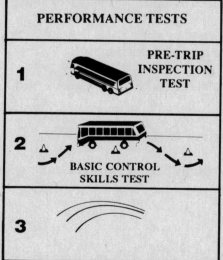

PERFORMANCE TESTS

1   PRE-TRIP INSPECTION TEST

2   BASIC CONTROL SKILLS TEST

3

FIGURE 3-7: CDL TESTS

What are **_performance tests_**? Mostly, they are the tests in which
you show your driving skills and road safety sense. They answer
questions about your driving ability. How well can you handle the
bus? How completely do you do a safety inspection? How well do
you drive in traffic?

Performance tests are also called driving tests, road tests, or skill
tests. They are tests that require use of a vehicle. They allow you
to prove your driving ability.

Here are some key points to remember about the CDL performance tests:

1. You may take the CDL performance tests only after you
    have passed the required written tests.

2. There are three types of performance tests: a pre-trip
    safety inspection test; a basic control skills test; and a
    road test.

3. The vehicle safety inspection test is usually given first.
    Then you take the basic control skills test, and then the
    road test. In some cases, the basic control skills tests are
    given at points on the road test route. In most cases, they
    will test your basic skills first and then go on the road.
    This way, if you do poorly with the basic skills, you will
    not be taken on the road. It may not be safe to do so.

4. The state will fail you if you do not obey traffic laws or
    cause an accident during the tests.

5. Performance tests must be taken in the type of vehicle for
    which you wish to be licensed. The USDOT CDL rules say
    that an applicant must take the skill/road test in a "repre-
    sentative vehicle." This means any bus within the vehicle
    group or license class that you intend to drive. The driv-
    ing test(s) are given to find out if you can operate any bus
    within that vehicle group.

**Performance
Tests**

IF YOU WANT A
LICENSE TO DRIVE
THIS BUS...

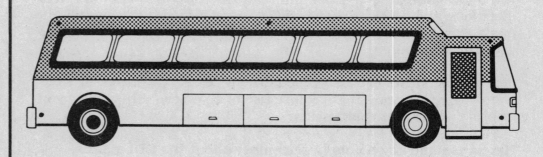

THEN YOU CAN TAKE A **CDL** DRIVING TEST IN A BUS SUCH AS
THESE......

FIGURE 3-8: CDL DRIVING TEST BY VEHICLE CLASS

6. All driving tests are conducted in on-street conditions or under a combination of on-street and off-street conditions.

7. You must pass all performance tests to get your bus CDL. To get a passing score on the driving tests, you must prove you can safely perform all required skills. A complete list of these skills is found in Part Five — Appendix G at the back of the book.

The performance tests are described briefly in the following paragraphs.

Vehicle Safety Inspection Test

The Vehicle Safety Inspection is also called the pre-trip inspection. The test is given to see if you know whether the bus is safe to drive. During the inspection, you must tell the examiner what is being inspected and why. The examiner will mark on a scoring form each item that was correctly inspected. Chapter Twelve tells you what you need to inspect.

Basic Control Skills Test

The purpose of this test is to measure your skill in controlling the bus. **Basic control skills** include starting, stopping, backing, turning, and changing gears. The examiner will explain how each test exercise is to be done. It is a good idea to practice these exercises. They are explained in Chapter Thirteen. The skills you learn through practice will help you pass the test. They will also help you drive better even if your job does not require exactly the same things.

Road Test

The Road Test measures your ability to drive safely in most on-the-road situations. The test drive is taken over a route set by the examiner. It will include, whenever possible, left and right turns, curves, upgrades and downgrades, intersections, country roads, city streets with several lanes, and expressway driving.

You will drive over a test route while following instructions from the examiner. The examiner will score you on the way you turn, change lanes, merge into traffic, and control speed. Scoring takes place at certain spots along the test route. The examiner will also score you on whether you signal correctly, search for hazards, control speed, and how you position your bus. Chapter Fourteen explains the road test.

Why So Many Different Tests?

It is easy to understand why there are three types of performance tests. A commercial bus driver must be a safe and skillful operator because of the valuable cargo he or she hauls. But what about all the written exams?

Only one written exam would be needed if all commercial drivers drove the same type vehicle and hauled the same type of cargo. The different vehicles they drive and many cargoes they haul require different types of knowledge and skills. The CDL tests were made to handle these differences.

The General Knowledge Test checks what every driver should know. That's why it is given to all drivers applying for a CDL. The other tests are specialized because they deal with different types of vehicles and cargoes. For example, drivers of vehicles with air brakes need to know more about the safe operation of air brakes. It would be unfair to ask all drivers to take a test having in-detail air brake questions when some have vehicles without air brakes. The same types of arguments can be made for the other specialized tests.

Another way of looking at the different tests is that each test result makes a decision about you. Results of the General Knowledge Test tell whether or not you should be licensed at all. Results of the Passenger Test indicate whether or not you should be permitted to drive a bus, and so forth.

Here are the general rules set by USDOT on passing the CDL Tests.

1. You must correctly answer at least 80 percent (80%) of the questions on each knowledge test in order to pass the test.

2. To get a passing score on the performance tests, you must show that you can successfully perform all of the required skills for your vehicle.

3. Two factors decide if you receive an air brake restriction on your CDL:

   a. The score you receive on the air brake knowledge test.
   b. The type of vehicle you drive during the driving skills test.

Here is how the air brake restriction works:

- If you score less than 80 percent (80%) on the air brake knowledge test, you will receive an air brake restriction on your CDL. That means you can drive only buses without air brakes.

- If you take the driving skill test in a bus not equipped with air brakes you will be restricted to driving buses which do not have air brakes.

The air brake restriction is now used by nearly all states.

- To avoid the restriction, take your driving skill test in a vehicle which has air brakes.

- An air brake restriction is shown on your CDL card or document.

For the driving skill test and the air brake restriction, air brakes mean any braking system that works fully or partly on the air brake principle.

Your state may have a separate air brake knowledge test. If it does not have the separate test, air brake questions will be found in the General Knowledge Test.

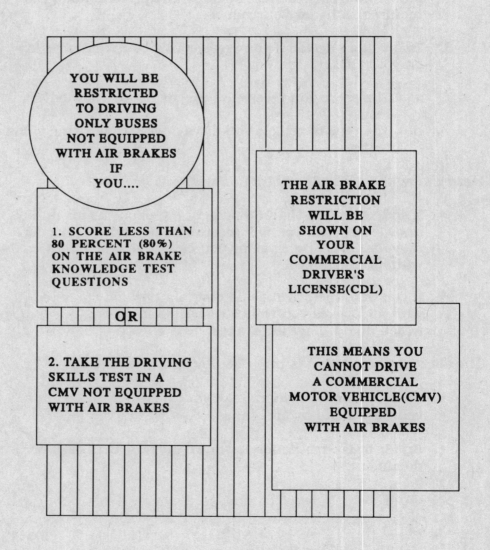

FIGURE 3-9: AIR BRAKE RESTRICTION

Exceptions

There are exceptions to the national CDL rules. For instance, you may not have to take a driving skill test because of your bus driving experience or good driving record. Who you work for or the type of work you do may free you from some CDL requirements. Your state is given some leeway in deciding this, so check your state's CDL rules. You may qualify for an exemption. You may be an exception to the CDL rule.

Substitute For Driving Skills Test

The USDOT knows that many CMV drivers are professionals. As a group, these drivers are highly experienced in the skills needed to operate trucks and buses. That is why the national CDL rules give states some options. The state can allow certain drivers to substitute a good driving record and experience for the driving skills tests.

The option would apply to a driver of CMVs who was currently licensed at the time of his or her application for a CDL. This driver must:

1. Have a good driving record and have previously passed the state driving skills test in a CMV;
   or
2. Have a good driving record along with certain driving experience.

A state using this option has certain rules to follow. One rule is that a driver must now be licensed to drive a CMV. Then he or she must:

1. Sign a paper that says they have not broken certain traffic laws.
   and
2. Sign that they have already passed the acceptable driving skills tests. They can also show that they have experience driving a CMV.

An "acceptable" test refers to a driving test given by a state with a classified licensing and testing system. This means a test taken in a vehicle of the class they want to be licensed to drive. This state option does not apply to the knowledge tests. The knowledge tests are required for all drivers — old or new.

Penalties

The Act of 1986 sets penalties for states that do not put the rules described in this chapter into force by September 30, 1993. These rules also require that CMV drivers take and pass the proper knowledge and skill tests by April 1, 1992. This is to make sure that all truck and bus drivers in the nation are qualified and licensed to operate the CMVs they drive.

As a minimum, each person to whom a CDL is issued must pass a written test and a driving test that meet uniform national standards.

To drive any bus, you will need a commercial driver's license.

Summary

Check your state's CDL rules. If you are currently licensed to drive a bus, you may not have to take and pass a driving skills test. These reasons may be used in place of the driving test.

- A good driving record

- Previously passed an acceptable skills test taken in a bus

- Good driving record and certain driving experience

A good driving record means that you were not convicted of a serious offense during the previous two years. It also means that your license to drive was not suspended, revoked, or canceled during this time, and you were not disqualified from driving a commercial motor vehicle.

You must also prove and certify that you are regularly employed as a bus driver and that:

1. You have previously taken and passed a skills test for a classified driver's license. This means the test was behind-the-wheel in a representative vehicle for that license class; or
2. For at least two years before your application for a CDL, you have operated a vehicle of the class for which you wish to be licensed (CDL).

WHAT IS A BUS?

ANY COMMERCIAL MOTOR VEHICLE DESIGNED TO SEAT AND CARRY 16 OR MORE PASSENGERS, INCLUDING THE DRIVER.

ALL BUS DRIVERS MUST HAVE A COMMERCIAL DRIVER'S LICENSE (CDL).

FIGURE 3-10: DEFINITION OF A BUS

SOME STATES HAVE STRICTER REQUIREMENTS. FOR EXAMPLE, CALIFORNIA REQUIRES YOU TO HAVE A CDL IF YOUR VEHICLE CARRIES 10 OR MORE PERSONS.

Key Words

Air brakes — A type of braking system on trucks and buses. A restriction will appear on the CDL if you take the test in a vehicle which does not have them.

Basic Control Skills Test — a test that checks how well you can control your bus.

Cargo — The load the truck or bus is carrying.

CDL Driver's Handbook — The official book put out by the state that tells the rules for commercial driver licensing.

Combination Vehicle — Tractor-trailers or truck and trailers.

General Knowledge Test — The written test that all drivers must take.

GCWR — Gross Combination Weight Rating (tractor-trailers or truck and trailers)

GVWR — Gross Vehicle Weight Rating (straight trucks and buses)

Manual transmission — One in which you have to shift the gears.

Performance tests — Tests of your driving skills and how well you check out your vehicle before you drive it.

Representative vehicle — One that is like the type an applicant intends to operate.

Specialized tests — Special tests for the CDL that measure special skills or requirements.

REVIEW QUESTIONS

1. As a bus driver you are under a national driver's licensing program. Who sets the rules for this national program?

   _____

2. Are states free to add rules that are stricter than the national rules?

   _____

3. Which drivers are covered by the national CDL program?

   _____

   _____

4. Which of these statements are true?
   A. All drivers must have a CDL if they drive a single or combination vehicle which weighs more than 26,000 pounds.
   B. CDL rules apply only to interstate drivers.
   C. Any driver who operates a bus which can carry 16 or more passengers must have a CDL.
   D. The driver of any size vehicle carrying hazardous material must have a CDL.

   _____

5. What are the classes of commercial vehicles which need a CDL to be driven? Can you name examples of vehicles in each class?

   _____

   _____

   _____

6. What are four kinds of CDL endorsements used?

   _____

   _____

   _____

   _____

7. What do these CDL Codes stand for?

A _____

B _____

C _____

N _____

T _____

P _____

H _____

X _____

8. What is the one CDL restriction?

_____

9. What is a "representative vehicle"?

_____

_____

10. What are the two kinds of CDL tests? The CDL tests a
    driver must take will usually depend upon what factor?

_____

_____

_____

11. A CDL applicant will have to take one or more written
    knowledge tests. What are these tests?

_____

_____

_____

12. What drivers will have to take an air brakes test? A
    tanker test? A combination vehicles test?

_____

_____

_____

13. What are the tests a bus driver will have to pass?

_____

_____

14. What are performance tests? Name the three types of performance tests.

_____

_____

_____

15. What do these tests measure?

A. Vehicle Inspection Test _____

B. Basic Control Skills Test _____

C. Road Test _____

16. Why are there so many CDL tests?

_____

_____

17. What two factors decide if you receive an air brake restriction on your CDL?

_____

_____

18. What are the exceptions to the national CDL rules?

_____

_____

PART TWO
BUS DRIVER'S MANUAL

This part of the book is a manual in itself. It was written to help you pass the bus driver's tests for a Commercial Driver's License. There are four chapters that apply to the buses you may want to drive. The chapters are listed below. They contain information you need to pass the knowledge tests.

Chapter 4: What All Commercial Drivers Should Know
This chapter should be studied by all drivers who want a CDL. It applies to both truck drivers and bus drivers.

Chapter 5: Carrying Passengers Safely
This chapter should be studied by all CDL applicants who want to drive buses.

Chapter 6: Does Your Bus Have Air Brakes?
This chapter should be studied by all CDL drivers who want to drive vehicles with air brakes. If you do not pass the air brake test questions you will be restricted to driving only vehicles without air brakes. This restriction will be placed on your CDL card.

Chapter 7: Driving A Tractor-Trailer Bus
If you want a CDL to drive a tractor-trailer bus you should study this chapter. The information is the same for all combination vehicles. It is the information you need to know to pass the test for:

- Tractor-trailers,
- Straight trucks pulling heavy trailers,
- Doubles,
- Triples,
- Tractor-trailer buses.

WHAT EVERY COMMERCIAL DRIVER SHOULD KNOW

CHAPTER

FROM NOW ON,

ONLY THE BEST WILL DRIVE

Chapter Objectives

Define what is a commercial driver

Explain reasons for vehicle safety inspections

List in detail the parts of the vehicle which must
be examined during an inspection

Define types of vehicle safety inspections

Explain basic procedures for maintaining
control of the vehicle

Explain safe procedures for backing, braking,
and shifting

Detail safe driving techniques for all types
of weather conditions

Discuss types of hazards and emergencies
a commercial driver may encounter

List correct procedures to be followed in the case of an
accident or a fire or when transporting
hazardous materials

Acquaint the driver with the dangers of using
drugs or alcohol and driving

CHAPTER 4

WHAT EVERY COMMERCIAL DRIVER SHOULD KNOW

As a truck or bus driver you must have a good general knowledge of safe driving practices. That's what this chapter is about — the information that all commercial drivers should know.

You must take a test on this information to get your CDL. This book will test you with the General Knowledge Test (Chapter Eight).

There is information on hazardous materials. As a commercial driver, you must know what materials require a hazardous material endorsement on your CDL.

This chapter does not contain information on combination vehicles (tractor-trailers, doubles, or triples), air brakes, or buses. This special information is found in other chapters.

Who is a Commercial Driver?

Who are the truck and bus drivers that need to know this information? Who is considered a commercial vehicle driver?

You are a **commercial driver** if you operate a truck weighing over 26,001 pounds (GVWR) or if you drive a bus which transports more than 16 passengers, including yourself. You are also a commercial driver if you haul **hazardous materials**. For example, each vehicle shown in Figure 4-1 is driven by a commercial driver.

This chapter is for all commercial drivers. It contains the general information and tells about the safe driving practices all truck and bus drivers should know.

Remember, the CMVSA/86 requires all commercial drivers to have a CDL. To get your CDL, you must be qualified. This includes taking the **General Knowledge Test**. This means you will be tested on facts found in this chapter — no matter for what class of commercial driver's license you are applying!

Vehicle Safety Inspections

There are three very good reasons for inspecting your truck or bus. The most important reason is safety. You inspect your vehicle to insure that it is safe to drive.

The second reason for the **vehicle safety inspection (VSI)** is economy. By doing a complete inspection every day, you become more familiar with your equipment. This helps you spot small problems before they become big problems. Small problems always cost less to fix than big ones. If you break down due to a careless VSI, it will cost you and your company time and money.

The third reason for the VSI is the law. Federal and state laws require certain inspections to be done on a regular basis. Remember, the VSI is not just a good idea, it is the law. Because it is the law, federal and state inspectors inspect commercial vehicles. An unsafe vehicle can be put "out-of-service" until the driver or owner fixes it.

FIGURE 4-1: EXAMPLES OF VEHICLES DRIVEN
BY COMMERCIAL DRIVERS

Certain defects will place your vehicle out-of-service immediately because they are considered very dangerous by the USDOT. These include:

- Serious air losses.

- Cracked wheels.

- Loose lug nuts.

- Cracked or broken brake drums.

- Defective steering.

- Defective suspension systems.

Most other defects must be corrected as soon as possible.

The USDOT uses these rules to define "out-of-service."

- *Driver* — When driver has driven more than the maximum permitted hours or has not prepared a duty status record.

- *Vehicle* — When motor vehicle by reason of its mechanical condition or loading would very likely cause an accident or breakdown.

To review, the three reasons for doing a proper VSI are safety, economy, and the law. By far, the most important of these reasons is safety!

Types of Vehicle Safety Inspections

There are three types of vehicle safety inspections: the pre-trip, the in-trip, and the post-trip.

The pre-trip inspection will usually be the most complete inspection each day. You do a pre-trip inspection before each trip to find problems that can cause a crash or breakdown. This VSI is required by law and by your company. It may include filling out a *vehicle condition report.*

The in-trip inspection is done as you drive and each time you stop. The reason for the in-trip is that parts do not break and wear out just at convenient times. This can happen anytime.

During a trip, for safety you should:

- Watch gauges for signs of trouble.

- Use your senses to check for problems (look, listen, smell, feel).

- Check these critical items when you stop.

    Tires, wheels and rims

    Brakes

    Lights

    Brake and electrical connections to trailer

    Trailer coupling devices

    Cargo securement devices

The post-trip is the inspection you do at the end of the trip, day, or tour of duty. It may include filling out a vehicle condition report listing any problems you find. The inspection report (vehicle condition report) helps the owner know when to fix something.

The post-trip inspection is required by law for "company drivers" when more than one driver uses the same vehicle. A vehicle condition report is filled out by the driver leaving the vehicle. The next driver would fill out the VCR from his or her pre-trip inspection. The post-trip report from the last driver should match the pre-trip report from the next one.

A good VSI does not have to take a lot of time. You may spend more time in the beginning until you know what to look for. Your VSI should be done in the same order every day. When you follow the same steps each time, your inspection will become more efficient and you will reduce the amount of time it takes to complete it.

A good VSI must be thorough, efficient, and consistent. You do not need to be a trained mechanic to do a thorough inspection. The things a driver can spot are the ones most likely to cause an accident or a breakdown.

To do a proper VSI, you must first know what to examine. Here are some ideas.

Tire Problems

It is dangerous to drive with bad tires. Look for these problems:

- Too much or too little air pressure

- Bad wear. You need at least 4/32 inch tread depth in every major groove on front wheels. You need 2/32 inch on the other wheels. No fabric should show through the tread or sidewall.

- Cut or other damage

- Tread separation

- Dual tires that come in contact with each other or parts of the vehicle

- Sizes that do not match

- Radial and bias-ply tires used together

- Cut or cracked valve stems

- Do not use regrooved, recapped, or retreaded tires on the front wheels of a bus.

Wheel and Rim Problems

- Bad wheels or rims: These could cause a crash.

- Damaged rims: These can cause tires to lose pressure or come off.

- Rust around wheel nuts: This may mean the nuts are loose. Check tightness. After a tire has been changed, stop a short while later and recheck tightness of the nuts.

- Missing clamps, spacers, studs, or lugs: These mean danger.

- Mismatched, bent, or cracked lock rings

- Wheels or rims that have had welding repairs: These are not safe to use.

Bad Brake Drums or Shoes

- Cracked drums

- Brake shoes or pads with oil, grease, or brake fluid on them

- Shoes worn thinner than 1/32-inch at any point, or shoes which are missing or broken

Steering System Defects

- Missing nuts, bolts, cotter keys, or other parts

- Bent, loose, or broken parts, such as steering column, steering gear box, or tie rods

- If power steering equipped — hoses, pumps, and fluid level; check for leaks.

- Steering wheel play of more than 10 degrees (approximately 2 inches movement at the rim of a 20-inch steering wheel). This can make it hard to steer.

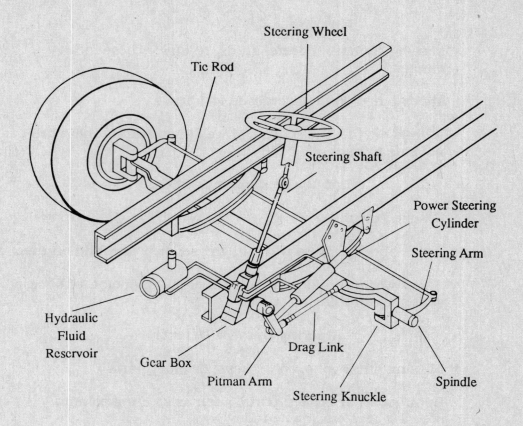

Steering Wheel

Tie Rod

Steering Shaft

Power Steering
Cylinder

Steering Arm

Hydraulic
Fluid
Reservoir

Gear Box

Pitman Arm

Drag Link

Steering Knuckle

Spindle

FIGURE 4-2: KEY PARTS OF STEERING SYSTEM

Suspension System Defects

The **suspension system** holds up the vehicle and its load and keeps the axles in place. Therefore, broken suspension parts can be very, very dangerous. You should check for:

• Spring hangers that let the axle move from its proper position.

• Cracked or broken spring hangers.

- Missing or broken leaves in any leaf spring. (If one-fourth of the leaves or more are missing, it will put the vehicle "out of service." Any defect can be dangerous though.)

- Broken leaves in a multi-leaf spring or leaves that have shifted so they might hit a tire or other part.

- Leaking shock absorbers.

- Torque arm U-bolts, spring hangers or other axle positioning parts that are cracked, damaged, or missing.

- Air suspension systems that are damaged and/or leaking.

- Any loose, cracked, broken, or missing frame members.

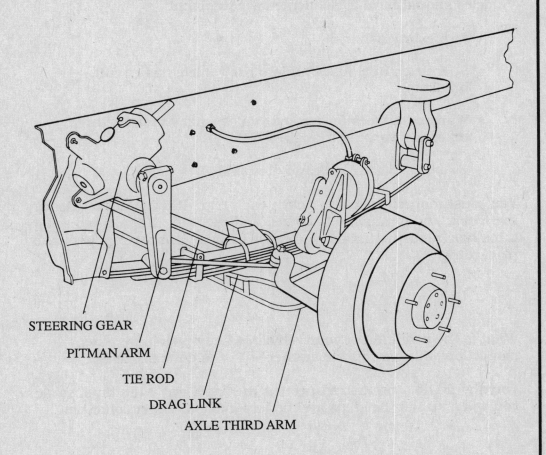

STEERING GEAR

PITMAN ARM

TIE ROD

DRAG LINK

AXLE THIRD ARM

FIGURE 4-3: KEY PARTS OF THE SUSPENSION SYSTEM

Exhaust System Defects

A broken exhaust system can let poison fumes into the cab or sleeper berth. You should check for:

- Loose, broken, or missing exhaust pipes, mufflers, tailpipes, or vertical stacks.

- Loose, broken, or missing mounting brackets, clamps, bolts, or nuts.

- Exhaust system parts that are leaking.

Emergency Equipment

Vehicles should have this emergency equipment:

- Fire extinguisher(s)

- Spare electrical fuses (unless the vehicle has circuit breakers)

- Warning devices for parked vehicles (for example, three reflective warning triangles)

Cargo (Trucks)

You must inspect the cargo before each trip. It must not overload the truck, and it must be balanced and secured. If the cargo contains hazardous materials, you must inspect for proper papers and placarding.

A Seven-Step Pre-Trip Inspection

What is the condition of your vehicle? A complete seven-step inspection will give you the answer — if it is done properly.

You should do a pre-trip inspection the same way each time, so you will learn all the steps and be less likely to forget something.

1. Approach checks: As you approach the vehicle, look at its overall condition. Check for fuel, oil, or water leaks and for damage.

2. Check the engine *compartment:* Raise the hood or cab, or open the engine compartment door, and complete the inspection.

3. Start the engine and check inside the vehicle: Get in, start the engine warm up, and check the controls and instruments. Check the condition of all emergency equipment (fire extinguisher, electrical fuses, reflective triangles, etc.).

4. Check lights: Put on the parking brake (chock wheels if you have to), get out and check high/low beam headlights and four-way warning flashers.

5. Conduct walkaround inspection: Turn off headlights and four-way flashers, turn on marker, clearance, and ID lights, put on right turn signal and then walk around the vehicle and inspect it.

6. Check lights: Turn off all lights, turn on left turn signal and stop lights (you may need a helper). Make sure they work.

7. Check brake system: Get in, turn lights on/off as required for driving. Do brake system tests and a final instrument check.

Each of these seven steps is described in greater detail later in the chapter. Vehicle Inspection Test Helpers are shown in Figure 4-4, Figure 4-5, and Figure 4-6. They may help you remember important things to look for. You can cut them out and bring them with you when you take your CDL test.

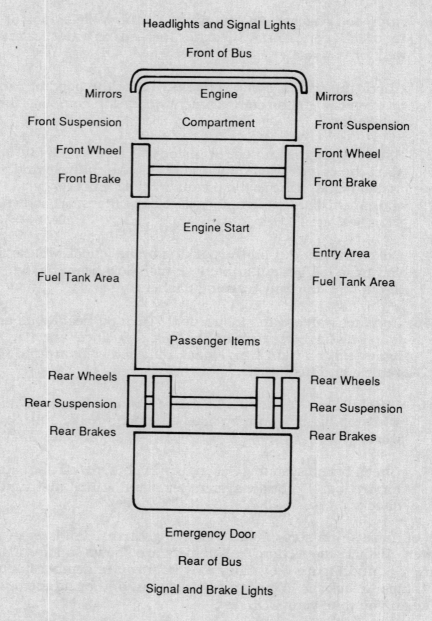

FIGURE 4-4: VEHICLE INSPECTION TEST HELPER
SCHOOL BUS

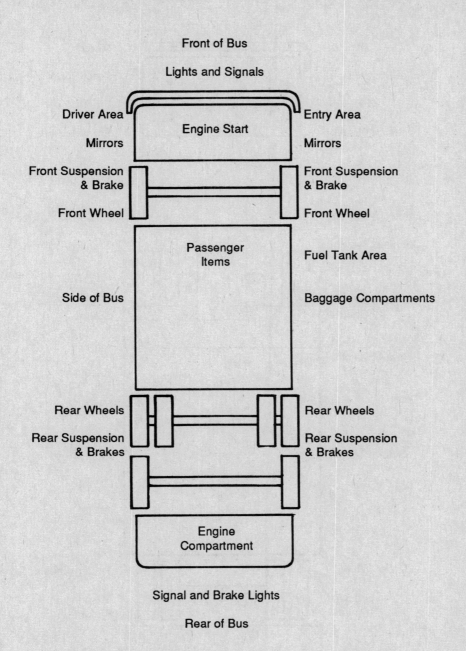

FIGURE 4-5: VEHICLE INSPECTION TEST HELPER
INTERCITY/TRANSIT BUS

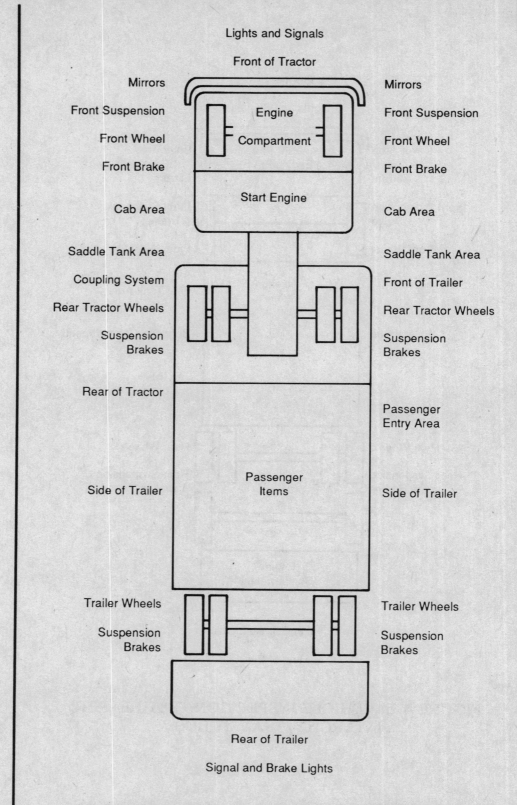

Lights and Signals

Front of Tractor

Mirrors	Engine	Mirrors
Front Suspension	Compartment	Front Suspension
Front Wheel		Front Wheel
Front Brake		Front Brake
	Start Engine	
Cab Area		Cab Area
Saddle Tank Area		Saddle Tank Area
Coupling System		Front of Trailer
Rear Tractor Wheels		Rear Tractor Wheels
Suspension Brakes		Suspension Brakes
Rear of Tractor		Passenger Entry Area
Side of Trailer	Passenger Items	Side of Trailer
Trailer Wheels		Trailer Wheels
Suspension Brakes		Suspension Brakes

Rear of Trailer

Signal and Brake Lights

FIGURE 4-6: VEHICLE INSPECTION TEST HELPER
TRACTOR-TRAILER BUS

SEVEN-STEP
PRE-TRIP INSPECTION
CHECKLIST

1. **Approach Vehicle — Look for Leaks**

2. **Check Under Hood or Cab**

3. **Start Engine and Check Inside Cab**

4. **Check Headlights and Warning Lights**

5. **Conduct Walkaround Inspection**

6. **Check Signal Lights**

7. **Check Air Brake System**

FIGURE 4-7: SEVEN-STEP PRE-TRIP INSPECTION
CHECKLIST

One: Approach Checks

Walk toward the vehicle. Look at the general condition. Look for damage or if the vehicle is leaning to one side. Look under it for fresh oil, coolant, grease or fuel leaks. Check the area around the vehicle for anything that may be a danger when you move it (people, other vehicles, objects, low hanging wires, tree limbs.)

Review the last vehicle inspection report. Drivers may have to make a vehicle inspection report in writing each day. The vehicle owner should repair any items listed in the report that affect safety. You should look at the last report to find out what was the matter, if anything. Check the vehicle to find out if the problems were fixed.

Two: Check the Engine Compartment

Check to be sure that the parking brakes are on and/or wheels chocked. Raise the hood, tilt the cab (secure loose things so they don't fall and break something), or open the engine compartment door. Check the following:

- Engine oil level

- Coolant level in radiator and condition of hose

- Level of power steering fluid and condition of hoses (if so equipped)

- Level of windshield washer fluid

- Battery fluid level and battery connections and tie downs (battery may be located elsewhere)

- Level of automatic transmission fluid (you may have to run the engine)

- Check alternator, water pump, and air compressor belts for tightness and excessive wear. Learn how much "give" the belts should have when they are adjusted correctly. Check each one.

- Leaks in the engine compartment (fuel, coolant, oil, power steering fluid, hydraulic fluid, battery fluid)

- Cracked or worn electrical wiring insulation

Lower and secure the hood or cab. Shut the engine compartment door.

Three: Start the Engine and Inspect Inside the Cab

- Get in and start the engine.

- Make sure the parking brake is on.

- Put the gearshift in neutral (or "park" if automatic).

- Start the engine; listen for strange noises.

Look at all Gauges

- Oil pressure — should come up to normal within seconds after engine is started

- Ammeter and/or voltmeter — should be in normal range(s)

- Coolant temperature — should begin slow rise to normal operating range

- Engine oil temperature — should begin gradual rise to normal operating range

- Warning lights and buzzers — oil, coolant, charging circuit warning lights should go out right away

Check Condition of Controls

Check all of the controls listed below for looseness, sticking, damage, or improper setting.

- Steering wheel

- Clutch

- Accelerator (gas pedal)

- Brakes
  Foot brake
  Trailer brake (if there is one)
  Parking brake
  Retarders (if vehicle has them)

- Transmission

- Interaxle differential lock (if there is one)

- Horn(s)

- Windshield wiper/washer

- Lights
  Headlights
  Dimmer switch
  Turn signal
  4-way flashers
  Clearance, identification, marker light switch(es)

Check Mirrors and Windshield

Inspect mirrors and windshield for cracks, dirt, illegal stickers, or anything that would prevent the driver from seeing. Clean and adjust if needed.

Check Emergency Equipment

Check for safety equipment:

- Spare electrical fuses (unless vehicle has circuit brakers)
- Three red reflective triangles
- Properly charged and rated fire extinguishers

Check for optional items such as:

- Tire chains (where winter conditions require them)
- Tire changing equipment
- List of emergency phone numbers
- Accident reporting kit (packet)

Apply the parking brake, turn on headlights (low beams) and four-way flashers, and get out.

Four: Check Lights

- Go to the front of the vehicle and check that low beams are on and both of the four-way flashers are working.
- Push the dimmer switch and check that high beams work.

Five: Do Walkaround Inspection

- Turn off headlights and four-way hazard warning flashers.
- Turn on the parking, clearance, side-marker and identification lights.
- Turn on the right turn signal. Walk around the vehicle and inspect it.
- Clean all lights, reflectors, and glass as you go along.

Walkaround Sequence

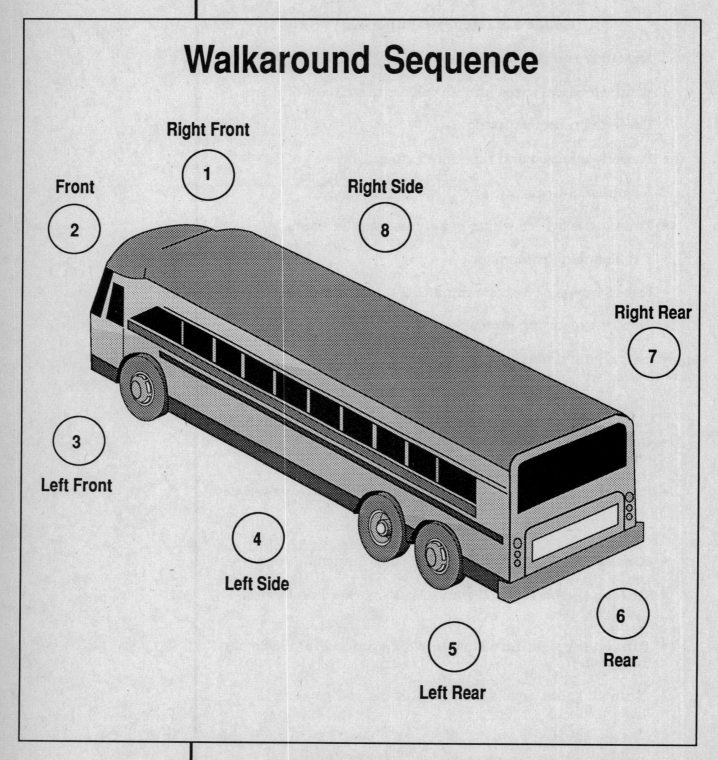

FIGURE 4-8: BUS WALKAROUND INSPECTION

Right Side

- Passenger entry door glass should be clean.

- Door latch or locking mechanism should work.

- Right front wheel

    Check the condition of wheels and rims — no missing, bent, or broken studs, clamps, lugs, or any signs of not being aligned.

    Condition of tires — properly inflated, valve stem and cap OK; no serious cuts, bulges, or tread wear.

    Use wrench to test rust-streaked lug nuts for looseness.

    Hub oil level OK with no leaks.

- Right front suspension

    Check the condition of springs, spring hangers, shackles, and U-bolts.

    Check the condition of the shock absorbers.

- Right front brake

    Brake drum should be in good condition.

    Condition of hoses (no leaks or signs of failure).

Right Rear

- Check the condition of wheels and rims — no missing, bent, broken spacers, studs, clamps, or lugs.

- Condition of tires — They should be properly inflated; valve stems and caps OK; no serious cuts, bulges, or tread wear; and not rubbing against each other or anything stuck between them.

- Tires should be of the same type. Do not mix radial and bias types.

- Tires should be evenly matched (same size).

- Be sure the wheel bearings and seals are not leaking.

- Suspension

    Check the condition of the spring(s), spring hangers, shackles, and U-bolts.

    The axle should be secure.

    Powered axle(s) should not be leaking lube (gear oil).

    Make sure the torque rod arms and bushings are in good condition.

    Check the condition of the shock absorber(s).

    If the vehicle has retractable axles, check the condition of the lift mechanism. If air powered, check for leaks.

- Brakes

    Check the condition of the brake drum(s).

    Make sure the hoses are in good condition — look for any wear due to rubbing.

- Lights and reflectors

    Side-marker lights should be clean, operating, and of the proper color (red at rear, others amber).

    Side-marker reflectors should be clean and of the proper color (red at rear, others amber).

Rear

- Lights and reflectors

    Rear clearance and ID lights should be clean, operating, and of the proper color (red at rear).

- *Reflectors* should be clean and of the proper color (red at rear).

- Taillights should be clean, operating, and of the proper color (red at rear).

- Right rear turn signal operating and of the proper color (red, yellow, or amber at rear).

- Be sure license plate(s) are present, clean, and secured.

- Splash guards should be present, not damaged, properly fastened, and not dragging on the ground or rubbing the tires.

Left Rear

- Check all in the same way as you did on the right rear.

Left Side

- Left front: Check all items in the same way as you did on the right side.
- Fuel tank(s)

  Should be securely mounted and not damaged or leaking

  Fuel line should be secure

  Tank(s) contain enough fuel

  Cap(s) on and secure

Front

- Check the condition of the front axle.

- Check the condition of the steering system.

  No loose, worn, bent, damaged or missing parts. Must grab steering mechanism to test for looseness.

- Windshield

  Check for damage and clean if dirty.

  Check windshield wiper arms for proper spring tension.

  Check wiper blades for damage, "stiff" rubber, and securement.

- Lights and reflectors

  Parking, clearance, and ID lights clean, operating and of the proper color (amber at front)

  Reflectors clean and of the proper color (amber at front)

- Front turn signal lights clean, operating, and of the proper color (amber or white on signals facing forward)

General

- Condition of visible parts

    Engine — not leaking

    Transmission — not leaking

    Exhaust system — secure, not leaking, and not touching wires or fuel lines

    Frame and cross members — no bends or cracks

    Electrical wiring — secured against snagging, rubbing, wearing

Six: Check Signal Lights

- Get in and turn off lights.

- Turn on stop lights (apply trailer hand brake or have a helper put on the brake).

- Turn on left turn signal lights.

- Get out and check lights.

- Left front turn signal light should be clean, operating, and of the proper color (amber or white on signals facing the front).

- Left rear turn signal light and both stop lights should be clean, operating and of the proper color (red, yellow, or amber).

Seven: Check Brake System

- Get in the vehicle.

- Turn off lights not needed for driving.

- Test for hydraulic leaks.

    If the vehicle has hydraulic brakes, pump the brake pedal three times. Then apply firm pressure to the pedal and hold for five seconds. The pedal should not move. If it does, there may be a leak or other problem. Get it fixed before driving.

- If the vehicle has air brakes, do the checks described in Chapters Six and Seven of this book.

- Test parking brake
  Fasten seat belt.
  Allow vehicle to move slowly.
  Apply parking brake.
  If it does not stop vehicle, it is faulty. Get it fixed.

- Test service brake stopping action
  Go about five miles per hour.
  Push brake pedal firmly.
  "Pulling" to one side or the other can mean brake
     trouble.
  Any unusual brake pedal "feel" or delayed stopping
     action can mean trouble.

Final Check

- Check for all required papers, trip manifests, permits, etc.

- Secure all loose articles in cab (they might interfere with operation of the controls or hit you in a crash).

This completes the pre-trip inspection.

IF YOU FIND ANYTHING THAT IS NOT SAFE DURING THE PRETRIP INSPECTION, GET IT FIXED. FEDERAL AND STATE LAWS FORBID OPERATING AN UNSAFE VEHICLE.

Inspection During a Trip

Check vehicle operation regularly. You should check:

- Instruments.

- Air pressure gauge (if you have air brakes).

- Temperature gauges.

- Pressure gauges.

- Ammeter/voltmeter.

- Mirrors.

- Tires.

- Cargo and cargo covers.

If you see, hear, smell, or feel anything that may mean trouble, check it out.

Safety Inspection

Truck drivers should inspect after the first 25 miles of a trip and every 150 miles or every 3 hours (whichever comes first) afterward. Check these things:

- Cargo doors and/or cargo securement

- Tires — Enough air pressure and not overheated

- Brakes — not overheated (put back of hand near brake drums to test)

- Coupling devices

After-Trip Inspection and Report

You may have to write a report each day on the condition of the vehicle(s) you drove. Report anything affecting safety or that can possibly lead to a mechanical breakdown.

The vehicle inspection report tells the vehicle owner about problems that may need fixing. Keep a copy of your report in the vehicle for one day. In that way, the next driver can learn about any problems you have found.

Basic Control

To drive a vehicle safely, you must be able to control its speed and direction. Safe operation of a commercial vehicle requires skill in:

- Accelerating.

- Steering.

- Shifting gears.

- Braking.

Fasten your seat belt when on the road. Apply the parking brake when you leave your vehicle.

Accelerating

Do not roll back when you start. You may hit someone behind you. Partly engage the clutch before you take your right foot off the brake. Put on the parking brake when you need to keep from rolling back. Release the parking brake only when you have applied enough engine power to keep from rolling back.

Speed up smoothly and slowly so the vehicle does not jerk. Rough or sudden acceleration can cause mechanical damage. When pulling a trailer, rough acceleration can damage the coupling.

Speed up very gradually when traction is poor, or in rain or snow. If you give it too much power, the drive wheels may spin and you can lose control. If the drive wheels begin to spin, take your foot off the accelerator.

Steering

Steering a large truck, tractor-trailer, or bus requires special skills. This is mainly due to their length. Hold the wheel correctly. Allow for "off-tracking" as you steer.

Hold the Wheel Right

Your grip on the wheel should be firm. If you hit a curb or pot-hole, the wheel could pull away from your hands unless you have a firm hold. Sit with your elbows free. This allows you to move easily and quickly. Both hands grasp the wheel's rim, not the spokes. Knuckles are outside the wheel with thumbs on top of it. Your hands should balance each other on opposite sides of the wheel.

THINK OF THE WHEEL AS A CLOCK. PLACE YOUR LEFT HAND BETWEEN THE EIGHT AND TEN O'CLOCK POSITIONS AND YOUR RIGHT HAND BETWEEN THE TWO AND FOUR O'CLOCK POSITIONS. THIS DOUBLE GRIP HELPS YOU MAINTAIN CONTROL OF YOUR BUS.

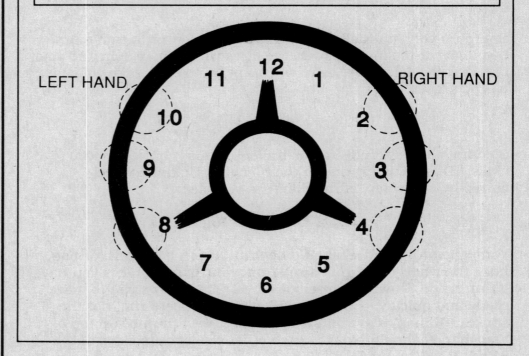

FIGURE 4-9: STEERING HANDHOLD

Off-Tracking

Any time you steer around corners and curves you should think about where your rear wheels are tracking. They follow a shorter path than the front wheels. This is called *off-tracking*. Notice the off-track of the rear inside wheels of the tractor-trailer in Figure 4-10.

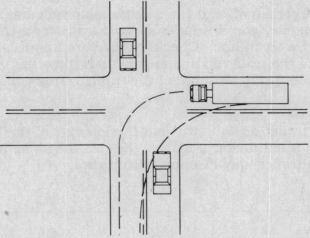

FIGURE 4-10: OFF-TRACKING

Tractor-trailers have a greater off-track than straight trucks or buses. In fact, tractor-trailers have two off-tracks. There is an off-track of the rear wheels of the tractor. There is an even greater off-track of the rear wheels of the trailer. These two off-tracks are shown in Figure 4-11.

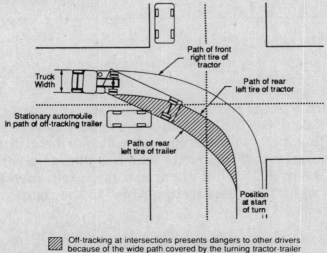

Off-tracking at intersections presents dangers to other drivers because of the wide path covered by the turning tractor-trailer

FIGURE 4-11: TRACTOR-TRAILER OFF-TRACKING

No matter what kind of big vehicle you drive, you must keep track of where your rear wheels are. If you do not, you can hit other vehicles or objects during turns. So, as you steer, allow for off-tracking.

Straightaways

Straight stretches of road can also cause problems for a tractor-trailer. The way you drive a truck and trailer or a tractor-trailer keeps the trailer in line. Check the mirrors frequently. If you can see more of the trailer in one mirror than the other, steer toward the side where you see more of the trailer. This will straighten out the rig.

When the trailer drifts to the left, the left side of the trailer fills up more of your left mirror (Figure 4-12). At the same time, the right side of the trailer may disappear from view.

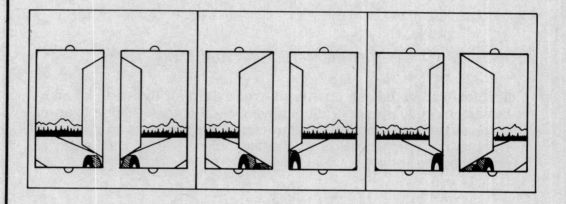

FIGURE 4-12: TRAILER DRIFTING

If the trailer drifts to the right, the view in the right mirror widens while the left side of the trailer disappears from view. To correct for minor drifting, turn your steering wheel toward the drift. In other words, turn toward the mirror which is filling up with a view of the side of the trailer. When the trailer drifts left, turn left. When it drifts right, turn the steering wheel to the right.

Backing with a Trailer

When backing a car, straight truck, or bus, you turn the top of the steering wheel toward the direction you want to go. When backing a trailer, you turn the steering wheel in the opposite direction. Once the trailer starts to turn, you must turn the wheel the other way to follow the trailer.

When you back with a trailer, try to position your vehicle so you can back in a straight line. If you must back on a curved path, back to the driver's side so you can see.

Back slowly. This will let you make corrections before you get too far off course.

Use the mirrors. The mirrors will help you see whether the trailer is drifting to one side or the other.

Correct drift at once. As soon as you see the trailer getting off the proper path, correct it by turning the top of the steering wheel in the direction of the drift.

Drive forward. When you must back, make pull-ups (drive forward) to reposition your vehicle as needed.

Backing Safely

Because you cannot see everything behind your vehicle, backing is always dangerous. Avoid backing whenever you can. When you park, try to park so you will be able to pull forward when you leave. When you have to back, here are a few simple safety rules:

- Look at your path.

- Back slowly.

- Back and turn toward the driver's side whenever possible.

- Use a helper whenever possible.

These rules are discussed on the next page.

Look at Your Path

Look at the line of travel before you begin. Get out and walk around the vehicle. Check your clearance to the sides and above the vehicle in and near the path your vehicle will take.

Back Slowly

Always back as slowly as possible. Use the lowest reverse gear. That way you can more easily correct any steering errors. You can also stop quickly if needed.

Back and Turn Toward the Driver's Side

Back toward the driver's side so you can see better. Backing toward the right side is very dangerous because you cannot see as well. If you back and turn toward the driver's side, you can watch the rear of your vehicle by looking out the side window. Use driver-side backing — even if it means going around the block to put your vehicle in this position. The added safety is worth it.

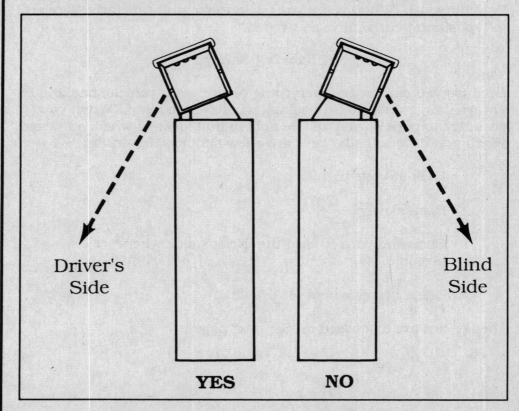

FIGURE 4-13: DRIVER'S SIDE BACKING

Use a Helper

Use a helper when you can. There are blind spots you cannot see. A helper is important to aid you in seeing all areas.

The helper should stand near the back of your vehicle where you can see him or her. Before you begin backing, work out a set of hand signals that you both understand. Agree on a signal to be used for "stop."

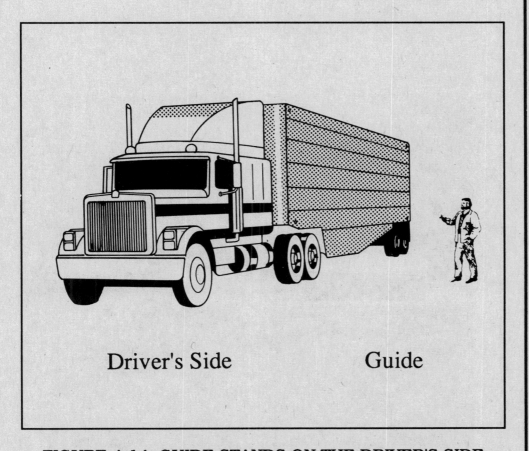

Driver's Side   Guide

FIGURE 4-14: GUIDE STANDS ON THE DRIVER'S SIDE

You need to have at least one convex spot mirror on the right side of your tractor. This mirror gives you a wide-angle view of your "blind side." Since this is most useful when you are turning, you should put your tractor at a 45° angle to the trailer as shown below before adjusting it.

While at this angle, you should be able to see the entire side of your trailer in this mirror.

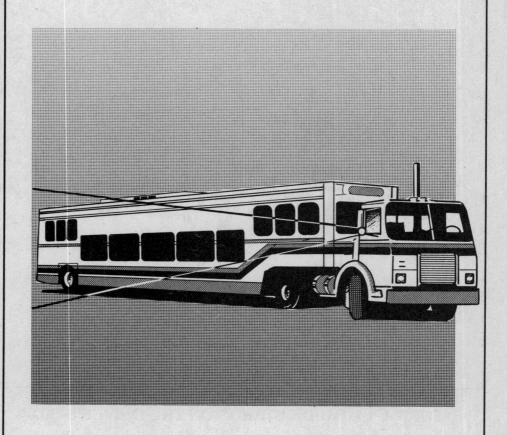

FIGURE 4-15: SPOT MIRRORS

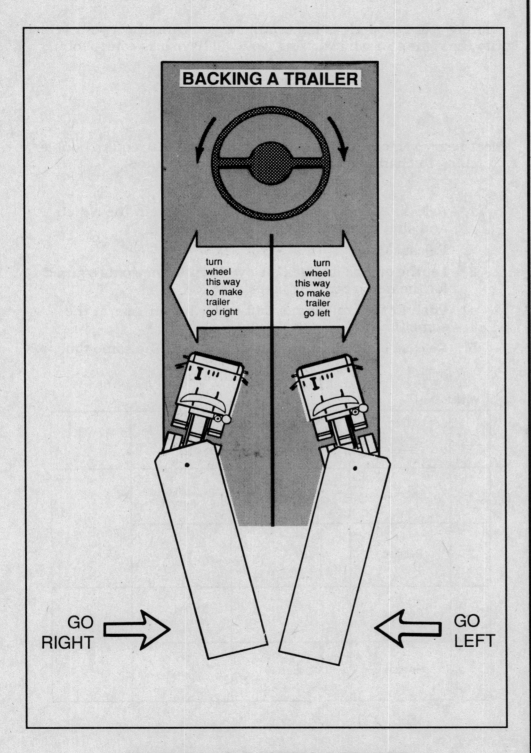

FIGURE 4-16: BACKING A TRAILER

Shifting Gears

Shifting gears properly is important. If you cannot get your vehicle into the right gear while driving, you will have less control of it.

Manual Transmissions

Basic Method For Shifting Up

Most heavy vehicles with manual *transmissions* require double clutching to change gears. This is the basic method:

1. Release the accelerator (gas pedal), push in the clutch and shift to neutral at the same time.
2. Release clutch.
3. Let the engine and gears slow down to the rpm required for the next gear (this takes practice).
4. Push in the clutch and shift to the higher gear at the same time.
5. Release clutch and press accelerator at the same time.

What to Do:

Step	Clutch 	Accelerator 	Stickshift 	
1	Depress	Release	Shift to Neutral	First Shift
2	Release			
3	Depress		Shift to Next Gear	Second Shift
4	Release	Depress		

FIGURE 4-17: DOUBLE CLUTCHING: UPSHIFT

Shifting gears while using double clutching requires practice. If you remain in neutral too long, you may have difficulty putting the vehicle into the next gear. If so, do not try to force it. Return to neutral, release the clutch, increase the engine speed to match the road speed, and try again.

Knowing When to Shift Up

There are two ways of knowing when to shift:

Use the engine speed (rpm). Study the driver's manual for your vehicle and learn the operating rpm range. Watch your tachometer, and shift up when your engine reaches the top of the range. Some newer vehicles use "progressive" shifting: the rpm at which you shift becomes higher as you move up in the gears. Find out what is right for the vehicle you will operate.

Use road speed (mph). Learn what speeds are best for each gear. Then, you can use the speedometer to know when to shift up. With either method, you may learn to use engine sounds to know when to shift.

Basic Method for Shifting Down

1. Release the accelerator, push in the clutch and shift to neutral at the same time.

2. Release the clutch.

3. Press down the accelerator, increase engine and gear speed to the rpm required in the lower gear.

4. Push in the clutch and shift to the lower gear at the same time.

5. Release the clutch and press the accelerator at the same time.

What to Do:

Step	Clutch	Accelerator	Stickshift	
1	Depress	Release	Shift to Neutral	First Shift
2	Release			First Shift
3		Depress		Rev
4	Depress	Release	Shift to Next Gear	Second Shift
5	Release			Second Shift

FIGURE 4-18: DOWNSHIFTING

Downshifting, like upshifting, requires knowing when to shift. Use either the tachometer or the speedometer and downshift at the right rpm or road speed.

Special Conditions Where You Should Downshift:

Before starting down a hill. Slow down and shift down to a speed that you can control without using the brakes hard. Otherwise, the brakes can get hot and lose their braking power. Downshift before starting down the hill. Make sure you are in a low enough gear, usually lower than the gear required to climb the same hill.

Before entering a curve. Slow to a safe speed, and downshift to the right gear before entering the curve. This lets you use some power through the curve to help the vehicle be more stable while turning. It also lets you speed up as soon as you are out of the curve.

Multiple-speed Rear Axle and Auxiliary Transmissions

These are used on many vehicles to provide extra gears. You usually control them by a knob or switch on the gearshift lever of the main transmission. There are many different shift patterns. Learn the right way to shift gears in the vehicle you will drive.

Automatic Transmissions

Some vehicles have automatic transmissions. You can select a low range to get greater engine braking when going down grades. The lower ranges prevent the transmissions from shifting up beyond the selected gear (unless the governor rpm is exceeded). It is very important to use this method when going down grades.

Retarders

Some vehicles have "retarders." Retarders help slow a vehicle, reducing the need to use the brakes. They reduce brake wear and give you another way to slow down. There are many types of retarders (exhaust, engine, hydraulic, or electric). All retarders can be turned on or off by the driver. On some vehicles, the retarding power can be adjusted. When turned "on," retarders apply their braking power to the drive wheels only when you let up on the gas pedal all the way.

Caution. When your drive wheels have poor traction, the retarders may cause them to skid. Turn them off when the road is wet, icy, or snow covered.

Braking

The most important part of your vehicle is the brakes. For safety's sake, it is far more important to be able to stop your truck or bus than to start it. Get into the habit of checking your brakes so that you may always safely stop.

It is to your advantage to develop good braking skills. Use gears to help slow down your big vehicle. Think ahead. Apply brakes early. It is to your disadvantage to "slow" using the brakes.

Good braking techniques demand that you do five things:

- Watch the road.

- Drive at a safe speed.

- Fit your driving to weather, road, and traffic conditions.

- Think ahead about what other drivers may do.

- Know the braking limits of your vehicle.

Brakes and braking are so vital to your driving that this book has a full chapter on these subjects. Chapter Six provides the basic braking information you will need to get your CDL.

Seeing

To be a safe driver, you need to know what is going on all around your vehicle. Not looking carefully is a major cause of accidents.

Seeing Ahead

All drivers look ahead, but many do not look far enough ahead.

The Importance of Looking Far Enough Ahead

Because stopping or changing lanes can take a lot of distance, knowing what traffic is doing is very important. You need to look well ahead of yourself to make sure you have room to make these moves safely.

How Far Ahead to Look

Most good drivers look 12 to 15 seconds ahead. That means looking ahead the distance you will travel in 12 to 15 seconds. At lower speeds, that is about one block. At highway speeds, it is about a quarter of a mile. If you're not looking that far ahead, you may have to stop too quickly or make quick lane changes. You must also look at things that are closer. Good drivers shift their attention back and forth, from near to far.

What to Look For

Traffic: Look for vehicles coming onto the highway, moving into your lane, or turning. Watch for brake lights from slowing vehicles. By seeing these things far enough ahead, you can change your speed or change lanes, if necessary, to avoid a problem.

Road conditions: Look for hills and curves — anything for which you will have to slow down or change lanes. Pay attention to traffic signals and signs. If a light has been green for a long time, it will probably change before you get there. Start slowing down and be ready to stop. Traffic signs can alert you to road conditions where you may have to change speed.

Seeing to the Sides and Rear

It is important to know what is going on behind your vehicle and to the sides. Check your mirrors regularly. Check more often in special situations.

Regular Checks

You need to make regular checks of your mirrors to be aware of traffic and to check your vehicle.

Traffic: Check the mirrors for vehicles on either side and in back of you. In an emergency, you may need to know whether you can make a quick lane change. Use your mirrors to spot vehicles that are behind you and going faster than you are. There are "blind spots" that your mirrors cannot show you. Check your mirrors regularly to know where other vehicles are around you and to see if they move into your blind spots.

Check your vehicle: Use the mirrors to keep an eye on your tires. It is one way to spot a tire fire. If you are carrying open cargo, you can use the mirrors to check it. Look for loose straps, ropes, or chains. Watch for a flapping or ballooning tarp.

Special Situations

Special situations require more care than just regular mirror checks. These special situations are lane changes, turns, merges, and tight maneuvers.

Lane changes: You need to check your mirrors to make sure no one is alongside you or about to pass you. Check your mirrors:

- Before you change lanes to make sure there is enough room.

- After you have signaled, so you can check to see that no one has moved into your blind spot.

- Right after you start the lane change in order to double-check that your path is clear.

- After you complete the lane change.

Turns: In turns, check your mirrors to make sure the rear of your vehicle will not hit anything.

Merges: When merging, use your mirrors to make sure the gap in traffic is large enough for you to enter safely.

Tight maneuvers: Any time you are driving in close quarters, check your mirrors often. Make sure you have enough clearance.

How to Use Mirrors

Use mirrors correctly by checking them quickly and understanding what you see.

Checking quickly: When you use your mirrors while driving on the road, check quickly. Look back and forth between the mirrors and the road ahead. Do not focus on the mirrors for too long. If you do, you will travel quite a distance without knowing what is happening ahead.

Understanding what you see: Many large vehicles have curved (convex) mirrors. These mirrors, also known as "fisheye," "spot," or "bugeye" mirrors, show a wider area than flat mirrors. This is often helpful. But everything appears smaller in a convex mirror than it would if you were looking at it directly. Things also seem farther away than they really are. It is important to realize this and to allow for it.

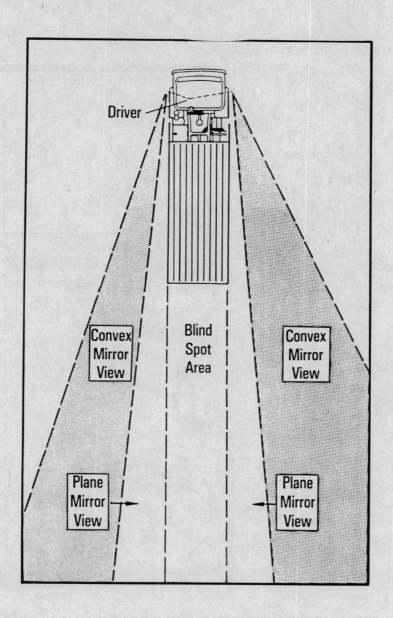

FIGURE 4-19: FIELD OF VISION
USING A CONVEX MIRROR

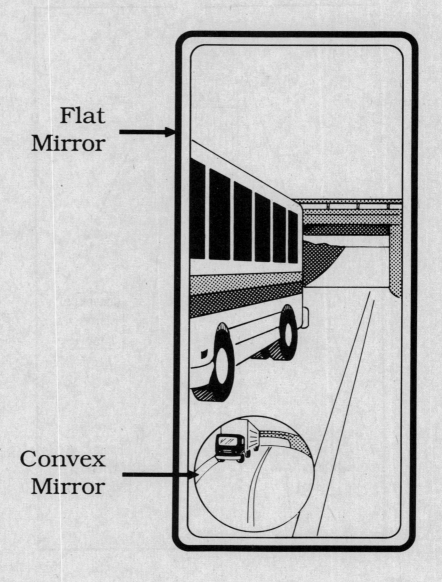

Flat
Mirror

Convex
Mirror

FIGURE 4-2O: DISTORTION OF CONVEX MIRRORS

Communicating

Other drivers cannot know what you are going to do until you tell them. One way to tell them is to signal your plans.

Signal What You Intend To Do

Signaling what you intend to do is important for safety. Here are some general rules for signaling.

Turns

There are three good rules for using turn signals: 1) Signal early; 2) Signal continuously; and 3) Turn off your signal (if you don't have self-canceling signals).

1. Signal early. Signal for some time before you turn. It is the best way to keep others from trying to pass you.

2. Signal continuously. You need both hands on the wheel to turn safely. Do not cancel the signal until you have completed the turn.

3. Cancel your signal after you have turned.

Lane Changes

Put on your turn signal before changing lanes. Change lanes slowly and smoothly. In that way, a driver you did not see may have a chance to honk the horn or avoid your vehicle.

Slowing Down

Warn drivers behind you when you see you will need to slow down. A few light taps on the brake pedal — enough to flash the brake lights — should warn drivers who are following. Use the 4-way emergency flashers when you are driving very slowly or are stopped. Warn other drivers in any of the following situations:

Trouble ahead: The size of your vehicle may make it hard for the drivers behind you to see the hazards ahead of you. If you see a hazard that will require slowing down, warn the drivers behind by flashing your brake lights.

Tight turns: Most car drivers do not know how slowly you have to drive to make a tight turn in a large vehicle. Give drivers behind you warning by braking early and slowing gradually.

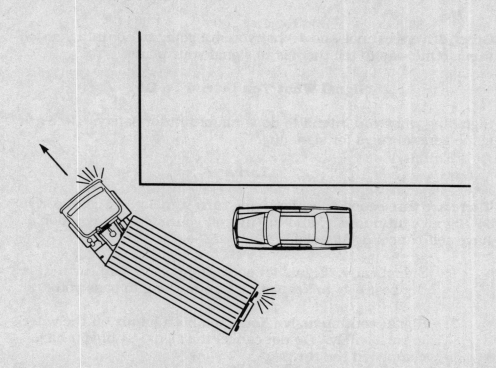

FIGURE 4-21: MAKING A RIGHT TURN FROM THE WRONG POSITION

 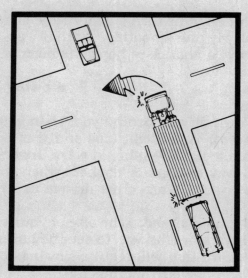

When Changing Lanes, Merging, Passing, or Turning

FIGURE 4-22: COMMUNICATE YOUR INTENT

Stopping on the road: Truck and bus drivers sometimes stop in the road to unload cargo or passengers or to stop for a railroad crossing. Warn drivers who are following by flashing your brake lights. Do not stop suddenly.

Driving Slowly

Drivers often do not realize how fast they are catching up to a slow vehicle until they are very close. If you must drive slowly, alert drivers who are behind you by turning on your emergency flashers (if it is legal). Laws regarding the use of flashers differ from one state to another. Check the laws of the states where you will drive.

Do Not Direct Traffic

Some drivers try to help out others by signaling when it is safe to pass. Do not do this. You can cause an accident. If you are blamed for it, you may have to pay many thousands of dollars in damages.

Communicate Your Presence

Other drivers may not notice your vehicle even when it is in plain sight. Let them know you are there. This will help prevent accidents.

When Passing

When you are about to pass a vehicle, a person on foot or bicycle, assume they do not see you. They could suddenly move in front of you. When it is legal, tap the horn lightly or, at night, flash your lights from low to high beam and back. Always try to drive carefully enough to avoid a crash even if others do not see or hear you.

When It is Hard to See

At dawn or dusk or in rain or snow, you need to make yourself easier to see. If you are having trouble seeing other vehicles, other drivers are having trouble seeing you. Turn on your lights. Use the headlights, not just the identification or clearance lights. Use the low beams; high beams can bother people in the daytime as well as at night.

When Parked At the Side of the Road

When you pull off the road and stop, be sure to turn on the 4-way emergency flashers. This is important at night. Do not trust the taillights to give warning. Drivers have crashed into the rear of a parked truck because they thought it was moving normally.

If you must stop on a road or the shoulder of a road, you should put out your reflective triangles within ten minutes. Place your warning devices at the following locations:

- On the traffic side of the vehicle — within ten feet of the front or rear corners — to mark the location of the vehicle. See Figure 4-23.

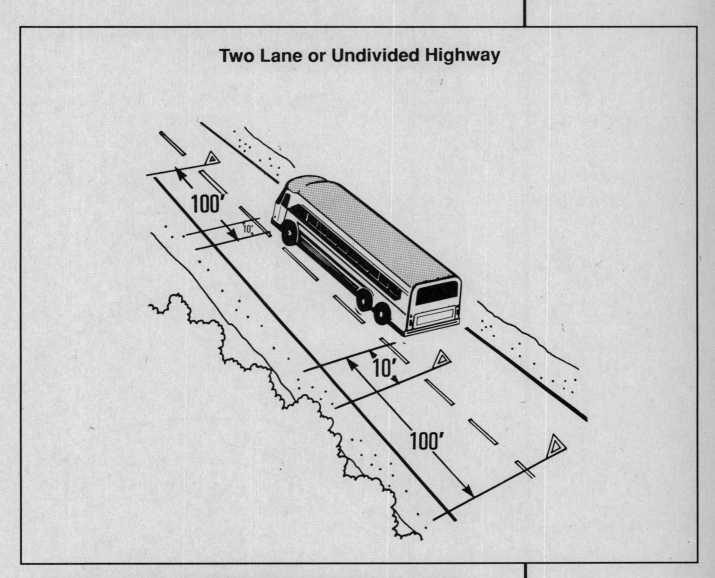

Two Lane or Undivided Highway

FIGURE 4-23: PLACING WARNING MARKERS CORRECTLY
ON AN UNDIVIDED HIGHWAY

- About 100 feet ahead of and behind the vehicle — on the shoulder or lane in which you are stopped. See Figure 4-23.

• Back beyond a hill, curve, or anything that prevents other drivers within 500 feet of the vehicle from seeing it. See Figure 4-24.

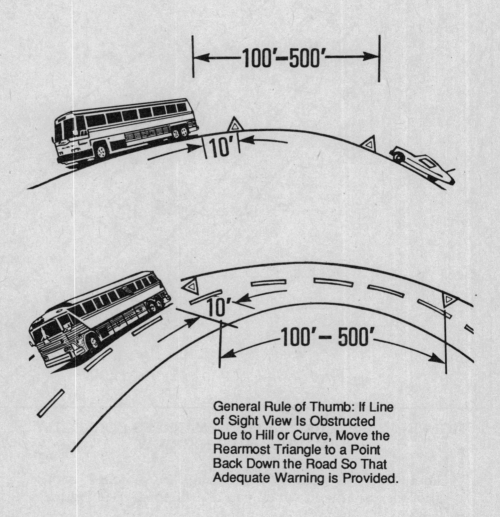

General Rule of Thumb: If Line of Sight View Is Obstructed Due to Hill or Curve, Move the Rearmost Triangle to a Point Back Down the Road So That Adequate Warning is Provided.

FIGURE 4-24: PLACING WARNING MARKERS WHEN THERE IS AN OBSTACLE IN THE LINE OF VIEW

- If you must stop on or by a one-way or divided highway, place warning markers 10 feet, 100 feet, and 200 feet toward the approaching traffic. See Figure 4-25.

One Way or Divided Highway

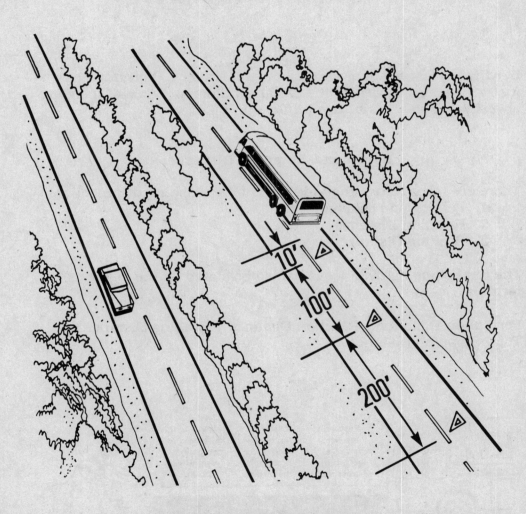

FIGURE 4-25: PLACING WARNING MARKERS WHEN STOPPED ON A DIVIDED HIGHWAY

Hold the triangles between yourself and the oncoming traffic for your own safety when walking down the highway to place them.

Use Your Horn When Needed

Your horn can let others know you are there. It can help to avoid a crash. Use your horn when needed. Remember, it can startle others and can be dangerous when used carelessly.

Speed Control

Driving too fast is a major cause of fatal crashes. You must adjust your speed according to several conditions. Some of them are *traction*, curves, *visibility*, traffic, and hills.

Speed and Stopping Distance

There are three things that add up to total stopping distance:
1. Perception Distance
2. Reaction Distance
3. Braking Distance

The total stopping distance may also be stated by the following formula.

Perception Distance + Reaction Distance + Braking Distance = Total Stopping Distance

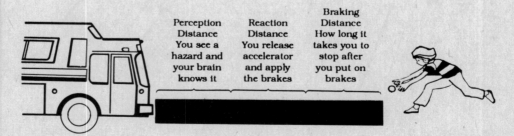

Perception Distance You see a hazard and your brain knows it

Reaction Distance You release accelerator and apply the brakes

Braking Distance How long it takes you to stop after you put on brakes

The total distance covered by the vehicle before you can brake to a full stop. The time to cover this distance is about six seconds at 55 mph.

FIGURE 4-26: TOTAL STOPPING DISTANCE

- **Perception distance**: This is the distance your vehicle goes from the time your eyes see a hazard until your brain knows it. The perception time for an alert driver is about 3/4 of a second. At 55 mph, you travel 60 feet in 3/4 of a second.

- **Reaction distance**: This is the distance your vehicle travels from the time your brain tells your foot to move from the gas pedal until your foot actually pushes the brake pedal. The average driver has a reaction time of 3/4 of a second. This accounts for an additional 60 feet traveled at 55 mph.

- **Braking distance**: This is the distance it takes to stop once the brakes are put on. At 55 mph on dry pavement with good brakes, it takes a truck about 170 feet to stop.

- **Total stopping distance**: At 55 mph, it will take about 6 seconds to stop, and your vehicle will travel about the distance of a football field (60 + 60 + 170 = 290 feet).

The Effect of Speed on Stopping Distance

When you double your speed, it will take about four times the distance to stop. The vehicle will have four times the destructive power if it crashes. High speeds increase stopping distances greatly. By slowing down a little, you can gain a lot in reduced braking distance.

The Effect of Vehicle Weight on Stopping Distance

If a vehicle is heavier, brakes have to do more work (and absorb more heat) to stop it. The brakes, tires, springs, and shock absorbers on heavy vehicles are designed to work best when the vehicle is fully loaded, so you will find that empty trucks require greater stopping distances because they have less traction. They can bounce and lock up their wheels. This gives much poorer braking power.

Matching Speed to the Road Surface

You cannot steer or brake a vehicle unless you have traction. Traction is the friction between the tires and the road. There are some road conditions that reduce traction and call for lower speeds. These are slippery surfaces, shaded areas, bridges, ice, and rain.

Slippery Surfaces

It will take longer to stop, and it will be harder to turn without skidding when the road is slippery. You must drive slower to be able to stop in the same distance as on a dry road. Wet roads can double stopping distance. Reduce speed by about one-third (slow from 55 to about 35 mph). On packed snow, reduce speed by half, or more. If the surface is icy, reduce speed to a crawl and stop driving as soon as you can safely do so.

Identifying Slippery Surfaces

Sometimes it is hard to know if the road is slippery. Here are some signs of slippery roads.

Shaded areas: Shady parts of the road will remain icy and slippery long after open areas have melted.

Bridges: When it gets cold, bridges will freeze before the road does. Be especially careful when the temperature is close to 32°F.

Melting ice: Slight melting will make ice wet. Wet ice is much more slippery than ice that is not wet.

Black ice: Black ice is a thin layer of ice that is clear enough you can see the road beneath it. It makes the road look wet. Any time it is below freezing and the road looks wet, watch out for black ice.

Vehicle icing: An easy way to check for ice is to open the window and feel the front of the mirror. If there is ice on the mirror, the road surface is probably starting to ice up.

Just after rain begins: Right after it starts to rain, the water mixes with the oil left on the road by vehicles. This makes the road very slippery. As the rain continues, the oil will wash away.

Hydroplaning

In some weather, water or slush collects on the road. When this happens, your vehicle can hydroplane. This is like water skiing. The tires lose their contact with the road and have little or no traction. You may not be able to steer or brake. You can regain control by releasing the gas pedal and pushing in the clutch. This will slow your vehicle and let the wheels turn freely. If the vehicle is hydroplaning, do not use the brakes to slow down. If the drive wheels start to skid, push in the clutch to let them turn freely.

It does not take a lot of water to cause hydroplaning. Hydroplaning can occur at speeds as low as 30 mph if there is a lot of water. It is more likely if the tire pressure is low or the tire tread is worn. (The grooves in a tire carry away the water; if they are not deep they do not work well). Be very careful driving through puddles. The water is often deep enough to cause hydroplaning.

Speed and Curves

Drivers must adjust their speed for curves in the road. If you take a curve too fast, two things can happen: 1) The wheels can lose their traction and continue straight ahead so you skid off the road; or 2) the wheels may keep their traction and the vehicle rolls over. Tests have shown that vehicles with a high center of gravity can roll over at the posted speed limit for a curve.

Slow to a safe speed before you enter a curve. Braking in a curve is dangerous because that makes it easier to lock the wheels and cause a skid. Slow down as needed. Never exceed the posted speed limit for the curve. Drive in a gear that will let you speed up slightly in the curve. This will help you stay in control.

Speed and How Far You Can See

You should always be able to stop within the distance you can see ahead. At night, low beams let you see about 250 feet ahead. You should not drive more than 40 mph with the low beams on. During the day, conditions such as fog or rain may require you to slow down so you will be able to stop in the distance you can see ahead.

Speed and Traffic Flow

When you are driving in heavy traffic, the safest speed is the speed of the other vehicles. Vehicles going the same direction at the same speed are not as likely to run into one another. Drive at the speed of the traffic if you can do so without going at an illegal or unsafe speed. Keep a safe following distance between you and the vehicles ahead.

The main reason drivers exceed speed limits is to try to save time. Anyone who tries to drive faster than the speed of traffic will not save much time, and the risks involved are not worth the few minutes saved. If you go faster than the speed of other traffic:

- You will have to keep passing other vehicles. This increases the chance of a crash.

- It is more tiring. Fatigue increases the chance of a crash.

Going with the flow of traffic is safer and easier.

Speed on Downgrades

Driving slowly is the most important thing to remember when going down long steep hills. This lets you drive more safely. If you do not go slowly enough, your brakes can become so hot they will not slow you down. Shift the transmission to a low gear before starting down the grade. Pay attention to signs warning of long downhill grades, and check your brakes before starting down the hill. Keep a light, steady pressure on the brake pedal.

Going down steep hills safely is discussed more fully in "Mountain Driving." Read that section carefully.

Managing Space

To be a safe driver, you need space all around your vehicle. When things go wrong, space gives you time to think and more time to take action.

To have space available when something goes wrong, you need to manage space. While this is true for all drivers, it is very important for drivers of large vehicles. Their vehicles take up more space and also require more space for stopping and turning.

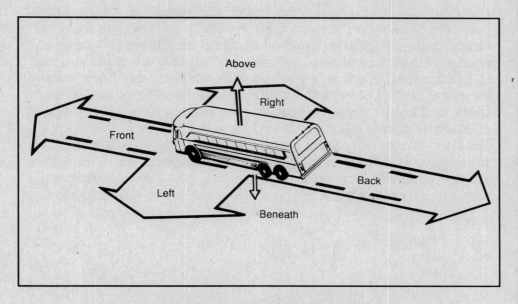

FIGURE 4-27: SPACE CUSHION

Space Ahead

Of all the space around your vehicle, it is the area ahead of the vehicle — the space you are driving into — that is the most important. You need space ahead in case you must suddenly stop. According to accident reports, the vehicle that trucks and buses most often run into is the one in front of them. The most frequent cause is following too closely. Remember, if the vehicle ahead of you is smaller than yours, it can probably stop faster than you can. You may crash if you are following too closely.

How Much Space?

How much space should you keep in front of you? One good rule says you need at least one second for each 10 feet of vehicle length at speeds below 40 mph. At greater speeds, you must add one more second for safety. For example, if you are driving a 40-foot vehicle, you should leave 4 seconds between you and the vehicle ahead. In a 60-foot rig, you will need 6 seconds. Over 40 mph, you will need 5 seconds for a 40-foot vehicle and 7 seconds for a 60-foot vehicle.

To know how much space you have, wait until the vehicle ahead passes a shadow on the road, a pavement marking, or some other clear landmark. Then count off seconds in this way, "one thousand-and-one, one thousand-and-two" and so on, until you reach the same spot. Compare your count with the rule of one second for every 10 feet of vehicle length. If you are driving a 40-foot truck and count up to 2 seconds, you are too close. Drop back a little and count again until you have 4 seconds of following distance (5 seconds if you are going over 40 mph). After a little practice, you will know how far back you should be. Remember to add one second for speeds above 40 mph. Also remember when the road is slippery, you need much more space to stop.

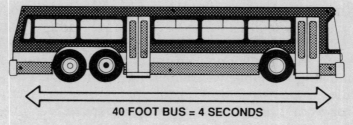

- 1 Second Required for Each 10 Feet of Vehicle Length - at Speeds Under 40 MPH

- Above 40 MPH Use same Formula, Then Add 1 Second for the Additional Speed

40 FOOT BUS = 4 SECONDS

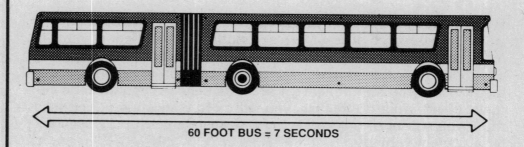

60 FOOT BUS = 7 SECONDS

FIGURE 4-28: FORMULA FOR FOLLOWING DISTANCE

Space Behind

You cannot stop others from following you too closely, but there are things you can do to make it safer.

- Stay to the right.

- Handle tailgaters safely.

Stay to the Right

Heavy vehicles are often *tailgated* (followed too closely by another vehicle) when they cannot keep up with the speed of traffic. This often happens when you are going uphill. If a heavy load slows you down, stay in the right lane. When you are going uphill, you should not pass another slow vehicle unless you can get around quickly and safely.

Handling Tailgaters Safely

In a large vehicle, it is often hard to see whether a vehicle is close behind you. You may be tailgated:

- When you travel slowly. Drivers trapped behind slow vehicles often follow closely.

- In bad weather. Many car drivers follow large vehicles closely during bad weather, especially when it is hard to see the road ahead.

If you find yourself being tailgated, here are some things you can do to reduce the chances of a crash:

- Avoid quick changes. If you have to slow down or turn, signal early and reduce speed very gradually.

- Increase your following distance. Opening up room in front of you will help you avoid having to make sudden speed or direction changes. It also makes it easier for the tailgater to get around you.

- Do not speed up. It is safer to be tailgated at a low speed than a high speed.

- Avoid confusing signals. Do not turn on your tail lights or flash your brake lights. Follow the suggestions above.

Space to the Sides

Commercial vehicles are often wide and take up most of a lane. Safe drivers will manage what little space they have. You can do this by keeping your vehicle in the center of your lane. Avoid driving next to others.

Staying Centered in a Lane

You need to keep your vehicle centered in the lane to keep safe clearance on both sides. If your vehicle is wide, you have little room to spare.

Traveling Next to Others

There are two dangers in traveling next to other vehicles:

- Another driver may change lanes suddenly and run into you.

- You may be trapped when you need to change lanes.

Find an open spot where you are not near other traffic. When traffic is heavy, it may be hard to find an open spot. If you must travel near other vehicles, try to keep as much space as possible between you and them. Also, drop back or pull forward so that you are sure the other driver can see you.

Strong Winds

Strong winds make it hard to stay in your lane. The problem is usually worse for lighter vehicles. This problem can be very bad coming out of tunnels. Do not drive beside others when it is windy if you can avoid it.

Space Overhead

Hitting overhead objects is a danger. Always make sure you have enough clearance so the top of the vehicle does not hit anything.

- Do not assume that the heights posted at bridges and overpasses are correct. Repaving or packed snow may have reduced the clearances since the time the heights were posted.

- The weight of a cargo van changes its height. An empty van is higher than a loaded one. Getting under a bridge when the van is loaded does not mean that the van will be able to do so when the van is empty.

- If you doubt you have safe space to pass under an object, go slowly. If you are not sure you can make it, take another route. Warnings are usually posted on low bridges or underpasses, but not always.

- Some roads can cause a vehicle to tilt. When this happens, there can be a problem clearing objects, such as signs or trees, along the edge of the road. Where this is a problem, drive a little closer to the center of the road.

- Before you back into an area, get out and check for overhanging objects such as trees, branches, or electrical wires. It is easy to miss seeing them while you are backing. Also check for any other hazards at the same time.

Space Below

Many drivers forget about the space under their vehicles. That space can be very small when a vehicle is heavily loaded. Railroad tracks can stick up several inches. This is often a problem on dirt roads or in unpaved yards where the surface around the tracks can wear away. Do not take a chance on getting hung up halfway across. Drainage channels across roads can cause the end of some vehicles to drag. Cross such areas carefully.

Space for Turns

The space around a truck or bus is important when turning. Because of a wide turning radius and off tracking, large vehicles can hit objects or other vehicles during turns.

Right Turns

Here are some rules to help prevent right-turn crashes:

- Turn slowly to give yourself and others more time to avoid problems.

- If you are driving a truck or bus that cannot make a right turn without swinging into another lane, turn wide as you complete the turn. This is shown in Figure 4-29A

- Do not turn wide to the left as you start the turn (Figure 4-29B). A driver behind you may think you are turning left and try to pass you on the right. This could cause you to crash into the other vehicle as you complete your turn.

- If you must cross into the oncoming lane to make a turn, watch out for vehicles coming toward you. Give them room to go by or to stop. However, do not back up for them because you could hit someone behind you.

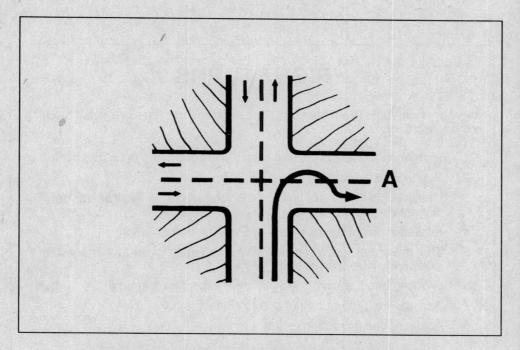

FIGURE 4-29A: RIGHT TURN — DO THIS

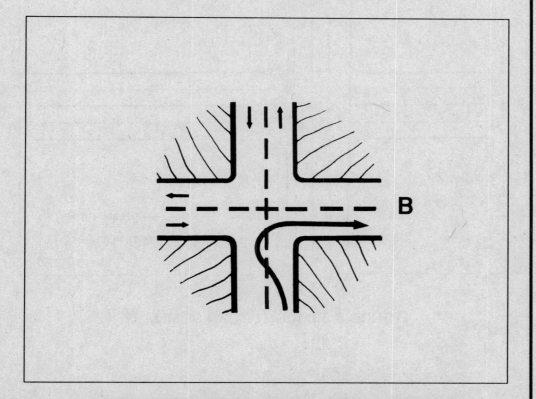

FIGURE 4-29B: RIGHT TURN — DO NOT DO THIS

RIGHT TURNS

Improper right turns are a leading cause of accidents. Here is a set of steps to reduce accidents:

1. Plan Ahead - Look at the turn before you get there. Set up for your turn.
2. Signal Your Turn
3. Check Right Mirror - Leave sufficient clearance from all obstacles without drifting out of your lane.
4. Have the unit in the gear that you will make the turn in.
5. Turn the wheel right when the trailer is halfway past the stationary object (telephone pole, car, or curb).
6. Proceed into the turn, checking the mirrors for clearance.
7. Assume the proper lane (the lane closest to the curb).
8. Adjust speed accordingly.

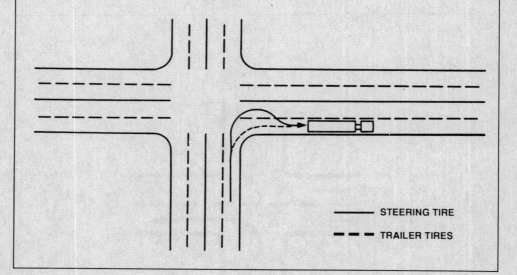

———— STEERING TIRE

– – – TRAILER TIRES

FIGURE 4-30: RIGHT TURN SUMMARY

Left Turns

When making a turn, be sure you have reached the center of the intersection before you start the left turn. If you turn too soon, the left side of your vehicle may hit something because of off-tracking. If you are turning into a multi-lane street, enter the right lane as shown in Figure 4-31.

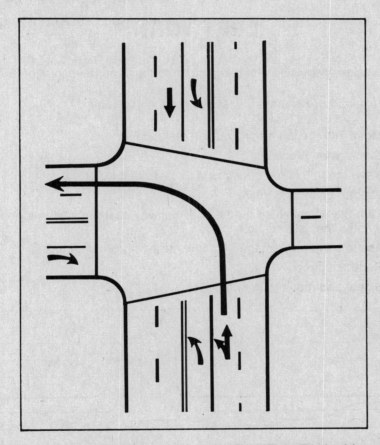

If There Are Two Left Turn Lanes, Use The Right Hand Lane

FIGURE 4-31: LEFT TURN LANES

If there are two turning lanes, always take the right-hand turn lane as shown in Figure 4-31. Do not start the turn from the inside lane because you then may have to swing right to make the turn. Drivers on your right will be hard for you to see, so you could crash into them.

If there are two turning lanes, always take the right-hand turn lane as shown in Figure 4-31. Do not start the turn from the inside lane because you then may have to swing right to make the turn. Drivers on your right will be hard for you to see, so you could crash into them.

LEFT TURNS

You have greater visibility making left turns than you have in right turns.

Once again, there is a set of steps to reduce accidents

1. Move into the left turning lane in advance
2. Signal your intentions
3. Have the unit in the gear you will make the turn in.
4. Yield to oncoming traffic.
5. Turn the wheel when the trailer is halfway past the stationary object (center line, island, etc.)
6. Assume the proper lane (left lane, farthest from the curb).
7. Reduce speed.
8. Signal and move to the right lane.

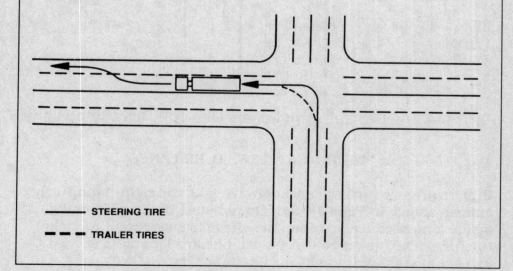

STEERING TIRE

TRAILER TIRES

FIGURE 4-32: LEFT TURN SUMMARY

Space Needed to Cross or Enter Traffic

Be aware of the size and weight of your vehicle when you cross or enter traffic. Here are some important things to keep in mind:

- Because of slow acceleration and the space large vehicles require, you may need a much larger gap to enter traffic than you would need in a car.

- Acceleration varies with the load. Allow more room if your vehicle is heavily loaded.

- Before you start across a road, make sure you can get all the way across before before the traffic reaches you.

Night Driving

Driving at night is more dangerous. More than half of all traffic accidents happen at night. Drivers do not see hazards as soon as they do in daylight, so they have less time to act. Drivers caught by surprise are less able to avoid a crash.

The problems of night driving involve the driver, the roadway, and the vehicle. We will discuss each of these factors.

Human Factors

Vision: People cannot see as well at night or in the dim light. The eyes need time to adjust to seeing in dim light. Most people will notice this when walking into a dark movie theater.

Glare: Drivers can be blinded for a short time by bright light. It takes time to recover from this blindness. Most people have been temporarily blinded by camera flash units or by the high beams of an oncoming vehicle. It can take several seconds to recover from glare blindness. Even two seconds can be dangerous. A vehicle going 55 mph will travel more than half the distance of a football field during that time. Do not look directly at bright lights when driving. Look at the right side of the road. Watch the sidelines when someone coming toward you has bright lights.

Fatigue and Not Being Alert: Fatigue (being tired or sleepy) and not being alert are bigger problems at night. The body naturally wants to sleep. This is beyond a person's control. Most people are less alert at night, especially after midnight. Drivers may not see hazards as soon or react as quickly, so the chance of a crash is greater. If you are sleepy, the only safe cure is to get off the road and get some sleep. If you do not, you risk your life and the lives of others.

Roadway Factors

Poor Lighting: In the daytime, there is usually enough light to see well. This is not true at night. Some areas may have bright street lights, but many areas will have poor lighting. On most roads, you may have to depend on your headlights for any light.

Less light means you will not be able to see hazards as well as in the daytime. Road users who do not have lights are hard to see. There are many accidents at night involving people who are walking, jogging, or riding bicycles and animals.

Even when there are lights, the road scene can be confusing. Traffic signals and hazards can be hard to see against a background of signs, shop windows, and other lights.

Drive slower when lighting is poor or confusing. Drive slowly enough to be sure you can stop in the distance you can see ahead.

Drunk Drivers: Drunk drivers are a hazard to themselves and to you. Be very alert near the closing times for bars and taverns. Watch for drivers who have trouble staying in their lanes or maintaining speed, stop without reason, or show other signs of being drunk.

Vehicle Factors

Headlights: At night your headlights will usually be the main source of light for you to see and for others to see you. You cannot see nearly as much with your headlights as you see in the daytime. With low beams, you can see about 250 feet ahead, and with high beams about 350-500 feet. You must adjust your speed to keep your stopping distance within your sight distance. This means driving slowly enough to be able to stop within the range of your headlights. Otherwise, by the time you see a hazard, you will not have time to stop.

Night driving can be more dangerous if you have problems with your headlights. Dirty headlights may give only half the light they should. This cuts down on how far you can see and makes it harder for others to see you. Make sure your lights are clean and working. Headlights can be out of adjustment. If they do not point in the right direction, they will not give you a good view and may blind other drivers. Have a qualified person check them for adjustment.

Other Lights: In order for you to be seen easily, the following must be clean and working properly:

- Reflectors
- Marker lights
- Clearance lights
- Tail lights
- Identification lights

Turn Signals and Brake Lights: At night your turn signals and brake lights are even more important for telling other drivers what you intend to do. Make sure your turn signals are clean and the stoplights work.

Windshields and Mirrors: It is more important to have clean windshields and mirrors at night than in the day. Bright lights at night can cause dirt on the windshield or mirrors to create a glare of its own. This can block your view. Most people have driven toward the sun just as it has risen or as it is about to set and found that they could barely see through a windshield that had seemed to be all right in the middle of the day. Clean your windshield on the inside and outside for safe driving at night.

Pre-Trip Procedures

Make sure you are rested and alert. If you are drowsy, sleep before you drive! A nap can save your life or the lives of others.

If you wear glasses, make sure they are clean and not scratched. Do not wear sunglasses at night.

Do a complete pre-trip inspection of your vehicle. Check all lights and reflectors. Clean those you can reach.

On the Road

Avoid blinding others with glare from your headlights. This can cause problems for drivers coming toward you. It may also bother drivers going in the same direction you are if your lights shine in their rearview mirrors. Dim your lights before they can bother other drivers. Dim your lights when you are within 500 feet of an oncoming vehicle. When you are following another vehicle, dim your lights when you are within 500 feet of it.

Avoid the glare from oncoming vehicles. Do not look directly at the lights of oncoming vehicles. Look slightly to the right at a right lane or edge marking. If other drivers do not put their low beams on, do not try to "get back at them" by putting on your high beams. This increases glare for oncoming drivers and the chance of a crash.

Use high beams when you can. Many drivers make the mistake of always using low beams. This seriously cuts down your ability to see ahead. Use high beams when it is safe and legal to do so. Do not use them within 500 feet of another vehicle, but as soon as you are farther away, turn them on. Also, do not let the inside of your cab get too bright. This makes it harder to see what is outside. Keep the interior light off, and adjust your instrument lights as low as possible. Be sure you can read the gauges though.

If you get sleepy, stop driving. People often do not realize how close they are to falling asleep even when their eyelids are falling shut. If you can safely do so, look at yourself in a mirror. If you look sleepy, stop driving! If you just feel sleepy, stop driving. You are in a very dangerous condition. The only safe cure is to sleep.

Night Driving Checklist

The Driver

- Clean Glasses
- Do Not Wear Sunglasses
- Be Rested

The Roadway

- Plan Your Route
- Know Location of Rest Stops
- Know Where Nighttime Hazards Are
  Ramps, Roadside Bars
- Be Extra Careful on Unfamiliar Roads

The Vehicle

- Perform Pre-trip Inspection
- Check All Lights
- Use Flashlights

FIGURE 4-33: NIGHT DRIVING CHECKLIST

Winter Weather Driving

Vehicle Checks

Make sure your vehicle is ready before driving in winter weather. You should make a regular pre-trip inspection. Pay close attention to the following items.

Coolant Level and Antifreeze Amount

Make sure the cooling system is full and there is enough antifreeze in the system to protect it against freezing. This can be checked with a special coolant tester.

Defrosting and Heating Equipment

Make sure the defrosters work. They are needed for safe driving. Be sure the heater works and you know how to operate it. If you use other heaters and expect to need them (mirror heaters, battery box heaters, fuel tank heaters), check their operation.

Wipers and Washers

Make sure the windshield wiper blades are in good condition. Be sure the wiper blades press against the window hard enough to wipe the windshield clean. Otherwise, they may not sweep off snow properly. Be sure the windshield washer works and there is liquid in the washer container. Use windshield washer antifreeze to prevent freezing of the washer liquid. If you cannot see well while driving (for example, if your wipers fail), stop safely and fix the problem.

Tires

Make sure you have enough tread on your tires. The drive tires must provide traction to push the rig over wet pavement and through snow. The steering tires must have traction to steer the vehicle. Enough tread is especially important in winter conditions. You should have at least 4/32-inch tread depth in every major groove on the front wheels and at least 2/32-inch on the other wheels. Deeper grooves would be better. Use a gauge to measure the depth. You need to be sure you have enough tread for safe driving.

Tire Chains

You may find yourself in conditions where you cannot drive without chains, even to get to a place of safety. Carry the right number of chains and extra cross links. Make sure they will fit your drive tires. Check the chains for broken hooks, worn or broken crosslinks, and bent or broken side chains. Learn how to put on the chains before you need to do it in snow and ice.

Lights and Reflectors

Make sure the lights and reflectors are clean. Lights and reflectors are especially important during bad weather. Check from time to time during bad weather to make sure they are still clean and working right.

Windows and Mirrors

Remove any ice or snow from the windshield, windows, and mirrors before starting. Use a windshield scraper, snow brush, or windshield defroster as they are needed to remove ice or snow.

Handholds, Steps, and Deck Plates

Remove all ice and snow from handholds, steps, and deck plates which you must use to enter the cab or to move about on the vehicle. This will reduce the danger of slipping.

Radiator Shutters and Winterfront

Remove ice from the radiator shutters. Make sure the winterfront is not closed too tightly. If the shutters freeze shut or the winterfront is closed too much, the engine may overheat and stop.

Exhaust System

Exhaust system leaks are especially dangerous when air flow in the cab may be poor (windows rolled up, etc.). Loose connections can permit poisonous carbon monoxide to leak into the vehicle. Carbon monoxide gas will make you sleepy. In large enough amounts, it can kill you. Check the exhaust system for loose parts and for sounds and signs of leaks.

Slippery Surfaces

Drive slowly and smoothly on slippery roads. If it is very slippery, you should not drive at all. Stop at the first safe place.

Safe Driving

The following are some safe driving guidelines for driving safely in bad weather. Start gently and slowly. As you begin driving, get the feel of the road. Do not hurry.

Adjust turning and braking to the road conditions. Make turns as gentle as possible. Do not brake any harder than necessary, and do not use the engine brake or speed retarder. They can cause the driving wheels to skid on slippery surfaces.

Adjust your speed to the conditions. Do not pass slower vehicles unless you must do so. Go slowly and watch far enough ahead to keep a steady speed. Try not to slow down and speed up. Take curves at slower speeds and do not brake while in curves. Be aware that as it warms up, the ice begins to melt, and the roads become more slippery. Slow down even more.

Adjust your space to the conditions. Do not drive beside other vehicles. Keep a longer distance between you and the vehicle ahead of you. When you see a traffic jam ahead, slow down or stop to wait for it to clear. Try hard to plan stops ahead of time and slow down gradually.

Wet Brakes

When driving in heavy rain or deep standing water, your brakes will get wet. Water on the brakes can weaken the brakes, or cause them to apply unevenly, or to grab. This can cause a lack of braking power, wheel lockups, pulling to one side or the other, or even cause the vehicle to *jackknife* if you pull a trailer.

Avoid driving through deep puddles or flowing water if possible. If you cannot avoid it, you should:

- Slow down.

- Place the transmission in a low gear.

- Gently put on the brakes. This presses the linings against the brake drums or discs and keeps mud, silt, sand, and water from getting inside.

- Increase the engine rpm and cross the water while keeping a light pressure on the brakes.

- When you are out of the water, maintain light pressure on the brakes for a short distance to heat them up and dry them out.

- Make a test stop when it is safe to do so. Check behind to make sure no one is following, then apply the brakes to be sure they work right. If they do not, dry them out as described above. (CAUTION: Do not apply too much pressure to the brakes and gas pedal at the same time because you can overheat the brake drums and linings.)

Like driving in winter weather, driving in very hot weather can cause problems. Make sure you and your vehicle are ready to handle summer driving conditions.

Summer Weather Driving

Vehicle Check

Do a normal pre-trip inspection, but pay special attention to the tires, engine oil, engine coolant, engine belts, and hoses.

Tires

Check the tire mountings and air pressure. Inspect the tires every two hours or every 100 miles when driving in very hot weather. Air pressure increases with temperature. Do not let air out, or the pressure will be too low when the tires cool off. If a tire is too hot to touch, remain stopped until the tire cools off. If you do not, the tire may blow out or catch fire. Pay special attention to recapped or retreaded tires. Under high temperatures, the tread may separate from the body of the tire.

Engine Oil

The engine oil helps keep the engine cool and lubricates it. Make sure there is enough engine oil. If you have an oil temperature gauge, check to see that the temperature remains within the proper range while you are driving.

Engine Coolant

Before starting out, check to be sure the engine's cooling system has the amount of water and antifreeze recommended by the engine manufacturer. Antifreeze helps the engine when the weather is hot as well as when the weather is cold. When driving, check the water or coolant temperature gauge from time to time. Make sure that it remains in the normal range. If the gauge goes above the highest safe temperature, there may be something wrong that can lead to engine failure or possibly a fire. Stop driving as soon as you safely can, and try to find out what is wrong.

Some vehicles have sight glasses or see-through coolant overflow or recovery containers which let you check coolant level while the engine is hot. If the container is NOT part of the pressurized system, the cap can be safely removed and coolant added even when the engine is at operating temperature.

Never remove the radiator cap or any part of the pressurized system until the system has cooled. Steam and boiling water can spray under pressure and cause severe burns. If you can touch the radiator cap with your bare hand, it is probably cool enough to open. If it is too hot to touch, wait until it has cooled down before opening it.

If coolant has to be added to a system without a recovery or overflow tank, follow these steps.

- Shut off the engine.

- Wait until the engine has cooled.

- Protect your hands (use gloves or a thick cloth).

- Turn the radiator cap slowly to the first stop. This releases the pressure seal.

- Step back while the pressure is released from the cooling system.

- When all pressure has been released, press down on the cap and turn it further to remove it.

- Look at the level of the coolant, and add more coolant if necessary.

- Replace the cap and turn it all the way to the closed position.

Engine Belts

Learn how to check V-belt tightness on your vehicle by pressing on the belts. Loose belts will not turn the water pump or fan properly. Then the engine will overheat. Also check the belts for cracking or other signs of wear.

Hoses

Make sure the coolant hoses are in good condition. A hose that breaks while you are driving can lead to engine failure or even a fire.

Safe Driving Tips

Watch for bleeding tar. The tar in road surfacing often rises to the surface in very hot weather. Spots where tar "bleeds" to the surface are very slippery. Watch for them and use care when you must drive over them.

Drive slowly enough to prevent overheating. High speeds create more heat for the tires and engine. In desert conditions, the heat may build up to the point where it is dangerous. The heat will increase the chances of tire failure, fire, or engine failure.

In mountain driving, the force of gravity plays a major role. If you have a heavy load, you will have to use lower gears and go slower to climb hills. In coming down steep hills, gravity will tend to speed you up. You must drive slowly enough that your brakes can hold your vehicle back without getting too hot. If the brakes become too hot, they may start to "fade." This means that you

Mountain Driving

have to push them harder and harder to get the same stopping power. If the brakes continue to be used hard, they can fade until you cannot slow down or stop at all. These dangers can be avoided by going down hills slowly.

Use of Gears While Driving Downhill

No matter what the size of your vehicle, driving down long, steep grades can cause your brakes to fail if you go too fast. Using lower gears will help keep you from going too fast. Lower gears allow engine compression and friction to slow the vehicle. This is true for both automatic and manual transmissions.

If you have a large vehicle with a manual transmission, do not wait until you have started down the hill to shift down. You could get hung up in neutral and lose the benefit of engine braking. You would find yourself coasting down the hill. This is both illegal and dangerous. Be in the right gear before starting down the hill.

With older trucks, the rule for choosing gears was to use the same gear going down the hill that you would need to climb the hill. Now, new trucks have low friction parts and streamline shapes for fuel economy. They may also have more powerful engines. This means they can go up hills in higher gears as well as have less friction and air drag to hold them back when going down hills. For that reason, drivers of modern trucks may have to use lower gears going down a hill than they will need to go up the hill. Find out what is right for your vehicle.

Proper Braking

When going downhill, brakes will always heat up. They are designed so brake shoes or pads rub against brake drums or discs to slow the vehicle. This creates heat. Brakes can take a lot of heat. However, brakes can be made to fail from too much heat by trying to slow down from too high a speed too many times or too quickly. Brakes will fade (have less stopping power) when they get very hot, and they can get to the point where they will not work.

The right way to use your brakes for long downhill grades is to drive slowly enough that a fairly light use of the brakes will keep your speed from increasing. If you go slowly enough, the brakes will be able to get rid of the heat, and will not get too hot.

Some people believe that letting up on the brakes from time to time will allow them to cool enough not to become too hot. Tests have proven this is not true. Brake drums cool very slowly, so the amount of cooling between applications is not enough to prevent overheating. This type of braking requires heavier brake pressure than a steady application does. The heavier pressure builds up more heat than a light continuous pressure does. Be sure to select the right gear, go slowly enough, and keep a light, steady foot on the brakes.

Escape Ramps

Escape ramps have been built on many steep mountain grades. Escape ramps are made to stop runaway vehicles safely without injuring drivers and passengers. They use a long bed of loose soft material (pea gravel) to slow a runaway vehicle. Sometimes this bed of gravel is used with an upgrade.

Know where the escape ramps are on your route. Signs show drivers where ramps are located. Escape ramps save lives, equipment, and cargo. Use them if you lose your brakes.

ESCAPE RAMPS

Types

- Gravity
- Arrester Beds
- Combination Ramp and Arrester Bed
- Sandpiles

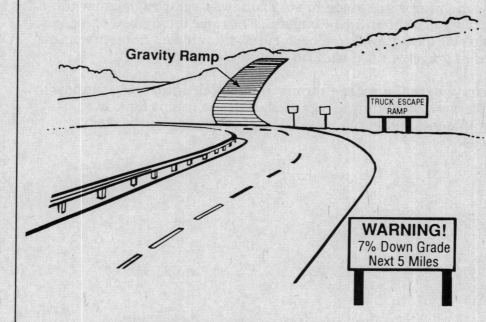

- Escape Ramps Rely on Loose Surface Material (e.g., Pea Gravel,Sand) to Stop Vehicles
- Some Also Use Steep Positive Grades (e.g., Gravity Type Ramp)

FIGURE 4-34: ESCAPE RAMPS

Figure 4-35 shows a "7% Grade..." sign. What does this sign mean? When you see such a sign at the start of a downhill grade, do this:

- Draw a pretend straight line off the top of the hill for 100 feet. If the distance from the end of the line to the road surface below is seven feet, then you are on a 7% grade. If the distance is eight feet, then you are on an 8% grade, and so on.

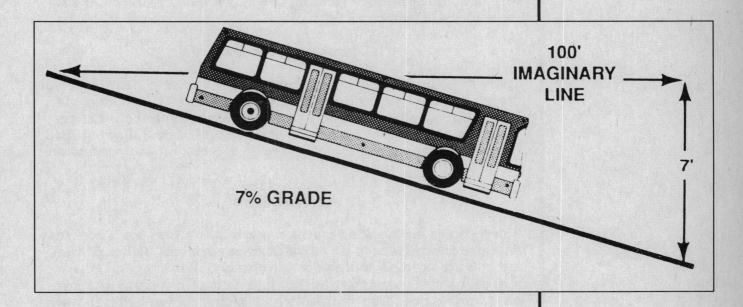

FIGURE 4-35: HOW TO FIGURE THE PERCENT OF GRADE

The Importance of Seeing Hazards

What is a hazard? A hazard is any road condition or road user (driver, bicyclist, pedestrian) that is a possible danger. For example, a car in front of you is headed toward the freeway exit, but the brake lights come on and he or she begins braking hard. This could mean that the driver is uncertain about taking the offramp. He or she may suddenly return to the highway. This car is a hazard. If the driver of the car cuts in front of you, it is no longer just a hazard, it is an emergency.

Seeing Hazards

Seeing Hazards Lets You Be Prepared

You will have more time to act if you see hazards before they become emergencies. In the example above, you may make a lane change or slow down to prevent a crash if the car suddenly cuts in front of you. Seeing this hazard gives you time to check your mirrors and signal a lane change. Being prepared reduces the danger. A driver who did not see the hazard until the slow car pulled back on the highway in front of him would have to do something very suddenly. Sudden braking or a quick lane change is much more likely to lead to a crash.

Learning to See Hazards

There are often clues that will help you see hazards. The more you drive, the better you can get at seeing hazards. This section will talk about hazards that you may not have thought about before. Slow down and be very careful if you see any of the following road hazards: work zones, drop offs, foreign objects, off-ramps, and on-ramps.

Work Zones

When people are working on the road, this is a hazard. There may be narrow lanes, sharp turns, or uneven surfaces. Other drivers are often distracted and do not drive safely. Workers and construction vehicles may get in the way. Drive slowly and with care near work zones. Use your 4-way flashers or brake lights to warn drivers behind you.

Drop Off

Sometimes the pavement drops off sharply near the edge of the road. Driving too near the edge can tilt your vehicle toward the side of the road. This can cause the top of your vehicle to hit roadside objects such as signs or tree limbs. Your vehicle can also be hard to steer as you cross the drop off when going off the road or coming back on it.

Foreign Objects

Things that have fallen on the road can be hazards. They can be a danger to your tires and wheel rims. They can damage electrical and brake lines. They can be caught between the dual tires and cause severe damage. Some items which appear to be harmless can be very dangerous. For example, cardboard boxes may be empty, or they may also contain something solid or heavy which can cause damage. The same is true of paper and cloth sacks. It is important to remain alert for objects of all sorts, so you can see them in time to avoid making sudden, unsafe moves.

Off-ramps/On-ramps

Freeway and turnpike exits can be very dangerous for commercial vehicles. Off-ramps and on-ramps often have speed limit signs posted. These speeds may be safe for cars but may not be safe for large or heavily loaded vehicles. Exits which go downhill and turn at the same time can be most dangerous. The downgrade makes it hard to reduce speed. Braking and turning at the same time can be a dangerous practice. Make sure you are going slowly enough before you get on the curved part of an off-ramp or on-ramp.

People Who are Hazardous

In order to protect yourself and others, you must be able to know when other drivers may do something hazardous. You must also be able to recognize other people who are a danger. Some clues to this type of hazard are discussed below:

Blocked Vision

People who cannot see others are very dangerous. Be alert for drivers whose vision is blocked. Drivers of vans, loaded station wagons, and cars with the rear window blocked are examples. Rental trucks should be watched carefully. Their drivers are often not used to the limited vision they have to the sides and rear of the truck. In winter, vehicles with frosted, ice covered, or snow covered windows are hazards.

Vehicles may be partly hidden by blind intersections or alleys. If you can see only the rear or front end of a vehicle but not the driver, then he cannot see you. Be alert because he may back out or enter into your lane. Always be prepared to stop.

Delivery trucks can present a hazard. The driver's vision is often blocked by packages or vehicle doors. Drivers of step vans, postal vehicles, and local delivery vehicles often are in a hurry and may suddenly step out of the vehicle or drive it into the traffic lane.

Parked vehicles can be hazards because people may get out of them or drive into your way. Watch for movement inside the vehicle or movement of the vehicle itself that shows people are inside. They may get out, or the vehicle may pull out into traffic. Watch for brake lights or backup lights, exhaust, or other clues that say a driver is about to move.

Be careful of a stopped bus. Passengers may cross in front of or behind the bus, and often they cannot see you.

Pedestrians and bicyclists can also be hazards. Walkers, joggers, and bicyclists may be on the road with their backs to the traffic, so they cannot see you. Sometimes, they wear portable radios with head sets, so they cannot hear you either. This can be very dangerous. On rainy days, pedestrians may not see you because of hats or umbrellas. They may be hurrying to get out of the rain and may not pay attention to the traffic.

Distractions

Distracted people: These people are hazards. Watch where they are looking. If they are looking at something else, they are not seeing you. Be alert even when they are looking at you. They may believe that they have the right of way.

Children: Children tend to act quickly without checking traffic. Children playing with one another may not look for traffic and are a serious hazard.

Talkers: Drivers or pedestrians talking to one another may not be paying close attention to the traffic.

Workers: People working on or near the roadway are a hazard. The work creates a distraction for drivers, and the workers themselves may not see you.

Ice cream truck: Someone selling ice cream is a clue to a hazard. Children may be nearby and not see you.

Disabled vehicle: People changing a tire or fixing an engine often do not pay attention to the danger that roadway traffic is to them. They are often careless. Jacked up wheels or raised hoods are hazard clues.

Accidents: Accidents are very hazardous. People involved in the accident may not look for traffic. Passing drivers tend to look at the accident. People often run across the road without looking. Vehicles may slow or stop suddenly.

Shoppers: People in and around shopping areas often are not watching traffic because they are looking for stores or looking into store windows.

Confused Drivers

Confused drivers often change direction suddenly or stop without warning. Confusion is common near freeway or turnpike interchanges and major intersections. Tourists unfamiliar with the area can be very hazardous. Clues pointing to tourists include car-top luggage and out-of-state license plates. Unexpected actions (stopping in the middle of a block, changing lanes for no apparent reason, backup lights suddenly going on) are clues to confusion. Hesitation is another clue. This includes driving very slowly, using brakes often, or stopping in the middle of an intersection. You may also see drivers who are looking at street signs, maps, and house numbers. These drivers may not pay attention to you.

Slow Drivers

Motorists who fail to drive at a normal speed are hazards. Seeing slow moving vehicles early can prevent a crash. Some vehicles by their nature are slow, and seeing them is a clue they are hazards (mopeds, farm machinery, construction machinery, tractors). Some of these will have the "slow moving vehicle" symbol to warn you. This is a red triangle with an orange center. Watch for it.

Drivers signaling a turn may be hazards. They may slow down more than you expect them to or even stop. If they are making a tight turn into an alley or driveway, they may proceed very slowly. If they are blocked by pedestrians or other vehicles, they may have to even stop on the roadway. Vehicles turning left may also have to stop because of oncoming vehicles.

Drivers in a Hurry

Some drivers may feel your commercial vehicle is keeping them from getting to where they want to go on time. Such drivers may pass you without a safe gap in the oncoming traffic and cut too closely in front of you. Drivers entering the road may pull in front of you in order to avoid being stuck behind you. You may have to brake for these people. Be aware of this and watch for drivers who are in a hurry.

Impaired Drivers

Drivers who are sleepy, ill, on drugs, or have had too much to drink are hazards. Some clues to these drivers are:

- Weaving across the road or drifting from one side to the other.

- Leaving the road (dropping the right wheels onto the shoulder or bumping across a curb when making a turn).

- Stopping at the wrong time (stopping at a green light or waiting for too long at a stop).

- Opening the window in cold weather.

- Speeding up or slowing down suddenly.

- Driving too fast or too slowly.

Be alert for drunk drivers and sleepy drivers late at night.

Driver Body Movement As A Clue

Drivers look in the direction they are going to turn. You may sometimes get a clue from a driver's head and body movements that he or she may be going to make a turn even though the turn signals are not on. Drivers making over-the-shoulder checks may be going to change lanes. These clues are most easily seen in motorcyclists and bicyclists. Watch other road users and try to tell whether they may do something hazardous.

Conflicts

You are in conflict when you have to change speed and/or direction to avoid hitting someone. Conflicts occur at intersections where vehicles meet, at merges (such as turnpike on-ramps), and where there are needed lane changes (such as the end of a lane, forcing a move to another lane of traffic). Other conflicts occur when there are slow moving or stalled vehicles in a traffic lane or when there is an accident. Watch for other drivers who are in conflict because they are a hazard to you. When they react to their conflict, they may do something that will put them in conflict with you.

Always Have a Plan

You should always be looking for hazards. Continue to learn how to see hazards on the road. Always look for them. However, do not forget why you are looking for the hazards — they may turn into emergencies. You look for the hazards in order to have time to plan a way out of any emergency. When you see a hazard, think about the emergencies that can develop and figure out what you will do. Always be ready to act on your plans. In this way, you will be a prepared, defensive driver who will increase not only your own safety but the safety of all road users.

Emergencies

Traffic emergencies occur when two vehicles or a vehicle and another object are about to crash. Vehicle emergencies occur when tires, brakes, or other critical parts fail. Following the safety practices in this manual can help prevent emergencies. If an emergency does happen, your chances of avoiding a crash depend upon how well you take action. Actions you can take are discussed in the paragraphs that follow.

Steering to Avoid a Crash

Stopping is not always the safest thing to do in an emergency. When you do not have enough room to stop, you may have to steer away from what is ahead. Remember, you can almost always turn quicker than you can stop. Use care, however. Top-heavy vehicles and tractors with multiple trailers may flip over.

Keep Both Hands on the Steering Wheel

In order to turn quickly, you must have a firm grip on the steering wheel with both hands. The best way to have both hands on the wheel when there is an emergency is to keep them there all of the time.

How to Turn Quickly and Safely

A quick turn can be made safely if it is done the right way. Here are some pointers that safe drivers use:

- Do not apply the brakes while you are turning. It is very easy to lock your wheels when turning. If that happens, you will skid out of control before you know it.

- Do not turn any more than is needed to clear the object in your way. The more sharply you turn, the greater the chances of a skid or rollover.

- Be prepared to "*countersteer*." This means you turn the wheel back in the other direction as soon as you have passed whatever was in your path. Unless you are prepared to countersteer, you will not be able to do it quickly enough. You should think of emergency steering and countersteering as two parts of one driving action.

Where to Steer

If an **oncoming driver** has drifted into your lane, a move to your right is best. If the driver realizes what has happened, the natural response will be to return to his or her own lane. If he or she does not return to the proper lane, you may still be able to avoid an accident.

If something is blocking your path, the best thing to do will depend on the situation:

- If you have been using your mirrors, you will know which lane is empty and can be safely used.

- If the shoulder is clear, going to the right may be best. No one is likely to be driving on the shoulder, but someone may be passing you on the left. You will know if you have been using your mirrors.

- If you are blocked on both sides, a move to the right may be best. At least you will not force anyone into an opposing traffic lane and a possible head-on collision. If a stopped vehicle is in front of you, a lane change may be better than running into it.

Leaving the Road

In some emergencies, you may have to drive off the road. This may be less risky than a collision with another vehicle. Most shoulders are strong enough to support the weight of a large vehicle and offer an escape route. Here are some guidelines if you must leave the road.

Avoid braking. If possible, avoid using the brakes until your speed has dropped to about 20 mph. Then brake very gently to avoid skidding on a loose surface.

Keep one set of wheels on the pavement if possible. This helps maintain control.

Stay on the shoulder. If the shoulder is clear, stay on it until your vehicle has come to a stop. Signal and check your mirrors before pulling back onto the road.

Return to the road. If you are forced to return to the road before you can stop, do the following:

- Turn sharply back onto the road. Do not try to edge gradually back on the road. If you do, your tire may grab suddenly and you can be halfway across the road before you know it.

- When both front tires are on the paved surface, counter-steer immediately. The two turns should be made as a single "steer-countersteer" move.

How to Stop Quickly and Safely

If someone suddenly pulls out in front of you, your natural response is to hit the brakes. This is a good response if there is enough distance to stop and you use the brakes correctly.

You should brake in a way that will keep your vehicle in a straight line and allow you to turn if needed. You can use either the "controlled braking" method or the "stab braking" method.

Controlled braking: With this method, you apply the brakes as hard as you can without locking the wheels. Keep the steering wheel movements very small while you are doing this. If you need to make a larger steering movement or if the wheels lock, release the brakes. Put on the brakes again as soon as you can.

Stab braking: Apply your brakes hard. Release the brakes when the wheels lock up. As soon as the wheels start rolling, put on the brakes fully again. It can take up to one second for the wheels to start rolling after you release the brakes. If you reapply the brakes before the wheels start rolling, the vehicle will not straighten out.

Do not jam on the brakes. Emergency braking does not mean pushing down on the brake pedal as hard as you can. That will only keep the wheels locked up and cause a skid. If the wheels are skidding, you cannot control the vehicle. Emergency braking means applying the brakes as hard as you need to without skidding.

Hydraulic Brake Failure

Brakes kept in good condition rarely fail. Most hydraulic brake failures occur for one of two reasons:

- Loss of hydraulic pressure

- Brake fade on long hills

Loss of Hydraulic Pressure

When the system will not build up pressure, the brake pedal will feel spongy or go to the floor. Here are some things you can do to help.

Downshift: Put the vehicle into a lower gear. This will help to slow down the vehicle.

Pump the brakes: Sometimes pumping the brake pedal will create enough hydraulic pressure to stop the vehicle.

Use the parking brake: The parking, or emergency, brake is separate from the hydraulic brake system, so it can be used to slow the vehicle. Be sure to press the release button or pull the release lever at the same time you use the emergency brake so you can adjust the brake pressure and keep the wheels from locking up.

Find an escape route: While slowing the vehicle, look for an escape route — an open field, a side street, or an escape ramp. Turning uphill is a good way to slow and stop the vehicle. Make sure the vehicle does not start rolling backward after you stop. Put it in low gear, apply the parking brake, and if necessary, roll back into some obstacle that will stop the vehicle.

Brake Failure on Downgrades

Going slowly enough and braking properly will almost always prevent brake failure on long downgrades. Once the brakes have failed, however, you are going to have to look outside your vehicle for something to stop it.

Your best hope is an escape ramp. If there is one, there will be signs telling you about it. Use it. Ramps are usually placed a few miles from the top of the downgrade. Every year, hundreds of drivers avoid injury to themselves or damage to their vehicles by using escape ramps. Some ramps use soft gravel that resists the motion of the truck and brings it to a stop. Others turn uphill, using the hill to stop the vehicle and soft gravel to hold it in place.

Any driver who loses brakes going downhill should use an escape ramp if there is one. If you do not use one, your chances of having a serious crash will be much worse.

If there is no escape ramp, take the best escape route you can see — an open field or a side road that flattens out or turns up- hill. Make the move as soon as you know your brakes do not work. The longer you wait, the faster the vehicle will go, and the harder it will be to stop.

Air Brakes and failure of air brakes are discussed in Chapter Six.

Tire Failure

There are four important things that qualified drivers do to handle tire failure safely:

- Know that a tire has failed.

- Hold the steering wheel firmly.

- Stay off the brakes.

- After stopping, check all of the tires.

Recognize Tire Failure

Knowing quickly you have a tire failure will let you have more time to react. Having just a few seconds to remember what it is you are to do can help you. The major signs of tire failure are:

Sound: The loud "bang" of a blowout is an easily recognized sign. Because it can take a few seconds for the vehicle to react, you may think it is some other vehicle. Any time you hear a tire blow, you will be safest to assume it is yours.

Vibration: If the vehicle thumps or vibrates heavily, it may be a sign that one of the tires has gone flat. With a rear tire, that may be the only sign you get.

Feel: If the steering feels "heavy," it is probably a sign that one of the front tires has failed. Failure of a rear tire can cause the vehicle to slide back and forth, or "fishtail." However, dual rear tires will usually prevent this.

Any of the above signs is a warning of possible tire failure. When a tire fails, you should do the following things.

Hold the Steering Wheel Firmly: If a front tire fails, it can twist the steering wheel out of your hand. The only way to prevent this is to have a firm grip on the steering wheel with both hands. The best way to have a firm grip on the steering wheel when a front tire fails is to keep a firm grip on it at all times.

Stay Off the Brakes: It is natural to want to brake in an emergency. However, braking when a tire has failed can cause you to lose control of the vehicle. Unless you are about to run into something, stay off the brakes until the vehicle has slowed down. Then brake very gently, pull off the road, and stop.

Check the Tires: After you have come to a stop, get out and check all of the tires. Do this even if the vehicle seems to be handling all right. If one of your dual tires goes, the only way you may know it is by getting out and looking at it.

Fires

Truck and bus fires can cause damage and injury. Learn the causes of fires and how to prevent them. Know what to do to put out fires.

Causes of Fire

The following are some causes of vehicle fires:

After accidents: Spilled fuel or improper use of flares

Tires: Not enough air in the tires or dual tires that touch

Electrical system: Short circuits due to damaged insulation or loose connections.

Fuel: Driver smoking, improper fueling, and loose fuel connections

Cargo: Flammable cargo, improperly sealed or loaded cargo, or poor ventilation in the cargo area

Fire Prevention

Pay attention to the following:

Pre-trip inspection: Make a complete inspection of the electrical, fuel, and exhaust systems, the tires, and the cargo.

Enroute inspection: Check the tires, wheels, and truck body for signs of heat whenever you stop during a trip.

Follow safe procedures: Use approved safety methods for fueling the vehicle, using brakes, handling flares, and other activities that can cause a fire.

Checking: Check the instruments and gauges often for signs of getting too hot. Use the mirrors to look for signs of smoke from tires or the vehicle itself.

Caution: Be careful when you handle anything flammable.

Firefighting Methods

- Attempt to Get Off Highway Before Stopping

- Notify Fire Department

- Do Not Risk Your Life

Type of Fire	*Precaution*
Engine Fire	Do Not Open Hood Wide
Electric Fire	Disconnect Battery Cables
Fuel Fires	Do Not Use Water on Oil
Cargo Fires	Open Door Cautiously
	Remove Cargo Until Source is Found
Tire Fires	Check for Heated Tires and Cool Them
	Do Not Drive With Tire Fire
	Do Not Pull Into Service Station
	Do Cool With Water and Remove Tire

FIGURE 4-36: FIREFIGHTING METHODS

Fire Fighting

Knowing how to fight fires is important. Fires have been made worse by drivers who did not know what to do. Here are some procedures to follow in case of fire:

Pull off the road. The first step is to get the vehicle off the road and stop. In doing so:

- Park in an open area. Park away from buildings, trees, brush, other vehicles, or anything that may catch fire.

- Do not pull into a service station!

- Use your CB (if you have one) to notify the police of your problem and your location.

Keep the fire from spreading. Before trying to put out the fire, make sure it does not spread any further.

- With an engine fire, turn off the engine as soon as you can. Do not open the hood if you can avoid it. Shoot extinguishers through louvers, the radiator, or aim it from the underside of the vehicle.

- For a cargo fire in a van or box trailer, keep the doors shut, especially if your cargo contains hazardous materials. Opening the van doors will supply the fire with oxygen and can cause it to burn very fast.

Use the Right Fire Extinguisher

- The "B:C" type of fire extinguisher is for electrical fires and burning liquids. The A:B:C type is for burning wood, paper, and cloth.

- Water can be used on wood, paper, or cloth but not on an electrical fire. You can get shocked. Water on a gasoline fire will just spread the flames.

- A burning tire must be cooled. Lots of water may be needed to cool it.

Extinguish the fire. Here are some rules to follow in putting out a fire:

- Know how the fire extinguisher works. Study the instructions printed on the extinguisher before you need to use it.

- When using the extinguisher, stay as far away from the fire as possible.

- Aim at the base of the fire, or the source of it, not up into the flames.

- Stand upwind. Let the wind carry the contents of the extinguisher to the fire rather than bringing the flames to you.

- Keep trying to put out the fire until whatever was burning has been cooled. No smoke or flame does not mean the fire is out or cannot begin again.

- Try to extinguish the fire only if you know what you are doing, and it is safe to do so.

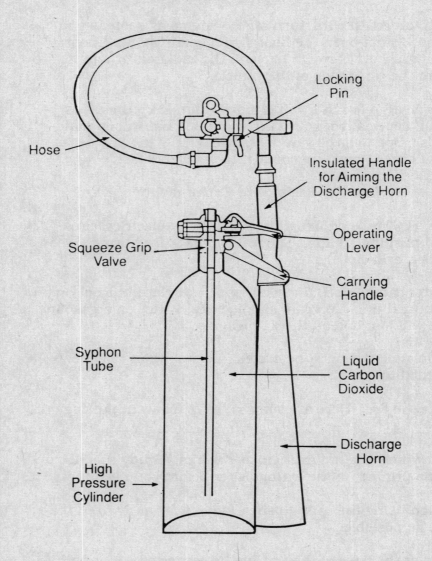

FIGURE 4-37: FIRE EXTINGUISHER

Basic Fire Prevention Steps

- Drive Defensively and Avoid Accidents
- Don't Be Careless With Cigarettes
- Check for Fire Hazards During Pretrip
- Monitor for Fire Hazards Enroute

Cause	Prevention
Tires	• Check for Low Pressure and "Kissing" Duals • Check at Each Stop
Brakes	• Inspect for Fire Hazards • Use Properly
Electrical System	• Inspect for Damage or "Shorts" • Use Proper Fuses
Exhaust System	• Inspect for Loose Parts • Don't Park Over Vegetation
Fuel System	• Inspect for Leaks • Fuel Safely and Legally
Fuses and Flares	• Follow Rules for Use and Storage
Cargo Heaters	• Follow Carrier Rules

FIGURE 4-38: BASIC FIRE PREVENTION STEPS

Skids

A skid happens when the tires lose their grip on the road. This is caused by one of four ways:

Overbraking: Braking too hard can lock up the wheels and cause you to skid. Skids can also occur by using the speed retarder when the road is slippery.

Oversteering: Turning the wheels more sharply than the vehicle can turn.

Overacceleration: Supplying too much power to the drive wheels. This will cause them to spin.

Driving too fast: Most serious skids result from driving too fast for the road conditions. Drivers who adjust their driving to the conditions do not overaccelerate and do not have to overbrake or oversteer from too much speed.

Drive-wheel Skids

By far, the most common skid is the one in which the rear wheels lose traction because of too much braking or acceleration. Skids caused by speeding up usually happen on ice or snow. They can be easily stopped by taking your foot off the accelerator and pushing in the clutch. Acceleration skids usually are not as dangerous as other types.

Rear wheel braking skids occur when the rear drive wheels lock. Because locked wheels have less traction than rolling wheels, the rear wheels usually slide sideways in an attempt to "catch up" with the front wheels. In a bus or straight truck, the vehicle will slide sideways in a "spin out." With vehicles towing trailers, a drive-wheel skid can let the trailer push the towing vehicle sideways. This can cause the vehicle to jackknife very suddenly.

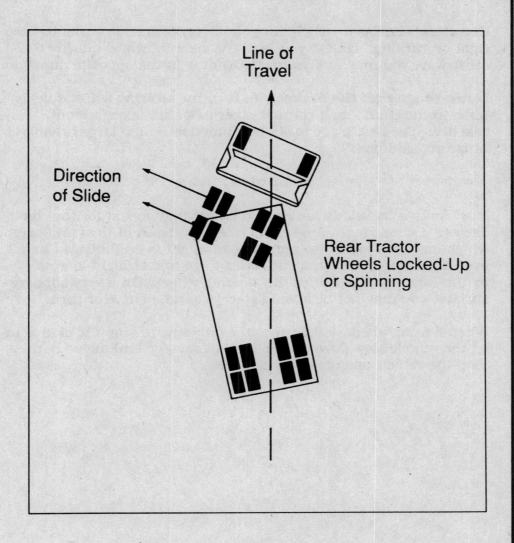

Line of Travel

Direction of Slide

Rear Tractor Wheels Locked-Up or Spinning

FIGURE 4-39: TRACTOR JACKKNIFE

Correcting a Rear-wheel Braking Skid

Do the following to correct a drive-wheel braking skid.

Stop braking: This will keep the rear wheels from sliding any further and let them roll again. If you are on ice, push in the clutch to let the wheels turn freely.

Turn quickly: When a vehicle begins to slide sideways, quickly steer in the direction you want the vehicle to go (down the road). You must turn the wheel quickly.

Countersteer: As a vehicle turns back on course, it wants to keep right on turning. Unless you turn the steering wheel quickly the other way, you may find yourself skidding in the opposite direction.

Learn to stay off the brakes: To turn the steering wheel quickly, push in the clutch, and counter-steer in a skid takes a lot of practice. The best place to get this practice is on a large driving range or "skid pad."

Front-wheel Skids

Most front-wheel skids are caused by driving too fast for the conditions. Other causes are lack of tread on the front tires and cargo which has been loaded so not enough weight is on the axle. In a front-wheel skid, the front end tends to go in a straight line no matter how much you turn the steering wheel. On a very slippery surface, you may not be able to steer around a curve or turn.

When a front-wheel skid occurs, the only way to stop the skid is to let the vehicle slow down. Stop turning and/or braking so hard. Stop the vehicle as quickly as possible.

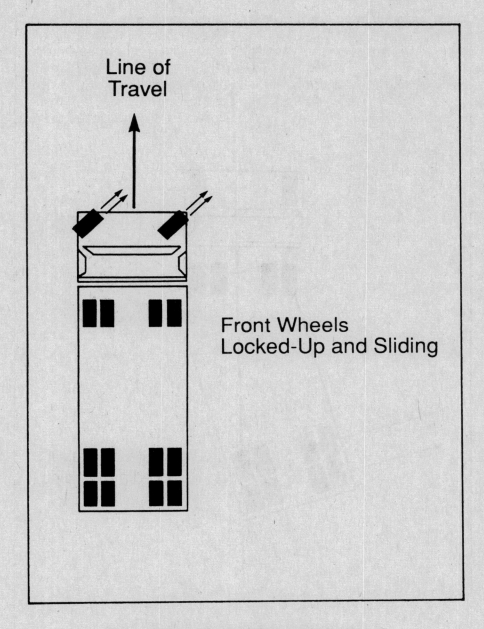

FIGURE 4-40: FRONT WHEEL SKID

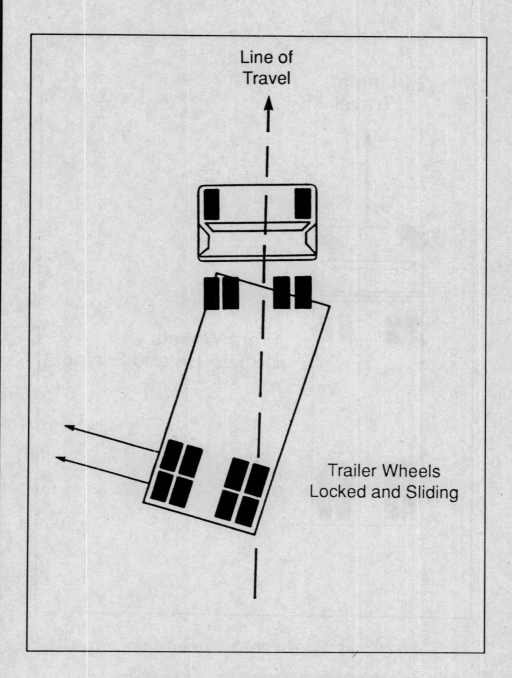

Line of
Travel

Trailer Wheels
Locked and Sliding

FIGURE 4-41: TRAILER JACKKNIFE

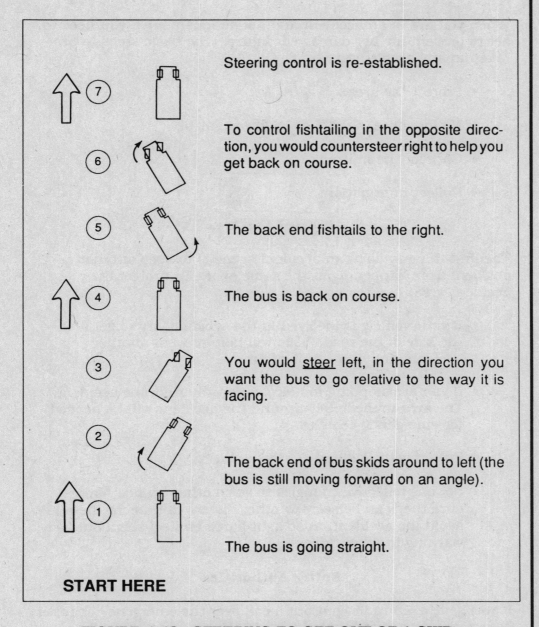

⑦ Steering control is re-established.

⑥ To control fishtailing in the opposite direction, you would countersteer right to help you get back on course.

⑤ The back end fishtails to the right.

④ The bus is back on course.

③ You would <u>steer</u> left, in the direction you want the bus to go relative to the way it is facing.

② The back end of bus skids around to left (the bus is still moving forward on an angle).

① The bus is going straight.

START HERE

FIGURE 4-42: STEERING TO GET OUT OF A SKID

Accidents

When you are in an accident and not seriously hurt, you need to act to prevent further damage or injury. The basic steps to be taken in any accident are to:

- Protect the area.

- Notify police, sheriff, or Highway Patrol.

- Care for the injured.

- Collect information.

Protect the Area

The first thing to do at an accident scene is to keep another accident from happening at the same spot. To protect the accident area:

- If your vehicle is involved in the accident, try to get it to the side of the road. This will help prevent another accident and allow traffic to move.

- If you are stopping to help, park away from the accident. The area immediately around the accident will be needed for emergency vehicles.

- Put on your flashers.

- Set out reflective triangles to warn other traffic. Make sure they can be seen by other drivers in time for them to avoid the accident. Also light flares and set them out as a warning to other drivers.

Notify Authorities

If you have a CB radio, put out a call over the emergency channel before you get out of your vehicle. If not, wait until after the accident scene has been properly protected, then phone the police or send someone to phone them. Try to find out where you are so you can give the exact location.

Care for the Injured

If a qualified person is at the accident and helping the injured, stay out of the way unless you are asked to assist. If there is no one else, do the best you can to help any one who is injured.

Here are some simple steps to follow:

- Do not move a badly injured person unless the danger of fire or passing traffic makes it necessary.

- Stop heavy bleeding by applying direct pressure to the wound.

- Keep the injured person warm.

Collect Information

If you were involved in the accident, you or your employer will have to file an accident report. You will need to know the following information for the report.

- Names, addresses, and driver license numbers of other drivers involved in the accident.

- License numbers and types of vehicles involved in the accident.

- Names and addresses of the owners of the other vehicles (if different from the drivers).

- A description of the damage to other vehicles and property.

- The name and address of anyone who was injured.

- The name, badge number, and agency of any officer investigating the accident.

- Names and addresses of witnesses.

- The exact location of the accident.

- The direction each of the vehicles was going at the time of the accident and the direction they were headed following it.

This section is about a driver's fitness to drive. Lack of rest, use of alcohol and drugs, and illness are just some of the problems that can cause a driver to be unfit to drive.

**Fitness
to Drive**

Be Ready to Drive

Driving a vehicle for long hours is tiring. Even the best drivers will become less alert. However, there are things that good drivers do to help stay alert and safe. Here are a few helpful hints.

Get enough sleep. Leaving on a long trip when you are already tired is dangerous. If you have a long trip planned, make sure you get a good sleep before you go.

Schedule trips safely. Your body gets used to sleeping during certain hours. If you are driving during those hours, you will be less alert. Try to plan trips for the hours you are usually awake.

Avoid medication. Many medicines can make you sleepy. Those that do will have a label warning against operating vehicles or machinery. The most common medicine of this type is an ordinary cold pill. If you have to drive with a cold, you are better off suffering from the cold than from the effects of the medicine.

Keep cool. A hot, poorly **ventilated** cab can make you sleepy. Keep the window or vent cracked, or use the air conditioner if you have one.

Take breaks. Short breaks can keep you alert. The time to take them is before you feel really drowsy or tired. Stop often. Walk around. Inspect your vehicle. It can help to do some physical exercises.

If You Do Become Sleepy

When you are sleepy, trying to "push on" is far more dangerous than most drivers think. It is a major cause of fatal accidents. Here are some important rules to follow:

Stop to sleep. When your body needs sleep, sleep is the only thing that will work. If you have to make a stop, make it when you feel the first signs of sleepiness, even if it is earlier than you planned. If you get up a little earlier the next day, you can keep on schedule without the danger of driving when you are not alert.

Take a nap. If you cannot stop for the night, at least pull off the road and take a nap. A nap as short as half an hour will do more to overcome fatigue than a half-hour coffee stop.

Avoid drugs. There are no drugs that can overcome being tired. They may keep you awake for a while but will not make you alert. Sooner or later, you will be even more tired than if you had not taken them at all. Sleep is the only thing that can cure fatigue.

Alcohol and Driving

Drinking alcohol and then driving is a very serious problem. People who drink alcohol are involved in traffic accidents which kill over 20,000 people every year. You should know:

- How alcohol works in the human body.

- How it affects driving.

- Laws regarding drinking and driving.

- Legal, financial, and safety risks of drinking and driving.

The Truth About Alcohol

There are many dangerous ideas about the use of alcohol. The driver who believes these wrong ideas will be more likely to get into trouble. Here are some examples:

Wrong Idea	The Truth
• Alcohol increases your ability to drive.	• Alcohol is a drug that will make you less alert and reduce your ability to drive safely.
• Some people can drink a lot and not be affected by it.	• Everyone who drinks is affected by alcohol.
• If you eat a lot first, you will not get drunk.	• Food will slow down the effects of alcohol but will not prevent them.

Wrong Idea	The Truth
• Coffee and a little fresh air will help a drinker sober up.	• Time is the only thing that will help a drinker sober up — other methods just do not work.
• Stick with beer — it is not as strong as wine or whiskey.	• A few beers are the same as a few shots of whiskey or a few glasses of wine.

It is the alcohol in drinks that affects human action. It makes no difference whether that alcohol comes from a couple of beers, two glasses of wine, or two shots of hard liquor.

All of the following drinks contain the same amount of alcohol:

- 12 ounce glass of 5% beer

- 5 ounce glass of 12% wine

- 1-1/2 ounce shot of 80 proof liquor

How Alcohol Works

Alcohol goes directly from the stomach into the blood stream. A drinker can control the amount of alcohol which he or she takes in by having fewer drinks or none. However, the drinker cannot control how fast the body gets rid of alcohol. The body gets rid of alcohol at a rate of about 1 drink per hour. If you have drinks faster than the body can get rid of them, you will have more alcohol in your body and will be more affected. The amount of alcohol in your body is measured by the *Blood Alcohol Concentration (BAC)*.

What Determines Blood Alcohol Concentration

BAC is determined by the amount of alcohol you drink (more alcohol means a higher BAC), how fast you drink (faster drinking means a higher BAC), and your weight (a small person does not have to drink as much to reach the same BAC).

Alcohol and the Brain

Alcohol affects more and more of the brain as BAC builds up. The first part of the brain which is affected controls judgment and self-control. One of the bad things about this is that it can keep drinkers from knowing they are getting drunk. Of course, good judgment and self-control are musts for safe driving.

As BAC continues to build up, muscle control, vision, and coordination are affected more and more. In time, a person will pass out.

How Alcohol Affects Driving

All drivers are affected by drinking alcohol. Alcohol affects judgment, vision, coordination, and reaction time. It causes serious driving errors, such as:

- Driving too fast or too slow
- Driving in the wrong lane
- Driving over the curb
- Weaving
- Driving between lanes
- Quick, jerky starts
- Not signaling
- Failure to use lights
- Running stop signs and red lights
- Improper passing

These effects mean more chances of a crash and losing your driver's license. Accident statistics show that the chance of a crash is much greater for drivers who have been drinking than for drivers who have not.

Remember, if you commit a first violation of driving your CMV while under the influence, you will lose your license for one year. If you have a second violation, you will lose it for at least ten years. Even driving your own car while you are under the influence can put you out of service for 24 hours.

Other Drugs

Besides alcohol, legal and illegal drugs are being used more often. Laws state you must not possess or use certain drugs while on duty. They say you must not be under the influence of any "controlled substance": an amphetamine (including "pep pills" and "bennies"); narcotics; or any other substance which can make a driver unsafe. This could include many prescription and over-the-counter drugs (cold medicines) which may make the driver sleepy or in some way affect safe driving ability. However, you may have and use drugs prescribed by a doctor if they will not affect safe driving ability.

Pay attention to warning labels on prescribed drugs and medicines and listen to the doctor's orders about possible effects. Stay away from illegal drugs. Do not use anything that hides fatigue — the only cure for fatigue is rest. Alcohol can make the effects of drugs worse. The safest rule is to not mix drugs with driving at all.

Use of alcohol or drugs can lead to traffic accidents resulting in death or injury and property damage. It can also lead to arrest, fines, and jail sentences. It can mean the end of a person's driving career.

Illness

Once in a while, you may become so ill or tired you cannot operate a motor vehicle safely. If this happens to you, you must not drive. In the case of an emergency, you may drive to the nearest place where you can safely stop.

Hazardous Materials

All commercial drivers must know the basic rules about hauling dangerous materials. Even if you do not plan to haul these materials, you still need to know what you cannot haul unless you have a hazardous material endorsement on your CDL.

What are Hazardous Materials?

The Federal Hazardous Materials Table names substances that pose a risk to health, safety, and property during transportation. You must follow many rules about transporting them. The intent of the rules is to:

- Contain the product.

- Communicate the risk.

- Ensure safe drivers and equipment.

What do These Rules Mean?

To contain the the product: Many hazardous products can injure or kill on contact. In order to protect drivers and others from contact with the product, the rules tell shippers how to package it safely. Other rules tell drivers how to load, transport, and unload bulk tanks. These are the containment rules.

To communicate the risk: The shipper uses a shipping paper and package labels to warn dockworkers and drivers of the risk. Shipping orders, bills of loading, and manifests are all examples of shipping papers.

There are 22 different classes of hazards. A material's hazard class reflects the risks associated with it. Here are the 22 classes of hazards.

EXPLOSIVE A	COMBUSTIBLE LIQUID
EXPLOSIVE B	NONFLAMMABLE GAS
EXPLOSIVE C	ORGANIC PEROXIDE
POISON A	IRRITATING MATERIAL
POISON B	FLAMMABLE SOLID
ORM-A	FLAMMABLE LIQUID
ORM-B	ETIOLOGIC AGENTS
ORM-C	BLASTING AGENTS
ORM-D	RADIOACTIVE MATERIAL
ORM-E	CORROSIVE MATERIAL
OXIDIZER	FLAMMABLE GAS

The initials ORM stand for "other regulated materials." Shippers write the name of the hazard class of hazardous products in the item description section on the shipping paper. The four-inch diamond shaped labels on the containers of hazardous materials should also contain that name. If the diamond label will not fit on the container, shippers should put the label on a tag. For example, compressed gas cylinders that will not hold a label have tags. Labels look like the examples shown in Figure 4-42 on the following page.

After an accident or hazardous material leak, the driver may be unable to speak when help arrives. Fire fighters and police must know the hazards involved in order to prevent more damage or injury. The driver's life, and the lives of others, may depend on quickly finding the shipping papers for hazardous cargo. For that reason, you must mark shipping papers related to hazardous materials with tabs or keep them on top of the other shipping papers. You must also keep shipping papers:

- In a pouch on the driver's door.

- In clear view within reach.

   or

- On the driver's seat.

Drivers must use placards to warn others of their hazardous cargo. Placards are signs placed on the outside of a vehicle to show the hazard class(es) of products on board. There are 19 different DOT placards. Each is turned upright on a point, like a diamond shape. The person who does the loading must place the placards on the front, rear, and both sides of the vehicle.

FIGURE 4-43: EXAMPLES OF HAZARDOUS
MATERIAL LABELS

Not all trucks that carry hazardous materials need to have placards. Any person with a CDL can drive a truck that carries hazardous materials if it does not require placards. If it requires
placards, a driver must not drive it unless his or her driver's
license has the hazardous materials endorsement.

To ensure safe drivers and equipment: The rules say that all drivers of placarded trucks must learn how to safely load and transport hazardous products. They must have a commercial driver's
license with the hazardous materials endorsement.

To get the required endorsement, they must pass a written test.
They also will need a tank endorsement if they transport hazardous products in a cargo tank on a truck larger than 26,000
pounds GVW.

Drivers who need the hazardous materials endorsement must
learn the placard rules. If you do not know whether your truck
needs placards, ask your employer. Never drive a vehicle needing
placards unless you have the hazardous materials endorsement.
To do so is a crime. When you are stopped, you will be cited. You
will not be allowed to drive your truck any further. It will cost you
and your company time and money. Failure to placard a truck
when it is needed will risk your life and others if you have an
accident. Emergency help will not know of your hazardous cargo.

Hazardous materials drivers must also know which products they
can load together, and which they cannot. Before loading a truck
with more than one type of product, you must know if it is safe to
load them together. If you do not know, ask your employer.

Summary

This chapter has presented a summary of general information
which is important for all drivers of commercial vehicles to know.
Various road and weather conditions were presented, and ways to
handle hazardous and emergency situations were discussed.
Knowledge in all of these areas is a must for the holder of a CDL.

Key Words

Acceleration — Speeding up

BAC — Blood alcohol concentration

Bicyclist — A person riding a bicycle

Billowing — Blowing up and about or ballooning

Carbon dioxide — A gas that can make a person very ill or even kill him or her

CB — Citizen band radio

Collision — Crash

Commercial driver — A driver who operates a commercial motor vehicle, such as haevy truck, tractor-trailer, bus, tanker, or a vehicle carrying hazardous material

Compartment — A section that is partitioned off from the rest of the vehicle for a particular use. The engine compartment is an example.

Countersteer — Turn the steering wheel in the opposite direction from the way you previously turned it

Emergency equipment — Equipment which is used by the driver when problems arise. It includes fire extinguishers, spare fuses, and warning devices.

Extinguisher — Equipment used to spray substances on a fire that will put it out

Financial — Having to do with money

Flammable — Material which will burn

Force of Gravity — A force of nature that pulls things downward

General Knowledge Test — A required test for the CDL that asks for information all commercial drivers must know

Hazardous materials — Materials which are dangerous to transport, such as dynamite and gasoline. A CDL must have a hazardous materials endorsement for the driver to be able to haul hazardous materials.

Hydraulic brakes — Brakes which are operated by fluid pressure

Hydroplaning — A condition that permits the tires to stop gripping the road in wet weather. The vehicle can then skid very easily.

Jackknife — A type of accident in which the tractor and trailer turn so as to make a V-shape

Off-tracking — A term which describes the path the rear wheels of a large vehicle take. This path is different from that of the front wheels.

Oncoming driver — A driver coming toward you (in front of you)

Oxygen — A gas in the air that lets things burn

Pedestrian — A person on foot

Poisonous — Containing a substance which can make a person ill or even cause death

Reflector — Equipment which casts back or reflects light

Retractable — Can be pulled up or back (retracted)

Securement — Properly attaching something such as cargo to a vehicle using bracing, chains, or other necessary equipment

Suspension system — The system of the vehicle which holds the vehicle and its load up and keeps the axles in place

Tachometer — A device which measures rpm (revolutions per minute)

Tailgate — Follow very closely behind another vehicle

Tourist — Someone who is visiting in an area

Traction — The ability of the tire to grip the pavement

Transmission — An enclosed unit for gears and related equipment. It may be manual if gears have to be shifted or automatic if the gears shift themselves.

Vehicle condition report — A written report made by the driver which lists any conditions of the vehicle which may be unsafe

Ventilate — To let air flow through freely

Visibility — How far a driver can see

Witness — Someone who sees something happen

REVIEW QUESTIONS

1. Who is considered a commercial driver? Do all commercial drivers have to pass a general knowledge test?
   _____
   _____

2. Which of these statements about Chapter Four is true?
   A. Chapter Four contains information on combination
       vehicles, air brakes and buses.
   B. There is information on hazardous material.
   _____

3. What are three good reasons for inspecting your bus?
   What is the most important reason?
   _____
   _____
   _____

4. What things should you check before a trip? During the
   trip?
   _____
   _____
   _____
   _____

5. Certain defects will place your vehicle "out-of-service"
   because they are considered dangerous by USDOT. Can
   you name six of these defects?
   _____
   _____
   _____

6. What are some key parts of the steering system?
   _____
   _____

7. Name some suspension system defects.

    _____

    _____

8. What three kinds of emergency equipment must you have?

    _____

    _____

    _____

9. What is the minimum tread depth for front tires? Other tires?

    _____

10. What are some items you should check on the front of your bus during the walkaround inspection?

    _____

    _____

    _____

11. What are the steps of the seven-step pre-trip inspection?

    _____

    _____

    _____

    _____

12. How do you test hydraulic brakes for leaks?

    _____

13. Can you use the "Vehicle Inspection Test Helpers" or memory aids during your State's inspection test?

    _____

14. Why should you back toward the driver's side? When backing, why is it important to use a helper?

    _____

    _____

    _____

15. What is a "pull-up?"

_____

16. If you are stopped on a hill, how can you start moving without rolling back.

_____

_____

17. What are the two special conditions when you should downshift?

_____

_____

18. When should you downshift automatic transmissions?

_____

19. What are two ways to know when to shift?

_____

_____

20. Retarders keep you from skidding when the road is slippery. True or false?_____

21. How far ahead should you look when driving on city streets? Highways?

_____

_____

22. What are the two main things to look for ahead of your vehicle?

_____

_____

23. What is your most important way to see to the sides and rear?

_____

_____

24. What does "communicating" mean in safe driving?

_____

_____

25. Where should your reflectors be placed when you are stopped on a divided highway?

_____

_____

26. What three distances add up to total stopping distance?

_____

_____

_____

27. If you go twice as fast, will your stopping distance increase by two or four times?

_____

28. Empty vehicles have the best braking. True or false?

_____

29. What is "black ice"?

_____

30. What is hydroplaning?

_____

31. Which of these statements is true?
    A.   You should decrease your following distance if somebody is tailgating you.
    B.   If you swing wide to the left before turning right, another driver may try to pass you on the right.

_____

32. How do you find out how many seconds of following distance space you have?

_____

_____

33. If you are driving a 40-foot vehicle at 55 mph, how many seconds of following distance space should you allow?

    _____

34. You should use your low beam headlights whenever you can. True or false?_____

35. You can safely remove the radiator cap at any time. True or false?_____

36. You should let air our of a hot tire tube so the pressure goes back to normal. True or false?_____

37. What effects can wet brakes cause? How can you avoid these problems?

    _____

    _____

38. If you are drowsy, what should you do before you drive?

    _____

39. Why should you be in the right gear before starting down a hill?

    _____

    _____

40. What gear should you use to go down a steep hill? Is there a rule for this?

    _____

    _____

41. What is one way to prevent brake fade?

    _____

42. What is a hazard? What are some roadway hazards?

    _____

    _____

43. What is a hazardous materials placard? Why are placards used?

_____

_____

44. You look for hazards in order to have time to do what?

_____

45. What is an escape ramp? Where are they found?

_____

_____

46. Stopping is always the safest thing to do in an emergency. True or false?_____

47. What are some advantages of going right instead of left around an obstacle?

_____

_____

48. What should you do if a tire blows out?

_____

49. What are some things to do at an accident scene to prevent another accident?

_____

_____

_____

50. What are two causes of tire fires? What are some cause of other vehicle fires?

_____

_____

_____

51. On what kinds of fires would you use a B:C extinguisher?

_____

_____

52. What are some rules to follow in putting out a fire?

_____

_____

_____

53. Which statements are true?
     A.   Coffee will help a drinker sober up.
     B.   Fresh air will help a drinker sober up.
     C.   Common medicines for colds can make you sleepy.

_____

CARRYING PASSENGERS SAFELY

CHAPTER

5

FROM NOW ON,

ONLY THE BEST WILL DRIVE

Chapter Objectives

Define who is a bus driver

List parts of vehicle to be inspected

Identify proper safety procedures

List conditions which often lead to crashes

CHAPTER FIVE

CARRYING PASSENGERS SAFELY

Bus drivers must have a commercial driver's license (CDL) with a Passenger Endorsement. To get the endorsement, you must pass a written test on the facts found in this chapter. You are tested on this information with the Passenger Test in Chapter Nine.

You must also pass the performance test for the class of bus you will drive. This chapter has the information you must know to drive a bus safely.

The federal law defines bus driver as a person who operates any vehicle designed to seat more than 15 persons, including the driver. Bus drivers must have a commercial driver's license. You are not classed as a bus driver if you carry only family members on personal trips. You are a commercial bus driver if you transport people who are not members of your family in a bus.

Who is a Bus Driver?

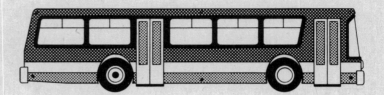

ARE YOU A BUS DRIVER?

The federal law states that you are legally a bus driver if you transport passengers in any vehicle designed to seat more than 15, including the driver. All bus drivers must have a commercial driver's license. You are a bus driver even if you only:

- Drive a school bus.

- Transport passengers for nonprofit groups, such as church groups, schools, scouting groups, senior citizen centers.

- Drive a hotel or car rental shuttle that seats more than 15.

- Drive an airport limousine that seats more than 15.

You are not a commercial bus driver if you only transport family members for nonbusiness purposes, even if your vehicle seats more than 15.

Note: Some states may have stricter laws. For example, California requires a CDL to transport more than 10 passengers.

FIGURE 5-1: ARE YOU A BUS DRIVER?

Pre-Trip Bus Inspection

Before driving your bus, make sure it is safe. During the pre-drive inspection, check defects reported by previous drivers. If the defects reported earlier have been fixed, sign the previous driver's report. This is your statement that the defects reported earlier have been fixed.

Make sure these things are in good working order before driving.

- Service brakes, including air hose couplings if your bus has a trailer or semitrailer

- Parking brake

- Steering mechanism

- Lighting devices and reflectors

- Tires (front wheels must not have recapped or regrooved tires)

- Horn

- Windshield wiper or wipers

- Rear-vision mirror or mirrors

- Coupling devices

- Wheels and rims

As you check the outside of the bus, close any open emergency exits. Also close any open baggage, restroom, service, or engine access panels before driving.

People sometimes damage empty buses. Always check the inside of the bus before driving it to be sure it is safe for the riders. Aisles and stairs must always be clear. The following parts of your bus must be in safe working condition.

- Each handhold and railing

- Floor covering

- Signaling devices, including the restroom emergency buzzer if the bus has a restroom

- Emergency exit handles

The seats must be safe for riders. All seats must be securely fastened to the bus. There is one exception to this rule. A charter bus carrying farm workers may have as many as eight folding seats in the aisle.

Never drive with an open emergency exit door or window. The "Emergency Exit" sign on an emergency door must be clearly visible at all times. If there is a red emergency door light, it must work. Turn it on every time you use your outside lights.

You may lock some emergency roof hatches in a partly open position for fresh air. Do not leave them open as a regular practice. Keep in mind the bus' need for higher clearance while driving with them open.

Make sure your bus has a fire extinguisher and the emergency reflectors required by law. The bus must also have spare electrical fuses unless it has circuit brakers.

The driver's seat should have a seat belt. Always use it for safety.

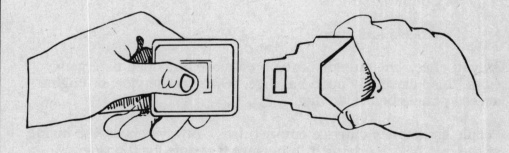

FIGURE 5-2: ALWAYS WEAR YOUR SEAT BELT

Loading And Trip Start

Do not allow riders to leave carry-on baggage in a doorway or aisle. Be sure there is nothing in the aisle that may trip riders. Secure baggage and freight in ways that avoid damage and:

- Allow the driver to move freely and easily.

- Allow riders to exit by any window or door in an emergency.

- Protect riders from injury if carry-ons fall or shift position.

Watch for cargo or baggage containing hazardous material. Most hazardous material cannot be carried on a bus.

The Federal Hazardous Materials Table shows which materials are hazardous (see page 225). They pose a risk to health, safety, and property during transportation. The rules require shippers to mark containers of hazardous material with the material's name, ID number, and a hazard label. There are 22 different 4-inch diamond-shaped hazard labels. Figure 5-3 shows some examples.

FIGURE 5-3: EXAMPLES OF WARNING LABELS

DO NOT transport any hazardous material unless you are sure the rules allow it. Watch for diamond-shaped labels.

Buses may carry small-arms ammunition labeled ORM-D, emergency hospital supplies, and drugs. Buses can also carry small amounts of certain other hazardous materials if the shipper cannot send them any other way. Buses must never carry:

- Class A poison, liquid Class B poison, tear gas, or irritating materials.

- More than 100 pounds of Solid Class B poisons.

- Explosives in the space occupied by people; the exception is small arms ammunition.

- Radioactive materials (which are labeled) in the space occupied by people.

- More than a total of 500 pounds of allowed hazardous materials. You also cannot carry more than 100 pounds of any one class of hazardous material.

Riders sometimes board a bus with an unlabeled hazardous material. They may not know it is unsafe. Do not allow riders to carry on common hazards such as car batteries or gasoline.

Intercity and urban mass transit buses may have riders who have never riden a bus before. They may be uneasy about their trip. Giving them information will help. Drivers for intercity buses should announce the destination before leaving the terminal. This will reassure riders and give those who have made a mistake a chance to get off. If the stops are different from the usual stops, tell the riders. This will help put them at ease and ensure their cooperation. If you are driving a route that is new or an express service, be sure the tell the riders about it. Always explain an unscheduled delay or stop. Before starting, remind riders to keep arms, heads, and legs inside the bus. If the bus has a restroom, tell them how to use the light and door lock.

No rider may stand in front of the back of the driver's seat. Buses designed to allow standing must have a 2-inch line on the floor or some other means of showing riders where they cannot stand. This is the standee line. All standee riders must stay behind it.

When you stop the bus, you should announce the:

- Location.

- Reason for stopping.

- Next departure time.

- Bus number.

Remind the riders to take carry-ons with them if they get off the bus. You should also tell them where to reclaim their checked luggage. If the aisle is on a lower level than the seats, remind riders of the step down. It is best to tell them before the bus comes to a complete stop.

Charter bus drivers should not allow riders on the bus until departure time. This will help prevent theft or damage to the bus.

Control of passengers while driving: Many charter and inter-city buses have passenger rules for comfort and safety. Mention rules about smoking, drinking, or the use of a radio or tape player at the start of the trip. If you explain the rules at the start, you may avoid trouble later on.

While driving, scan the inside of your bus as well as the road ahead, to the side, and to the rear. You may have to remind riders about rules, or to keep their arms, feet, and heads inside the bus.

Riders can stumble while getting on or off and when the bus starts or stops. To help prevent this caution riders to watch their step when leaving the bus. Wait for them to sit down or brace themselves before starting the bus. Starting and stopping the bus should be as smooth as possible to avoid injury to your riders.

Occasionally, you may have a drunk or disorderly rider. You must ensure this rider's safety as well as that of others. Do not let such riders off where it would be unsafe for them. It may be safer at another stop or a well lighted area where there are other people. Many carriers have guidelines for handling these riders.

Common bus crashes: Crashes often happen at intersections. Use caution, even if a traffic signal or stop sign controls the other traffic. School and mass transit buses sometimes scrape off mirrors or hit passing vehicles when pulling out from a bus stop. Remember the clearance your bus needs, and watch for poles and tree limbs at stops. Know the size of the gap your bus needs to start up and merge with traffic. Wait for the gap to open before leaving the stop. Never assume other drivers will brake to give you room when you signal or start to pull out.

Crashes on curves kill people and destroy buses. They result from too much speed or when rain or snow has made the road

On the Road

slippery. Every banked curve has a safe "design speed." Because of the banking, the forces at the design speed actually push the bus downward into the banked roadway, rather than sideways off the curve. The design speed is often less than the posted speed for the curve. Although the posted speed is safe for cars, it may be too high for buses. With good traction, the bus may roll over. With poor traction, it will simply slide off the curve. Reduce speed for curves! If your bus leans toward the outside on a banked curve, you are driving too fast.

Stop at railroad crossings: Stop your bus between 50 and 15 feet before railroad crossings. Look in both directions for trains. Listen carefully for them also. You should open your forward door if it improves you ability to see or hear an approaching train. Before crossing after a train has passed, make sure there is not another train coming from either direction or on other tracks. If your bus has a manual transmission, do not change gears while crossing the tracks.

You do not have to stop, but must slow down and look:

- At streetcar crossings.

- At railroad tracks used only for industrial switching.

- When a policeman or flagman is directing traffic.

- When a traffic signal shows green.

- At crossings marked "exempt crossing."

1. Turn on 4-way flashers unless state law prohibits.
2. Slow down gradually.
3. Pull as far to the right as safety allows.
4. Make a full, complete stop, no closer than 15 feet or farther than 50 feet from the track.

FIGURE 5-4: RAILROAD CROSSING

Stop at drawbridges: Stop at drawbridges that do not have a signal light or traffic control attendant. Stop at least 50 feet before the draw of the bridge. Make sure the draw is completely closed before crossing it.

You do not need to stop, but you must slow down and make sure it is safe when:

- There is a traffic light showing green.

- The bridge has an attendant or traffic officer who controls traffic when the bridge opens.

After-Trip Bus Inspection

Inspect your bus at the end of each shift. If you work for an interstate carrier, you must complete a written inspection report for each bus you have driven. The report must list each bus and state any defect that would affect safety or result in a breakdown. If there are no defects, the report should say so.

FIGURE 5-5: INSPECT YOUR BUS AT THE END OF EACH SHIFT

Riders sometimes damage safety-related parts such as handholds, seats, emergency exits, or windows. If you report this damage at the end of a shift, mechanics can make repairs before the bus goes out again. Mass transit drivers should also make sure the door locks and signals for passenger use work properly.

Avoid fueling your bus with riders on board unless you have to. Never refuel in a closed building with riders on board. Do not talk with riders or engage in any activity which may distract you while driving.

Do not tow or push a disabled bus with riders aboard either vehicle unless it would be unsafe to have them get off. If it is unsafe to discharge passengers, tow or push the vehicle only as far as the nearest safe spot and let the passengers off there. Follow your employer's guidelines for towing or pushing disabled buses.

Safety Measures

Urban mass transit coaches may have a brake and accelerator interlock system. The interlock applies the brakes and holds the throttle in idle position when the rear door is open. The interlock releases when you close the rear door. Do not use this safety feature in place of the parking brake when safety requires using the parking brake.

Use of Brake-Door Interlocks

Passenger safety must be the first consideration for a bus driver. To help insure this, this chapter has presented the proper procedures for inspecting a bus. Inspections should always be done before driving a bus and at the end of a shift. Examples of hazardous materials which may not be carried on a bus and ways of controlling potentially unsafe situations and preventing riders from being injured were mentioned. Finally, specific rules for driving a bus across railroad tracks and drawbridges were given as well as advice for avoiding crashes.

Summary

REVIEW QUESTIONS

1. Bus drivers must have a CDL with a passenger endorsement. True or false? _____

2. Chapter 5 contains information a driver must know to drive a bus safely. True or false? _____

3. To get a bus driver's CDL, you must pass a written knowledge test. True or false? _____

4. When are you considered a bus driver?

    _____

5. You are not considered a bus driver if you only carry family members for non-business purposes. True or false? _____

6. What are some items to check in the interior of a bus during pre-trip inspection?

    _____

    _____

    _____

7. What are some hazardous materials you can transport by bus?

    _____

    _____

    _____

8. What are some hazardous materials you cannot transport by bus?

    _____

    _____

    _____

9. What items must be in good working order before driving the bus?

    _____

    _____

    _____

10. You should always use your seat belt, even on short trips. True or false? _____

11. Do not transport hazardous materials unless you are sure the rules allow it. True or false? _____

12. What are the most common bus crashes?

    _____

    _____

13. Does it matter where you make a passenger get off the bus? Why?

    _____

    _____

14. How far from a railroad crossing should you stop?

    _____

15. When must you stop before crossing a drawbridge?

    _____

    _____

    _____

16. Which of these statements are true?
    a. Inspect your bus at the end of each shift.
    b. If you work for an interstate carrier, you must complete a written inspection report for each bus driven.
    c. You need not complete a report if there are no defects.

    _____

17. When can you push or tow a disabled bus with riders aboard either vehicle?

    _____

    _____

18. What guidelines should you follow on towing or pushing disabled buses?

_____

_____

19. What are the safety rules to follow when refueling your bus?

_____

_____

_____

20. What is the brake-door interlock found on transit buses? How does it work?

_____

_____

_____

DOES YOUR BUS HAVE AIR BRAKES?

CHAPTER

Three Braking Systems
The Parts of an Air Brake System
Dual Air Brake Systems
Inspecting the Air Brake System
Using Air Brakes
Summary
Key Words
Review Questions

FROM NOW ON,

ONLY THE BEST WILL DRIVE

Chapter Objectives

Understand the types of braking systems and their uses

Discuss the parts and equipment used in
air brake systems

Present the types of switches and gauges that are used
to monitor the air brake system

Explain the types of brakes and controls that are used

Detail proper inspection procedures for braking systems

Present correct braking techniques

CHAPTER SIX

DOES YOUR BUS HAVE AIR BRAKES?

This chapter tells you about air brakes. You need this information to operate the air brakes on trucks and buses safely. If you want to drive a tractor-trailer bus with air brakes, you will also need to read Chapter Seven.

Air brakes provide a safe way of stopping large vehicles, but they must be well maintained and used properly. Because of this, it is very important that you study this chapter. A test on these facts will be given to drivers intending to drive a bus equipped with air brakes. Air brake test questions are found in Chapter Ten.

Air brakes use compressed air to make the brakes work. The system stores air under pressure and then sends it when needed to the air chambers located at each wheel. You can apply all the braking force you need to each of the wheels of a heavy vehicle, even rigs pulling two or three trailers.

Three Braking Systems

Air brake systems are three braking systems combined: the service brake system, the parking brake system, and the emergency brake system.

- The *service brake* system applies the brakes when you press the brake pedal and releases them when you let up on the brake pedal during normal driving.

- The *parking brake* system applies and releases the parking brakes when you use the parking brake control.

- The *emergency brake* system uses parts of the service and parking brake systems to stop the vehicle if there is a brake system failure.

The Parts of an Air Brake System

The *air compressor* pumps air into the air storage tanks (reservoirs). The air compressor is connected to the engine through gears or a V-belt. The compressor may be cooled by air or by the engine cooling system. It may have its own oil supply or be lubricated by engine oil. If the compressor has its own oil supply, check the oil level before driving.

Air Compressor Governor

The *governor* controls when the air compressor will pump air into the air storage tanks. When the air tank pressure rises to the "cut-out" level (around 125 pounds per square inch, or "*psi*"), the governor stops the compressor from pumping air. When the tank pressure falls to the "cut-in" level (around 100 psi), the governor allows the compressor to start pumping again.

Air Storage Tanks

Air *storage tanks* are used to hold compressed air. The number and size of air tanks varies among vehicles. The tanks will hold enough air to allow the brakes to be used several times even if the compressor stops working.

Air Tank Drains

Compressed air usually has some water and compressor oil in it. This is bad for the air brake system. For example, the water can freeze in cold weather and cause brake failure. The water, oil, etc. tend to collect in the bottom of the air tank. This is why each air tank is equipped with a drain valve in the bottom, so it can be emptied if necessary. There are two types of air tank drains:

- Manual — This is operated by turning the valve a quarter turn, shown in Figure 6-1 below, or by pulling a cable. You must drain the tanks yourself at the end of each day of driving.

- Automatic — The water and oil are automatically forced out from the valve as they collect in it. These valves are equipped for manual draining as well.

The automatic type can also have electric heating devices to prevent freeze-up in cold weather.

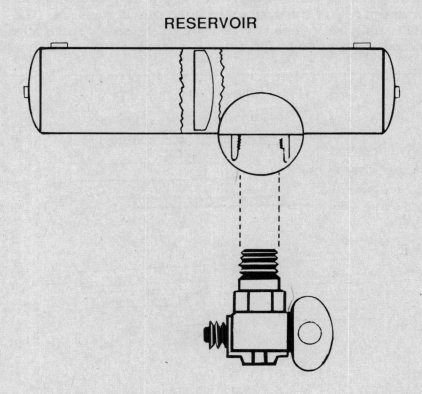

RESERVOIR

FIGURE 6-1: MANUAL DRAIN VALVE

Alcohol Evaporator

Some air brake systems have an alcohol *evaporator* to put alcohol into the air system. This reduces the risk of ice in air brake valves and other parts during cold weather. Ice inside the system can make the brakes stop working.

Check the alcohol container and fill it as needed during cold weather. This may be as often as every day. Daily air tank drainage is still needed to get rid of water and oil unless the system has automatic drain valves.

Safety Valve

A safety relief valve is placed in the first tank to which air is pumped by the air compressor. The safety valve protects the tank and the rest of the system from too much pressure. The valve is usually set to open at 150 psi. If the safety valve releases air, something is wrong. Have the problem fixed by a mechanic.

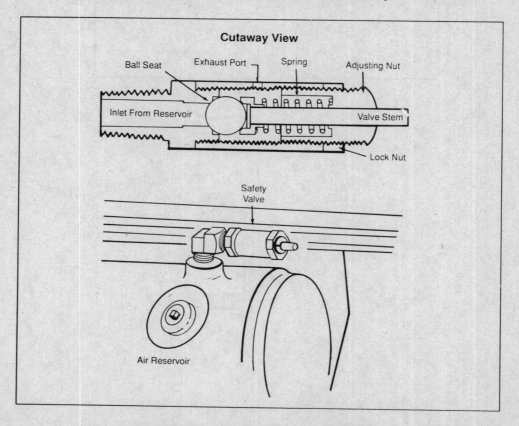

FIGURE 6-2: SAFETY VALVE

The Brake Pedal

You put on the brakes by pushing down the brake pedal. It is also called the foot valve, or treadle valve. Pushing the pedal down harder applies more air pressure. Letting up on the brake pedal reduces the air pressure and releases the brakes. Releasing the brakes lets some air go out of the system, so the air pressure in the tanks is reduced. It must be replaced by the air compressor. Pressing and releasing the pedal needlessly can let out air faster than the compressor can replace it. If the pressure gets too low, the brakes will not work.

When you push the brake pedal down, two forces push back against your foot. One force comes from a spring. The second force comes from the air pressure going to the brakes. This lets you feel how much air pressure is being applied to the brakes.

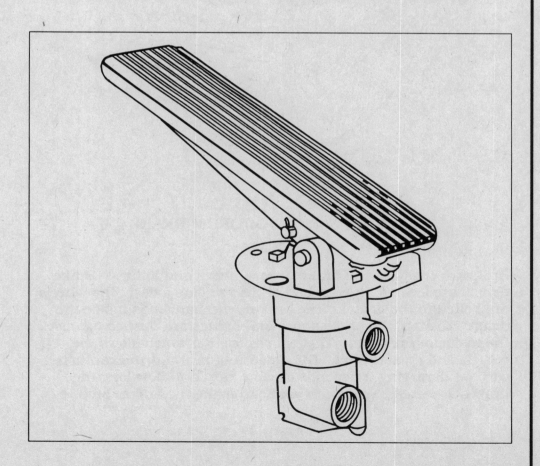

FIGURE 6-3: FOOT VALVE — THE BRAKE PEDAL

Foundation Brakes

Foundation brakes are used at each wheel. The most common type is the S-cam drum brake shown in Figure 6-4. The parts of the brake are described below.

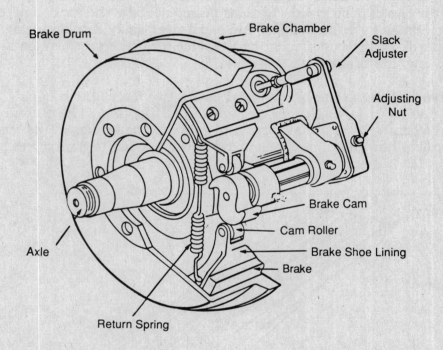

FIGURE 6-4: S-CAM DRUM BRAKE

Brakes are made up of brake drums, shoes and linings. Brake drums are located on each end of the vehicle's axles. The wheels are bolted to the drums. The braking mechanism is inside the drum. To stop, the brake shoes and linings are pushed against the inside of the drum. This causes friction which slows the vehicle and creates heat. The amount of heat a drum can take without damaging it depends on how hard and how long the brakes are used. Too much heat can make the brakes stop working.

S-Cam Brakes

When you push the brake pedal, air is let into each brake chamber (see Figure 6-4). Air pressure pushes the rod out. This moves the slack adjuster which twists the brake cam shaft. This turns the S-cam. It is called an S-cam because it is shaped like the letter "S." The S-cam forces the brake shoes away from one another and presses them against the inside of the brake drum. When the brake pedal is released, the S-cam rotates back, and a spring pulls the brake shoes away from the drum.This lets the wheels roll freely again.

Wedge Brakes

In this type of brake, the brake chamber push rod pushes a wedge directly between the ends of two brake shoes. This shoves them apart and against the inside of the brake drum. Wedge brakes may have one or two brake chambers. Each brake chamber push rod pushes wedges in at the ends of the brake shoes. Wedge brakes may be self-adjusting or may need manual adjustment.

Disc Brakes

In air operated disc brakes, air pressure acts on a brake chamber and slack adjuster in the same way it does with S-cam brakes. But instead of the S-cam, a "power screw" is used. The pressure of the brake chamber on the slack adjuster turns the power screw. The power screw clamps the disc, or rotor, between the brake lining pads of a caliper. This process works like a large C-clamp.

S-cam brakes are used in more vehicles than wedge brakes and disc brakes.

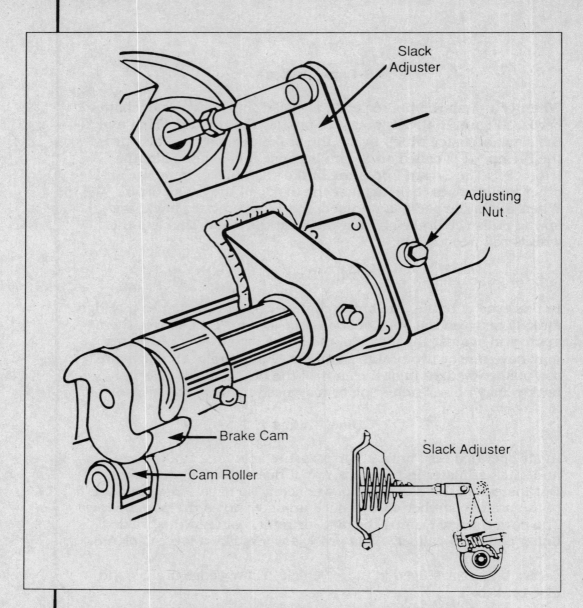

FIGURE 6-5: MANUAL SLACK ADJUSTER

One-Way Check Valve

A one-way check valve allows air to flow in one direction only. All air tanks on vehicles with air brakes must have a check valve. The check valve keeps air from going out of the tank if the air compressor develops a leak.

Supply Pressure Gauges

All vehicles with air brakes have a pressure gauge connected to the air tank. If the vehicle has a dual air brake system, there will be a gauge for each half of the system. On some vehicles, there will be one gauge with two needles. Dual systems will be discussed later. These gauges tell you how much pressure is in the air tanks.

The **air pressure gauge** indicates the usable air supply you have for items such as air brakes, windshield wipers, etc. Normal operating range of your air pressure gauge is 90 to 120 pounds per square inch. (psi). Your gauge must indicate at least 90 pounds before moving the vehicle. As you drive and use the air systems, your gauge will normally fluctuate up and down between 90 and 120 pounds. At 90 pounds the compressor should start to bring the system back to full capacity (120 pounds). When this level is obtained the compressor should shut off. If the air pressure should drop below 90 pounds without apparent cause, such as overusing the brakes, the system should be checked.

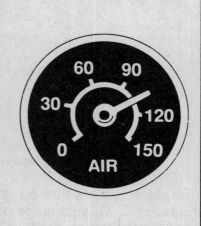

FIGURE 6-6: AIR PRESSURE GAUGE

The **air application gauge**, which is not available on all tractors, indicates the amount of air being used at any one time when brakes are applied.

FIGURE 6-7: APPLICATION PRESSURE GAUGE

Application Pressure Gauge

This gauge shows how much air pressure you are applying to the brakes. This gauge is not found on all vehicles. When going down steep grades, putting on more application pressure to hold the same speed means the brakes are fading. You should slow down and use a lower gear. The need for more pressure can also be caused by brakes which need adjusting, air leaks, or mechanical problems.

Low Air Pressure Warning

A low air pressure warning signal is required on vehicles with air brakes. A warning signal you can see must come on before the air pressure in the tanks falls below 60 psi. This is one-half the compressor governor cut-out pressure on older vehicles. The warning is usually a red light. A buzzer may also sound.

Another type of warning is the "wigwag." This device drops a mechanical arm into your view when the pressure in the system drops below 60 psi. An automatic wigwag will rise out of your view when the pressure in the system goes above 60 psi. The manual reset type must be placed in the "out of view" position by hand. It will not stay in place until the pressure in the system is above 60 psi.

On large buses, it is common for the low pressure warning devices to signal at 80-85 psi instead of 60 psi.

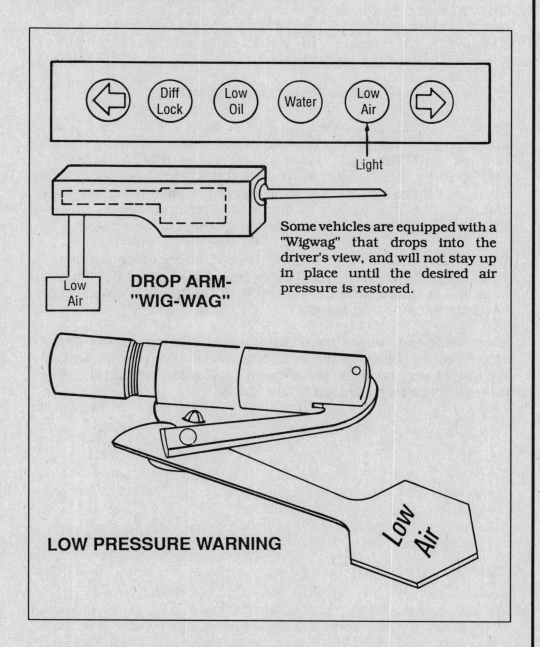

Some vehicles are equipped with a "Wigwag" that drops into the driver's view, and will not stay up in place until the desired air pressure is restored.

FIGURE 6-8: LOW PRESSURE WARNING DEVICE

Stop Light Switch

Drivers behind you must be warned when you put on your brakes. An air brake system does this with an electric switch that is operated by air pressure. The switch turns on the brake lights when you put on the air brakes.

Front Brake Limiting Valve

Some older vehicles (made before 1975) have a front brake limiting valve with a control in the cab. The control is usually marked "normal" and "slippery." When you put the control in the "slippery" position, the limiting valve cuts the "normal" air pressure to the front brakes by half. Limiting valves are used to reduce the chance of the front wheels skidding on slippery surfaces. However, they also reduce the stopping power of the vehicle.

We now know front wheel braking is good under all conditions. Tests have shown front wheel skids from braking are not likely even on ice. Make sure the control is in the "normal" position to have normal stopping power.

Many vehicles have automatic front wheel limiting valves. These valves reduce the air to the front brakes except when the brakes are put on very hard (60 psi or more application pressure). These valves cannot be controlled by the driver.

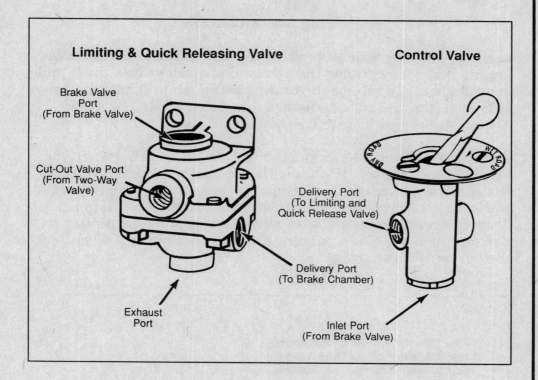

Limiting & Quick Releasing Valve

Brake Valve Port (From Brake Valve)

Cut-Out Valve Port (From Two-Way Valve)

Exhaust Port

Delivery Port (To Brake Chamber)

Control Valve

Delivery Port (To Limiting and Quick Release Valve)

Inlet Port (From Brake Valve)

FIGURE 6-9: FRONT BRAKE LIMITING VALVE

Spring Brakes

All trucks, truck tractors, and buses must be equipped with emergency brakes and parking brakes. They must keep the vehicle braked by mechanical force. This is necessary because air pressure can eventually leak away. Spring brakes are generally used to meet this need. When driving, powerful springs are held back by air pressure. If the air pressure is removed, the springs put on the brakes.

A parking brake control in the cab allows the driver to let the air out of the spring brakes. This lets the springs put the brakes on. A leak in the air brake system which causes all the air to be lost will also cause the springs to put on the brakes.

The braking power of spring brakes depends on proper adjustment of the brakes. If the brakes are not adjusted right, neither the regular brakes nor the emergency and parking brakes will work as they should.

Parking Brake Controls

In newer vehicles with air brakes, you put on the parking brakes (spring brakes) by pulling the diamond shaped, yellow, push-pull control knob. To release the brakes, you push in the knob. In older vehicles, the parking brakes may be controlled by a lever. Always use the parking brakes when you park.

A word of caution: Never push down the brake pedal when the spring brakes are on. If you do, the brakes could be damaged by the combined forces of the springs and the air pressure. Many, but not all, brake systems are designed so this cannot happen. This safeguard may not always work, so it is much better to develop the habit of not pushing down the brake pedal when the spring brakes are on.

To the right of the driver on the control panel are two push-pull type valves. The top knob is termed the **System Parking Brake Valve**, or parking brake, and is yellow. When pulled, the brakes will actuate for the entire unit. This is the brake which you would use for parking at *all* times. When pushed in, all brakes release and the vehicle is ready for movement. The knob on the bottom, colored red, is called the **Trailer Air Supply Valve**. When this knob is pulled, only the trailer brakes are applied, When hooking to a new trailer, this valve must be depressed to release your trailer brakes before driving. When you bob-tail, this button should be pulled to keep the air from leaking out of the lines on the back of your tractor.

FIGURE 6-10: PARKING BRAKE AND TRAILER AIR SUPPLY

Modulating control valves: In some vehicles, a control handle on the dashboard may be used to apply the spring brakes gradually. This is called a *modulating valve*. It is spring loaded so you can feel the braking action. The farther you move the control lever, the harder the spring brakes come on. They work in this way so you can still control the spring brakes even if the service brakes fail. When parking a vehicle with a modulating control valve, move the lever as far as it will go and hold it in place with the lock.

Dual parking control valves: When the main air pressure is lost, the spring brakes come on. Some vehicles, such as buses, have a separate air tank which can be used to release the spring brakes. This is so you can move the vehicle in an emergency. One of the valves is a push-pull type and is used to put on the spring brakes for parking.

The other valve is spring loaded when the valve is pulled out. When you push the control in, air from the separate air tank releases the spring brakes so the vehicle can move. When you release the control, the spring brakes come on again. There is only enough air in the separate tank to do this a few times, so plan carefully if you must do this. If you do not, you may be stopped in a dangerous location when the separate air supply runs out.

Other Brake System Parts

There are many parts of air brake systems that we have not covered. Knowledge about these parts is not needed for safe operation of a large vehicle.

Most newer heavy-duty vehicles use dual air brake systems for safety. A dual air brake system has two separate air brake systems which use a single set of brake controls. Each system has its own air tanks, hoses, lines, etc. One system usually operates the regular brakes on the rear axle or axles. The other system operates the regular brakes on the front axle (and sometimes one rear axle). Both systems supply air to the trailer (if there is one). The first system is called the "*primary*" system. The other is called the "*secondary*" system.

Dual Air Brake Systems

Before driving a vehicle with a dual air brake system, allow time for the air compressor to build up at least 100 psi pressure in both the primary and secondary systems. Watch the primary and secondary air pressure gauges (or needles, if the system has two needles on one gauge). Pay attention to the low air pressure warning light and buzzer. The warning light and buzzer should shut off when air pressure in both systems rises to the value set by the manufacturer. This value must be greater than 60 psi.

The warning light and buzzer should come on before the air pressure drops below 60 psi in either system. If this happens while you are driving, stop right away and safely park the vehicle. If one air system is very low on pressure, either the front or rear brakes will not operate fully. This means it will take you longer to stop. Bring the vehicle to a safe stop and have the air brake system fixed.

Tractor and straight truck spring brakes will come on fully when the air pressure drops to a range of 20 to 45 psi (typically 20 to 30 psi). Do not wait for the brakes to come on automatically. When the warning light and buzzer first come on, bring the vehicle to a safe stop while you can still control the brakes.

Inspecting the Air Brake System

You should use the basic seven-step inspection procedure described in Chapter Four to inspect your vehicle. There are more things to check on a vehicle with air brakes than on one without them. These items are discussed below in the order that they should be inspected using the seven-step method.

Engine Compartment Checks

During Step Two, check the air compressor drive belt if the compressor is belt driven. Check the condition and tightness of the belt. It should be in good condition. If it is not, have it replaced.

Walkaround Inspection

During Step Five, check the manual slack adjusters on S-Cam brakes. Park on level ground and chock the wheels to prevent the vehicle from moving. Turn off the parking brakes so you will be able to move the slack adjusters. Wear gloves to protect your hands and pull hard on each slack adjuster you can reach. If a slack adjuster moves more than one inch at the point where the push rod attaches to it, adjust it or have it adjusted.

Vehicles with too much brake slack can be very hard to stop. The problem most often found in roadside inspections is brakes that are not adjusted properly. Be safe; check the slack adjusters.

Check the brake drums (or discs), linings, and hoses. Brake drums must not have any cracks longer than one-half the width of the friction area. Linings (friction material) must not be loose or soaked with oil or grease. They must not be thinner than 1/32 inch at the thinnest point. This is the minimum thickness permitted. For increased safety, the lining should be thicker. Mechanical parts must be in place, not broken or missing. Check the air hoses connected to the brake chambers to make sure they are not cut or worn due to rubbing.

Final Air Brake Check

Do these checks instead of the hydraulic brake check shown in Chapter Four, "Step Seven: Check Brake System."

Test the low pressure warning signal. Shut off the engine when you have enough air pressure to turn off the low pressure warning signal. Turn on the electrical power and step on and off the brake pedal to reduce air tank pressure. The low air pressure warning signal must come on before the pressure drops to less than 60 psi in the air tank. In dual air systems, this will be the tank with the lowest air pressure.

If the warning signal does not work, you can lose air pressure and not know about it. This can cause sudden emergency braking in a single circuit air system. In dual systems, the stopping distance will be increased, and only limited braking can be done before the spring brakes come on.

Check to be sure the spring brakes come on automatically. Chock the wheels, release the parking brakes when you have enough air pressure to do it, and shut off the engine. Step on and off the brake pedal to reduce the air tank pressure. The "parking brake" knob should pop out when the air pressure falls to the manufacturer's specification (usually in a range between 20 and 40 psi). This causes the spring brakes to come on.

Check the rate of air pressure buildup. With the engine at operating rpm, the pressure should build from 85 psi to 100 psi within 45 seconds in dual air systems. If the vehicle has larger than minimum size air tanks, the buildup time can be longer and still be safe. Check the manufacturer's specifications. In single air systems (pre-1975), typical requirements are pressure buildup from 50 to 90 psi within 3 minutes when the engine is at an idle speed of 600-900 *rpm*.

If air pressure does not build up fast enough, the pressure may drop too low during driving. Then you will have to make an emergency stop. Do not drive the vehicle until the problem is fixed.

Test the air leakage rate. With a fully charged air system (typically 125 psi), turn off the engine, release the service brake, and time the air pressure drop. The loss rate should be less than 2 psi in one minute for single vehicles and less than 3 psi in one minute for combination vehicles. Apply 90 psi or more with the brake pedal. If the air pressure falls more than 3 psi in one minute for single vehicles or more than 4 psi for combination vehicles after the initial pressure drop, the air loss rate is too much. Check for air leaks and fix them before driving the vehicle. Otherwise, you could lose your brakes while driving.

Check the air compressor governor cut-in and cut-out pressures. Pumping should start at about 100 psi and stop at about 125 psi. (Check manufacturer's specifications.) Run the engine at a fast idle. The air governor should cut out the air compressor near the manufacturer's specified cut-out pressure. The air pressure shown by the gauge(s) will stop rising. With the engine idling, step on and off the brake to reduce the air tank pressure. The compressor should cut back in near the manufacturer's specified cut-in pressure. The pressure should begin to rise.

If the air governor does not work as described above, it may need repairs. A governor that does not work right may not keep enough air pressure for safe driving.

Test the parking brake. Stop the vehicle, put the parking brake on, and gently pull against it in a low gear to test if the parking brake will hold.

Test the service brakes. Wait for normal air pressure, release the parking brake, move the vehicle forward slowly (about 5 *mph*), and put on the brakes firmly using the brake pedal. Note if the vehicle "pulls" to one side, has an unusual feel, or has a delayed stopping action. This test may show you problems which you would not know about until you needed the brakes on the road.

Normal Stops

Push down the brake pedal. Push as hard as you need to on the pedal so the vehicle comes to a smooth, safe stop. If you have a manual transmission, do not push the clutch in until the engine rpm is down almost to idle. When stopped, select a starting gear.

Emergency Stops

You should brake so you can steer and so your vehicle stays in a straight line. Use one of the following two methods.

Controlled braking. This method is also called "squeeze" braking. Put on the brakes as hard as you can without locking the wheels. Do not turn the steering wheel while doing this. If you need to make large steering adjustments or if you feel the wheels sliding, release the brakes. Brake again as soon as the tires get traction.

Stab braking. Press down on the brake pedal as hard as you can. Release the brakes when the wheels lock up. As soon as the wheels start rolling, again put on the brakes hard. It can take up to one second for the wheels to start rolling after you release the brakes. Make sure you stay off the brakes long enough to get the wheels rolling again. Otherwise the vehicle may not stay in a straight line.

Stopping Distance

In Chapter Four, you read about stopping distance under "Speed and Stopping Distance." With air brakes there is an added delay in coming to a stop: the time it takes for the brakes to work after the brake pedal is pushed. With hydraulic brakes (used on cars

Using Air Brakes

and smaller trucks), the brakes work at once. However, with air brakes, it takes a little time (up to half a second) for the air to flow through the lines to the brakes. Thus, the total stopping distance for vehicles with air brake systems is made up of four different factors.

> Perception Distance
> Reaction Distance
> Brake Lag Distance
> + Effective Braking Distance
> _____
> TOTAL STOPPING DISTANCE

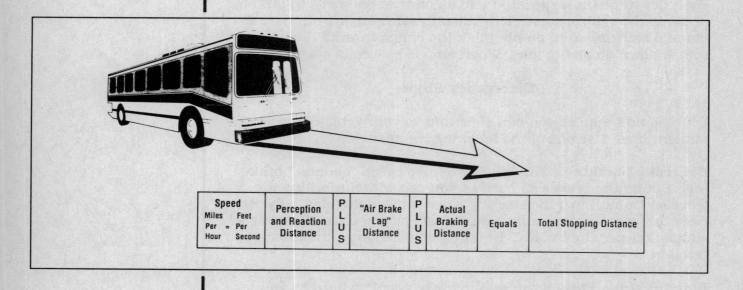

Speed Miles = Feet Per = Per Hour = Second	Perception and Reaction Distance	P L U S	"Air Brake Lag" Distance	P L U S	Actual Braking Distance	Equals	Total Stopping Distance

FIGURE 6-11: TOTAL STOPPING DISTANCE

The air brake lag distance at 55 mph on dry pavement adds about 32 feet to the total stopping distance. So the average driver with good traction and brakes will need over 300 feet to stop when going 55mph. This is longer than a football field.

Braking on Downgrades

When you use the brakes, they get hot. Brakes can take a lot of heat, but they will stop working if there is too much heat. This is caused by trying to slow down from too high a speed too many times or too quickly. Brakes will fade (have less stopping power) when they get too hot. They can fade so badly they will not slow you down.

The right way to go down long grades is to use a low gear and drive slowly enough that a fairly light, steady use of the brakes will keep you from speeding up. If you go slowly enough, the brakes will be able to get rid of the heat so they will work as they should.

Some people believe that using the brakes hard going downhill and letting up on them from time to time will allow them to cool. Tests have shown this is not true. Brakes cool very slowly, so the cooling periods between the times of hard braking are not enough to prevent overheating. Also, the vehicle picks up speed when the brakes are released. This means more hard braking to slow it back down. Braking in this way, on-and-off, builds up more heat than the light, steady method does. Because of this, drive slowly, use the right gear, and maintain light, steady pressure on the brakes.

It is important to remember that brakes should always be adjusted properly. This is especially so when going down steep grades. In addition to proper slack adjustment, the air brake system should be balanced to give the same braking at each of the wheels. If this is not done, some brakes will do more work than others. They will heat up and lose some of their stopping power. Brake balance can be tested and fixed by good air brake mechanics.

Brake Fade

Brake fade is caused by heat in the brakes. As brake drums heat and expand, the brake shoes have to travel farther. If the slack adjusters are not set right (too much slack), the brakes will not work as well as they should. Too much heat also causes the friction material used in brakes not to work well.

Too much heat can mean you will have to push the brake pedal harder to get the same stopping force. If this happens, it means the brakes are being overloaded. Notice how hard you must step on the brake pedal to control or slow your speed. If your brakes begin to fade, you should slow down and shift to a lower gear. Going slower gives the brakes time to get rid of heat.

Low Air Pressure Warning

If the low air pressure warning comes on, stop and safely park your vehicle as soon as possible. There may be an air leak in the system. Controlled braking is possible only while enough air is in the air tanks. The spring brakes will come on when the air pressure drops into the range of 20 to 45 psi. A heavily loaded vehicle will take a long distance to stop because the spring brakes do not work on all axles. Lightly loaded vehicles or vehicles on slippery roads may skid out of control when the spring brakes come on. It is much safer to stop while there is enough air in the tanks to use the foot brake.

Parking Brakes

You should always use the parking brakes when you park except for the situations discussed in the next paragraph. To put on the parking brakes, pull out the parking brake control knob. Push it in to release them. The control is a yellow diamond-shaped knob labeled "parking brakes" on newer vehicles. On older vehicles, it may be a knob of a different shape and color. Often, it is a round blue knob. It can even be a lever that swings from side to side or up and down.

Do not use the parking brakes if the brakes are very hot (from just having come down a steep grade) or if the brakes are very wet and the temperature is below freezing. If they are used while they are very hot, they can be damaged by the heat. If they are used in freezing temperatures when the brakes are very wet, they can freeze so the vehicle cannot move. Use wheel chocks to hold the vehicle. Let hot brakes cool before using the parking brakes. If the brakes are wet, use the brakes lightly while driving in a low gear. This will heat and dry them.

Drain Air Tanks

If your vehicle does not have automatic air tank drains, drain your air tanks at the end of each working day to remove moisture and oil. If you do not, the brakes could fail.

Summary

This chapter has explained the parts and operation of an air brake system. Different types of brakes, air tank drains, valves, gauges, switches, and other controls were described. The importance of knowing the correct braking procedures and how to properly inspect the braking system was emphasized.

NEVER LEAVE YOUR BUS UNATTENDED WITHOUT SETTING THE PARKING BRAKES.

YOUR BUS MIGHT ROLL AWAY AND CAUSE INJURY AND DAMAGE.

FIGURE 6-12: NEVER LEAVE YOUR BUS WITHOUT
APPLYING THE PARKING BRAKES.

Key Words

Air Compressor — The part of the braking system that pumps air into the air storage tanks

Emergency Brake System — The braking system that uses parts of the service and parking brake systems to stop the vehicle if the brake system fails

Evaporator — A device that changes a liquid into a gas

Governor — The device that keeps the right amount of air pumping into the air storage tanks by stopping the flow of air when the air pressure rises to the cut-out level and starting it again when the pressure falls to the cut-in level

Manufacturer's Specifications — The limits the maker has built the equipment to work within

Modulating Valve — A device that regulates or adjusts the action of spring brakes

MPH — Miles per hour

Parking Brake System — The braking system used by the vehicle when the driver uses the parking brake control

Primary — First in order

PSI — Pounds per square inch

RPM — Revolutions per minute (engine speed)

Secondary — Second in order

Service Brake System — The braking system on your vehicle that is activated by using the brake pedal

REVIEW QUESTIONS

1. Air brake systems use a combination of three braking systems. What are these three systems? What is the purpose of each?

   _____

   _____

   _____

2. How many parts of these braking systems can you name and locate on your vehicle?

   _____

   _____

   _____

3. Why do you need to know about air brake systems?

   _____

   _____

4. When must air tanks be drained?

   _____

   _____

5. For what is a supply pressure gauge used?

   _____

   _____

6. All vehicles with air brakes must have a low air pressure warning signal. True or false?

   _____

7. What are spring brakes? Foundation brakes?

   _____

   _____

   _____

8. In newer vehicles with air brakes, what control do you use to put on the parking brakes? What does the control look like?

_____

_____

9. On older vehicles, the parking brakes may be controlled by a lever. True or false?

_____

10. Use the parking brakes whenever you park. True or false?

_____

11. What is a dual air brake system?

_____

_____

12. What are slack adjusters?

_____

_____

13. What are the steps in inspecting the air brake system?

_____

_____

_____

14. How can you check slack adjusters?

_____

_____

15. How can you test the low air pressure warning signal?

_____

_____

16. Do air brakes work instantly like hydraulic brakes? Why?

   _____

   _____

17. Why is it important to drive slowly on downgrades?

   _____

   _____

18. What causes "brake fade"?

   _____

   _____

19. What should you do if the low air pressure warning signal comes on?

   _____

   _____

20. When should you use the parking brakes? When should you not use them?

   _____

   _____

21. How often should you drain air tanks?

   _____

DRIVING A TRACTOR-TRAILER BUS

CHAPTER

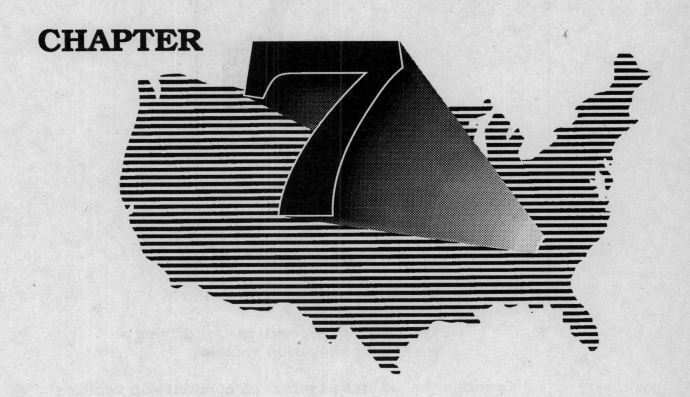

FROM NOW ON,

ONLY THE BEST WILL DRIVE

Chapter Objectives

Define a combination vehicle

Explain safety precautions for driving a
combination vehicle

Describe the air brake system on combination vehicles

Explain correct coupling and uncoupling procedures

Specify additional items which are to be checked during
a walkaround inspection

Describe how to check the brake system of a
combination vehicle

CHAPTER SEVEN

DRIVING A TRACTOR-TRAILER BUS

If you intend to drive a tractor-trailer bus, you will need to pass the test on combination vehicles. Under CDL rules, your tractor-trailer bus is a combination vehicle. This chapter provides information needed to pass the test for these vehicles, but the facts give you only the minimum knowledge needed for driving a combination vehicle.

A separate knowledge test for combination vehicles is found in Chapter Eleven. Some states add the combination vehicle test questions to the General Knowledge Test found in Chapter Eight. In either case, you need to know the basic information for driving a tractor-trailer bus safely.

What is a Combination Vehicle?

A *combination vehicle* is a straight truck or tractor with one or more trailers or semitrailers. The three-axle tractor-trailer bus is one example (Figure 7-1). The tractor-trailer with five axles and 18 wheels shown in Figure 7-2 and a straight truck (Figure 7-3) are other examples. Additional types of combination vehicles are shown in Figure 7-4.

As a tractor-trailer bus driver you must hold a Class A commercial driver's license (CDL) for combination vehicles. Under CDL rules, a combination vehicle is any combination of vehicles weighing over 26,001 pounds. The weight of the trailer being towed must be over 10,000 pounds. A tractor-trailer bus fits this definition. As a driver, you must think of yourself as both a:

- Bus driver

  and

- Tractor-trailer driver

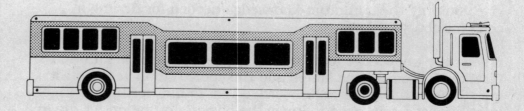

FIGURE 7-1: THREE-AXLE TRACTOR-TRAILER BUSES

FIGURE 7-2: FIVE-AXLE TRACTOR-SEMITRAILERS

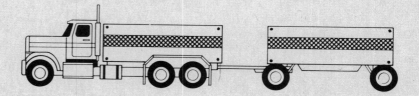

NOTE: THE WEIGHT OF THE TRAILER BEING TOWED MUST BE OVER 10,000 POUNDS (GVWR).

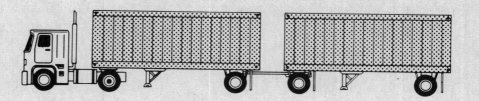

FIGURE 7-3: TRACTOR WITH DOUBLE TRAILERS

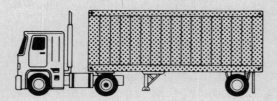

THREE AXLE RIG

FOUR AXLE RIG

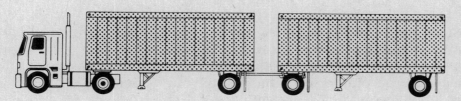

DOUBLE TRAILERS
(FIVE AXLES)

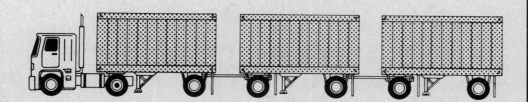

TRIPLE TRAILERS
(SEVEN AXLES)

FIGURE 7-4: TYPES OF COMBINATION VEHICLES

Driving Combination Vehicles Safely

It is important to know the safety measures a driver of a tractor-trailer or combination vehicle must take. Combination vehicles are usually heavier and longer. This requires more driving skill than single trucks or buses. This means that drivers of tractor-trailer buses need more knowledge and skill than drivers of single vehicles. In this section, we discuss important safety factors that apply mainly to combination vehicles.

Rollovers

Rollovers happen when you turn too fast. Drive slowly around corners. Slow down for on-ramps and off-ramps. Avoid quick lane changes, especially when fully loaded. Fully loaded rigs are 10 times more likely to roll over in a crash than empty rigs.

To help yourself prevent a rollover, you need to be aware of your passenger load. If one side of the bus is so heavily loaded it makes the trailer lean, a rollover is more likely to occur.

Steer Gently

Steer gently and smoothly when you are pulling a trailer. If you make a sudden movement with your steering wheel, you can tip over a trailer. Follow at a safe distance behind other vehicles (at least one second for each ten feet of your vehicle length, plus another second if you are going over 40 mph). Look far enough down the road to avoid being surprised and having to make a sudden lane change. At night, drive slowly enough to see obstacles with your headlights before it is too late to change lanes or stop gently. Slow to a safe speed before going into a turn.

Brake Early

Control your speed whether fully loaded or empty. Large combination vehicles that are empty take more time and distance to stop than fully loaded ones. When lightly loaded, the stiff suspension springs and strong brakes give poor traction and make it very easy to lock up the wheels. If this happens, your trailer can swing out and strike other vehicles. Your tractor can also jackknife very quickly (Figure 7-5). You also must be very careful about driving *"bobtail" tractors* (tractors without semi-trailers). Tests have shown that bobtails can be very hard to stop smoothly. It takes them longer to stop than a tractor-semitrailer loaded to maximum gross weight.

In any combination rig, allow plenty of following distance and look far enough ahead that you can brake early. You do not want to be caught by surprise and have to make a "panic" stop.

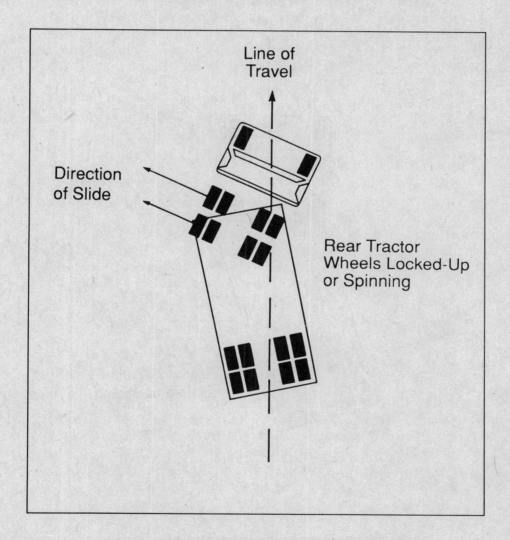

FIGURE 7-5: TRACTOR JACKKNIFE

Prevent Trailer Skids

When the wheels of a trailer lock up, the trailer will tend to swing around. This is more likely to happen when the trailer is empty or lightly loaded. This type of jackknife is often called a "trailer jackknife." This is shown in Figure 7-6.

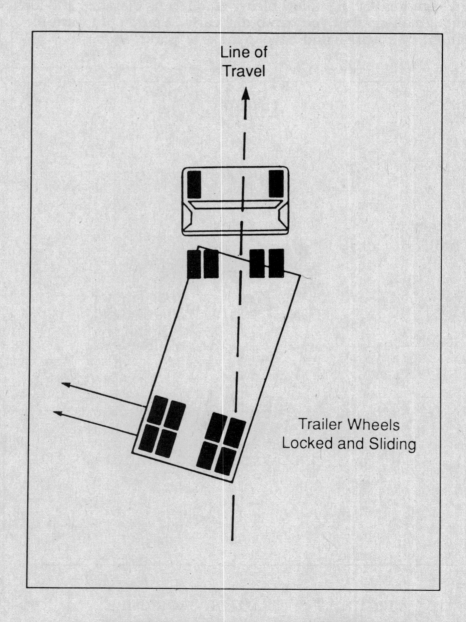

FIGURE 7-6: TRAILER JACKKNIFE

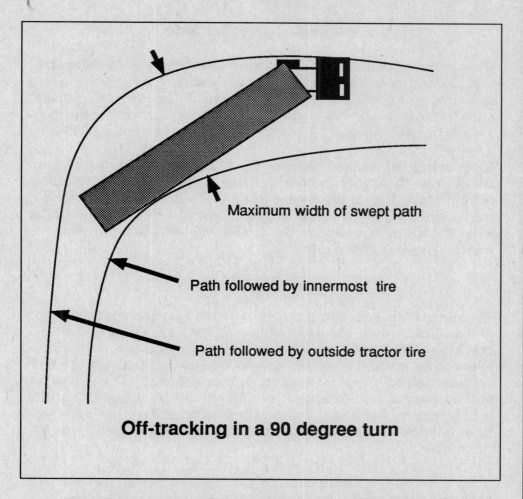

Maximum width of swept path

Path followed by innermost tire

Path followed by outside tractor tire

Off-tracking in a 90 degree turn

FIGURE 7-7: OFF-TRACKING IN A 90 DEGREE TURN

If you must cross into another lane to turn right, swing wide as you complete the turn. If you swing left before the turn, cars may try to pass you on the right.

FIGURE 7-8: SWING WIDE AS YOU COMPLETE THE TURN

Stopping a Trailer Skid

Recognize it as a skid. The earliest and best way to recognize that the trailer has started to skid is by seeing it in your mirrors. Any time you apply the brakes hard, check the mirrors to make sure the trailer is staying where it should be. Once the trailer swings out of your lane, it is very difficult to prevent a jackknife.

Stop using the brake. Release the brakes to get back traction. Do not use the trailer hand brake (if you have one) to "straighten out the rig." This is the wrong thing to do since the brakes on the trailer wheels caused the skid in the first place. Once the trailer wheels grip the road again, the trailer will start to follow the tractor and straighten out.

Turning Wide

When a vehicle goes around a corner, the rear wheels follow a different path than the front wheels follow. This is called **off-tracking**. Figure 7-7 shows how off-tracking causes the path followed by a tractor-semi to be wider than the rig itself. Longer vehicles will off-track more than shorter vehicles. The rear wheels of the powered unit (truck or tractor) will off-track some, but the rear wheels of the trailer will off-track even more. If there is more than one trailer, the rear wheels of the last trailer will off-track the most.

Steer the front end wide enough around a corner so the rear end does not run over the curb, pedestrians, other vehicles, etc. If you cannot complete your turn without entering another traffic lane, turn wide as you complete the turn (Figure 7-8). This is better than swinging wide to the left before starting the turn. If you swing wide before starting the turn, other drivers may pass you on the right causing you to crash into them as you turn.

Combination Vehicle Air Brakes

You should study Chapter Six before reading this section. Chapter Six explains air brakes in single vehicles. The braking system in combination vehicles has additional parts to control trailer brakes. This chapter will discuss these parts.

Trailer Hand Valve

The *trailer hand valve* (also called the trolley valve or Johnson bar) operates the trailer brakes. The trailer hand valve should be used only to test the trailer brakes. Do not use it when driving because it can make the trailer skid. The foot brake sends air to all of the brakes on the vehicle. This includes the brakes on the trailer(s). There is much less danger of causing a skid or jackknife when using just the foot brake.

Never use the hand valve for parking because all the air may leak out. This will unlock the brakes in trailers that do not have spring brakes. Always use the parking brakes when you park. If the trailer does not have spring brakes, use wheel *chocks* to keep the trailer from moving.

Tractor Protection Valve

The *tractor protection valve* keeps air in the tractor or truck braking system if the trailer should break away or develop a bad leak. The tractor protection valve is controlled by the trailer air supply control valve. This valve is found in the cab. The control valve allows you to open and shut the tractor protection valve. The tractor protection valve will close automatically if air pressure is low (in the range of 20 to 45 psi). When the tractor protection valve closes, it stops any air from going out of the tractor's system. It also lets the air out of the trailer emergency line. This causes the trailer emergency brakes to come on. (Emergency brakes are covered later.)

Trailer Air Supply Valve

On newer vehicles, the *trailer air supply control* is a red 8-sided knob which controls the tractor protection valve. You push it in to supply the trailer with air, and pull it out to shut off the air and put on the trailer's emergency brakes. The valve will pop out (thus closing the tractor protection valve) when the air pressure drops into the range of 20 to 45 psi.

The tractor's protection valve controls, or "emergency" valves on older vehicles, may not operate automatically. Some vehicles have a lever instead of a knob. The "normal" position is used for pulling a trailer. The "emergency" position is used to shut the air off and put on the trailer's emergency brakes.

Trailer Air Valves

Every combination vehicle has two air lines — the service line and the emergency line. They run between each section of a combination vehicle (tractor to trailer, trailer to dolly, dolly to second trailer, etc.).

Service Air Line: The service air line (also called the control line or signal line) carries air which is controlled by the foot brake or the trailer hand brake. The pressure in the service line is connected to relay valve(s) on the trailer(s). Depending on how hard you press the foot brake or hand valve, more or less pressure is applied to the trailer brakes. A relay valve connects the trailer air tanks to the trailer air brakes. As pressure builds up in the service line, the relay valve opens and sends air pressure from the trailer air tank to the trailer brake chambers. This action puts on the trailer brakes.

Emergency Air Line: The emergency air line has two purposes. The first is to supply air to the trailer air tanks. The second is to control the emergency brakes on combination vehicles. Loss of air pressure in the emergency line causes the trailer emergency brakes to come on. The pressure loss can be caused by a trailer breaking loose. This tears apart the emergency air hose. Loss of pressure can also be caused by a hose, metal tubing, or other part which breaks, letting the air out. When the emergency line loses pressure, it also causes the tractor protection valve to close (the air supply knob will pop out).

Emergency lines are often coded with the color red (red hose, red couplers, or other parts) to keep them from getting mixed up with the blue service line.

Hose Couplers (Glad Hands)

Glad hands are coupling devices used to connect the service and emergency air lines from the truck or tractor to the trailer. The couplers have a rubber seal which prevents air from escaping.

Clean the couplers and rubber seals before making a connection. To connect the glad hands, press the two seals together with the couplers at a 90-degree angle to each other. Turn the glad hand attached to the hose to join and lock the couplers.

Some vehicles have "dead end" or dummy couplers to which the hoses may be attached when they are not in use. This prevents water and dirt from getting into the couplers and the air lines. Use the dummy couplers when the air lines are not connected to a trailer. If there are no dummy couplers, the glad hands can sometimes be locked together. This will depend on the couplings. It is very important to keep the air supply clean.

When coupling, make sure to couple the proper glad hands together. To help avoid mistakes, colors are sometimes used. Blue is used for the service lines and red for the emergency (supply) lines. Sometimes, metal tags with the words "service" or "emergency" stamped on them are attached to the lines.

If you do cross the air lines, supply air will be sent to the service lines instead of going to charge the trailer air tanks. This will release the trailer spring brakes (parking brakes). If the spring brakes do not release when you push the trailer air supply control, check the air line connections.

Older trailers do not have spring brakes. If the air supply in the trailer air tank has leaked away, there will be no emergency brakes, and the trailer wheels will turn freely. If you cross the air lines, you can drive away, but you will have no trailer brakes. This is very dangerous. Always test the trailer brakes before driving. Test them by using the hand valve or by pulling the air supply (tractor protection valve) control. Pull forward gently against the brakes in a low gear to make sure they work.

Trailer Air Tanks

Each trailer and converter dolly has one or more air tanks. They are filled by the emergency (supply) line from the tractor. They provide the air pressure used to operate the trailer's brakes. Air pressure is sent from the air tanks to the brakes by relay valves. The pressure in the service air line indicates how much pressure the relay valves should send to the trailer brakes. The pressure in the service line is controlled by the brake pedal and the trailer hand brake.

It is important not to let water and oil build up in the air tanks. If it does, the brakes may not work right. Each tank has a drain valve on it, and you should drain them every day. If your tanks have automatic drains, they will keep most moisture out, but you should still open the drains to make sure any moisture that may have built up will be emptied out.

Shut-Off Valves

Shut-off valves (also called cut-out cocks) are used in the service and supply air lines at the back of trailers which tow other trailers. These valves permit closing off the air lines when another trailer is not being towed. Check to see that all shut-off valves except the ones at the back of the last trailer are in the open position. Those at the back of the last trailer must be closed.

Service, Parking, and Emergency Brakes on Trailers

Newer trailers have spring brakes just like trucks and truck tractors. However, converter dollies and trailers built before 1975 are not required to have spring brakes. Those that do not have spring brakes have emergency brakes which work from the air stored in the trailer air tank. The emergency brakes come on whenever air pressure in the emergency line is lost.

These older trailers also have no parking brake. The emergency brakes come on whenever the air supply knob is pulled out or the trailer is disconnected. These brakes will hold only as long as there is air pressure in the trailer air tank. The air will finally leak away, and then there are no brakes. Therefore, it is very important for safety that you use wheel chocks when you park trailers without spring brakes.

A major leak in the emergency line will cause the tractor protection valve to close and the trailer emergency brakes to come on. You may not notice a major leak in the service line until you try to put on the brakes. When you put on the brakes, the air loss from the leak will lower the air tank pressure quickly. If it goes low enough, the trailer emergency brakes will come on.

Coupling and Uncoupling

Knowing the right way to couple and uncouple combination vehicles is basic to their safe operation. Improper coupling and uncoupling can be very dangerous. General coupling and uncoupling steps are listed below. There are differences among rigs, so learn the details of correctly coupling and uncoupling the truck(s) you will operate.

Coupling Tractor-Semitrailers

Step 1.   Inspect the Fifth Wheel.

• Check for damaged or missing parts.

• Check to see that the mounting to the tractor is secure with no cracks in the frame, etc.

• Be sure the fifth wheel plate is completely greased. Failure to keep the fifth wheel plate lubricated can cause steering problems because of friction between the tractor and trailer.

• Check to be sure the fifth wheel is in the proper position for coupling.

Wheel tilted down toward the rear of the tractor jaws open
Safety unlocking handle in the automatic lock position
If you have a sliding fifth wheel, make sure it is locked.

• Make sure the trailer **kingpin** is not bent or broken.

Step 2.   Inspect Area and Chock Wheels.

• Make sure the area around the vehicle is clear.

• Be sure the trailer wheels are chocked or the spring brakes are on.

• Check that cargo (if any) is secured against movement when the tractor is coupled to the trailer.

Step 3.   Position Tractor.

• Put the tractor directly in front of the trailer.   (Never back under the trailer at an angle because you may push the trailer sideways and break the landing gear).

• Check the position of the vehicle by using the outside mirrors and looking down both sides of the trailer.

Step 4.   Back Slowly.

• Back until the fifth wheel just touches the trailer.

• Do not hit the trailer.

Step 5.   Secure the Tractor.

• Put on the parking brake.

• Put the transmission in neutral.

Step 6.   Check the Height of the Trailer.

• The coupling surface of the trailer should be just below the middle of the fifth wheel. Raise or lower the trailer as needed. If the trailer is too low, the tractor may strike and damage the nose of the trailer. If the trailer is too high, it may not couple correctly.

• Check to be sure the kingpin and fifth wheel are aligned.

Step 7.   Connect the Air Lines to the Trailer.

• Check the glad hand seals and connect the tractor emergency air line to the trailer emergency glad hand.

• Check the glad hand seals and connect the tractor service air line to the trailer service glad hand.

• Make sure the air lines are safely supported where they will not be crushed or caught while the tractor is backing under the trailer.

Step 8.   Supply Air to the Trailer.

• From the cab, push in the "air supply" knob or move the tractor protection valve control from the "emergency" position to the "normal" position. This will supply air to the trailer brake system.

• Wait until the air pressure is normal.

• Check the brake system for crossed air lines.

Shut off the engine so you can hear the brakes.
Apply and release the trailer brakes. Listen for the sound of trailer brakes being applied and released. You should hear the brakes move when they are applied and air escape when the brakes are released.
Check the air brake system pressure gauge for signs of major air loss.

- When you are sure the trailer brakes are working, start the engine.

- Make sure the air pressure is up to normal.

Step 9. Lock the Trailer Brakes.

- Pull out the "air supply" knob or move the tractor protection valve control from "normal" to "emergency."

Step 10. Back Under the Trailer.

- Use the lowest reverse gear.

- Back the tractor slowly under the trailer to avoid hitting the kingpin too hard.

- Stop when the kingpin is locked into the fifth wheel.

Step 11. Check to be Sure the Connection is Secure.

- Raise the trailer landing gear slightly off the ground.

- Pull the tractor gently forward while the trailer brakes are still locked to check that the trailer is locked onto the tractor.

Step 12. Secure the Vehicle.

- Put the transmission into neutral.

- Put on the parking brakes.

- Shut off the engine and take the key with you so no one will move the truck while you are under it.

Step 13. Inspect the Coupling.

   • Use a flashlight if necessary.

   • Make sure there is no space between the upper and lower fifth wheel. If there is space, something is wrong. If the kingpin is on top of closed fifth wheel jaws, the trailer can come loose very easily.

   • Go under the trailer and look into the back of the fifth wheel. Make sure the fifth wheel jaws have closed around the shank of the kingpin. See Figure 7-9.

   • Check that the locking lever is in the "lock" position.

   • Be sure the safety catch is in position over the locking lever. On some fifth wheels the catch must be put in place by hand.

   • If the coupling is not right, do not drive the coupled unit. Get it fixed.

Step 14. Connect the Electrical Cord and Check the Air Lines.

   • Plug the electrical cord into the trailer and fasten the safety catch.

   • Check both the air lines and the electrical line for signs of damage.

   • Make sure the air and electrical lines will not hit any moving parts of vehicle.

Step 15. Raise the Front Trailer Supports (Landing Gear).

   • Use the low gear range (if so equipped) to begin raising the landing gear. Once free of weight, switch to the high gear range.

   • Raise the landing gear all the way up. Never drive with landing gear only part way up because it may catch on railroad tracks or other things.

   • After raising the landing gear, secure the crank handle safely.

- When the full weight of the trailer is resting on the tractor:
  Check for enough clearance between the rear of the tractor frame and the landing gear. When the tractor turns sharply it must not hit the landing gear.
  Check to be sure there is enough clearance between the top of the tractor tires and the nose of the trailer.

Step 16.   Remove the Trailer Wheel Chocks.

- Remove and store the wheel chocks in a safe place.

Uncoupling Tractor-Semitrailers

Step 1.   Position the Rig.

- Make sure the surface of the parking area can support the weight of the trailer.

- Have the tractor lined up with the trailer. Pulling out at an angle can damage the landing gear.

Step 2.   Ease the Pressure on the Locking Jaws.

- Shut off the trailer air supply to lock the trailer brakes.

- Ease the pressure on the fifth wheel locking jaws by backing up gently (this will help you release the fifth wheel locking lever).

- Put on the parking brakes while the tractor is pushing against the kingpin. This will hold the rig with pressure off of the locking jaws.

Step 3.   Chock the Trailer Wheels.

- Chock the trailer wheels if the trailer does not have spring brakes or if you are not sure it does. The air can leak out of the trailer air tank and release its emergency brakes. If this happens, the trailer can move if it does not have chocks.

Step 4.   Lower the Landing Gear.

• If the trailer is empty, lower the landing gear until it
makes firm contact with the ground.

• If the trailer is loaded, turn the crank in low gear a few
extra turns after the landing gear makes firm contact
with the ground. This will lift some weight off the
tractor. Do not lift the trailer off the fifth wheel.
Doing this:
    Makes it easier to unlatch fifth wheel.
    Makes it easier to couple the next time.

Step 5.   Disconnect the Air Lines and Electrical Cable.

• Disconnect the air lines from the trailer. Connect the
air line glad hands to the dummy couplers at the back
of the cab, or couple them together.

• Hang the electrical cable with the plug down to
prevent moisture from entering it.

• Make sure lines are supported so they will not be
damaged while driving the tractor.

Step 6.   Unlock the Fifth Wheel.

• Raise the release handle lock.

• Pull the release handle to the "open" position.

• Keep legs and feet clear of the rear tractor wheels to
avoid serious injury in case the vehicle moves.

Step 7.   Pull the Tractor Partially Clear of the Trailer.

• Pull the tractor forward until the fifth wheel comes
out from under the trailer.

• Stop with the tractor frame under the trailer. This
prevents the trailer from falling to the ground if the
landing gear collapses or sinks.

Step 8.   Secure the Tractor.

• Put on the parking brake.

• Place the transmission in neutral.

Step 9.   Inspect the Trailer Supports.

• Make sure the ground is supporting the trailer.

• Make sure the landing gear is not damaged.

Step 10.   Drive the Tractor Clear of the Trailer.

• Release the parking brakes.

• Check the area and drive the tractor clear of the trailer.

Use the seven-step inspection procedure described in Chapter Four to inspect a tractor-trailer bus. There are more things to inspect on a combination vehicle than on a single vehicle. Many are just more of the same things that are to be checked on a single vehicle. For example, tires, wheels, lights, reflectors, etc. However, there are also some new things to check. These are discussed below.

Additional Things to Check During a Walkaround Inspection

Do these checks as well as those listed in the Chapter Four "Step Five: Do Walkaround Inspection."

Coupling System Areas

• Check the fifth wheel (lower).
   It should be securely mounted to the frame.
   No missing or damaged parts.
   Enough grease.
   No visible space between the upper and lower fifth wheel.
   Locking jaws should be around the shank, not the head of kingpin.
   The release arm should be properly seated and the safety latch/lock engaged.

Inspecting a Combination Vehicle

- Fifth wheel (upper).
  Glide plate should be securely mounted to the
    trailer frame.
  Kingpin not damaged.

- Check the air and electric lines to the trailer.
  The electrical cord should be firmly plugged in and
    secured.
  The air lines should be properly secured with
    enough slack for turns.
  All lines should be free from damage.

- Slide fifth wheel.
  Be sure the slide is not damaged or missing parts.
  Properly greased.
  All locking pins should be present and locked in
    place.
  If air powered—no air leaks.
  Check to see that fifth wheel is not so far forward
    that the tractor frame will hit the landing gear or
    the cab hit the trailer during turns.

Landing Gear

- Should be fully raised, no missing parts, and not bent
  or otherwise damaged.

- The crank handle should be in place and secured.

- If power operated, no air or hydraulic leaks.

Double and Triple Trailers

- Shut-off valves (at rear of trailers and in service and
  emergency lines):
    Rear of front trailers: OPEN.
    Rear of last trailer: CLOSED.
    Converter dolly air tank drain valve: CLOSED.

- Be sure air lines are supported and glad hands are
  properly connected.

- If a spare tire is carried on the converter gear (dolly),
  make sure it is secured.

- Be sure the pintle eye of the dolly is in place in the pintle hook of trailer(s).

- Make sure pintle hook is latched.

- Safety chains should be secured to trailer(s).

- Be sure light cords are firmly in their sockets on trailers.

Combination Vehicle Brake Check

Do these checks in addition to those already listed in Chapter Four, "Step Seven: Check Brake System." The hydraulic brake test and "Inspecting Your Air Brake System" test are not needed.

Check That Air Flows to All Trailers (Double and Triple Trailers)

Use the tractor parking brake and/or chock the wheels to hold the vehicle. Wait for the air pressure to reach normal, then push in the red "trailer air supply" knob. This will supply air to the emergency (supply) lines. Use the trailer hand brake to provide air to the service line.

Go to the rear of the rig. Open the emergency line shut-off valve at the rear of the last trailer. You should hear air escaping. This shows the entire system is charged. Close the emergency line valve. Open the service line valve to check that service air pressure goes through all the trailers. This test assumes that the trailer hand brake or the service brake pedal is on. Close the valve. If you do NOT hear air escaping from both lines, check to see if the shut-off valves on the other trailer(s) and dolly(s) are in the OPEN position. You MUST have air all the way to the back for all of the brakes to work.

Test the Tractor Protection Valve

Charge the trailer air brake system. Build up normal air pressure and push the "air supply" knob in. Shut off the engine. Step on and off the brake pedal several times to reduce the air pressure in the tanks. The trailer air supply control (also called the tractor protection valve control) should pop out (or go from the "normal" to the "emergency" position) when the air pressure falls into the pressure range specified by the manufacturer. This is usually within the range of 20 to 45 psi.

If the tractor protection valve does not work right, an air hose or trailer brake leak can drain all of the air from the tractor. This will cause the emergency brakes to come on, causing possible loss of control of the vehicle.

Test the Trailer Emergency Brakes

Charge the trailer air brake system and check to be sure the trailer rolls freely. Then stop and pull out the trailer air supply control (also called tractor protection valve control or trailer emergency valve) or move it to the "emergency" position. Pull gently on the trailer with the tractor to check that the trailer emergency brakes are on.

Test the Trailer Service Brakes

Check for normal air pressure, release the parking brakes, move the vehicle forward slowly, and put on the trailer brakes with the hand control (trolley valve), if there is one. You should feel the brakes come on. This tells you the trailer brakes are connected and working. The trailer brakes should be tested with the hand valve but controlled during normal operation with the foot pedal. This applies air to the service brakes at all of the wheels.

Summary

This chapter defines and shows examples of combination vehicles. Safety procedures to be used when driving a combination vehicle were examined. The air brake system, including how to check it, was described in detail. The correct ways to couple and uncouple combination vehicles were also explained. Finally, additional items to be checked in a walkaround inspection were discussed.

Bobtail Tractor — A tractor without a semitrailer

Chock — A wedge-shaped block placed behind the wheels to keep the vehicle from rolling

Combination Vehicle — A straight truck or tractor with one or more trailers or semitrailers

Emergency Air Line — An air line which supplies air to the trailer air tanks and also controls the emergency brakes on combination vehicles

Glad Hands — Coupling devices that are used to connect the service and emergency air lines from the truck or tractor to the trailer

Kingpin — The part of the trailer that fits into the tractor on a fifth wheel combination vehicle

Off-tracking — The rear wheels following a different path than the front wheels follow when a CMV turns a corner

Service Air Line — An air line which runs between the sections of a combination vehicle that is controlled by the foot brake or the trailer hand brake

Tractor Protection Valve — A device which keeps air in the tractor or truck braking system in the event the trailer breaks away or develops a bad leak

Trailer Air Supply Control — A knob on newer vehicles which is used to control the tractor protection valve

Trailer Hand Valve — A device, also called a trolley valve or Johnson bar, that operates the trailer brakes

Key Words

REVIEW QUESTIONS

1. What is a combination vehicle?

    _____

2. A tractor-trailer bus is a combination vehicle. True or false? _____

3. Is there a written knowledge test for driving combination vehicles?

    _____

4. What two actions can prevent rollovers?

    _____

5. What causes trailer skids?

    _____

6. What is meant by "trailer jackknife"?

    _____

    _____

7. Should you use the trailer hand brake to straighten out a jackknifing trailer? Why or why not?

    _____

    _____

8. What is "off-tracking"?

    _____

    _____

9. In combination vehicles, the braking system has parts to control trailer brakes. What are these parts?

    _____

    _____

10. Why should you not use the trailer hand brake while driving?

_____

11. Describe what the trailer air supply valve does?

_____

_____

12. What is the service line for? What is the emergency air line for?

_____

_____

13. Why should you use chocks when parking a trailer without spring brakes?

_____

14. What are "glad hands"?

_____

_____

15. What are the steps in coupling or hooking up tractor and trailer?

_____

_____

16. What are the uncoupling steps?

_____

_____

17. What might happen if the trailer is too high when you try to couple?

_____

_____

18. What additional checks must be made on a combination vehicle during the walkaround inspections?

_____

_____

_____

19. How should you go about testing the trailer emergency brakes? The trailer service brakes?

_____

_____

_____

_____

PART THREE
KNOWLEDGE TESTS

This part of the book describes and provides the CDL knowledge tests for bus drivers. There are four chapters. You should study all chapters that apply to the tests you will need to take. The chapters tell you exactly who will need to take each test.

Knowledge tests are given so that you can show that you have the knowledge about safe driving needed to operate a commercial vehicle, particularly your bus. The CDL rules do not expect each test to cover every detailed item of required knowledge. This would take hundreds of questions. Instead, the tests sample what you know. This method requires fewer questions.

The CDL national rules also recognize that your state may want to ask special questions about its own laws and rules. The test information given in this book does not cover such special state questions. You will need to read your state's CDL driver manual for this information.

Your state is also free to choose its testing method. The knowledge tests can be paper and pencil tests, oral tests (someone reads the questions), or they may be given by a testing machine. For this reason, we have included both multiple-choice and true-false questions in the chapters which follow. The true-false questions are the ones most likely to be used for oral testing.

The four chapters and the tests they cover are as follows:

Chapter 8: General Knowledge Test
Every driver who wants any kind of CDL must first pass the General Knowledge Test. This test covers the information every commercial driver must know. The test is the same for all drivers. It applies to every type of commercial vehicle. Study Chapter Four to prepare for the General Test.

Chapter 9: Passenger Test
This test measures the knowledge required to drive vehicles equipped with air brakes. Every person who wants to drive a commercial vehicle with air brakes must pass this test.

Chapter 10: Air Brakes Test

This test measures the knowledge required to drive vehicles equipped with air brakes. Every person who wants to drive a commercial vehicle with air brakes must pass this test.

Your state may or may not have a separate test for air brakes. Your state may include air brake questions on the General Test. These questions would be considered the air brake test. In this case, air brake questions will be graded separately. You will need to study Chapter Six to prepare for the air brake test or air brake questions.

Chapter 11: Combination Vehicle Test

This test measures the knowledge required to drive a combination vehicle such as a tractor-trailer bus. The test applies only to CDL Class A vehicles. Like the air brake test, you may or may not have to take a separate test for combination vehicles. Questions about driving a tractor-trailer, bus or a straight truck and trailer rig may be included on the Class A General Knowledge Test.

You must be prepared to answer test questions on driving a combination vehicle if you want to drive a Class A vehicle. If you need to review what you need to know, go back and study Chapter Seven.

GENERAL KNOWLEDGE TEST

CHAPTER

8

FROM NOW ON,

ONLY THE BEST WILL DRIVE

Chapter Objectives

Provide a review of the information every commercial driver should know

Define who must take the General Knowledge Test

Help the CDL applicant become familiar with testing procedures and questions

Test the general knowledge of CDL applicants

CHAPTER EIGHT

GENERAL KNOWLEDGE TEST

This chapter covers the things you need to know about the General Knowledge Test. All bus and truck drivers who apply for any type of CDL must take this test. The General Knowledge Test covers information that applies to the operation of any commercial vehicle.

The practice tests in this chapter will help you learn what you need to study and know for the test. You will also receive actual training in taking the test. The tests provide you with a review of Chapter Four. If you have trouble with a test question, go back to Chapter Four to find the answer.

Purpose of the General Knowledge Test

There is some information all commercial drivers need to know. This knowledge does not depend on the type of vehicle you drive or the cargo you haul. For example, all drivers need to know how to choose a safe speed at which to drive and how to react to an emergency. This type of knowledge — which all drivers need to know — is the what is measured by the General Knowledge Test.

Who Must Take the General Test?

Every driver who wants a CDL must first pass the General Knowledge Test. If you do not make a passing score on the General Knowledge Test, you cannot take the performance tests.

If you fail the General Knowledge Test you must take it again. When you pass the test, you will then go on to take the other tests for your license class and endorsements. The main point is that you must first pass the General Knowledge Test.

Here are some of the rules for the knowledge test you must pass:

1. If you are seeking a CDL for the first time, you must pass the General Knowledge Test.

2. If you want a Class A license, you must pass not only the General Knowledge Test but also the Air Brake Test and the Combination Vehicle Test.

3. If you are a Class B or Class C applicant, you must pass the General Knowledge Test and the Air Brake Test if your vehicle has air brakes.

4. All drivers seeking a bus driver's CDL must pass the Passenger Endorsement Test.

To pass the General Knowledge test for a given license class, you must obtain a passing score on every knowledge test required for that class.

Here are some directions to follow for taking the General Knowledge Test. These are general rules only. Your State may have more specific rules to follow. The first rule is to make sure you FOLLOW THE DIRECTIONS given to you by the examiner. Now for the other rules:

- Do not start the test until you have read ALL of the instructions and understand them.

- Read each question. Decide which answer is best. There is only one best answer for each question.

- Make sure you mark your answer sheet as directed. Do not make any other marks on your answer sheet.

- Do not mark more than one answer for each question. If you mark more than one answer to a question, it will be graded as a wrong answer.

- If you do not know the answer to a question, you should guess. Answer all of the questions on the test.

- Make sure you know how much time you have to take the test. If the test is not timed, take as long to work on the test questions as you need.

General Directions

The instructions which follow are a sample of what you may have to read before taking the General Knowledge Test.

This is a test of your mastery of knowledge required to drive a bus or other commercial vehicle. It consists of 50 multiple-choice questions.

You are not to make any marks on this booklet. All your answers are to be made on the answer sheet that you have been given. Before going any further, please *print* your name, social security number, and the date in the spaces provided on the answer sheet.

Test Instructions

For each of the 50 test questions, begin by reading the question carefully. Decide which *one* (and *only* one) answer is most clearly correct. Then mark that answer on your answer sheet by circling the letter corresponding to it.

Look at the Example box on the answer sheet. It shows how you are to mark your answers. Notice that you must *circle* the answer you wish to mark. You may change an answer if you wish, but be sure that you erase completely the old answer.

You are to mark only *one* answer for each question; if you mark more than one, you will not be given credit for the question.

You should answer each question. You will not be given credit for the unanswered questions. Thus, if you are not sure of the answer, you should take a guess.

You may begin whenever you are ready. Work entirely through the 50 items on this test. If you have any questions, you may ask the examiner.

Practice Tests

Each practice test is a set of multiple-choice questions. Read the Sample Instructions on pages 319 and 320 and use the sample answer sheet forms to mark your answers. The answers to the test questions are found on pages 345 and 346.

Sample Answer Sheets

General Knowledge Test answer sheets are found on pages 321 and 322. These answer sheets may or may not be like the ones you will use for your state's CDL General Knowledge Test, but they will help you practice taking the test. You can mark your answers for the two practice tests which follow on these sheets.

ANSWER SHEET: GENERAL TEST — PRACTICE SET A

Name: _____

SSN: _____

Date: _____

EXAMPLE

          X.   A   B   (C)   D

1.	A	B	C	D		26.	A	B	C	D
3.	A	B	C	D		27.	A	B	C	D
4.	A	B	C	D		28.	A	B	C	D
5.	A	B	C	D		29.	A	B	C	D
6.	A	B	C	D		30.	A	B	C	D
7.	A	B	C	D		31.	A	B	C	D
8.	A	B	C	D		32.	A	B	C	D
9.	A	B	C	D		33.	A	B	C	D
10.	A	B	C	D		34.	A	B	C	D
11.	A	B	C	D		35.	A	B	C	D
12.	A	B	C	D		36.	A	B	C	D
13.	A	B	C	D		37.	A	B	C	D
14.	A	B	C	D		38.	A	B	C	D
15.	A	B	C	D		40.	A	B	C	D
16.	A	B	C	D		41.	A	B	C	D
17.	A	B	C	D		42.	A	B	C	D
18.	A	B	C	D		43.	A	B	C	D
19.	A	B	C	D		44.	A	B	C	D
20.	A	B	C	D		45.	A	B	C	D
21.	A	B	C	D		46.	A	B	C	D
22.	A	B	C	D		47.	A	B	C	D
23.	A	B	C	D		48.	A	B	C	D
24.	A	B	C	D		49.	A	B	C	D
25.	A	B	C	D		50.	A	B	C	D

ANSWER SHEET: GENERAL TEST - PRACTICE SET B

Name: _____

SSN: _____

Date: _____

EXAMPLE

X.   A   B   Ⓒ   D

1.	A	B	C	D		26.	A	B	C	D
3.	A	B	C	D		27.	A	B	C	D
4.	A	B	C	D		28.	A	B	C	D
5.	A	B	C	D		29.	A	B	C	D
6.	A	B	C	D		30.	A	B	C	D
7.	A	B	C	D		31.	A	B	C	D
8.	A	B	C	D		32.	A	B	C	D
9.	A	B	C	D		33.	A	B	C	D
10.	A	B	C	D		34.	A	B	C	D
11.	A	B	C	D		35.	A	B	C	D
12.	A	B	C	D		36.	A	B	C	D
13.	A	B	C	D		37.	A	B	C	D
14.	A	B	C	D		38.	A	B	C	D
15.	A	B	C	D		40.	A	B	C	D
16.	A	B	C	D		41.	A	B	C	D
17.	A	B	C	D		42.	A	B	C	D
18.	A	B	C	D		43.	A	B	C	D
19.	A	B	C	D		44.	A	B	C	D
20.	A	B	C	D		45.	A	B	C	D
21.	A	B	C	D		46.	A	B	C	D
22.	A	B	C	D		47.	A	B	C	D
23.	A	B	C	D		48.	A	B	C	D
24.	A	B	C	D		49.	A	B	C	D
25.	A	B	C	D		50.	A	B	C	D

Do *not* start the test until you have read the instructions on pages 319 and 320. Mark your answers on Answer Sheet: General Test — Practice Set A.

1. Which of these is not part of the check of the engine compartment done for a pre-trip inspection?
   A. Engine oil level
   B. Valve clearance
   C. Condition of belts and hoses
   D. Worn wiring insulation

2. An enroute inspection should include checking:
   A. Cargo doors and/or cargo securement.
   B. Temperature.
   C. Brake temperature.
   D. All of the above

3. You are checking your wheels and rims for a pre-trip inspection. Which of these statements is true?
   A. Rust around wheel nuts may mean that they are loose.
   B. Cracked wheels or rims can be used if they have been welded.
   C. A vehicle can be safely driven with one missing lug nut on a wheel.
   D. Mismatched lock rings can be used on the same vehicle.

4. The proper way to hold a steering wheel is at clock positions _____.
   A. 6 and 12
   B. 5 and 7
   C. 1 and 11
   D. 3 and 9

5. Which of these statements about double-clutching and shifting is true?
   A. It should not be used when the road is slippery.
   B. You can use the sound of the engine to tell you when to shift.
   C. If you miss a gear while upshifting, you must bring the vehicle to a stop.
   D. It involves using two clutch pedals.

6. Which of these statements about engine overheating is true?
   A. If your engine overheats within 20 miles of the end of your trip, you should complete the trip and then check the problem.
   B. You should not shut off an overheated engine until it cools.
   C. You should never remove the radiator cap on a pressurized system while the engine is hot.
   D. Antifreeze is not needed when the weather is warm.

7. Which of these statements about brakes is true?
   A. The heavier a vehicle or the faster it is moving, the more heat the brakes have to absorb to stop it.
   B. Brakes have more stopping power when they get very hot.
   C. Brake drums cool very quickly.
   D. All of the above are true.

8. Retarders:
   A. Work better at very low speeds or very low rpms.
   B. Allow you to disconnect the steering axle brakes.
   C. Can cause the vehicle to skid when the road is slippery.
   D. Cannot be used on interstate highways.

9. You are testing the service brakes on a hydraulic system. Which of these can mean there is a problem with the service brakes?
   A. The vehicle pulls to one side when the brake pedal is pressed
   B. Delayed stopping action
   C. Any unusual brake pedal "feel"
   D. All of the above

10. You are driving a 40-foot vehicle at 45 mph. Driving conditions are ideal (dry pavement, good visibility). What is the least amount of space that you should keep in front of your vehicle to be safe?
    A. 2 seconds
    B. 3 seconds
    C. 4 seconds
    D. 5 seconds

11. If you are being tailgated, you should:
    A. Turn on your taillights.
    B. Increase the space in front of your vehicle.
    C. Speed up.
    D. Signal the tailgater when it is safe to pass you.

12. The most important reason for being alert to hazards is so:
    A. Accident reports will be accurate.
    B. Law enforcement personnel can be called.
    C. You will have time to plan your escape if the hazard becomes an emergency.
    D. You can help impaired drivers.

13. A moving vehicle ahead of you has a red triangle with an orange center on the rear. What does this mean?
    A. It is a law enforcement vehicle.
    B. The vehicle is hauling hazardous materials.
    C. It may be a slow moving vehicle.
    D. It is being driven by a student driver.

14. You are driving a long vehicle that makes wide turns. You want to make a left turn from Elm Street onto Oak Street. There are two left turn lanes on Elm Street, and Oak Street is a four-lane street with two lanes in each direction. You should:
    A. Use the leftmost left turn lane.
    B. Use the rightmost left turn lane.
    C. Start in the leftmost left turn lane and swing into the rightmost left turn lane just before entering the intersection.
    D. Start in the rightmost left turn lane and swing into the leftmost left turn lane just before entering the intersection.

15. Which of these statements about crossing or entering traffic with a heavy vehicle is true?
    A. Heavy vehicles need larger gaps in traffic than cars.
    B. The best way to cross traffic is to pull the vehicle partway across the road and block one lane while waiting for the other lane to clear.
    C. The heavier your load, the smaller the gap needed to cross traffic.
    D. Because heavy vehicles are easy to see, you can count on other drivers to move out of your way or slow down for you.

16. Heavy vehicles must sometimes travel more slowly than other traffic. Which of these is not a good rule to follow when you are driving such a vehicle?
    A. Signal other drivers when it is safe for them to pass you.
    B. Pass other vehicles only if you can do so quickly.
    C. Stay to the right.
    D. Turn on your flashers if it is legal to do so.

17. Which of these statements about overhead clearance is true?
    A. You should assume posted clearance signs are correct.
    B. A vehicle's clearance can change with the load carried.
    C. If the road surface causes your vehicle to tilt toward objects at the edge of the road, you should drive close to the shoulder.
    D. If you are not sure your vehicle will clear something above, driving fast will help because air pushes the vehicle down.

18. The distance that you should look ahead of your vehicle while driving amounts to about _____ at highway speed.
    A. One block
    B. 500 feet
    C. 800 feet
    D. 1/4 mile

19. You should use your mirrors to check:
    A. The condition of your tires and cargo.
    B. Where the rear of your vehicle is while you make turns.
    C. Traffic gaps before you merge.
    D. All of the above.

20. Which of these statements about using turn signals is true?
    A. When turning, you should cancel the signal just before you make the turn.
    B. You do not need to use your turn signal when changing lanes on a four-lane highway.
    C. When turning, you should signal early.
    D. You should use your turn signals to mark your vehicle when it is pulled off on the side of the road.

21. High beams should:
    A. Never be used while the vehicle is on a public road.
    B. Be used whenever it is wise and legal to do so.
    C. Be turned on when an oncoming driver does not dim his/her lights.
    D. Be dimmed when you are within 100 feet of another vehicle.

22. You must park on the side of a level, straight two-lane road. Where should you place the three reflective triangles?
    A. One within 10 feet of the rear of the vehicle, one about 100 feet to the rear, and one about 200 feet to the rear.
    B. One within 10 feet of the rear of the vehicle, one about 100 feet to the rear, and one about 100 feet from the front of the vehicle.
    C. One about 50 feet from the rear of the vehicle, one about 100 feet to the rear, and one about 100 feet from the front of the vehicle.
    D. One within 10 feet of the front of the vehicle, one about 100 feet from the front, and one about 100 feet to the rear.

23. Which of these statements about marking a stopped vehicle is true?
    A. If a hill or curve keeps oncoming drivers from seeing the vehicle within 500 feet, the rear reflective triangle should be moved back down the road to give adequate warning.
    B. You do not need to put out reflective triangles unless the vehicle will be stopped for 30 minutes or more.
    C. The vehicle's taillights should be kept on to warn other drivers.
    D. All of the above are true.

24. Which of these is a good rule to follow when steering to avoid a crash?
    A. Apply the brakes while turning.
    B. Steer with one hand so you can turn the wheel more quickly.
    C. Do not turn any more than needed to clear what is in your way.
    D. Avoid countersteering.

25. You are driving in the right lane of a four-lane, undivided road. You come over a hill and find a car stopped ahead in your lane. You do not have room to stop, and the hill blocks your view to the rear. Which of these is most likely the best action to take?
    A. Steer into the left lane.
    B. Steer into the oncoming lanes.
    C. Steer to the right.
    D. Use hard braking and brace for collision.

26. Controlled braking:
    A. Can be used while you are turning sharply.
    B. Involves locking the wheels for short periods of time.
    C. Is used to keep a vehicle from skidding.
    D. All of the above

27. Some traffic emergencies may require you to leave the road. Which of these is a good thing to remember?
    A. If you must leave the road, try to get all wheels off the pavement.
    B. Do not apply the brakes unless you are moving at a speed greater than 20 mph.
    C. Brake gently to avoid skidding.
    D. Most shoulders will not support a large vehicle.

28. Your vehicle has hydraulic brakes. While traveling on a level road, the system loses pressure and the brakes fail. Which of these statements is true?
    A. You should not downshift if you have an automatic transmission.
    B. Pumping the brake pedal may bring the pressure up so you can stop the vehicle.
    C. The parking brake will not work either because it is part of the same hydraulic system.
    D. All of the above

29. You are traveling down a long, steep hill. Your brakes begin to fade and then fail. What should you do?
    A. Downshift
    B. Pump the brake pedal
    C. Look for an escape ramp or escape route
    D. All of the above

30. Vehicle skids can be caused by which of the following conditions?
    A. New tires
    B. Air brakes
    C. Roads with too many curves
    D. Driving too fast for the road conditions

31. To correct a rear-wheel braking skid, you should:
    A. Apply more pressure to the brake pedal.
    B. Apply more pressure to the brake pedal and steer/countersteer.
    C. Release the brakes and accelerate.
    D. Release the brakes and steer/countersteer.

32. If a straight vehicle (no trailer or articulation) goes into a front-wheel skid, it will:
    A. Slide sideways and spin out.
    B. Go straight ahead but will turn if you turn the steering wheel.
    C. Go straight ahead even if the steering wheel is turned.
    D. Cause a vibration in the vehicle.

33. Which of these statements about cold weather driving is true?
    A. There is no need to worry about the engine overheating when the weather is very cold.
    B. Exhaust system leaks are less dangerous in cold weather.
    C. Wiper blades should be adjusted so that they do not make direct contact with the windshield.
    D. Windshield washer antifreeze should be added to the washer reservoir.

34. Which of these statement about tires and hot weather driving is true?
    A. You should inspect your tires more often because the air pressure is more likely to get too high.
    B. If a tire is too hot to touch, you should drive on it to cool it off.
    C. Recapped tires are less likely to fail in hot weather than new tires.
    D. All of the above are true.

35. Hydroplaning:
    A. Only occurs when there is a lot of water.
    B. Only occurs at speeds above 50 mph.
    C. Cannot occur when driving through a puddle.
    D. Is more likely if tire pressure is low.

36. When the roads are slippery, you should:
    A. Drive alongside other vehicles.
    B. Make turns as gently as possible.
    C. Stop and test the traction while going up hills.
    D. Decrease the distance that you look ahead of your
        vehicle.

37. Your brakes can get wet when you drive through a heavy
    rain. What can this cause when the brakes are applied?
    A. Wheel lockup
    B. Trailer jackknife
    C. Lack of braking power
    D. All of the above

38. Which of these statements about downshifting is true?
    A. It should not be done with automatic transmissions.
    B. It allows engine compression and friction to help the
        brakes slow the vehicle.
    C. The proper time to downshift is just after the vehicle
        starts down the hill.
    D. It is not necessary if the vehicle has retarders.

39. Which of these statements about escape ramps is true?
    A. They are used to stop vehicles that lose their brakes on
        downhill grades.
    B. They are designed to prevent injury to drivers and
        passengers.
    C. They protect equipment and cargo from severe
        damage.
    D. All of the above are true.

40. Which of these is *not* a good rule to follow when caring for
    the injured at an accident scene?
    A. If a qualified person is helping them, stay out of the
        way unless asked to assist.
    B. Stop heavy bleeding by applying direct pressure to the
        wound.
    C. Keep injured persons cool.
    D. Move severely injured persons if there is a danger
        due to fire or passing traffic.

41. Which of these statements about vehicle fires is true?
    A. If cargo in a van or box trailer catches on fire, you should open the cargo doors as soon as possible.
    B. If your engine is on fire, you should open the hood as soon as you can.
    C. If a trailer is on fire, you should drive fast to put out the flames.
    D. A burning tire must be cooled.

42. On which fires can you use the "B:C" fire extinguisher?
    A. Electrical fires
    B. Burning liquids
    C. Burning cloth
    D. All of the above

43. Which of these is a good rule to follow when using a fire extinguisher?
    A. Keep as close to the fire as possible.
    B. Stay downwind of the fire.
    C. Aim at the base of the fire.
    D. All of the above

44. Which of these statements about drinking alcohol is true?
    A. Some people are not affected by drinking.
    B. A few beers have the same effect when driving as a few shots of whiskey.
    C. Coffee and fresh air can sober up a person.
    D. All of the above are true.

45. As the Blood Alcohol Concentration (BAC) goes up, what happens?
    A. The drinker more clearly sees how alcohol is affecting him/her.
    B. The effects of alcohol decrease.
    C. The person becomes more dangerous if allowed to drive.
    D. The drinker can sober up in less time.

46. Which of these can help you stay alert while driving?
    A. Scheduling trips during hours that you are normally asleep
    B. Taking a cold pill
    C. Keeping the cab warm
    D. Taking short breaks before you get drowsy

47. Which of these statements about drugs is true?
    A. A driver can use any prescription drug while driving.
    B. Amphetamines (pep pills or bennies) can be used to help the driver stay alert.
    C. Use of drugs can lead to accidents and/or arrest.
    D. All of the above are true.

48. You do not have a Hazardous Materials Endorsement on your Commercial Driver's License. You are asked to haul hazardous materials in a placarded vehicle. You should:
    A. Refuse to haul the load.
    B. Take the placards off the vehicle.
    C. Haul the load, but only to the nearest place where a driver with a Hazardous Materials Endorsement can take over.
    D. Haul the load, but file a report with the Department of Transportation after the trip.

49. A vehicle is loaded with most of the weight on the steering axle. What may result?
    A. Better handling
    B. A need to disconnect the steering axle brakes
    C. Too little traction on the steering axle
    D. Hard steering

50. Which of these statements about cargo loading is true?
    A. The legal maximum weight allowed by a state can be considered safe for all driving conditions.
    B. Slight overloading of a vehicle can make its brakes work better.
    C. If cargo is loaded by the shipper, the driver is not responsible for overloading.
    D. State laws dictate legal weight limits.

Do not start the test until you have read the instructions on pages 319 and 320. Mark your answers on Answer Sheet: General Knowledge Test — Practice Set B.

General Test Practice Set B

1. Which of these items are checked in a pre-trip inspection?
    A. Whether vehicle lights are working and clean
    B. Wiper blades
    C. Cargo securement
    D. All of the above

2. You are checking your tires in a pre-trip inspection. Which of these statements is true?
    A. Dual tires should be touching each other.
    B. Radial and bias-ply tires can be used together on the same vehicle.
    C. 2/32 inch tread depth is safe for the front tires.
    D. Different types of tires or mismatched sizes should not be used on the same vehicle.

3. You are checking your steering and exhaust systems in a pre-trip inspection. Which of these statements is true?
    A. Steering wheel play of more than 10 degrees (2 inches on a 20-inch steering wheel) can make it hard to steer.
    B. Leaks in the exhaust system are not a problem if they are outside the cab.
    C. Some leakage of power steering fluid is normal.
    D. All of the above are true.

4. You are putting your vehicle in motion from a stop. As you apply power to the drive wheels, they start to spin. You should:
    A. Try a lower gear.
    B. Press harder on the accelerator.
    C. Take your foot off the accelerator.
    D. Take your foot off the accelerator and put on the brakes.

5. Which of these statements about downshifting is true?
   A. When you downshift for a curve, you should do so before you enter the curve.
   B. When you downshift for a hill, you should do so after you start down the hill.
   C. When double-clutching, you should let the rpms decrease while the clutch is released and the shift lever is in neutral.
   D. All of the above are true.

6. Which of these is a sign of tire failure?
   A. Steering that feels heavy
   B. A loud "bang"
   C. Vibration
   D. All of the above

7. The purpose of retarders is to:
   A. Provide emergency brakes.
   B. Help slow the vehicle while driving and reduce brake wear.
   C. Apply extra braking power to the non-drive axles.
   D. Help prevent skids.

8. To test the service brake on a hydraulic system, you push down the pedal firmly to see if the braking action is correct. Where and when should this be done.
   A. In a parking lot when the vehicle is not moving
   B. On the road when the vehicle is moving at about 5 mph
   C. At a special Brake Testing Center only
   D. When the vehicle is traveling downhill with a load

9. The parking brake should be tested while the vehicle is:
   A. Parked.
   B. Moving slowly.
   C. Going downhill.
   D. Moving at highway speed.

10. How do you test the foot brake on a hydraulic system?
   A. Move the vehicle slowly to see if it stops when the brake is applied.
   B. Measure the free play in the pedal with a ruler.
   C. With the vehicle stopped, pump the pedal three times, apply firm pressure, then hold down pedal and see if the pedal moves.
   D. Step on the brake pedal and the accelerator at the same time to see if the vehicle moves.

11. Which of these is a good rule to follow when driving at night?
     A. Keep your speed slow enough thatyou can stop within the range of your headlights.
     B. Look directly at oncoming headlights.
     C. Wear sun glasses.
     D. Keep your instrument lights as bright as you can.

12. While driving, you see a small (1 foot square) cardboard box ahead in your lane. You should:
     A. Stop and direct traffic around it.
     B. Stop and see if it is something valuable.
     C. Hit it with your vehicle to knock it off the road.
     D. Steer around it when it is safe to do so.

13. You are driving a long vehicle that makes wide turns. You want to turn left from Pine Street onto Cedar Street. Both are two-lane, two-way streets. You should:
     A. Begin the turn with your vehicle in the left lane of Pine Street.
     B. Turn into the left lane of Cedar Street and then move to the right lane when the traffic is clear.
     C. Begin turning your vehicle as soon as you enter the intersection.
     D. Begin turning your vehicle when you are halfway through the intersection.

14. You are driving a heavy vehicle. You must exit a highway using an off-ramp that curves downhill. You should:
     A. Drive at the posted speed limit for the off-ramp.
     B. Slow down to a safe speed before the turn.
     C. Come to a full stop at the top of the ramp.
     D. Wait until you are in the turn before downshifting.

15. Which of these should you *not* do when passing a vehicle?
     A. Lightly tap your horn (if it is legal) just before you pull out to pass.
     B. At night, flash your lights from low to high beam and back just before you pull out to pass.
     C. Assume the other driver does not see you.
     D. Move as close to the other vehicle as you can before pulling into the passing lane.

16. Which of these statements about backing a heavy vehicle is true?
    A. You should avoid backing whenever you can.
    B. When you use a helper, he or she should use clear voice (spoken) signals.
    C. It is safer to back toward the right side of the vehicle than to the driver's side.
    D. All of the above are true.

17. How far should a driver look ahead of the vehicle while driving?
    A. 6-9 seconds
    B. 9-12 seconds
    C. 12-15 seconds
    D. 18-21 seconds

18. When looking ahead of your vehicle while driving, you should:
    A. Look straight ahead.
    B. Look to the right side of the road.
    C. Look to the left side of the road.
    D. Look back and forth.

19. Which of these statements about using mirrors is true?
    A. You should look at a mirror for several seconds at a time.
    B. Convex mirrors make things look closer than they really are.
    C. There are "blind spots," so your mirror may not show you everything.
    D. A lane change requires you to look at the mirrors twice.

20. Which of these statements about turn signals is *false*?
    A. Turn on signal lights just as you start to turn at a corner.
    B. Cancel the signal only when you have completed the turn.
    C. Turn on signal lights well before turning.
    D. Put on your turn signals before changing lanes.

21. Which of these is a proper use of vehicle lights and flashers?
    A. Turning on your headlights during the day when visibility is reduced due to rain or snow
    B. Flashing your brake lights to warn someone behind you of a hazard that will require slowing down
    C. Flashing your brake lights to warn someone behind you that you are going to stop on the road
    D. All of the above

22. You must park on the side of a level, straight, four-lane divided highway. Where should you place the three reflective triangles?
    A. One within 10 feet of the rear of the vehicle, one about 100 feet to the rear, and one about 200 feet to the rear.
    B. One within 10 feet of the rear of the vehicle, one about 100 feet to the rear, and one about 100 feet from the front of the vehicle.
    C. One about 50 feet from the rear of the vehicle, one about 100 feet to the rear, and one about 100 feet from the front of the vehicle.
    D. One within 10 feet of the front of the vehicle, one about 100 feet from the front, and one about 100 feet to the rear.

23. Your vehicle is in a traffic emergency and may collide with another vehicle if you do not take action. Which of these is a good rule to remember at such a time?
    A. Stopping is always the safest action in a traffic emergency.
    B. Heavy vehicles can almost always turn more quickly than they can stop.
    C. Leaving the road is always more risky than hitting another vehicle.
    D. Open the door and jump out if you have time.

24. What is countersteering?
    A. Turning the steering wheel counterclockwise.
    B. Steering in the opposite direction from what other drivers expect you to do.
    C. Using the steering axle brakes to prevent oversteering.
    D. Turning the wheel in the opposite direction you were steering to avoid a traffic emergency.

25. You are driving on a two-lane road. An oncoming driver drifts into your lane and is headed straight for you. Which of these is generally the best action to take?
    A. Steer into the oncoming lane.
    B. Steer onto the left shoulder.
    C. Steer to the right.
    D. Brake hard.

26. Which of these is the most important thing to remember about emergency braking?
    A. It wears the brake linings.
    B. Disconnecting the steering axle brakes will help keep your vehicle in a straight line during emergency braking.
    C. Never do it without downshifting first.
    D. If the wheels are skidding, you cannot control the vehicle.

27. Stab braking:
    A. Should never be used.
    B. Should only be used on slick roads.
    C. Involves locking the wheels.
    D. Involves steady pressure on the brake pedal.

28. To avoid a crash, you had to drive onto the right shoulder. You are now driving at 40 mph on the shoulder. How should you move back onto the pavement?
    A. Come to a complete stop, if possible, before steering back onto the pavement.
    B. Brake hard to slow the vehicle, then steer sharply onto the pavement.
    C. Steer sharply onto the pavement and countersteer when both back wheels of your vehicle are on the pavement.
    D. Keep moving at the present speed and steer very gently back onto the pavement.

29. You are driving on a straight, level highway at 50 mph. There are no vehicles in front of you. Suddenly a tire blows out on your vehicle. What should you do first?
    A. Stay off the brake until the vehicle slows down on its own.
    B. Quickly steer onto the shoulder.
    C. Begin light braking.
    D. Begin controlled or stab braking.

30. The most common cause of serious vehicle skids is:
    A. Driving too fast for the road conditions.
    B. Poorly adjusted brakes.
    C. Bad tires.
    D. Poorly designed roads.

31. How do you correct a rear-wheel acceleration skid?
    A. Apply more power to the wheel.
    B. Downshift.
    C. Apply the brake.
    D. Stop accelerating and release the clutch.

32. You must drive on a slippery road. Which of these is a good thing to do in such a situation?
    A. Use a smaller following distance.
    B. Apply the brakes during turns.
    C. Slow down gradually.
    D. All of the above.

33. The road you are driving on becomes very slippery due to glare ice. Which of these is a good thing to do in such a situation?
    A. Stop driving as soon as it is safe to do so.
    B. Downshift to stop.
    C. Apply the brakes often to keep the linings clean.
    D. Drive at a varying speed.

34. Which of these will help keep an engine cool in hot weather?
    A. Avoiding high-speed driving.
    B. Making sure the engine has the right amount of oil.
    C. Keeping antifreeze in the radiator.
    D. All of the above

35. What should you do when your vehicle hydroplanes?
    A. Start stab braking.
    B. Accelerate slightly.
    C. Countersteer hard.
    D. Release the accelerator.

36. You should avoid driving through deep puddles or flowing water. But if you must, which of these steps can help keep your brakes working?
    A. Driving through quickly
    B. Gently pressing the brake pedal while driving through the water
    C. Applying hard pressure on both the brake pedal and accelerator after coming out of the water
    D. Disconnecting the steering axle brakes after coming out of the water

37. You are driving a modern (newer) truck with a manual transmission. What gear will you probably have to use to take a long downhill grade?
    A. The same gear used to climb the hill
    B. A lower gear than was used to climb the hill
    C. A higher gear than was used to climb the hill
    D. None; newer trucks can coast down hills

38. Which of these best describes how you should use the brake pedal on a steep downhill grade?
    A. Light, pumping action
    B. Light, steady pressure
    C. Repeated strong pressure, then release
    D. With stronger pressure as the vehicle goes downhill

39. Which of these is *not* a good rule to follow when protecting an accident scene?
    A. Do not move any of the involved vehicles off the road until law enforcement personnel arrive.
    B. Put on your flashers.
    C. Set out reflective triangles to warn other drivers.
    D. If you're stopping to help, park away from the scene.

40. Which of these can cause a fire.
    A. Tires with too low an air pressure
    B. Loose fuel connections
    C. Electrical short circuits
    D. All of the above

41. The first step to take if your vehicle catches fire while driving is:
    A. Immediately open the door and jump out.
    B. Head for the nearest service station.
    C. Park in the shade of a building.
    D. Get the vehicle off the road and stop in an open area.

42. On which fires can you use water?
    A. Tire fires
    B. Gasoline fires
    C. Electrical fires
    D. All of the above

43. Which of these pieces of emergency equipment should be carried at all times in your vehicle?
    A. Fire extinguisher(s)
    B. Spare electrical fuses (if the vehicle uses them)
    C. Warning devices for parked vehicles
    D. All of the above

44. Which of these statements about drinking alcohol is true?
    A. Alcohol first affects judgment and self-control, which are essential for safe driving.
    B. Statistics show that drivers who have been drinking have a much greater chance of being in a crash.
    C. A driver can lose his/her license for driving while under the influence of alcohol.
    D. All of the above are true.

45. It takes the body _____ hour(s) to get rid of the alcohol in four beers.
    A. 1
    B. 2
    C. 3
    D. 4

46. Which of these statements about staying alert when you drive is true?
    A. A half-hour break for coffee will do more to keep you alert than a half-hour nap.
    B. There are drugs that can overcome being tired.
    C. If you must stop to take a nap, it should be at a truck stop or other public area — never on the side of the road.
    D. The only thing that can cure fatigue is sleep.

47. Which of these will tell you that the cargo contains hazardous materials.
    A. The name of a hazard class on the shipping paper
    B. A four-inch, diamond-shaped hazardous materials label on the container
    C. A hazardous materials placard on the vehicle
    D. All of the above

48. You do not have a Hazardous Materials Endorsement on your Commercial Driver's License. When can you legally haul hazardous materials?
    A. Never
    B. Only when the vehicle does not require placards
    C. Only when the shipment will not cross state lines
    D. Only when an official from the Department of Transportation is present

49. A vehicle is loaded with very little weight on the drive axle. What may result?
    A. Poor traction
    B. A need to disconnect the steering axle brakes
    C. Damage to drive axle tires
    D. Better handling

50. Cargo inspections:
    A. Are most often *not* the responsibility of the driver.
    B. Should be performed at every change of duty status.
    C. Are needed only if hazardous materials are being hauled.
    D. Should be performed every 6 hours or 300 miles.

Summary

You must pass the General Knowledge Test to obtain your Commercial Driver's License. This applies to every class of vehicle and to all bus drivers and truck drivers. Every driver who wants any kind of CDL must first pass the General Knowledge Test.

There is some information that all commercial drivers need to know. This knowledge does not depend on the type of vehicle driven or the cargo hauled. For example, all drivers need to know how to choose a safe driving speed and how to react to emergencies. This type of knowledge is what is measured by the General Knowledge Test. To review the material, go back to Chapter Four.

If you do not pass the General Knowledge Test, you cannot take the CDL performance tests. You must correctly answer at least 80 percent (80%) of the questions to pass the knowledge test.

REVIEW QUESTIONS

1. What is the purpose of the General Knowledge Test?

    _____

    _____

2. Who must take the General Knowledge Test?

    _____

3. What is a passing score for the General Knowledge Test?

    _____

4. Did you answer every question on the General Knowledge
    Test — Practice Sets A and B? How many answers did
    you get wrong on Test A? Test B? Do you now know the
    correct answers for these questions?

    _____

    You will need to know the answers for all 100 questions
    asked on Practice Sets A and B. Chances are that your
    State's General Knowledge Test will include questions
    found on these two practice tests.

5. Besides passing the General Knowledge Test, what other
    tests must you pass to obtain a CDL to drive a:

    - Class A bus? _____
    - Class B bus? _____
    - Class C bus? _____

ANSWER KEY FOR GENERAL TEST: PRACTICE SET A

1.	B	26.	C
2.	D	27.	C
3.	A	28.	B
4.	D	29.	C
5.	B	30.	D
6.	C	31.	D
7.	A	32.	C
8.	C	33.	D
9.	D	34.	A
10.	D	35.	D
11.	B	36.	B
12.	C	37.	D
13.	C	38.	B
14.	B	39.	D
15.	A	40.	C
16.	A	41.	D
17.	B	42.	D
18.	D	43.	C
19.	D	44.	B
20.	C	45.	C
21.	B	46.	D
22.	B	47.	C
23.	A	48.	A
24.	C	49.	D
25.	C	50.	D

ANSWER KEY FOR GENERAL TEST: PRACTICE SET B

1.	D	26.	D
2.	D	27.	C
3.	A	28.	A
4.	C	29.	A
5.	A	30.	A
6.	D	31.	D
7.	B	32.	C
8.	B	33.	A
9.	B	34.	D
10.	C	35.	D
11.	A	36.	B
12.	D	37.	B
13.	D	38.	B
14.	B	39.	A
15.	D	40.	D
16.	A	41.	D
17.	C	42.	A
18.	D	43.	D
19.	C	44.	D
20.	A	45.	D
21.	D	46.	D
22.	A	47.	D
23.	B	48.	B
24.	D	49.	A
25.	C	50.	B

PASSENGER TEST

CHAPTER

9

FROM NOW ON,

ONLY THE BEST WILL DRIVE

Chapter Objectives

Measure the knowledge all bus drivers must have

Help the CDL applicant become familiar with the testing procedures used to obtain the Passenger Endorsement (P)

Review the information a driver needs to drive a bus

Provide questions with which the CDL applicant may practice taking a General Bus Test and the Passenger Test

CHAPTER NINE

PASSENGER TEST

Bus drivers must have a Passenger Endorsement on their CDL. To get this endorsement they must pass the Passenger Test. This chapter contains a CDL Passenger Test for your practice. The test questions on this practice test are similar to ones you will have to answer on your state's Passenger Test. If you need help in answering any test question, go back to Chapter Five to find the information you need.

A General Bus Test has been included in this chapter for your extra practice and review. While your State may not have such a test, we offer it so that you can review the general knowledge a bus driver is expected to have. If you have trouble answering any questions on the General Bus Test, refer back to Chapter Four for help.

Purpose of the Passenger Test

The Passenger Test measures the knowledge all bus drivers must have. Every person who intends to drive a vehicle that carries more than 15 passengers, including the driver, must pass this test to obtain a Passenger Endorsement (P).

Description of Tests

Two tests are provided in this chapter: the Passenger Test — Practice Set and the General Bus Test — Practice Set. Both tests are for your practice and review.

The Passenger Test is like the passenger endorsement test your state uses. There are 20 questions. All questions are multiple-choice and have four answers from which to choose. There is only one correct answer for each question. The Passenger Test has no time limit. Most persons will finish the test in 15 to 20 minutes.

The General Bus Test is offered for your interest only. Your state may or may not have a similar test. Some of the 32 questions we include may not be asked by your state, but they are questions every bus driver should be able to answer. That is why we think it may be of value to you.

Test Instructions

The instructions for taking each Test are similar to those provided in Chapter Eight on pages 319 and 320. You may want to read these test instructions again.

Remember, you are to mark only one answer for each question. If you mark more than one answer you will not be given credit for the question. It is in your best interest to answer every question. If you are not sure of the answer, you should guess which is right. After you have completed the tests, check your answers. The answers to the test questions are on page 366.

If you have any questions about the instructions you are to follow when you are taking your state's test, ask the examiner.

Sample Answer Sheets

The Passenger Test and General Bus Test answer sheets are found on pages 351 and 352. Use these sheets to mark your answers for the two practice tests which follow.

ANSWER SHEET: PASSENGER TEST — PRACTICE SET

Name:_____

SSN:_____

Date:_____

EXAMPLE

X.   A Ⓑ C D

1.	A	B	C	D
2.	A	B	C	D
3.	A	B	C	D
4.	A	B	C	D
5.	A	B	C	D
6.	A	B	C	D
7.	A	B	C	D
8.	A	B	C	D
9.	A	B	C	D
10.	A	B	C	D
11.	A	B	C	D
12.	A	B	C	D
13.	A	B	C	D
14.	A	B	C	D
15.	A	B	C	D
16.	A	B	C	D
17.	A	B	C	D
18.	A	B	C	D
19.	A	B	C	D
20.	A	B	C	D

ANSWER SHEET: GENERAL BUS TEST — PRACTICE SET

Name:_____

SSN:_____

Date:_____

EXAMPLE

X.   A   B   Ⓒ   D

1.	A	B	C	D	17.	A	B	C	D
2.	A	B	C	D	18.	A	B	C	D
3.	A	B	C	D	19.	A	B	C	D
4.	A	B	C	D	20.	A	B	C	D
5.	A	B	C	D	21.	A	B	C	D
6.	A	B	C	D	22.	A	B	C	D
7.	A	B	C	D	23.	A	B	C	D
8.	A	B	C	D	24.	A	B	C	D
9.	A	B	C	D	25.	A	B	C	D
10.	A	B	C	D	26.	A	B	C	D
11.	A	B	C	D	27.	A	B	C	D
12.	A	B	C	D	28.	A	B	C	D
13.	A	B	C	D	29.	A	B	C	D
14.	A	B	C	D	30.	A	B	Ⓒ	D
15.	A	B	C	D	31.	A	B	C	D
16.	A	B	C	D	32.	A	B	C	D

This test contains questions similar to those that will be on the Passenger Test given by your state. You must pass this test to get the Passenger Endorsement (P) on your CDL. Mark your answers on the Passenger Test Answer Sheet.

1. You must *not* permit standing riders:
    A. Between the wheel wells.
    B. In front of the standee line.
    C. Within two feet of an emergency exit.
    D. Within two feet of any window.

2. Your bus is disabled. The bus, with riders aboard, may be towed or pushed to a safe place only:
    A. By another bus with its 4-way flashers on.
    B. By a tow truck with a GVWR of at least 27,000 pounds.
    C. If the distance is less than 1 mile.
    D. If getting off the bus would be more risky for the riders.

3. Buses may have recapped or regrooved tires:
    A. On any or all of the wheels.
    B. Only when the average speed will be less than 40 mph.
    C. Only on the outside wheel of dual wheels.
    D. Anywhere except on the front wheels.

4. You may sometimes haul small-arms ammunition, emergency shipments of drugs, or hospital supplies on a bus. The total weight of all such hazardous materials must not be greater than _____ pounds.
    A. 100
    B. 250
    C. 500
    D. 750

5. How many folding aisle seats are allowed in a bus that is *not* carrying farm workers?
    A. 0
    B. 4
    C. 6
    D. 8

6. How many seats *not* securely fastened to the bus are usually allowed?
   A. 0
   B. 1
   C. 2
   D. 3

7. If your bus has an emergency exit door, it must:
   A. Be secured when the bus is operating.
   B. Always have a red door light turned on.
   C. Not have any signs, stickers, or markings near it.
   D. Meet all of the requirements listed in the three previous answers.

8. It is best to wear your seat belt:
   A. Only when you will be driving over 35 mph.
   B. Only when driving on sand, gravel, or ice covered roads.
   C. Only if your bus holds more than 27 people.
   D. At all times.

9. A bus may carry baggage or freight only if it is secured so that:
   A. The driver can move freely and easily.
   B. Any rider can use all exits.
   C. Riders are protected from falling or shifting packages.
   D. All of the above.

10. When you inspect your bus, you must make sure that:
    A. Every handhold and railing is secure.
    B. Rider signaling devices are working.
    C. Emergency exit handles are secure.
    D. All of the above.

11. When you discharge an unruly rider, you should choose a place that is:
    A. Off the regular route.
    B. Dark and poorly lighted.
    C. As safe as possible.
    D. The most convenient.

12. Which one of the following types of cargo can never be
    carried on a bus with riders?
    A. Small arms ammunition (ORM-D).
    B. Tear gas.
    C. Emergency hospital supplies.
    D. Emergency drug shipments.

13. If there is no traffic light or attendant, how far from the
    draw of a drawbridge must you stop?
    A. 5 feet
    B. 10 yards
    C. 50 feet
    D. 100 feet

14. To stop for railroad tracks, a bus driver should stop
    _____ feet before the nearest track.
    A. 20 to 5
    B. 35 to 10
    C. 50 to 15
    D. 65 to 20

15. If you have riders aboard, you must never fuel your bus:
    A. With a higher grade of fuel.
    B. In a closed building.
    C. Without a static chain.
    D. With any of the windows open.

16. If a rider wants to bring a car battery or a can of gasoline
    aboard your bus, you should:
    A. Not allow them to do it.
    B. Tell them they must go to the rear of the bus.
    C. Instruct them to sit next to an open window.
    D. Have the rider pay a second fare.

17. Which of the following answers lists the three types of
    emergency equipment you must have on your bus?
    A. Emergency reflectors, fire extinguisher, and tire
       repair kit
    B. Hydraulic jack, fire extinguisher, signal flares
    C. Fire extinguisher, spare electric fuses, and emergency
       reflectors
    D. Repair kit, spare electric fuses, and fire extinguisher

18. Some city transit buses may have a brake-door interlock system. This system:
     A. Works when the passenger exit doors are open.
     B. Should be used in place of the parking brake.
     C. Releases the brakes.
     D. Should be used in emergencies.

19. All of the following should be in good working order before driving. Which item MUST be in good working order before the bus can leave?
     A. Destination sign
     B. Service brakes
     C. Restroom service
     D. Windows

20. When it is carried on a bus, hazardous material must be:
     A. Labeled.
     B. Stored in the passenger compartment.
     C. Packed in a yellow box.
     D. All of the above.

This is another test of how well you know the information required to drive a bus. Mark your answers on the General Bus Test answer sheets.

NOTE: This test is a practice and review test. It includes questions that may not be asked on your state's CDL test. For instance, there are questions about Federal Motor Carrier Safety Regulations and CDL rules. Although they may not be included in CDL tests, these questions cover information important to every bus driver.

1. A straight bus weighing 20,000 pounds GVWR (Gross Vehicle Weight Rating) which hauls 20 passengers falls into which CDL class?
    A. A
    B. B
    C. C
    D. All of the above

2. You have passed all the requirements for a Class B bus driver's license. Which of these vehicles are you *not* licensed to drive?
    A. Class A bus
    B. Class B bus
    C. Class C bus
    D. All of these vehicles can be driven with a Class B bus license.

3. When you apply for a bus driving job, you must report to the Company all motor vehicle accidents you have been involved in during the past ____ year(s).
    A. 1
    B. 3
    C. 5
    D. 10

4. Federal regulations set an axle weight limit of ____ pounds on a tandem axle (four feet apart).
    A. 26,000
    B. 32,000
    C. 34,000
    D. 40,000

5. According to Federal regulations, the minimum depth required for tire tread on steering axle tires is ____ of an inch.
    A. 2/32
    B. 4/32
    C. 6/32
    D. 8/32

6. You must put a loaded bus into motion from a stopped position on a steep upgrade (4% or more). Which of these is the best technique to follow when you have a bus with a manual transmission?
    A. Hold the foot brake until the clutch has been fully released.
    B. Accelerate hard and release the clutch quickly.
    C. Slowly release the clutch while releasing the parking brakes.
    D. Use the same method that is used when starting on a level surface or downgrade.

7. Which of these statements about gear ranges in buses with automatic transmissions is true?
    A. The highest range should be used at all times except when roads are slippery.
    B. The highest range should only be used with heavy loads.
    C. Lower ranges should be used for greater engine braking on downgrades.
    D. Lower ranges should only be used by buses equipped with engine brakes.

8. The driver's seat should be adjusted:
    A. Only when the bus is at a stop.
    B. Only when the bus is moving at 30 mph or less.
    C. Whenever the driver finds it necessary while driving.
    D. None of the above.

9. If you increase your speed from 20 to 60 mph (original speed times 3), how much more braking distance is required at 60 mph than at 20 mph?
    A. 3 times
    B. 3 x 2 or 6 times
    C. 3 x 3 or 9 times
    D. 3 x 4 or 12 times

10. In general, the best braking technique to use in maintaining a safe speed when driving on a downgrade is:
    A. Fanning or pumping the brakes.
    B. Using only the parking brakes.
    C. Using only downshifting.
    D. Applying steady service brake pressure.

11. When driving at more than 40 mph, what is the safe minimum following distance for ideal daytime conditions?
    A. One second for every 10 feet of vehicle length (rounded upward to the nearest 10 feet)
    B. Answer "A" plus one second
    C. Four seconds
    D. None of the above

12. Which of these is the best general rule for night driving?
    A. Drive close to the shoulder of the road.
    B. Drive slightly faster than the other traffic.
    C. Drive slightly slower than the other traffic.
    D. Increase the normal (daytime) following distance by one second.

13. When you are not sure who has the right-of-way, the safest course of action is to:
    A. Let the faster vehicle have the right-of-way.
    B. Let the vehicle on the right have the right-of-way.
    C. Let whoever got there first have the right-of-way.
    D. Let the other driver have the right-of-way.

14. Off-tracking of the rear wheels is affected by:
    A. Faster speed on turns and curves.
    B. Sharper turns and curves.
    C. Greater distance between the front and rear wheels.
    D. All of the above.

15. As the driver of a bus, how can you best avoid hindering other traffic on the highway?
    A. By driving slightly faster than the other traffic.
    B. By passing only the slowest vehicles.
    C. By traveling in convoy packs with other heavy vehicles.
    D. By staying in the right-hand lane.

16. How are buses to handle most railroad grade crossings?
    A. Come to a complete stop before crossing.
    B. Slow down and prepare to stop if a train is
       approaching.
    C. Turn the vehicle flashers on before crossing.
    D. Tap the electric horn before crossing.

17. Which of these statements about speed management is
    true?
    A. The posted speed limit is safe for all conditions.
    B. You should be able to stop within the distance that you
       can see ahead.
    C. The heavier the bus, the less stopping distance
       required.
    D. All of the above are true.

18. Which of these is a good rule for backing a straight bus?
    A. Back toward the side opposite the driver.
    B. Turn the steering wheel so that its top moves away
       from the direction in which you want the back of the
       vehicle to go.
    C. Use voice signals to communicate with a helper.
    D. None of the above.

19. An oncoming vehicle keeps its high beams on. You should
    deal with this hazard by:
    A. Turning your high beams on.
    B. Putting down your visors to mask the beams.
    C. Blinking your trailer or side lights.
    D. Looking to the right side of your lane.

20. Which of these forms of signaling is *not* recommended?
    A. Signaling to others that it is safe to pass your bus
    B. Using four-way flashers to warn of danger ahead
    C. Signaling to others that you will change lanes
    D. All of the previous answers are proper to use.

21. Your bus is broken down on the right shoulder of a two-lane highway. How should you set out the warning devices?
   A. One against the bus, one about 50 feet behind it, and a third about 150 feet behind the bus
   B. One within 20 feet of the rear of the bus, a second about 100 feet behind the bus, and a third within 20 feet of the front of the bus
   C. One within 10 feet of the front of the bus, a second about 100 feet to the rear, and a third about 100 feet in front of the bus, facing oncoming traffic
   D. One within 10 feet of the front of the bus, a second within 100 feet of the front, and a third within 100 feet of the rear

22. The proper time to cancel your turn signal for a lane change or turn is:
   A. When the maneuver is complete.
   B. When you know that all other drivers have seen your signal.
   C. Just after starting the maneuver.
   D. About halfway through the maneuver.

23. Following are some situations that require special attention from all drivers. Which one is an even bigger problem for the driver of a vehicle with a low ground clearance?
   A. Backing on level ground
   B. Off-tracking on sloped curves
   C. Humps or dips in the road
   D. Driving in slippery conditions

24. When must a driver's vehicle inspection report be completed?
   A. At the start of every trip
   B. At the end of every work day
   C. At every duty status change
   D. After every rest break

25. In a pressurized cooling system, coolant level should be checked:
   A. Only by a mechanic.
   B. Only while the engine is hot.
   C. Every 90 days.
   D. None of the above.

26. Federal regulations prohibit the fueling of buses with passengers aboard more often than necessary. It is also prohibited to fuel buses:
   A. With a different grade of fuel.
   B. In a closed building.
   C. With no static chains.
   D. When the tank is less than 1/8 full.

27. In general, standees on a bus are not permitted:
   A. To stand between the fixed seats.
   B. In front of the standee line.
   C. Within five feet of an emergency exit.
   D. Within two feet of any window.

28. If you need to evacuate your bus in an emergency, passengers should be directed to a safe place no less than _____ feet from the bus.
   A. 75
   B. 100
   C. 150
   D. 200

29. If your bus becomes disabled on a freeway or expressway and you must stop on the left side of the road, it is best to stop so that the bus is:
   A. In line with traffic, against the farthest left wall, divider, or line.
   B. In line with traffic and centered between the left edge of the shoulder and the left edge of traffic.
   C. At an angle to traffic with the front door facing the downstream side of traffic.
   D. At an angle to traffic with the front door facing the upstream side of traffic.

30. If your bus has an emergency exit door, it must:
   A. Be secured when operating the bus.
   B. Have a red electric door light turned on at all times.
   C. Not have any signs, stickers, or markings anywhere near it.
   D. Meet all of the requirements listed in the answers above.

31. If a passenger is creating a disturbance on the bus, your first responsibility is to:
    A. Provide safe transportation for everyone aboard.
    B. Discharge that passenger immediately.
    C. Make sure that the bus is not damaged.
    D. Keep your schedule; whatever you do, you cannot delay the trip.

32. Federal regulations do *not* allow a driver to drive if he or she is:
    A. Ill or impaired, and the condition interferes with the ability to drive safely.
    B. Ill for longer than three hours.
    C. Taking medication of any kind.
    D. All of the above.

Summary

You must pass the Passenger Test to obtain a Passenger Endorsement on your CDL. One basic truth to keep in mind about your bus driver endorsement is that it is good only if you meet all the requirements for the commercial driver's license you are seeking.

When you pass the written test for the Passenger Endorsement, that endorsement is "conditional" until you complete all steps in the testing process for your license class. Suppose, for example, that you pass the General Test (Chapter Eight) and the Passenger Test (Chapter Nine) but fail the performance tests (Chapters Twelve, Thirteen, and Fourteen). You cannot drive a bus and haul passengers until you pass all of the bus driver tests.

Usually, all required written tests must be passed before you take the performance tests. This lets the State know that you have the knowledge for operating a bus safely before getting on the road. If you fail one or more of the written tests, you must take the failed test(s) again and pass them before you can take the performance tests.

REVIEW QUESTIONS

1. What is the purpose of the Passenger Test?

   _____

   _____

2. Did you answer every question on the Passenger
   Test — Practice Set? How many questions did you
   answer correctly? How many questions did you miss?
   Do you now know the correct answers for the missed
   questions?

   _____

   _____

3. Did you answer every question on the General Bus
   Test — Practice Set? How did you do? If you missed
   any of the questions on this test, do you now know the
   correct answers?

   _____

   _____

4. Besides passing the Passenger (Endorsement) Test,
   what other tests must you pass to obtain a bus
   driver's CDL in your state?

   _____

   _____

   _____

ANSWER KEY FOR PASSENGER TEST — PRACTICE SET

1. B	6. A	11. C	16. A
2. D	7. A	12. B	17. C
3. D	8. D	13. C	18. A
4. C	9. D	14. C	19. B
5. A	10. D	15. B	20. A

ANSWER KEY FOR GENERAL BUS TEST — PRACTICE SET

1. C	9. C	17. B	25. D
2. A	10. D	18. D	26. B
3. B	11. B	19. D	27. B
4. C	12. D	20. A	28. B
5. B	13. D	21. C	29. C
6. C	14. D	22. A	30. A
7. C	15. D	23. C	31. A
8. A	16. B	24. B	32. A

AIR BRAKE TEST

CHAPTER 10

ONLY THE BEST WILL DRIVE

Chapter Objectives

Provide a review of Chapter Six

Help the CDL applicant become familiar with testing procedures and questions

Measure the knowledge needed to safely drive vehicles which have air brakes

Provide questions with which the CDL applicant may practice taking the Air Brake Test

CHAPTER TEN

AIR BRAKE TEST

If you intend to drive a bus equipped with air brakes, you will need to pass a knowledge test and take your performance test in a bus with full or partial air brakes.

This chapter contains test questions on the information you need to know to drive vehicles with air brakes safely. If you need help in answering the air brake test questions, review Chapter Six.

This test measures the knowledge required to safely drive vehicles equipped with air brakes. Every person who wants to drive a bus with air brakes must pass the test regardless of which class license applies to the bus. Air brakes include any braking system operating fully or partly on the air brake principle.

Purpose of the Air Brake Test

Your state may test your knowledge in the use of air brakes in several ways. There may be a separate air brake test, or the General Test may include air brake questions which are graded separately.

Ways of Testing

For example, your state offers a 40-question basic General Knowledge Test including 10 air brake questions. If you score less than 80 percent on the air brake questions, you fail the air brake part of the test. However, you can still receive your CDL if you score 80 percent or better on the other 30 questions, but you will have an air brake restriction on your CDL.

Air Brake Restriction

This is how you can be restricted from operating a commercial motor vehicle with air brakes:

1.   You fail an air brake knowledge test.

2.   You fail the air brake questions that are included on a General Test. The practice General Tests we included in Chapter Eight did not ask a special set of questions about air brakes. However, general questions on braking, hydraulic brakes, and parking brakes were asked.

3.   You perform the skills test and road test in a vehicle not equipped with air brakes.

In each of these cases, your CDL will show that you are restricted from operating a CMV equipped with air brakes. This means, of course, that you cannot legally drive a commercial motor vehicle that has air brakes.

Test Instructions

The practice test offered in this chapter consists of 34 multiple-choice questions. There are four answers to choose from for each question. There is only one correct answer for each question. If you mark more than one answer you will not be given credit for the question.

Sample Answer Sheet

Like all other CDL knowledge tests, it is in your best interest to answer every question. If you are not sure of the answer, you should guess.

The Answer Sheet: Air Brake Test — Practice Set is found on the next page. Use this answer sheet to mark the answers for the practice test which follows.

After you have completed the test, check your answers. The answers to the practice test questions are found on page 381.

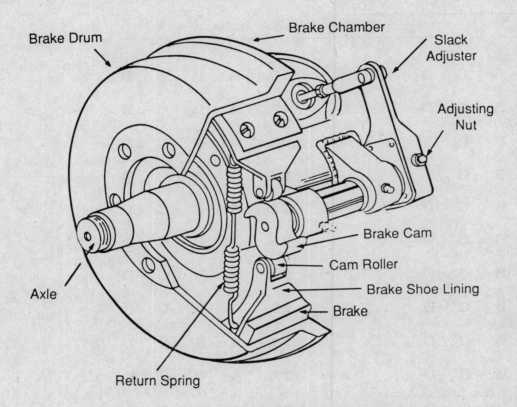

FIGURE 10-1: AIR BRAKE SYSTEM

ANSWER SHEET: AIR BRAKE TEST – PRACTICE SET

Name:_____   EXAMPLE

SSN:_____   **X.**   A   B   C   (D)

Date:_____

_____

1.	A B C D		18.	A B C D
2.	A B C D		19.	A B C D
3.	A B C D		20.	A B C D
4.	A B C D		21.	A B C D
5.	A B C D		22.	A B C D
6.	A B C D		23.	A B C D
7.	A B C D		24.	A B C D
8.	A B C D		25.	A B C D
9.	A B C D		26.	A B C D
10.	A B C D		27.	A B C D
11.	A B C D		28.	A B C D
12.	A B C D		29.	A B C D
13.	A B C D		30.	A B C D
14.	A B C D		31.	A B C D
15.	A B C D		32.	A B C D
16.	A B C D		33.	A B C D
17.	A B C D		34.	A B C D

The questions which follow are about air brakes and their safe use. Mark your answers on the answer sheet.

There is only one correct answer for each question. Answer every question.

1. Modern air brake systems combine three different systems.
    They are the service brake system, the parking brake
    system, and the:
    A. Emergency brake system.
    B. Foot brake system.
    C. S-cam brake system.
    D. Drum brake system.

2. The brake system that applies and releases the brakes
    when the driver uses the brake pedal is the:
    A. Emergency brake system.
    B. Service brake system.
    C. Parking brake system.
    D. None of the above

3. If the service brake system fails, the system you need to use
    to stop the vehicle is the:
    A. Parking brake system.
    B. Emergency brake system.
    C. Drum brake system.
    D. Hand brake system.

4. The air compressor governor controls:
    A. The speed of the air compressor.
    B. When the compressor is on or off.
    C. Air pressure applied to the brakes.
    D. When the compressor will pump air into the storage
        tanks.

5. Which of the following is OK to find in your air brake
    system?
    A. Oil
    B. Air
    C. Water
    D. All of the above

**Air Brake
Test —
Practice Set**

6. If your vehicle has an alcohol evaporator, it is there to:
   A. Rid the wet tank of alcohol that condenses in it.
   B. Let the driver skip the daily tank draining.
   C. Boost tank pressure the way superchargers boost engines.
   D. Reduce the risk of ice in air brake valves in cold weather.

7. If your vehicle has an alcohol evaporator, every day during cold weather you should:
   A. Check and fill the alcohol level.
   B. Change the alcohol from a new bottle.
   C. Oil the system with 5-weight oil.
   D. Check the oil for alcohol content.

8. The brake pedal in an air brake system:
   A. Is the main lever in the system.
   B. Can be a foot rest during normal driving.
   C. Controls the air pressure applied to operate the brakes.
   D. Exerts force on the slack adjusters by rods and linkages.

9. The most common type of foundation brake found on heavy vehicles is the:
   A. Disc brake.
   B. Wedge and drum brake.
   C. S-cam drum brake.
   D. None of the above

10. If the air system should develop a leak, what keeps the air in the tanks?
    A. The governor
    B. The tractor protection valve
    C. The emergency relay valve
    D. The one-way check valve

11. Which of the following is the right substance to hold a parking or emergency brake in position?
    A. Fluid pressure
    B. Spring pressure
    C. Air pressure
    D. Any of the above

12. During normal driving, parking and emergency brakes are usually held back by:
    A. Air pressure.
    B. Spring pressure.
    C. Centrifugal force.
    D. Bolts or clamps.

13. The effectiveness of the spring emergency or parking brakes:
    A. Has nothing to do with the condition of the service brakes.
    B. Can only be tested by highly trained brake service people.
    C. Depends on the adjustment of the service brakes.
    D. Increases when the service brakes are hot.

14. In air brake vehicles, use the parking brakes:
    A. When double clutching.
    B. As little as possible.
    C. Whenever you park the vehicle.
    D. Only during the pre- and post-trip inspections.

15. Your truck or bus has dual parking control valves. This means that you can use pressure from a separate tank to:
    A. Release the emergency brakes to move a short distance.
    B. Apply more brake pressure for stopping if the main tank is getting low.
    C. Stay parked without using up service air pressure.
    D. Balance the service brake system while you drive.

16. Air brake equipped vehicles must have:
    A. At least two air tanks.
    B. A hydraulic system in case the air system fails.
    C. An air pressure gauge to show the pressure available for braking.
    D. An air use gauge which shows the air used by the brake chambers for braking.

17. The driver must be able to see a warning that is given when air pressure in the service air tanks falls below:
    A. 40 psi.
    B. 50 psi.
    C. 60 psi.
    D. 80 psi.

18. The supply pressure gauge shows the driver how much pressure:
    A. Has been used in this trip.
    B. Is available in the air tanks.
    C. Is being sent to the brake chambers.
    D. None of the above

19. The application pressure gauge shows the driver how much pressure:
    A. Has been used on the trip.
    B. Is available in the air tanks.
    C. Is being sent to the brake chambers.
    D. None of the above

20. What turns on the stop light switch in an air brake system?
    A. Spring pressure
    B. Hydraulic pressure
    C. Air pressure
    D. The driver turns on the switch by hand.

21. You have a dual air brake system on a straight truck or bus. If a low air pressure warning comes on for only one system, what should you do?
    A. Reduce your speed and drive to the nearest service garage.
    B. Reduce your speed and test the remaining system.
    C. Try to find a repair station before the emergency brakes lock.
    D. Stop and safely park. Do not continue until the system has been repaired.

22. To check the free play in manual slack adjusters, you need to:
    A. Stop on level ground and apply the parking brakes.
    B. Park on level ground, chock the wheels, and release the parking brakes.
    C. Park on level ground and drain off air pressure before making adjustments.
    D. Apply the service brakes by hand at the brake chambers and watch the slack adjuster move.

23. A straight truck or bus air brake system cannot leak more than _____ psi per minute with the engine off and the brakes released.
    A. 1
    B. 2
    C. 3
    D. 4

24. A combination vehicle air brake system cannot leak more than _____ psi per minute with the engine off and the brakes released.
    A. 1
    B. 2
    C. 3
    D. 4

25. Air loss in a straight truck or bus should not be more than _____ with the engine off and the brakes on.
    A. 1 psi in 30 seconds
    B. 1 psi in 1 minute
    C. 2 psi in 45 seconds
    D. 3 psi in 1 minute

26. Experts do *not* recommend fanning (on-again off-again braking) for long downhill runs. Why?
    A. Air usage is less when fanning.
    B. Brake linings do not get hot when fanning.
    C. The short time off the brakes does not allow them to cool.
    D. None of the above

27. Drivers should know that their brakes are fading when:
    A. They need more brake pressure to keep the same speed on a downgrade.
    B. The brake pedal "fades away" when you press on it.
    C. You take your foot off of the brake pedal and speed increases.
    D. You need less pressure on the brake pedal for each stop.

28. Of the choices below, the first thing to do when a low air pressure warning comes on is:
    A. Stop and safely park as soon as possible.
    B. Upshift.
    C. Adjust the brake pedal for more travel.
    D. Open the air supply control valve.

29. Oil and water that collect in air tanks can make brakes fail. If you do not have automatic tank drains, when should you drain the air tanks?
    A. Every four hours
    B. Every day
    C. Every week
    D. Every other week

30. Air loss in a combination vehicle should not be more than ___ psi per minute with the engine off and the brakes on.
    A. 2
    B. 3
    C. 4
    D. 5

31. You must make a very quick stop. You should brake so you:
    A. Can steer hard while braking hard.
    B. Use the full power of the brakes and lock them.
    C. Stay in a straight line and can steer.
    D. Burn up the hand brake first.

32. To make an emergency stop using the stab braking method:
    A. Pump the brake pedal rapidly and lightly.
    B. Brake hard with the pedal until the wheels lock, then release the brakes until the wheels begin rolling again.
    C. Brake hard with the pedal until the wheels lock, then release the brakes for the same amount of time that the wheels were locked.
    D. Brake hard with the pedal and hand valve until you stop.

33. Air braking takes more time than hydraulic braking because air brakes:
    A. Use different brake drums.
    B. Need to have air flow through the lines to work.
    C. Require heavier return springs.
    D. Always have small air leaks.

34. Which of the following makes the total stopping distance longer for air brakes than hydraulic ones?
    A. Perception distance.
    B. Reaction distance.
    C. Brake lag distance.
    D. Effective braking distance.

The questions found on the Air Brake Practice Test are mainly for single unit vehicles such as a straight bus or truck. Air brake questions for combination vehicles such as a tractor-trailer bus are included in the Combination Vehicle Test: Practice Set found in Chapter Eleven.

All air brake questions found in CDL knowledge tests measure what you know about air brakes and their safe use. You need this knowledge for safe operation of the air brakes used on buses and trucks.

If you wish to drive a bus equipped with air brakes, you must pass a knowledge test on air brakes and take your skills and road tests in a vehicle equipped with air brakes. If you do not, your CDL will be restricted to driving only vehicles without an air brake system. For the purpose of the skills/road test and the CDL restriction, air brakes include any braking system operating fully or partially on the air brake principle.

You must correctly answer at least 80 percent (80%) of the questions to pass the air brake knowledge requirement.

Summary

REVIEW QUESTIONS

1. What is the purpose of testing a driver's knowledge of air brakes?

    _____

    _____

2. Who must pass the air brake knowledge requirement?

    _____

    _____

3. What are the two ways your state may test your knowledge of operating safely a vehicle which has air brakes?

    _____

    _____

4. What percent of air brake questions must you answer correctly in order to pass the test?

    _____

5. Did you answer every question on the practice test? How many questions did you answer correctly? Do you now know the correct answers for all of the questions you missed?

    _____

6. How can you be restricted from operating a commercial motor vehicle with air brakes? What does an air brake restriction on your CDL mean?

    _____

    _____

    _____

ANSWER KEY FOR AIR BRAKE TEST — PRACTICE SET

1.	A	18.	B
2.	B	19.	B
3.	B	20.	C
4.	D	21.	D
5.	B	22.	B
6.	D	23.	B
7.	A	24.	C
8.	C	25.	D
9.	C	26.	C
10.	D	27.	A
11.	B	28.	A
12.	A	29.	B
13.	C	30.	C
14.	C	31.	C
15.	A	32.	B
16.	C	33.	B
17.	C	34.	C

COMBINATION VEHICLES TEST

CHAPTER

11

FROM NOW ON,

ONLY THE BEST WILL DRIVE

Chapter Objectives

Provide a review of Chapter Seven

Help the CDL applicant become familiar with testing procedures and questions.

Measure the knowledge needed to drive combination vehicle safely

Provide questions with which the CDL applicant may practice taking the Combination Vehicles Test

CHAPTER ELEVEN

COMBINATION VEHICLES TEST

If you drive a tractor-trailer bus or any other combination vehicle you must pass the CDL Combination Vehicles Test. This chapter provides test questions on driving combination vehicles safely. If you need help in answering these test questions, review Chapter Seven: Driving A Tractor-Trailer Bus.

This test measures knowledge required to safely drive combination vehicles such as tractor-trailer buses. This test applies only to Class A vehicles.

A Class A license is needed to drive any combination of vehicles with a Gross Combination Weight Rating (GCWR) of 26,001 or more pounds. The Gross Vehicle Weight Rating (GVWR) of the vehicle(s) being towed must be over 10,000 pounds. Holders of a Class A CDL may also, with the proper endorsements, operate all commercial vehicles within Class B and Class C.

**Purpose
of the
Combination
Vehicles Test**

Examples of Class A Vehicles

Examples of Class A vehicles include but are not limited to the following.

FIGURE 11-1: Examples of Class A Vehicles

Combination vehicles are usually longer and heavier than single commercial vehicles. They require more knowledge and skill to drive. That is why there is a combination vehicle knowledge test. In addition to the knowledge required on the General Test, drivers of combination vehicles also know about:

- Combination vehicle air brakes.

- Proper coupling and uncoupling of tractor to semitrailer.

- Vehicle inspection procedures for combination vehicles.

- Safety factors that apply to pulling a trailer.

Required Knowledge

The practice test in this chapter consists of 32 questions. All questions are multiple-choice. There are four answers from which to choose for each question. There is only one correct answer for each question. If you mark more than one answer you will not be given credit for the question.

Like other CDL knowledge tests, it is in your best interest to answer every question. If you are not sure of the answer you should guess which is the best answer.

After you have completed the test, check your answers. The answers are found on page 397.

Test Instructions

The Combination Vehicle Practice Test answer sheet is found on the next page. Use this answer sheet to mark your answer for the practice test which follows.

Sample Answer Sheet

ANSWER SHEET: COMBINATION VEHICLES TEST — PRACTICE SET

Name:_____

SSN:_____

Date:_____

EXAMPLE

X. (A)   B   C   D

---

1. A   B   C   D   17. A   B   C   D

2. A   B   C   D   18. A   B   C   D

3. A   B   C   D   19. A   B   C   D

4. A   B   C   D   20. A   B   C   D

5. A   B   C   D   21. A   B   C   D

6. A   B   C   D   22. A   B   C   D

7. A   B   C   D   23. A   B   C   D

8. A   B   C   D   24. A   B   C   D

9. A   B   C   D   25. A   B   C   D

10. A   B   C   D   26. A   B   C   D

11. A   B   C   D   27. A   B   C   D

12. A   B   C   D   28. A   B   C   D

13. A   B   C   D   29. A   B   C   D

14. A   B   C   D   30. A   B   C   D

15. A   B   C   D   31. A   B   C   D

16. A   B   C   D   32. A   B   C   D

The questions on this test are about safely driving combination vehicles. You must pass this test if you want to drive a combination vehicle such as a tractor-trailer bus.

There is only one correct answer for each question. Answer all questions. Mark your answers on the answer sheet.

1. There are two things that a driver can do to prevent a roll-over. They are: 1) Keep the weight in your truck as close to the ground as possible; and 2):
   A. Make sure that the brakes are properly adjusted.
   B. Keep both hands firmly on the steering wheel.
   C. Drive slowly around turns.
   D. Keep the fifth wheel's free play as tight as possible.

2. There are two things that a driver can do to prevent a roll-over. They are: 1) Drive slowly around turns; and 2):
   A. Make sure that the brakes are properly adjusted.
   B. Keep both hands firmly on the steering wheel.
   C. Keep the weight in your truck as close to the ground as possible.
   D. Keep the fifth wheel's free play as tight as possible.

3. Which of the following statements is true?
   A. The brake and suspension systems of combination vehicles are most effective with a light load.
   B. Always delay braking of a heavy vehicle until you know no other choice.
   C. Light vehicles need more braking power to stop than heavy ones.
   D. "Bobtail" tractors take longer to stop than loaded combination vehicles.

4. When should you use the hand valve to park a combination vehicle?
   A. When you park at loading docks.
   B. When parking for less than two hours.
   C. When parking on a grade.
   D. Never use the hand valve for parking.

5. A device which corrects for brake lag on long air brake vehicles is the:
   A. Quick release valve.
   B. Relay valve.
   C. Front wheel limiting valve.
   D. One-way check valve.

6. Air lines on a truck are often color coded, so you will not mix them up. If they are color coded, the emergency line will be _____ and the service line _____.
   A. Red; blue
   B. Black; yellow
   C. Blue; red
   D. Orange; black

7. Using the hand valve before using the brake pedal to prevent trailer skids in normal driving:
   A. Should not be done.
   B. Results in the least skidding.
   C. Lets the driver steer with both hands.
   D. Is the best method for straight line braking.

8. The hand valve should be used:
   A. As a parking brake.
   B. Only when the trailer is fully loaded.
   C. To test the trailer brakes.
   D. Only if the trailer does not have spring brakes.

9. After you fully charge the tractor air tank, charge the trailer tank by:
   A. Pushing in the trailer air supply valve.
   B. Pulling out the trailer air supply valve.
   C. Connecting only the service line glad hand.
   D. Opening the tractor protection valve by pressing the brake pedal.

10. Why should you lock the glad hands to each other (or dummy couplers) when you are not towing another vehicle?
    A. The air circles back, getting cleaner each cycle.
    B. The connected brake circuit becomes a back-up air tank.
    C. It will keep dirt and water out of the lines.
    D. All of the above

11. You are driving a semi and the trailer breaks away, pulling apart the air lines. You expect the trailer brakes to come on and:
    A. The tractor to lose all air pressure.
    B. The tractor brakes to keep working.
    C. The trailer supply valve to stay open.
    D. Go off about every two seconds.

12. Your emergency air line breaks or gets pulled apart while you are driving. The loss of pressure will cause:
    A. The tractor's air to dump into the trailer tank through the service line.
    B. The emergency trailer brakes to come on.
    C. The air compressor to unload instead of pumping air.
    D. The trailer supply valve to open.

13. If only the service line comes apart while you are driving:
    A. The emergency tractor brakes will come on at once.
    B. The trailer's air tank will exhaust through the open line at once.
    C. The emergency trailer brakes will come on at once.
    D. Nothing may happen until you try to use the brakes.

14. If you use the foot pedal after the service line comes apart:
    A. The loss of pressure can cause the tractor protection valve to close.
    B. Only five stops can be made on the pressure left in the trailer tank.
    C. The trailer's spring brakes will lock on.
    D. The trailer's tank pressure will go to the tractor's system.

15. Air brake equipped trailers made before 1975:
    A. Often do not have spring brakes.
    B. Are more safe to use because they are heavier.
    C. Usually need a glad hand converter.
    D. All of the above

16. Why should you be sure that the fifth wheel has enough grease?
    A. For proper electrical grounding
    B. To prevent steering problems
    C. To keep the brake system in balance
    D. To reduce heat and noise

17. When you get ready to back under the trailer, line up:
    A. About 12 degrees off the line of the trailer.
    B. The kingpin to engage the driver's side locking jaw first.
    C. Directly in front of the trailer.
    D. The left rear outer dual wheel with the kingpin.

18. You are coupling a semitrailer to your tractor but have not yet backed under the tractor. The trailer is at the right height when the:
    A. Kingpin is about 1-1/4 inches above the fifth wheel.
    B. End of the kingpin is even with the top of the fifth wheel.
    C. Trailer is just below the middle of the fifth wheel.
    D. Trailer landing gears are fully extended.

19. You are coupling a tractor to a trailer and have backed up but are not under the tractor. What should you hook up before backing under it?
    A. The electrical service cable.
    B. The emergency and service air lines.
    C. The ground cable.
    D. Nothing. Back up and lock the fifth wheel.

20. After connecting the air lines but before backing under the trailer, you should:
    A. Pull ahead to test the glad hand connections.
    B. Supply air to the trailer system.
    C. Make sure that the trailer brakes are off.
    D. Walk around the rig to be sure that it is clear.

21. After you charge the trailer, check to see that the air lines are not crossed and the trailer brakes work properly by:
    A. Depressing the brake pedal.
    B. Turning on the parking brakes from the cab.
    C. Turning the trailer brakes on and off with the hand valve.
    D. Watching your mirrors to see if the trailer lights come on.

22. You have charged the trailer with the tractor engine off. You should not move the vehicle until the air system is:
    A. Empty.
    B. At normal pressure.
    C. Bled down to half the normal pressure.
    D. Between 60 and 80 psi.

23. Before you back under the trailer, make sure the:
    A. Air brakes are off.
    B. Tractor protection valve is normal.
    C. Trailer brakes are locked.
    D. Air supply knob is in.

24. After you lock the kingpin into the fifth wheel, check the connection by:
    A. Driving away and turning right and left.
    B. Backing up with the trailer brakes released.
    C. Pulling the tractor ahead sharply to release the trailer brakes.
    D. Pulling the tractor ahead gently with the trailer brakes locked.

25. What is the best way to test the tractor-trailer hookup?
    A. Look at it.
    B. Set the trailer wheels then rock the trailer with the tractor.
    C. Set the trailer brakes, and pull gently forward in low gear against the trailer brakes.
    D. Put the tractor in gear and pull ahead with a sharp jerk.

26. What part of the kingpin should the locking jaws close around?
    A. The shank
    B. The head
    C. The base
    D. It does not matter

27. How much space should be between the fifth wheel plate and fifth wheel?
    A. At least 1/2 inch
    B. About 1/4 inch
    C. Just enough to see light through it
    D. None

28. The fifth wheel locking lever is *not* locked after the jaws close around the kingpin. This means that:
    A. The trailer will swivel on the fifth wheel.
    B. You can set the fifth wheel for weight balance.
    C. The parking lock is off, and you may drive away.
    D. The connection is bad. You must fix it before driving.

29. The safety catch for the fifth wheel locking lever must be
_____ for a coupling to be complete.
   A. Straight up
   B. Under the locking lever
   C. Over the locking lever
   D. Through the locking lever

30. You have coupled a tractor with a trailer and want to drive
away. Where do you want the landing gear (front supports)
to be before driving away?
   A. Half-raised with the crank handle secured in its
      bracket.
   B. Three-fourths raised with the crank handle removed.
   C. Fully raised with the crank handle securely in its
      bracket.
   D. Three turns off the top with the crank handle secured
      in its bracket.

31. The landing gears are up and the trailer is resting on the
tractor. Make sure that:
   A. There is enough clearance between the tops of the
      tractor tires and the nose of the trailer.
   B. There is enough clearance between the tractor frame
      and the landing gear.
   C. Neither A nor B
   D. Both A and B

32. Why must you be sure that the lines are not crossed when
you hook up to an older trailer?
   A. The hand valve will apply the tractor brakes if the
      lines are crossed.
   B. The service brakes will work the trailer spring brakes
      instead of the air brakes.
   C. If the trailer has no spring brakes, there are no
      emergency brakes.
   D. The brake lights will come on when you press the
      pedal, but no braking will happen.

Summary

The Combination Vehicles Test applies only to Class A vehicles. Among bus drivers, this test is only for those who intend to drive a tractor-trailer bus.

To qualify for a Class A license with a passenger endorsement, a bus driver must pass the following knowledge tests:

- General Test
- Passenger Test
- Combination Vehicles Test
- Air Brake Test

The driver must get at least 80 percent (80%) of the questions right on each test to pass these knowledge tests.

Upon passing the knowledge tests, the driver must take and pass the performance tests described in Chapters Twelve, Thirteen, and Fourteen.

Holders of a Class A CDL may, with the passenger endorsement, operate all buses within CDL Class A, Class B, and Class C.

REVIEW QUESTIONS

1. What is the purpose of the Combination Vehicles Test?

    _____

    _____

2. The Combination Vehicles Test applies only to what class of commercial motor vehicles?

    _____

3. Who are the only bus drivers who must take this test?

    _____

4. What is a combination vehicle? How much must the vehicle (tractor or truck and trailer) weigh to be classed as a combination under CDL rules?

    _____

    _____

5. To obtain a Class A CDL with a passenger endorsement, what knowledge tests must you pass?

    _____

6. If you pass all the tests required for a Class A CDL with a passenger endorsement, what buses are you allowed to operate?

    _____

    _____

7. Did you answer every question on the practice test? How many questions did you miss? Do you now know the correct answers for these questions?

    _____

**ANSWER KEY
FOR COMBINATION VEHICLES TEST
PRACTICE SET**

1. C		17. C
2. C		18. C
3. D		19. B
4. D		20. B
5. B		21. C
6. A		22. B
7. A		23. C
8. C		24. D
9. A		25. C
10. C		26. A
11. B		27. D
12. B		28. D
13. D		29. C
14. A		30. C
15. A		31. D
16. B		32. C

PART FOUR
PERFORMANCE TEST

There are two basic kinds of CDL Examinations: knowledge test and performance test. This part of the book is about the CDL performance tests. Passing the knowledge test does not mean that you have the technical skill to properly inspect your bus or to drive it safely on the highway. Therefore, the CDL testing program includes several performance tests. A pre-trip inspection test is required for all Class A and Class B buses. A basic control skills test is required for all Class A and Class B vehicles. Finally, a road test is required for all three classes: Class A, Class B, and Class C.

Substitute for Performance Test: It is recognized that commercial motor vehicle drivers are professionals who are, as a group, highly experienced in the skills needed to operate such vehicles. In response to this fact, the CDL rules provide your state with an option. Your state can allow certain drivers to substitute a good driving record and experience for the driving skills test. This option does not apply to the CDL knowledge test.

In general, the option applies only to a driver of a commercial motor vehicle (CMV) who is currently licensed at the time of his or her application for a CDL, and who has either:

    1. A good driving record and has previously passed a state road test in a CMV:

    or

    2. A good driving record in combination with certain types of driving experience.

Check with your state's CDL agency or CDL driver's manual for the details.

These three test are covered in the following chapters

Chapter 12: Vehicle Inspection Test
This chapter covers the parts of the vehicle inspection test. The purpose of this test is to see if you know whether the bus is safe to drive. You will be asked to conduct a thorough inspection of the vehicle you will be using in the driving test. You will be asked to point to or touch the parts you are inspecting and explain what you are looking for. Chapter Twelve will help you learn all of the details of the vehicle inspection test.

Chapter 13: Basic Control Skills Test

This test evaluates your basic skill in controlling the bus. You will be asked to do several backing and parking exercises. The exercises may be given as part of the road test. Chapter Thirteen will let you know what to expect during the test. It will also describe the test exercises and how to practice them.

Chapter 14: Road Test

The road test evaluates your ability to drive safely in most on-the-road situations. The test drive will include, wherever possible, left and right turns, intersections, railway crossings, curves, hills, rural roads, city streets, and expressway driving.

VEHICLE INSPECTION TEST

CHAPTER

Purpose of the Test
General Instructions
Memory Aids
Safety Rules
Inspection Procedures
Examiner's Scoring Standards
Inspection Item Checklist
Inspection Routines
Review Questions

FROM NOW ON,

ONLY THE BEST WILL DRIVE

Chapter Objectives

Help the CDL applicant become familiar with the testing procedures

Explain the purpose of the Vehicle Inspection Test

Provide the applicant with Vehicle Inspection Test Helpers

Describe in detail 64 items that may be inspected

Provide inspection routines for different types of buses

CHAPTER TWELVE

VEHICLE INSPECTION TEST

To get your CDL, you will need to conduct a pre-trip inspection of the bus you will be using for the driving tests. During the inspection, you will have to explain to the examiner what is being inspected and why. The examiner will mark on a scoring form each item that was correctly inspected. This chapter tells you what you need to inspect.

The purpose of the vehicle inspection test is very clear. The examiner needs to find out if you know whether your bus is safe to drive. Another way of looking at this test is that it gives you a way to show that you have the technical knowledge and skill to inspect your bus.

You do not have to be an expert mechanic to do a good inspection, but you must be able to recognize and point to each key part or item that needs to be checked. This chapter should help you do that correctly.

Purpose of the Test

General Instructions

The examiner will give you some general instructions before the test. These instructions will be something like this:

"For the Vehicle Inspection Test, please conduct a thorough inspection of your bus. As you do the inspection, point to or touch the things you are inspecting. Explain to me what you are doing.

"Begin by inspecting the engine compartment. Then start the engine. After you have done the start-up checks, turn off the engine. Then do the rest of the inspection. Go ahead whenever you are ready."

The examiner will ask you if you understand the instructions. Ask questions if you do not understand. The examiner will read the instructions again or explain any points you do not understand.

The examiner wants you to follow these main steps:

1. Inspect the engine compartment

2. Perform in-vehicle checks

3. Shut down the engine

4. Perform the rest of the inspection

These are the main parts of the vehicle inspection test. The examiner will let you inspect individual items in whatever order you like.

Memory Aids

If you want to use a memory aid, most examiners will let you. To make sure, ask your examiner before you use one.

The next pages have Vehicle Inspection Test Helpers that you can use as memory aids. There are three different memory aids. There is one for a tractor-trailer bus, one for a coach/transit bus, and one for a school bus.

**Vehicle
Inspection
Test Helpers**

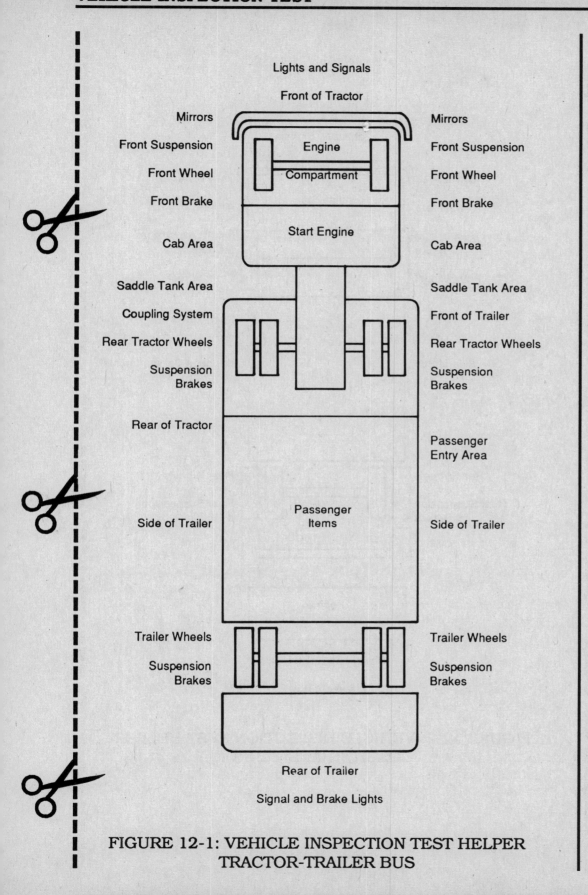

FIGURE 12-1: VEHICLE INSPECTION TEST HELPER
TRACTOR-TRAILER BUS

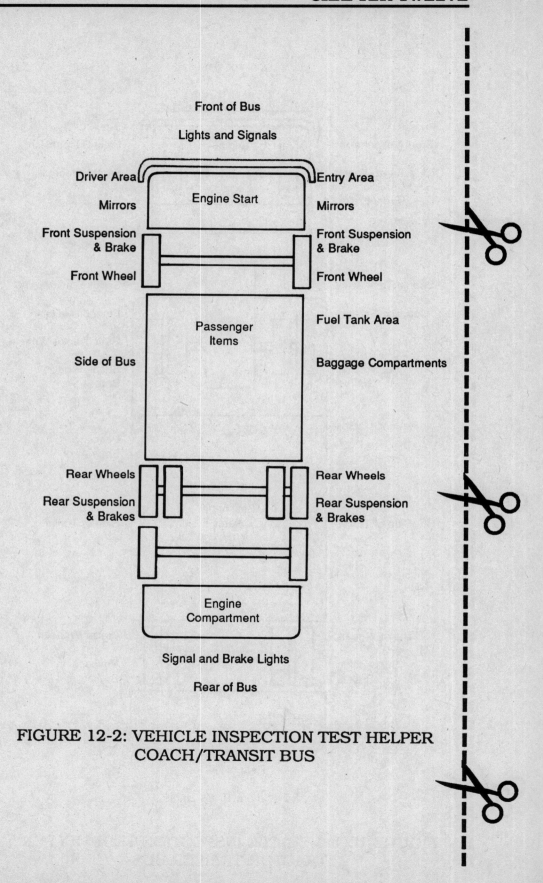

FIGURE 12-2: VEHICLE INSPECTION TEST HELPER
COACH/TRANSIT BUS

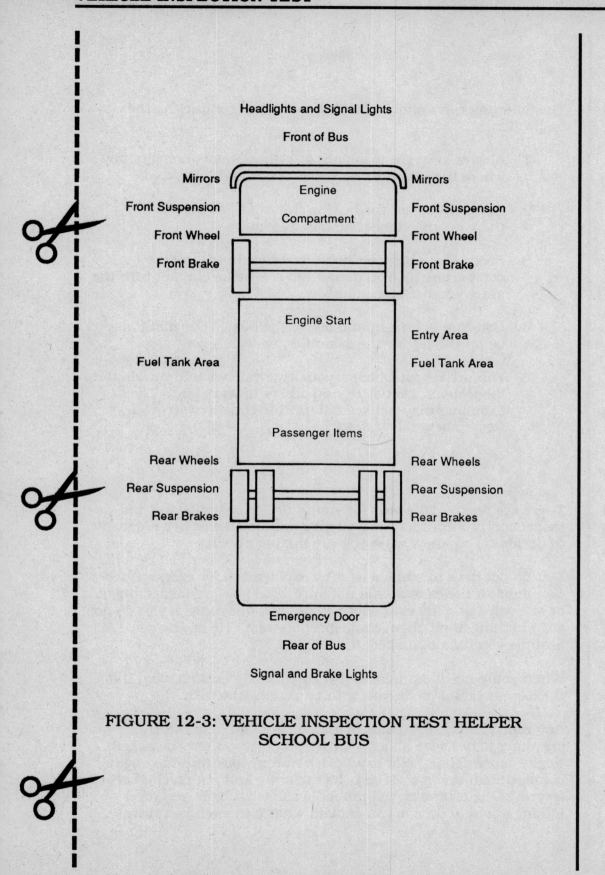

FIGURE 12-3: VEHICLE INSPECTION TEST HELPER
SCHOOL BUS

Safety Rules

The following rules should be observed when conducting the inspection:

1. Always keep the examiner in sight. Make sure you stay where the examiner can always see and hear you.

2. Never get under the bus, in front of it, or behind it if there is any chance the bus may move.

3. Be careful when you point to things in the engine compartment. You do not have to make contact with the parts you are inspecting.

4. Use care getting in and out of the bus. Your mind may be on the test or the examiner, so watch your step.

5. You are responsible for your own safety while you do the inspection. Do not rely on others to warn you. The examiner may not see a hazard in time to warn you. Remember, safety first!

Inspection Procedures

There are no special words for you to use to describe any one inspection procedure. The examiner will use his or her judgment to decide if you know what you are talking about.

You do not have to make a lengthy explanation for every inspection item. If the examiner is not sure what you are inspecting, he or she will ask. The examiner will not ask questions if you do not say anything at all about an inspection item. He or she will assume you did not inspect it.

When you point to an item and then correctly explain what it is, the examiner will credit you with inspecting the item.

Any time you inspect (point to and explain) an item but the examiner is not sure about your inspection, you may be asked to give more details. For example, you may look into the engine compartment and say, "The belts are snug and not cracked or frayed." The examiner will probably ask what belts you are talking about and have you explain what part each belt drives.

You may also be asked for more details if you point to an item, say its name, and just say it is in good condition. For example, you may say, "The brake chamber looks OK." The examiner will probably ask you how you know the brake chamber is in good condition.

The Examiner's Scoring Standards, which follow, will give you some pointers on what to look for and what to explain during your pre-trip inspection test.

Here is a review of the inspection procedures.

1. The examiner provides the instructions.

2. Begin the inspection when you are ready. Follow these steps:

    A. Inspect the engine compartment.

    B. Perform the in-vehicle checks.

    C. Shut down the engine after completing the engine checks.

    D. Conduct the passenger compartment checks.

    E. Perform the rest of the inspection.

3. As you inspect each item:

    A. Point to the item.

    B. Say the name of the item you are inspecting.

    C. Tell the examiner what you are looking for.

    D. Tell the examiner what you find.

This section shows you what the examiner may use to score your inspection. There are 64 inspection items listed. The items are listed in alphabetical order. For each item, there is a description and a scoring standard. The examiner uses information like this to decide if you have correctly inspected an item.

Examiner's Scoring Standards

The standards give the features or symptoms that show whether an item is in safe condition. You should be able to recognize and explain these key features or symptoms.

You do not have to give a word-for-word description of what the standards say. Use your own words. It is the examiner's job to judge whether you understand what to look for and if you can recognize when an item is unsafe. This listing should help you review what you must look for and recognize.

As you review the listing, remember that some items will not apply to you. For example, your bus may not have air brakes. Remember also that this is an examiner's listing. There will be items that apply only to tractor-trailers and trucks.

As you review, it may be helpful to place a checkmark by those items which apply to the bus you will be inspecting. You will need to inspect these items during your CDL pre-trip inspection test. Make sure you can describe the item and explain the inspection procedure because that is the standard on which you will be scored.

The 64 Inspection Items

1. AIR BRAKE CHECK

   Description: The procedure the driver uses to check the air brake system.

   Scoring Standard: The driver performs air brake system check in the following manner:

   A) Lets the air pressure build to the governed cut-out pressure. This should occur between 100-125 pounds per square inch (psi).

   B) With the engine off, wheels chocked, and parking brake released, the driver should fully apply the foot brake to see if the air pressure drops more than three pounds in one minute (single vehicle) or more than four pounds in one minute (combination unit). If the loss exceeds this amount, there is a defect somewhere in the system.

C)   Starts fanning off the air pressure by rapidly applying and releasing the foot brake: the low air pressure warning alarm should activate before the air pressure drops below 60 psi.

D)   Continues to fan off the air pressure: at approximately 40 pounds pressure on a tractor trailer, the tractor protection valve should close (pop out); on other vehicle types, the spring brake push-pull valve should pop.

Note: Air brake check procedures vary from vehicle to vehicle, and different drivers may have learned different ways. However, all procedures are designed to see that the safety devices operate at the correct times as the air pressure drops from normal to a nearly complete loss of air pressure.

2.   AIR BUZZER OR WARNING

Description: Low air pressure warning

Scoring Standard: The air pressure buzzer should be working. If it is, the warning will sound immediately after the engine starts but before the air compressor has built up pressure. The driver should let the air pressure build to the governed cut-out pressure. This should occur between 100-125 psi: The low air pressure warning should stop when the air pressure gets above 60 psi.

3.   AIR COMPRESSOR BELT

Description: Drives air compressor to maintain air pressure in air brake system

Scoring Standard: With the engine off, the driver points to, touches, or presses the belt to test that it is snug. The driver notes that the belt is not frayed, has no visible cracks, loose fibers, or signs of wear. If the belt appears worn or loose, the driver should push the belt with his or her hand. If it deflects more than 1/2 to 3/4 of an inch, the slippage is probably excessive.

Note: Check to see that the driver is inspecting the right belt. The compressor may not be belt driven — mark the item correct if the driver mentions this. Cross it off if there is no belt and the driver says nothing.

4. AIR LEAK

   Description: If present, will be in air brake and air suspension systems

   Scoring Standard: No air leaks can be heard from the air brake system or from the suspension system air bags.

5. AIR AND ELECTRIC LINES

   Description: Carry air and electricity to the trailer

   Scoring Standard: The driver checks that the air hoses are not cut, cracked, chafed, or worn (steel braid does not show through) and listens for audible air leaks. Air and electrical lines should not be tangled, crimped or pinched, or dragging against tractor parts. The wire covering is not cut, cracked, chafed, or worn (no wire showing through). None of the air or electrical lines should be spliced or taped.

6. AIR AND ELECTRIC CONNECTORS

   Description: Connect air supplies and electrical power to the trailer

   Scoring Standard: The driver checks that trailer air connectors are sealed and in good condition; checks that the glad hands are free of damage and locked in place, and there are no audible air leaks. Checks that the trailer electrical plug is firmly seated and locked in place.

7. AMMETER OR VOLTMETER

   Description: Shows if generator or alternator is functioning

   Scoring Standard: The driver checks the gauge that shows the alternator or generator is charging (warning light is off); then the needle jumps and flutters, then registers "charge."

8. **AXLE SEALS**

   Description: Seals for axle/wheel assembly lubrication

   Scoring standard: The driver checks to be sure there are no cracks or distortions in the wheel/axle mounting and no signs of leaking lubricants.

9. **BRAKE CHAMBER**

   Description: Converts air pressure to mechanical force to operate wheel brakes

   Scoring Standard: A check is made to be sure it is not cracked or dented, and it is securely mounted.

10. **BRAKE DRUM**

    Description: Mounting and container for brake shoes

    Scoring Standard: There should be no cracks, dents or holes and no loose or missing bolts.

11. **BRAKE HOSES**

    Description: Carry air or hydraulic fluid to wheel brake assembly

    Scoring Standard: Driver checks for cracked, worn, or frayed hoses and for secure couplings.

12. **BRAKE LININGS**

    Description: Brake shoe friction linings

    Scoring Standard: On some brake drums, there are openings where the brake linings can be seen from outside the drum. For this type of drum, the applicant should check that a visible amount of brake lining is showing. Do not score if a backing plate fully encloses the brake shoe assembly.

13. CAB CATWALK

Description: Platform at the rear of a tractor cab for the driver to stand on when connecting or disconnecting trailer lines

Scoring Standard: The catwalk is solid, securely bolted to tractor frame, and clear of loose objects.

14. COOLANT LEVEL

Description: Coolant is the fluid that cools the engine.

Scoring Standard: The driver looks at the sight glass of the reservoir or removes the radiator cap and looks to see the level (see note). An adequate level will show in the sight glass or be visible in the radiator when the cap is removed.

Note: If the engine is hot, do not let the driver remove the radiator cap. If there is no sight glass, mark the item correct if the driver indicates that he or she would remove the cap. Mark as incorrect if the driver removes radiator cap when a sight glass is available.

15. CLUTCH DEPRESSED (Before Starting Engine)

Description: Reduces load on starting motor

Scoring Standard: The driver depresses the clutch before turning on the starter and keeps it depressed until the engine reaches idling speed.

Note: Cross out this item if the vehicle has an automatic transmission.

16. DOORS CLOSED (Baggage Compartment of Bus)

Description: Bus baggage compartment doors and other doors or hatches not used by passengers

Scoring Standard: The baggage compartment doors should be securely closed. The doors should not be bent or broken; the hinges secure; and the latches secure and fully closed.

17. DRIVE SHAFT

   Description: Transmits power from the transmission to the drive axle

   Scoring Standard: The shaft should not be bent or cracked; the shaft couplings should appear to be secure.

18. EXHAUST SYSTEM

   Description: Pipes for carrying exhaust gases from the engine

   Scoring Standard: The driver checks to see that the outside visible parts are securely mounted and have no cracks, holes, or severe dents.

19. FRAME

   Description: Structure for supporting the vehicle body or trailer platform over wheels

   Scoring Standard: Checks to be sure there are no cracks or bends in the long part of the frame; no loose, cracked, bent, broken or missing cross pieces; no signs of breaks or holes in the body or bus floor.

20. FUEL TANK

   Description: Holds fuel

   Scoring Standard: The driver checks to be sure the tank is secure, the caps are secure, there are no leaks, and the tank is not damaged.

21. GEARSHIFT IN NEUTRAL (When starting engine)

   Description: Keeps engine power from causing the vehicle to move during engine start-up

   Scoring Standard: The driver checks to see that the gearshift is in neutral before starting the engine.

   Note: Do not score for automatic transmission.

22. GENERATOR BELT

Description: Drives the alternator or generator

Scoring Standard: With the engine off, the driver points to, touches, or presses the belt to test that the belt is snug. He or she should also note that the belt is not frayed and has no visible cracks, loose fibers, or signs of wear. The driver should push the belt with his or her hand. If the belt sags more than 1/2 to 3/4 of an inch there is probably too much slippage.

Note: Check to be sure the driver is inspecting the correct belt.

23. HEATER AND DEFROSTER

Description. Heats cab or passenger compartment; prevents frost from forming on windshield

Scoring Standard: The driver checks to see that the heater and defroster are working.

24. HORN(S)

Description: Air and/or electrical horns for warning other drivers or pedestrians

Scoring Standard: The driver checks electric and/or air horns to be sure they work.

25. HUB OIL SEAL

Description: Seals in lubrication for the wheel hub

Scoring Standard: The driver checks to see that the wheel hub oil seal is not leaking and, if there is a sight glass, that the oil level is adequate.

26. KINGPIN AND APRON

Description: Attaches trailer to tractor (kingpin) and provides a surface for resting the trailer on the fifth wheel

Scoring Standard: The driver checks to be sure the kingpin does not appear to be bent; that the apron lies flat on the fifth wheel skid plate; and that the visible part of the apron is not bent, cracked or broken.

27. LANDING GEAR

Description: Supports the front end of the trailer when the trailer is not coupled to a tractor.

Scoring Standard: The driver checks to be sure the landing gears are fully raised, there are no missing parts, the support frame is not bent or damaged; and the crank handle is present and secured. If the landing gear is power operated, it must be checked for air or hydraulic leaks.

28. LEAKS (ENGINE)

Description: Fluid leaks from the engine

Scoring Standard: The driver checks for fluid puddles or dripping fluids on the ground under the engine and on the underside of the engine.

29. LEAKS (FUEL)

Description: Leaks from the fuel tanks

Scoring Standard: The driver checks for any leaks from the fuel tanks.

Note: Signs of spillage from overfilling a fuel tank are not to be treated as a fuel leak.

30. LIGHTING INDICATORS

   Description: The dashboard indicator lights for signals, flashers, and the headlight's high beam

   Scoring Standard: The driver checks to see that the indicators illuminate when the respective lights are turned on.

31. LIGHTS (BRAKE)

   Description: Front and rear brake lights

   Scoring Standard: The driver checks to be sure both brake lights come on when the brakes are applied.

32. LIGHTS (FRONT OF VEHICLE)

   Description: Headlights, parking lights, and forward clearance lights

   Scoring Standard: The driver checks to see if the headlights function on both the high and low beams, and the parking lights function both as parking lights and as left and right signals.

   Note: The driver may mix checks of lighting functions in with other parts of the inspection. There is no requirement to check lights in a specific order. The examiner must keep track of which lights are checked.

33. LIGHTS (REFLECTOR)

Description: Lights and reflectors for showing vehicle clearances at night

Scoring Standard: The driver checks to see if the reflectors are clean; that none are missing or broken, and they are of proper color (red on rear, amber elsewhere). He or she also checks to make sure the clearance lights work, are clean, not broken, and of the proper color (red on rear, amber elsewhere). Checks the rear running lights to see that they are clean, not broken, and are of proper color. Rear running lights must be checked separately from the signal, flasher, and brake lights.

Note: Checks of running lights and clearance lights may be done at different times in the inspection. The examiner must keep track of the lighting functions that are checked.

34. LIGHTS (SIGNAL)

Description: Rear signal lights and four-way flashers

Scoring Standard: The driver checks to be sure each signal flashes and that the four-way flashers work.

35. LOCKING PINS (FIFTH WHEEL)

Description: Hold the sliding fifth wheel in a fixed position along the slider rails

Scoring Standard: The driver looks for loose or missing pins in the slide mechanism of the sliding fifth wheel; if it is air powered, he or she makes sure there are no air leaks. He or she also checks that the fifth wheel is not so far forward that the tractor frame will strike the landing gear during turns.

36. LUG NUTS

Description: Hold wheel on axle

Scoring Standard: The driver checks that all lug nuts are present; lugs are not loose (look for rust trails around nuts); there are no cracks radiating from lug bolt holes or distortion of the bolt holes.

37. MIRRORS

Description: Side mirrors for rear view of traffic

Scoring Standard: The driver checks for proper adjustment; that it is not cracked or loose (fittings); the visibility is not impaired due to dirty mirrors.

38. MOUNTING BOLTS (FIFTH WHEEL)

Description: Hold fifth wheel mount on tractor frame

Scoring Standard: The driver looks for loose or missing mounting brackets, clamps, bolts, or nuts; and that both the fifth wheel and slide mounting appear solidly attached in place.

39. OIL LEVEL

Description: Dipstick used to measure amount of oil for engine lubrication

Scoring Standard: With the engine stopped, the driver pulls out the dip stick and sees where the oil level is relative to the full or refill mark. The level must be above the refill mark.

40. OIL PRESSURE

Description: Ensures that engine oil is flowing

Scoring Standard: The driver checks that oil pressure is building to normal; the gauge shows increasing or normal oil pressure; the warning light goes off. The engine oil temperature should begin a gradual rise to the normal operating range.

41. PARKING BRAKE

Description: Keeps vehicle from rolling when parked

Scoring Standard: The driver checks that the parking brake will hold the vehicle by trying to pull the vehicle forward with the parking brake on.

42. PASSENGER EMERGENCY EXITS

    Description: Bus doors, roof hatches, or push-out windows used for emergency exits

    Scoring Standard: The driver checks that all emergency exit doors can be opened, and that they are firmly closed.

43. PASSENGER ENTRY

    Description: Bus door(s) used for normal entry or exit

    Scoring Standard: The door correctly opens and locks are closed; the entry steps are clear; treads are not loose or worn out enough to trip a passenger.

44. PASSENGER SEATING

    Description: Passenger seats

    Scoring Standard: No broken seat frames; all seats are firmly attached to the floor.

45. PLATFORM (FIFTH WHEEL)

    Description: Mounting holding the fifth wheel skid plate and locking jaws mechanism

    Scoring Standard: No cracks or breaks in the platform structure.

46. POWER STEERING FLUID

    Description: Hydraulic fluid that assists front wheels to respond to steering wheel action

    Scoring Standard: With the engine stopped, the driver pulls out the dip stick and sees where the fluid level is relative to the refill mark. The level must be above the refill mark.

47. RELEASE ARM (FIFTH WHEEL)

Description: Releases fifth wheel locking jaws so that the trailer can be uncoupled

Scoring Standard: The driver checks that release arm is in the engaged position and any safety latch is in place.

48. RIMS

Description: Keep the tires on the wheels

Scoring Standard: The driver checks for damaged or bent rims; rims should not have welding repairs or rust trails that indicate the rim is loose on the wheel (also see lug nuts).

49. SAFETY LATCH (FIFTH WHEEL)

Description: Locks locking jaws closed

Scoring Standard: The driver checks that the safety latch is engaged.

50. SAFETY AND EMERGENCY EQUIPMENT

Description: Equipment for use during a breakdown or at an accident scene

Scoring Standard: The driver checks for fuses, flares, red reflective triangles, and a properly charged and rated fire extinguisher. (Optional items: snow chains, tire changing equipment, spare lamps, bulbs, electrical tape, flashlight, pliers, screwdriver, wire, tire pressure gauge)

51. SHOCK ABSORBERS

Description: Tubular piston devices which damp out the extreme forces on wheels created by severe road bumps

Scoring Standard: The driver checks for loose or broken mountings and leaks from the shock absorbers.

52. **SLACK ADJUSTERS**

Description: Linkage from brake chamber to brake shoe which activates brakes

Scoring Standard: The driver checks for broken, loose, or missing parts. The angle between push rod and adjuster arm should be a little over 90 degrees when brakes are released, and not less than 90 degrees when brakes are applied.

53. **SPACERS (WHEEL)**

Description: The axle collar between the dual wheels which keeps the wheels evenly separated

Scoring Standard: The driver checks that dual wheels are evenly separated and that the tires are not touching one another.

54. **SPLASH GUARDS**

Description: Flaps mounted behind exposed dual wheels to prevent the wheels from throwing up water or debris from road

Scoring Standard: The driver checks that splash guards are present if required; are properly fastened; and not chaffing the wheels.

Note: Different states have different regulations about splash guard requirements. You must know the requirements of your state.

55. **SPRINGS**

Description: Leaf or coil springs which allow the axles to move up and down as the road surface changes

Scoring Standard: The driver looks for broken leaves, leaves that have shifted and are in, or nearly in, contact with the tires, rim, brake drum, frame or body; missing or broken leaves in the leaf spring (if one fourth or more of the leaves are missing, vehicle is out of service). For coil springs, the driver looks for broken or distorted springs.

56. SPRING MOUNTINGS

Description: All brackets, bolts, and bushings used for attaching the spring to the axle and vehicle frame

Scoring Standard: The driver checks for cracked or broken spring hangers; broken, missing, or loose bolts; missing or damaged bushings; broken, loose, or missing axle mounting parts.

57. STEERING BOX

Description: Container for the mechanism that transforms steering column action into wheel turning action

Scoring Standard: The driver looks for missing nuts, bolts, cotter keys, etc.; power steering fluid leaks; of damage to the power steering hose. The driver checks to be sure the steering box is secure.

58. STEERING LINKAGE

Description: Transmits steering action from the steering box to the wheel

Scoring Standard: The driver checks to be sure the connecting links, arms, and rods are not worn or cracked; joints and sockets are not worn or loose; and there are no loose or missing nuts or bolts.

59. STEERING PLAY

Description: Procedure to check for excessive looseness in the steering linkages

Scoring Standard: Non-power steering — the driver works the steering wheel back and forth. It should have less than 5-10 degrees of free play. Power steering — with engine running, the driver works the steering wheel from left to right and notes the degree of free play that occurs before the left front wheel barely moves. This should be less than 5-10 degrees.

60. TIRES

Description: Road wheel tires

Scoring Standard: The driver checks tread depth (see note); tire inflation (see note); to see if the tread is evenly worn; looks for cuts or other damage to the tread or walls; checks to see that the valve caps and stems are not missing, broken or damaged; the retread is not separating from the tire (no retreads on front wheels).

Note: Minimum tread depth is 4/32 inch on the front tires and 2/32 inch on the other tires. A proper check of inflation requires the use of a tire pressure gauge. A tire mallet can be used to check to be sure the tire is not flat. Score as incorrect if the applicant kicks a tire to see if it is flat.

61. TORSION BAR

Description: The steel bar, rod, or arm assembly that acts as a spring instead of using a leaf or coil spring that is usually on the rear tractor wheels

Scoring Standard: The driver checks that the torsion bar assembly or torque arm is not cracked, broken or missing.

62. WATER PUMP BELT

Description: The belt for driving the engine water pump

Scoring Standard: With the engine off, driver points to, touches, or presses the belt to test that it is snug. The driver should note that the belt is not frayed, there are no visible cracks, loose fibers, or signs of wear. If the belt appears worn or loose, the driver should push the belt with his or her hand. If it deflects more than 1/2 to 3/4 of an inch, the slippage is probably excessive.

Note: Check to be sure the driver is inspecting the correct belt.

63.   WINDSHIELD

Description: Glass in front of the driver through which he or she sees

Scoring Standard: The driver checks for cracks, dirt, illegal stickers, or other obstructions which could obscure the driver's view.

64.   WIPERS

Description: Windshield wipers

Scoring Standard: The driver checks for worn rubber on the blades; that the blades are secure on the wiper arm; and the wipers work.

Inspection Item Checklist

After you have reviewed each of the 64 items, you should check your bus. Which of the items are found on the type of bus you will be using for the CDL tests? Use the form on the next page to identify them. Place a check mark in the blank next to each item is found on your bus.

Passing the inspection test will depend on how thorough you are. In other words, you cannot afford to overlook an item that needs to be inspected. Make sure you know what items are found on your bus. If you are not sure, you are not ready for the test.

ITEM	ITEM	ITEM
___ 1. Air Brake Check	___22. Generator Belt	___44. Passenger Seating
___ 2. Air Buzzer or Warning	___23. Heater and Defroster	___45. Platform (Fifth Wheel)
___ 3. Air Compressor Belt	___24. Horn(s)	___46. Power Steering Fluid
___ 4. Air Leak	___25. Hub Oil Seal	___47. Release Arm (Fifth Wheel)
___ 5. Air and Electric Lines	___26. King Pin and Apron	___48. Rims
___ 6. Air and Electric Connectors	___27. Landing Gear	___49. Safety Latch (Fifth Wheel)
___ 7. Ammeter or Voltmeter	___28. Leaks (Engine)	___50. Safety and Emergency Equipment
___ 8. Axle Seals	___29. Leaks (Fuel)	___51. Shock Absorbers
___ 9. Brake Chamber	___30. Lighting Indicators	___52. Slack Adjusters
___10. Brake Drum	___31. Lights (Brake)	___53. Spacers (Wheel)
___11. Brake Hoses	___32. Lights (Front of Vehicle)	___54. Splash Guards
___12. Brake Linings	___33. Lights (Reflectors)	___55. Springs
___13. Cab Catwalk	___34. Lights (Signal)	___56. Spring Mountings
___14. Coolant Level	___35. Locking Pins (Fifth Wheel)	___57. Steering Box
___15. Clutch Depressed	___36. Lug Nuts	___58. Steering Linkage
___16. Doors Closed	___37. Mirrors	___59. Steering Play
___17. Drive Shaft	___38. Mounting Bolts (Fifth Wheel)	___60. Tires
___18. Exhaust System	___39. Oil Level	___61. Torsion Bar
___19. Frame	___40. Oil Pressure	___62. Water Pump Belt
___20. Fuel Tank	___41. Parking Brake	___63. Windshield
___21. Gearshift in Neutral	___42. Emergency Exits	___64. Wipers
	___43. Passenger Entry	

FIGURE 12-4: INSPECTION ITEM CHECKLIST

Inspection Routines

To make sure you do a thorough inspection, you should plan your inspection routine. A suggested routine for each major bus is outlined in the charts which follow.

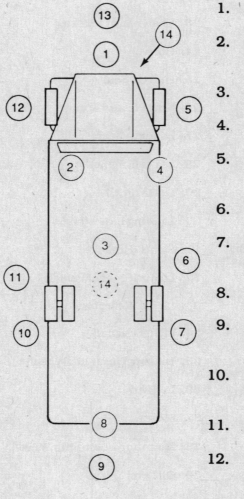

1.   Engine Compartment Checks

2.   Engine Start —
     Instrument and Controls Check

3.   Passenger Items

4.   Passenger Entry Area

5.   Front Right Wheel,
     Suspension and Brake Checks

6.   Right Side of Bus Checks

7.   Rear Right Wheel,
     Suspension and Brake Check

8.   Emergency Exit Check

9.   Rear of Bus —
     Signal and Brake Lights

10.   Rear Left Wheel,
      Suspension and Brake Checks

11.   Left Side of Bus Checks

12.   Front Left Wheel,
      Suspension and Brake Checks

13.   Front of Bus —
      Lights, Signals and Mirrors

14.   Under Vehicle Checks —
      Front and Rear

FIGURE 12-5:
SUGGESTED INSPECTION ROUTINE:
SCHOOL BUS (CONVENTIONAL)

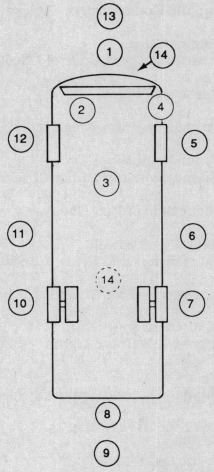

1. Engine Compartment Checks

2. Engine Start —
    Instrument and Control Checks

3. Passenger Items

4. Passenger Entry Area

5. Front Right Wheel,
    Suspension and Brake Checks

6. Baggage Compartment and
    Side Checks

7. Rear Right Wheel,
    Suspension and Brake Checks

8. Emergency Exit Checks

9. Rear Checks —
    Signal and Brake Lights

10. Rear Left Wheel,
    Suspension and Brake Checks

11. Left Side of Bus Checks

12. Left Front Wheel,
    Suspension and Brake Checks

13. Front Checks — Lights,
    Signals and Mirrors

14. Under Vehicle Checks

FIGURE 12-6:
SUGGESTED INSPECTION ROUTINE:
SCHOOL BUS (TRANSIT TYPE)

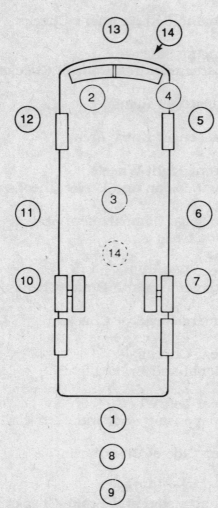

1. Engine Compartment Checks

2. Engine Start —
    Instrument and Control Checks

3. Passenger Items

4. Passenger Entry Area

5. Front Right Wheel,
    Suspension and Brake Checks

6. Right Side of Bus Checks

7. Rear Right Wheel,
    Suspension and Brake Checks

8. Emergency Exit Checks

9. Rear Checks —
    Signal and Brake Lights

10. Rear Left Wheel,
    Suspension and Brake Checks

11. Left Side of Bus Checks

12. Front Left Wheel,
    Suspension and Brake Checks

13. Front Checks —
    Lights, Signals and Mirrors

14. Under Vehicle Checks —
    Front and Rear

FIGURE 12-7:
SUGGESTED INSPECTION ROUTINE:
INTERCITY BUS (COACH)

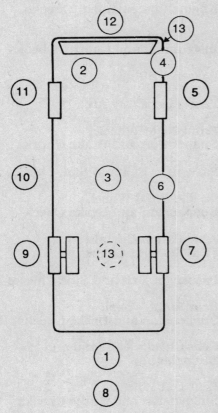

1. Engine Compartment Checks

2. Engine Start —
   Instrument and Control Checks

3. Passenger Items

4. Passenger Entry Area

5. Front Right Wheel,
   Suspension and Brake Check

6. Passenger Exit and
   Side of Bus Check

7. Rear Right Wheel,
   Suspension and Brake Checks

8. Rear Checks —
   Signal and Brake Lights

9. Rear Left Wheel,
   Suspension and Brake Checks

10. Left Side of Bus Check

11. Front Left Wheel,
    Suspension and Brake Checks.

12. Front Checks — Lights,
    Signals and Mirrors

13. Under Vehicle Checks

FIGURE 12-8:
SUGGESTED INSPECTION ROUTINE:
TRANSIT BUS

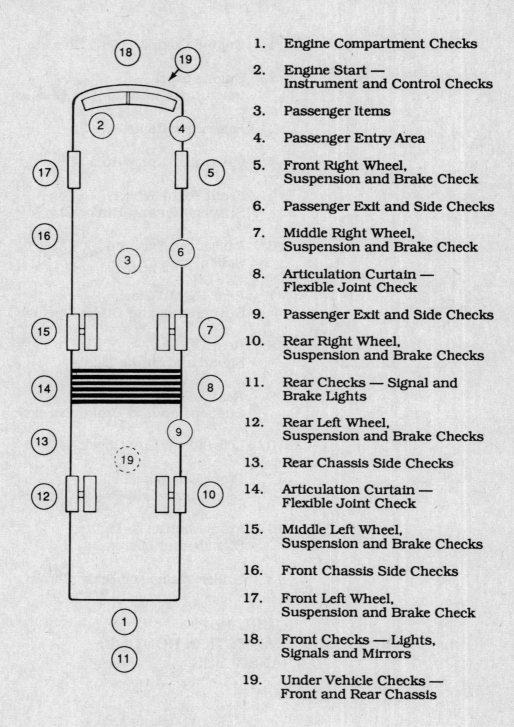

1. Engine Compartment Checks

2. Engine Start —
   Instrument and Control Checks

3. Passenger Items

4. Passenger Entry Area

5. Front Right Wheel,
   Suspension and Brake Check

6. Passenger Exit and Side Checks

7. Middle Right Wheel,
   Suspension and Brake Check

8. Articulation Curtain —
   Flexible Joint Check

9. Passenger Exit and Side Checks

10. Rear Right Wheel,
    Suspension and Brake Checks

11. Rear Checks — Signal and
    Brake Lights

12. Rear Left Wheel,
    Suspension and Brake Checks

13. Rear Chassis Side Checks

14. Articulation Curtain —
    Flexible Joint Check

15. Middle Left Wheel,
    Suspension and Brake Checks

16. Front Chassis Side Checks

17. Front Left Wheel,
    Suspension and Brake Check

18. Front Checks — Lights,
    Signals and Mirrors

19. Under Vehicle Checks —
    Front and Rear Chassis

FIGURE 12-9:
SUGGESTED INSPECTION ROUTINE:
ARTICULATED BUS

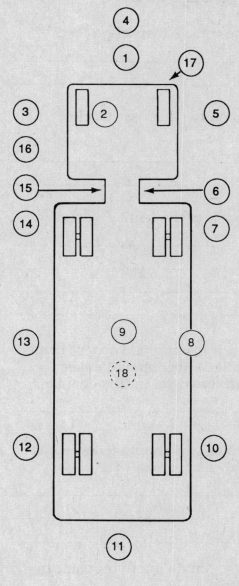

1. Engine Compartment Checks

2. Engine Start — Instrument and Control Checks

3. Front Left Tractor Wheel, Suspension and Brake Checks

4. Front of Tractor Checks — Lights, Signals and Mirrors

5. Front Right Tractor Wheels, Suspension and Brake Checks

6. Rear of Tractor Checks — Air/Electric Links, Coupling System Checks

7. Rear Right Tractor Wheels, Suspension and Brake Checks

8. Passenger Doors, Right Side Trailer Checks

9. Passenger Items

10. Right Tractor Wheels, Suspension and Brakes Check

11. Rear Checks, Signal and Brake Lights and Splash Guards.

12. Left Trailer Wheels, Suspension and Brake Checks

13. Left Side Tractor Check

14. Rear Left Tractor Wheels, Suspension and Brake Checks

15. Rear of Engine — Exhaust System, Frame Drive Shaft Check

16. Cab Area Checks — Both Sides — Saddle Tank

17. Under Tractor Checks

18. Under Trailer Checks

FIGURE 12-10:
SUGGESTED INSPECTION ROUTINE:
TRACTOR-TRAILER BUS

REVIEW QUESTIONS

1. What is the purpose of the vehicle inspection test?

   _____

   _____

2. What must you be able to do to pass the vehicle inspection test?

   _____

   _____

3. What are the four main parts of the test?

   _____

   _____

   _____

   _____

4. You may be allowed to use a memory aid or test helper during the vehicle inspection. How many Vehicle Inspection Test Helpers are provided in this chapter?

   _____

5. What are the five safety rules you should follow when conducting the inspection?

   _____

   _____

   _____

6. During the test, what must you do after you point to the items you are inspecting?

   _____

7. There is a list of 64 inspection items provided in the chapter. This is the examiner's list. Some of the items may not apply to your bus. Have you filled out the Inspection Item Checklist? How many items apply to your bus?

   _____

BASIC CONTROL SKILLS TEST

CHAPTER

FROM NOW ON,

ONLY THE BEST WILL DRIVE

Chapter Objectives

Help the CDL applicant become familiar with testing procedures

Provide sample exercises so the applicant may practice his or her driving skills

Define pass/fail standards

CHAPTER THIRTEEN

BASIC CONTROL SKILLS TEST

After you pass the required knowledge tests, you will take the CDL performance tests. One of the performance tests you will need to pass is the Basic Control Skills Test. This chapter will tell you about this test.

The test may include as many as seven test exercises. Each exercise is a test of your basic driving skill. You should practice these exercises. The skills you learn will help you pass the test and they will help you be a better driver.

The purpose of the test is to evaluate your basic driving skills. It is a test of your ability to control and maneuver your bus.

You must pass the Basic Control Skills Test if you intend to drive a Class A or Class B bus. In some cases, when applying for a Class A or B license, the driver may submit a Certificate of Driving Experience instead of taking a driving test. This certificate must be completed by an employer. The employer must be authorized by the State to issue such certificates. You will need to check with your employer for more information on the Certificates of Driving Experience and Training.

Purpose of the Basic Control Skills Test

Test Exercises

This test consists of various exercises to be completed in an area marked by traffic cones and boundary lines. The exercises may include the following kinds of maneuvers:

- A measured right turn.

- Driving forward into an alley or designated location and stopping close to the front of the alley or at a designated spot.

- Backing in a straight line.

- Backing into the alley from the sight (left) side to simulate docking.

- Backing into a parallel parking space from the sight (left) side.

- Backing into a parallel parking space from the conventional (curb or right) side.

- Backing around markers, beginning and ending with markers on the left side (serpentine).

The examiner will explain the rules to you. You will be scored on your ability to properly perform each exercise.

Sample Test Instructions

At the beginning of the test, the examiner will give you instructions such as these:

"This test consists of a series of basic control exercises.

"Try not to go over any exercise lines or hit any of the cones. Try to keep pullups to a minimum. However, remember it is better to do a pullup than to go over a boundary.

"The foot of each cone or marker marks the exercise boundary, so if a wheel passes over the foot of a cone, that counts the same as going over the exercise boundary.

"I will give you directions for each exercise as we come to it.

"When you complete each exercise, tap your horn to let me know.

"In all of the exercises, I will act as a driver's assistant to see that you do not accidentally run over any markers or barriers or come into conflict with any other vehicles.

"If you see me raise my arm like this (examiner raises arm straight up, palm out), stop the vehicle."

FIGURE 13-1: STOP SIGNAL

The Basic Control Skills Test exercises may be given at a single site or at several sites. Different sites may be used for the different exercises. They may be done off-road or on a road with very little, if any, traffic.

Test Site

The exercises may be conducted at an off-road site, and the road test on surface streets. The off-road site may be a large, paved lot like a parking area or a training ground. The on-street site will be a paved road with light traffic, such as an industrial area.

In either case, the test area will be suitable for heavy vehicles and must have the necessary overhead clearance. For off-road areas, boundary lines may be painted or marked with tape to help you. Cones or other markers will be used to mark the corners of the exercises. At on-street sites, cones or markers will be used.

Pullups and Errors

For each exercise, there is a list of things that can be scored. These are explained in detail in the Pass-Fail Standards section. The two most common scoring factors are pullups and errors in controlling the vehicle.

Pullups

When you intentionally stop and reverse direction to get a better position or make a correction, it is counted as a "pullup." Stopping without changing direction is not usually counted as a pullup. The examiner will keep track of each pullup or correction you make during an exercise.

Control Errors

If you touch or cross an exercise boundary line or hit a fixture (cone or marker) with the vehicle, it is counted as a control error. Control errors are scored or counted in the same way as pullups.

Doing the Exercises

The Basic Control Skills Test may include as many as seven test exercises. They are:

1. Right Turn.
2. Forward Stop.
3. Straight Line Backing.
4. Alley Dock.
5. Parallel Park (Sight Side).
6. Parallel Park (Right Side).
7. Backward Serpentine.

The details and scoring rules for each exercise may vary from state to state, so you will need to find out how your state does it. A general description of each exercise follows.

1. Right Turn

You will be asked to drive forward and make a right turn around a cone or marker. Your rear wheels should come as close as possible to the cone or marker without touching it.

This is what the examiner may tell you to do:

"Drive slowly forward and make a right turn around that cone. Try to bring your rear wheels as close to the cone as you can without hitting it. I will walk up to the cone. When I wave you forward, come ahead and make the turn."

After waving you forward, the examiner will check the clearance of your rear wheels coming around the cone.

The examiner will record the results on a scoring form. He or she will note how close you came to the cone, if you hit the cone, and if you needed to make a pullup to complete the turn.

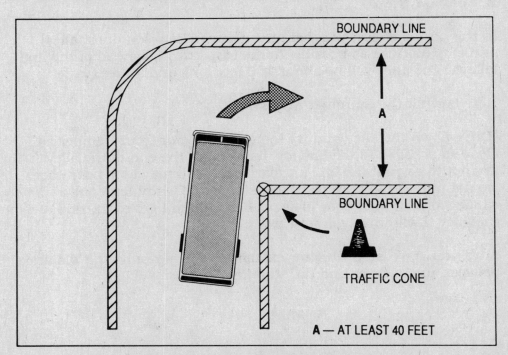

FIGURE 13-2: THE RIGHT TURN

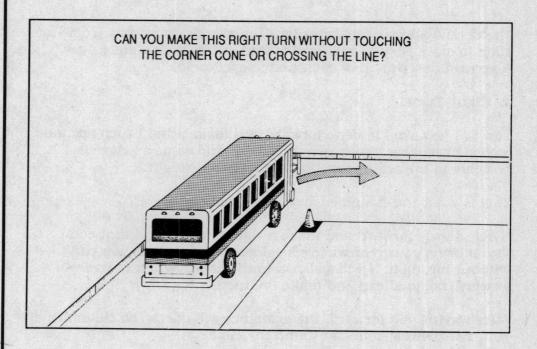

CAN YOU MAKE THIS RIGHT TURN WITHOUT TOUCHING
THE CORNER CONE OR CROSSING THE LINE?

FIGURE 13-2A: THE RIGHT TURN

2. Forward Stop

In this test exercise, you will drive forward between lines (alley) and stop as close as possible to the stop line at the end of the line (alley). The alley will be about 100 feet long and 12 feet wide.

Here is what the examiner may say:

"Drive down the alley and try to stop with your front bumper as close as possible to the line (or markers) at the end of the alley. Try not to go past the line (or markers). You may stop only once. Do not pull ahead once you have stopped. Do not lean out of the window or open the door to see better. When I get to the end of the alley, I will wave you forward."

After you have stopped, the examiner will measure the distance between the bumper and the stop line.

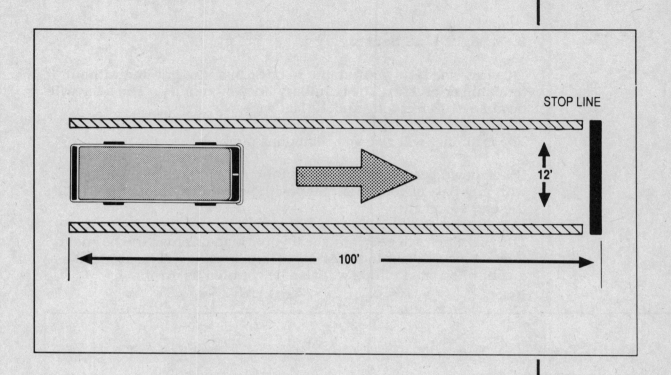

STOP LINE

12'

100'

FIGURE 13-3: FORWARD STOP

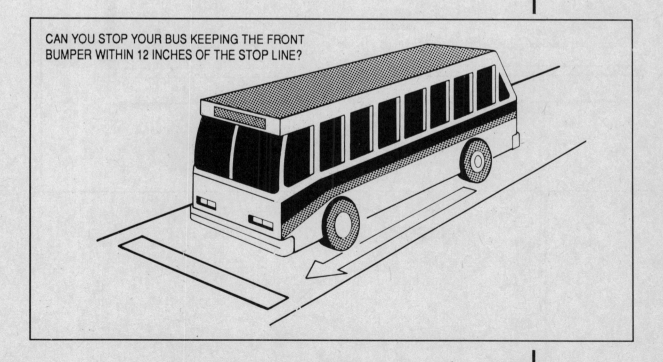

CAN YOU STOP YOUR BUS KEEPING THE FRONT
BUMPER WITHIN 12 INCHES OF THE STOP LINE?

FIGURE 13-3A: FORWARD STOP

3. Straight Line Backing

This exercise tests your ability to back in a straight line without touching or crossing the boundary lines of an alley. The alley will be about 100 feet long and 12 feet wide.

The examiner will give you directions such as:

"Back down the alley. Try not to touch either side of the alley with any part of your bus. Stop with your front bumper even with the end of the alley."

The examiner will check to see if you touch or cross the boundary lines. If you do not touch or cross any lines, it will be counted as a control error. Pullups will also be counted as errors.

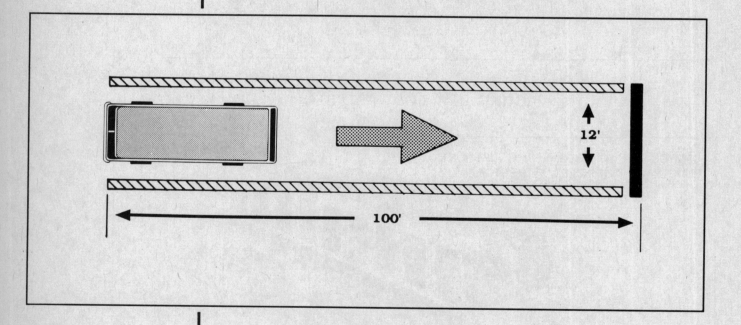

FIGURE 13-4: STRAIGHT LINE BACKING

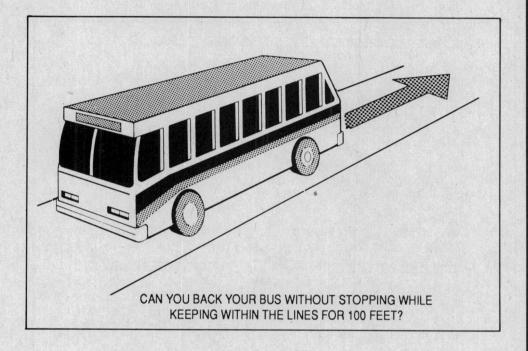

CAN YOU BACK YOUR BUS WITHOUT STOPPING WHILE
KEEPING WITHIN THE LINES FOR 100 FEET?

FIGURE 13-4A: STRAIGHT LINE BACKING

4. Alley Dock

The object of this exercise is to alley dock without touching any
markers or the curb. You will come by the alley so that the
entrance is on your left.

Here are the directions you may be given:

"Drive by the entrance to the alley and back into it. When you
back in, try to get as close as possible to the left side and to the
back of the alley without hitting it. Do not back past the end of
the alley. I will go over and stand at the entrance to the alley.
When I wave you forward, come ahead, then back into the alley.
Toot your horn when you are in position."

The examiner will watch for pullups as you start backing in. The
examiner will also see if you touch or cross boundary lines. When
you stop at the end of the exercise, the distance between the rear
of your vehicle and the stop line will be checked.

When the examiner has marked your score sheet, instructions for
the next exercise will be given.

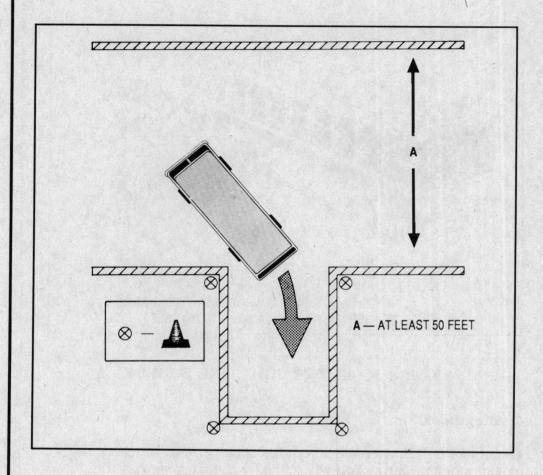

A — AT LEAST 50 FEET

FIGURE 13-5: ALLEY DOCK

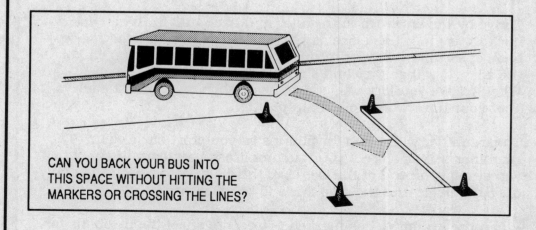

CAN YOU BACK YOUR BUS INTO
THIS SPACE WITHOUT HITTING THE
MARKERS OR CROSSING THE LINES?

FIGURE 13-5A: ALLEY DOCK

5. Parallel Park (Sight Side)

For this exercise, you will park in an area that is on your left.
The space in which you have to park will be 10 feet longer than
your vehicle.

After pointing out the parking space, the examiner will say:

"Drive by the parking space and back into it. Try to get your bus
as close to the rear and the curbside of the space as you can without crossing the lines or hitting the cones. Try to get your bus
completely in the space. When I wave you forward, drive ahead
and back into the space. Toot your horn when you are parked."

The examiner will look for pullups, hitting cones, and touching or
crossing boundary lines. When you toot your horn, the examiner
will record the distance your bus is from the back, front, and curb
lines.

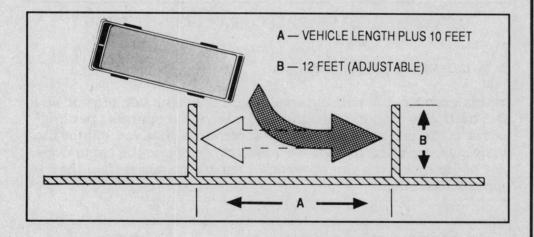

A — VEHICLE LENGTH PLUS 10 FEET

B — 12 FEET (ADJUSTABLE)

FIGURE 13-6: PARALLEL PARK (SIGHT SIDE)

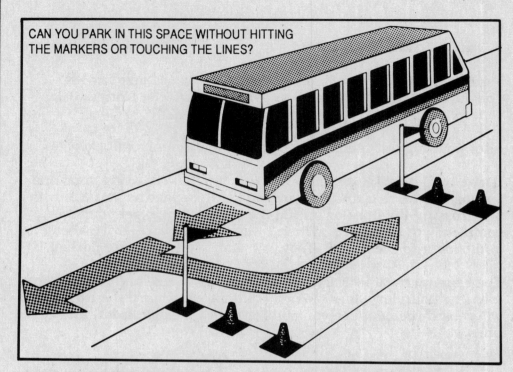

CAN YOU PARK IN THIS SPACE WITHOUT HITTING
THE MARKERS OR TOUCHING THE LINES?

FIGURE 13-6A: PARALLEL PARK (SIGHT SIDE)

6. Parallel Park (Right Side)

In this exercise, the parking space is on the right side of your bus.
The routine is exactly the same as the sight-side parallel parking
exercise. To perform it, follow the same steps that you did for the
sight-side exercise. In fact, the examiner may use the same exercise setup by having you approach the parking space from the
opposite direction.

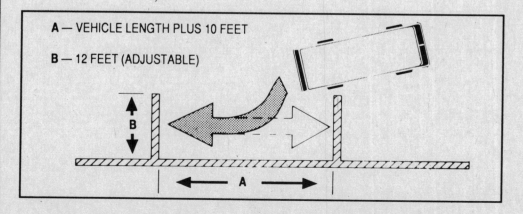

A — VEHICLE LENGTH PLUS 10 FEET

B — 12 FEET (ADJUSTABLE)

FIGURE 13-7: PARALLEL PARK (RIGHT SIDE)

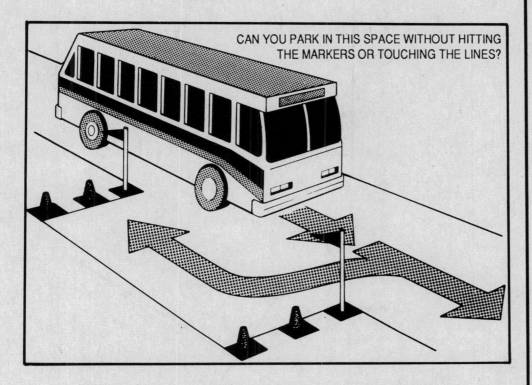

CAN YOU PARK IN THIS SPACE WITHOUT HITTING THE MARKERS OR TOUCHING THE LINES?

FIGURE 13-7A: PARALLEL PARK (RIGHT SIDE)

7. Backward Serpentine

The serpentine layout is a row of three cones. You are to back around the three cones in a serpentine manner without striking the cones or markers. One correction (pullup) is usually allowed. In some tests, you may open the door and step out of your vehicle to check your position.

To direct you, the examiner may say:

"Back up in a serpentine manner. Follow the directional arrows as shown in this diagram. Stop when you are past the last cone. Try not to touch any cones as you weave through."

A diagram of the path you must travel is on the next page.

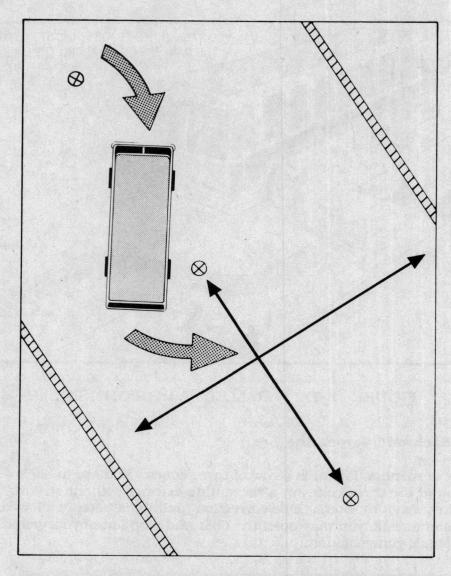

FIGURE 13-8: BACKWARD SERPENTINE MANEUVER

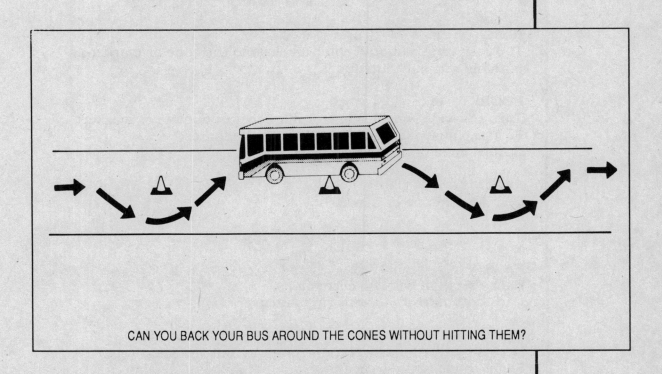

CAN YOU BACK YOUR BUS AROUND THE CONES WITHOUT HITTING THEM?

FIGURE 13-8A: BACKWARD SERPENTINE MANEUVER

Pass-Fail Standards

Your state may require you to perform all of the seven of skill exercises or only some of them. This will depend upon the space available at the examination site. It may also depend upon the type of bus you are driving.

A failure on any maneuver of the skill test may cause you to fail the complete test, or to have points deducted for each driving error. Make sure you know how the exercise will be scored before you take the skills test.

A listing of how each exercise may be judged is on the following page.

Right Turn

PASS
The rear wheels should come as close to the cone or marker as possible without touching it.

POOR
Turn too wide (wheel is one or more feet from cone or marker)
Turn too sharp (barely touches cone or marker)
Bumps cone or marker

FAIL
Drives over cone or marker

Forward Stop

PASS
Backs straight with no corrections
Uses both mirrors to perform maneuver

POOR
Begins by turning wheel the wrong way but recovers
Slight to moderate weave
Drives forward once or twice to straighten vehicle
Uses one mirror only or both mirrors only a time or two

FAIL
Cannot back up
Drives forward three or more times to straighten vehicle
Does not use mirrors

Alley Dock

PASS
Performs alley dock without touching markers or curb line

POOR
Bumps or touches marker or curb
Turns wheel wrong way but recovers
Makes two or three pullups

FAIL
Backs over marker
Wheel over curb
Cannot complete alley dock
Makes four or more pullups

Parallel Parking

PASS
Performs maneuver without touching marker or curb line

POOR
Touches marker or curb
Turns wheel wrong way but recovers
Needs one or two pullups

FAIL
Backs over marker or any wheel over curb
Cannot complete parallel park
Makes three or more pullups

Serpentine Backing

PASS
Backs around three markers without striking markers or curb line

POOR
Touches markers or curb line lightly
Turns wheel wrong way but recovers
Needs three or four pullups

FAIL
Backs over marker or any wheel on curb
Cannot complete serpentine maneuver
Makes five or more pullups

The Basic Control Skills Test may include as many as seven test exercises. Each exercise is a test of your basic skill in controlling and handling your bus. The seven test exercises are: Right Turn; Forward Stop; Straight Line Backing; Alley Dock; Parallel Park (Sight Side); Parallel Park (Right Side); and Backward Serpentine.

Summary

The test examiner will explain how you are to perform each exercise. You will be scored by the number and types of errors you make during each exercise. The most serious error is driving over a marker or boundary, so your objective should be to complete the exercise without going over any lines or hitting any of the cones. Try to keep pullups to a minimum, but, remember it is better to do a pullup than to hit a marker or go over a line.

You should practice these exercises. The skills you develop will help you pass the test, and they will help you become a better driver.

REVIEW QUESTIONS

1.   What is the purpose of the Basic Control Skills Test?
    _____
    _____

2.   In your state, which commercial drivers are required
    to take the Basic Control Skills Test?
    _____
    _____

3.   In your state, is this skills test conducted on an off-
    street test area or on surface streets during the
    road test?
    _____

4.   In your state, which exercises or maneuvers are
    used to test your ability to control your bus? Which
    of these exercises or maneuvers do you need to
    practice?
    _____
    _____
    _____
    _____

5.   What do each of these exercises attempt to measure?
    What do you have to do to pass the exercise? What
    will cause you to fail each exercise?
    A. The Right Turn _____
    B. The Forward Stop _____
    C. Straight Line Backing _____
    D. The Alley Dock _____
    E. Parallel Park (Sight Side) _____
    F. Parallel Park (Right Side) _____
    G. Backward Serpentine _____

6.   Have you checked how your State scores the basic
    control skill exercises?
    _____
    _____

ROAD TEST

CHAPTER

14

FROM NOW ON,

ONLY THE BEST WILL DRIVE

Chapter Objectives

Explain the purpose of the road test

Help the CDL applicant become familiar with the test procedures

Explain the driving maneuvers that the driver will be expected to perform

Identify scoring locations and performance ratings

CHAPTER FOURTEEN

ROAD TEST

Once you have completed all other tests, you are ready for the Road Test. You will need to take the Road Test in the type of vehicle for which you intend to be licensed.

The Road Test is also known as the "drive test." It is the test where you show your ability to drive in traffic, and demonstrate your safe driving skills. Since safety is of highest priority, if you do not obey a traffic law or if you cause an accident during the test, you will automatically fail the test.

Your application fee generally entitles you to several attempts at passing the Road Test. In some states, you may need to call for an appointment to take the Road Test. This is because of the length of the test.

The purpose of this performance test is to evaluate your ability to drive safely in on-the-road traffic situations. It will include, wherever possible, left and right turns, intersections, railway crossings, up- and downgrades, rural or semi-rural roads, city multi-lane streets, and expressway driving.

Purpose of the Road Test

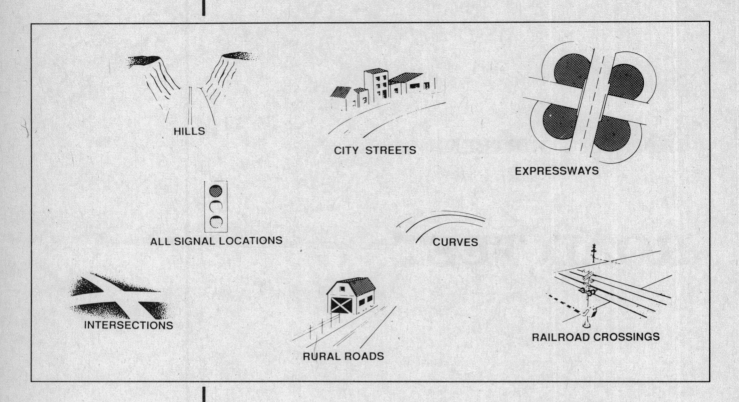

FIGURE 14-1: ROAD TEST SITUATIONS

Test Procedures

The test drive is taken over a route specified by the examiner. As you drive, you must follow instructions given by the examiner. The examiner will score you on how well you make turns, make lane changes, merge into traffic, and control your speed at specific places along the test route.

The examiner will also score you on how well you do such things as signal, search for hazards, shift gears, use mirrors, control speed, and position the bus in your lane.

Under the national CDL test rules, all road tests must be taken in the type of vehicle the applicant will be authorized to drive.

Test Route Locations

You will drive over a test route that has been set up in advance. This ideal test route includes the locations for the tests listed below. These test route locations are planned in advance. The examiner will score your driving performance at each location.

1. LEFT AND RIGHT TURNS: You will be asked to make turns at traffic lights, stop signs, and uncontrolled intersections. The turns will range from easy to somewhat difficult for heavy vehicles. You can expect to make from four to eight left turns and four to eight right turns.

2. CITY BUSINESS STREETS: This section will be one to two miles long. It will be a straight stretch in an urban business area. It will contain intersections with traffic lights and through intersections (no lights or stops). The traffic will be moderate. The section will require you to make lane changes somewhere along the route. This section will let you show how you cope with traffic in a typical business area.

3. INTERSECTIONS: These intersections may be located in the business area described above. The test will include your driving through:

    • Two uncontrolled intersections. These are through intersections — not controlled by traffic lights or stop signs.

    • Two controlled intersections. These intersections are controlled by lights and signs. They are street corners where a stop has to be made.

4. RAILWAY CROSSINGS: The test will try to include one uncontrolled crossing and one controlled crossing. The crossings should have enough sight distance so that youcan look for oncoming trains. You must look left and right as you approach the crossing. Your head movement is the only way the examiner will be able to tell if you have noticed the crossing and are searching for hazards.

5. LEFT AND RIGHT CURVES: This section includes two curves, one to the left, and one to the right. The curves will be fairly tight. Tight curves are used so that a noticeable off-tracking situation is produced.

6. TWO-LANE RURAL OR SEMI-RURAL ROAD: This section of the test will be about two miles long. If a rural road is not available in the test area, a street with few entrances and a higher speed limit will be used. This part of the test lets you show how you handle situations found on a two-lane rural road.

7. FREEWAY OR EXPRESSWAY: This is where you show your ability to handle freeway or expressway driving. The section should start with a ramp entrance and end with a ramp exit. The section should be long enough for a heavy vehicle to do two lane changes. A section of multi-lane highway may be used if there is no freeway or expressway available.

8. A DOWNGRADE: The grade should be steep enough and long enough to require you to gear down and brake. If a long grade is not available, a steep, short hill will probably be used.

9. AN UPGRADE: The grade should be steep enough and long enough to require gear changing to maintain your speed. The same grade may be used for both the upgrade and downgrade sections of the test.

10. A DOWNGRADE FOR STOPPING: This is a grade where a bus can be safely stopped and parked for a minute or so. The grade needs to be only steep enough to cause the bus to roll if you do not park properly. It takes just a gentle slope to cause a heavy vehicle to roll.

11. AN UPGRADE FOR STOPPING: This section checks your ability to safely park on an upgrade. The same grade used for the downgrade stop may be used for this part of the test.

12. UNDERPASS OR LOW CLEARANCE AND BRIDGE: One underpass or low clearance and one bridge are used for this section. The underpass should have a posted clearance height. The bridge should have a posted weight limit. If an underpass or bridge is not available, the examiner will have you drive to places that have signs a heavy vehicle driver should use. Examples of such signs are: "No Commercial Vehicles After 11:00 PM," or "Bridge With 10 Ton Weight Limit In 5 Miles." Figure 14-2 shows some other examples.

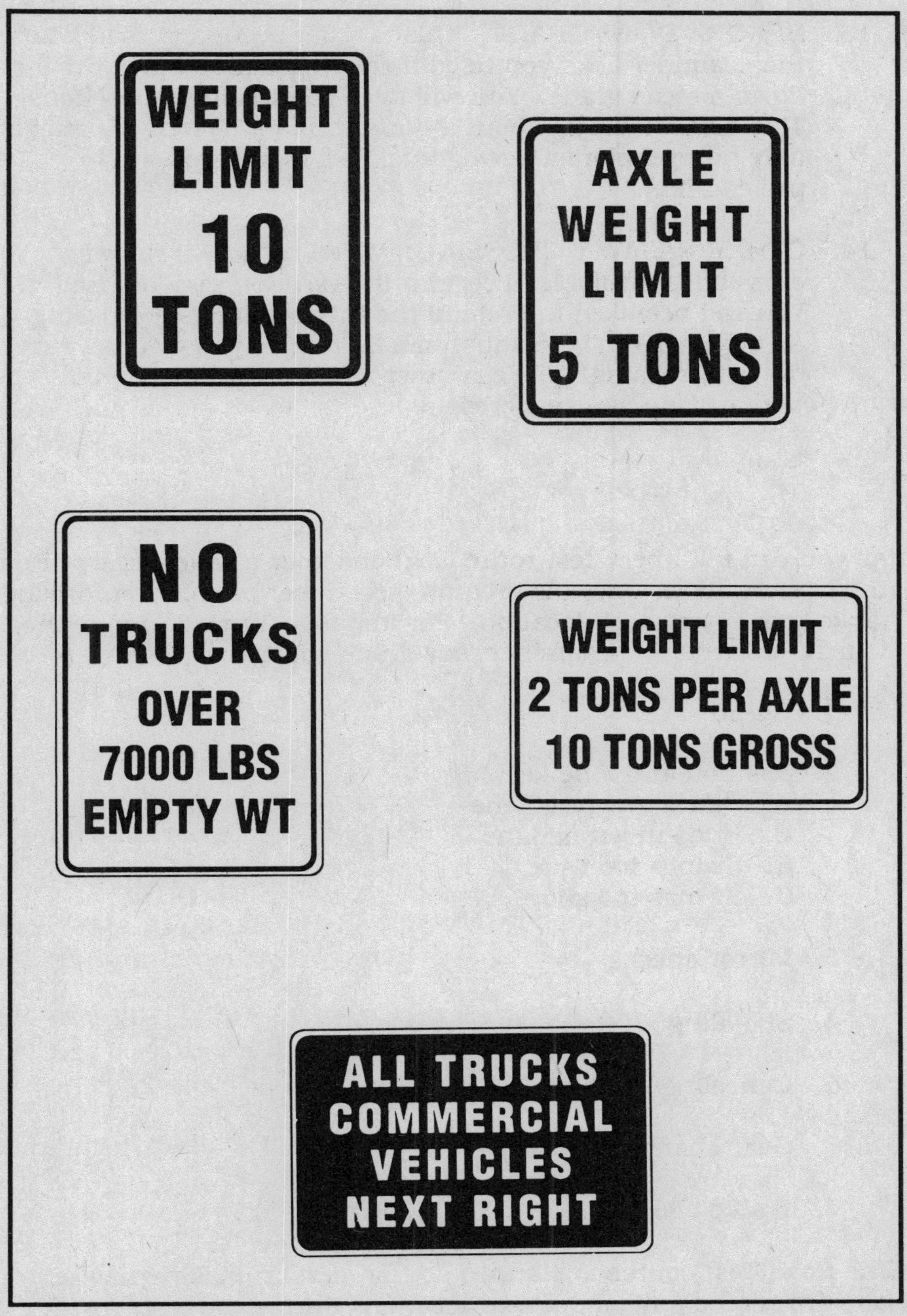

FIGURE 14-2: HEAVY VEHICLE SIGNS

13. BEFORE DOWNGRADE: This is a flat section of road where the examiner asks you to go through the motions of driving down a steep grade. You will need to explain your actions. This section will be about a quarter of a mile long. It may or may not be before a downgrade. If it is not, you are to pretend it is.

14. OTHER RAILWAY CROSSING: When no actual railway crossing is available, a regular intersection may be used. You will be asked to pretend the intersection is a crossing. As a bus driver, you must handle this as you would a real railway crossing. The examiner will score you as if you were driving at a real crossing.

Scoring Locations

As you can tell, these test route locations offer a wide variety of traffic situations. They also require you to perform certain driving tasks properly at each location. For instance, during each of the four right turns, the examiner may grade your:

1. Speed

2. Position and lane keeping
   A. Starts in wrong lane
   B. Ends in wrong lane
   C. Swings too wide
   D. Swings too short

3. Mirror checks

4. Signaling

5. Canceling signal

6. Gear changes

7. Traffic checks

The Road Test course is planned so that certain tasks or maneuvers are scored only at selected locations during the test. You may make 10 right turns during the test drive, yet only four of the turns may be used as scoring locations. The examiner will not deduct points for a maneuver that is performed improperly if it occurs at a location other than the pre-selected location. There is one big exception: an error that is grounds for "immediate failure" will be scored anywhere along the test drive course.

Each state will have its own special GFIF rules. Make sure you know your state's GFIF rules before the test.

The GFIF rules deal with serious errors. As soon as an error of this type is made, the test is stopped. Here is a listing of errors which may be grounds for immediate failure:

1. An accident occurs during the test drive that involves any amount of property damage or personal injury.

2. Refusal to perform any maneuver which is part of the test.

3. Any dangerous action in which:
    A. An accident is prevented by expert driving or action on the part of others.
    B. The examiner is forced to assist the test driver in avoiding an accident.
    C. The test driver drives over a curb or sidewalk and by doing so endangers others.
    D. The test driver creates a serious traffic hazard, such as:
        1. Driving the wrong way on a one-way street;
        2. Driving on the wrong side of a two-way street;
        3. Stalling the vehicle in a busy intersection.

4. The test driver is unable to properly operate vehicle equipment. Or, after a short distance on the test course, it becomes apparent that the test driver is dangerously inexperienced.

5. The test driver commits one of the following:
    A. Passes another vehicle which is stopped at a crosswalk while yielding to a pedestrian.
    B. Passes a school bus, with red lights flashing, while it is loading or unloading students.

Grounds for Immediate Failure (GFIF)

C. Makes or starts to make one turn from the wrong lane under traffic conditions that create a dangerous situation. An example of this would be a left turn from the right-turn lane or a right turn from the left-turn lane. This can occur on a two-way street with several lanes or a one-way street (See Figure 14-3).

D. Running through a red light or stop sign. This applies if the test driver has to be stopped from running the light or sign.

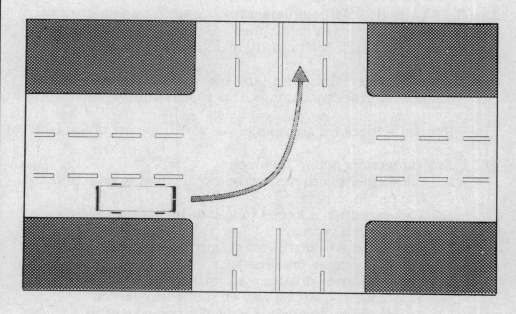

FIGURE 14-3: GROUNDS FOR IMMEDIATE FAILURE

Road Test Scoring Systems

The national CDL system allows each state to devise their own tests and scoring systems. The national rules, however, require that persons taking the road test must demonstrate they can successfully perform all of the skills in the road test to achieve a passing score. There are a number of road test scoring systems a state can use. Here are some examples.

Four-point demerit system: Under this system each maneuver is graded good, fair, poor or failing. A driver will be scored "good" for a maneuver if it is performed without points being deducted. Points are deducted for "fair" and "poor" performance. A passing score is usually 30 or fewer deductions.

Three-point demerit system: Good performance is not scored in this system. Incorrect performance is scored fair, poor, and fail. Fair is scored for the least degree of error. Poor is scored for a medium degree of error. Fail is for the greatest degree of error.

Fixed point demerit system: Under this system, a fixed point value is assigned for incorrect performance of each maneuver. Each maneuver is scored once. Since this value is applied only once, repeating the same error does not increase the deductions.

Multiple point demerit system: Point values are assigned to the maneuvers. The examiner records the number of times each error occurs. The total errors (occurrences) times the point value equals the deduction. Standard grounds for immediate failure are used.

California demerit system: This system assigns point values for poor performance or performances on which improvement is needed. Tally markers or checks are made for each incorrect performance. This is multiplied by the value established for the performance and entered under "improvement needed" or under "poor" to obtain the total point deduction. Total deductions are subtracted from 100 to obtain the score. Standard causes for immediate rejection are used.

The flexible point demerit system: A range of deductions from a low to a high number of points is set for each incorrect performance. For example, a test driver stalling his or her bus in an intersection may be given a one to ten point deduction, depending upon the situation and the degree of error. All maneuvers are scored in the same way. A passing score is usually 30 or fewer deductions. Immediate rejection or failure is based upon standard causes.

Percentage system: Under this system, each performance is graded as good or as indicating a need for further training. The final score is then figured on a percentage basis. This is done by dividing the number of good performances by the number of performances graded. Grounds for immediate failure are based on standard causes.

Merit system: Instead of deducting for maneuvers incorrectly performed, this system credits the driver with points for correct performance. The system is usually based on a road test that scores drivers on a 100-point basis. To pass the test, a minimum score must be reached by the driver.

As you can see, there are a number of scoring systems your state can use. Make sure you know:

- How you will be scored.

- What is the passing score.

- The grounds for immediate failure.

- The rules for repeating the test if you fail.

Your state will have materials available that tell what kind of a scoring system is used and the kind of road test you will be given.

Now look at a sample road test to learn on what you can be tested and how your performance(s) will be checked.

Performance Checks

Chances are your road test drive will:

- Use a pre-planned route.

- Require the examiner to grade your performance at certain locations on the test route.

What are these performances? What will be checked during the test drive? Your test may be made up of these 11 performance groups:

A. Starting.

B. Stopping.

C. Driving straight.

D. Driving around curves.

E. Lane changes.

F. Turning.

G. Merging.

H. Traffic restrictions.

I. Blind intersections.

J. Driving on hills.

K. Railway crossings.

Each performance group may consist of one or more performance checks. In the listing below there are 11 performance groups (in capital letters) with a total of 36 performance checks.

A. STARTING
    1. Pulling away — starting smoothly on a level surface
    2. Upshifting — correctly shifting up through the gear pattern

B. STOPPING
    3. Downshifting — correctly shifting down through the gear pattern
    4. Braking — using the brakes to come to a smooth, safe stop
    5. Stopping point — stopping the vehicle at the proper point

C. DRIVING STRAIGHT
    6. Mirror checks — checking the mirrors regularly for following traffic
    7. Speed — maintaining the proper speed on the straightaway
    8. Lane keeping — staying within the lane while driving straight

D. DRIVING AROUND CURVES
    9. Speed — entering curves at a safe and proper speed
    10. Lane Position — staying within the lane while in a curve

E. LANE CHANGING
    11. Mirror checks — checking mirrors prior to lane change
    12. Lane position — pausing to allow any unseen vehicles to get out of the way before crossing a lane line
    13. Cancel signal — manually cancel the turn signal following lane change

F. TURNING
    14. Speed — entering turns at a proper and safe speed
    15. Position/single lane — positioning the vehicle correctly for a turn within a single lane
    16. Position/multiple lane — positioning the vehicle correctly for a turn where more than one lane is available
    17. Mirror checks — checking the rear of the vehicle for clearance during the turn
    18. Lane keeping — staying within the lane while in a turn or using the best possible turn path
    19. Cancel signal — manually canceling the signal following a turn
    20. Upshifting — correctly shifting up through the gear pattern

G. MERGING
    21. Signaling — switching on the turn signal before a merge
    22. Mirror checks — lining up the vehicle and checking the mirrors before a merge
    23. Speed— merging at the speed of traffic
    24. Cancel signal — manually turning off the signal following a merge

H. TRAFFIC RESTRICTIONS
    25. Lane restrictions — obeying the lane bans imposed by signs, signals and roadway markings
    26. Travel restrictions — complying with restrictions for commercial motor vehicles such as bridge weight limits and underpass clearance limits

I. BLIND INTERSECTIONS
    27. Search — checking cross traffic when approaching a blind intersection
    28. Speed — adjusting your speed to meet the situation when approaching a blind intersection

J. DRIVING HILLS
  29. Starting uphill — starting smoothly while on an incline
  30. Shifting uphill — smoothness of downshifting on an incline as well as using the proper gear
  31. Speed downhill — maintaining a safe speed down a grade
  32. Stopping uphill — bringing the vehicle to a safe stop on an incline
  33. Stopping Downhill — bringing vehicle to a safe stop on a downgrade.

K. RAILWAY CROSSINGS
  34. Train Checks — checks for presence of trains
  35. Stops — correctly stops the vehicle at the proper point before the tracks
  36. Crossing Tracks — approaching and crossing tracks in a safe and proper manner

In addition to these performance checks, some tests include a General Driving group that checks your:

- Use of Controls — using the clutch, gears, accelerator, brake system, steering hand-hold, and auxiliary equipment such as the lights, wipers and defroster.

- Courtesy — keeping in the right hand lane on a hill; using four-way flashers when your speed is slower than the traffic flow; not following other vehicles too closely; communicating your intentions properly; and yielding to pedestrians and others.

- Rules of Road — obeying all signs, signals and markings; following the rules of safety; avoiding hazards; and using seat belts.

Test Scoring

The examiner judges each performance by using a specific set of criteria or rules. If the performance meets the criteria, it is scored as a "YES" or correct performance. If it does not, it is scored a "NO" or incorrect performance. Each score is marked accordingly on a test score sheet.

Here are the criteria or scoring rules for the 36 performances described above:

Starting

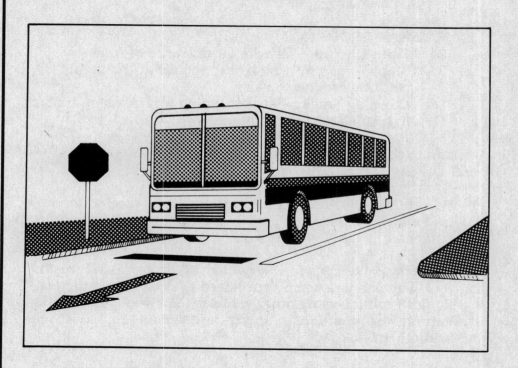

FIGURE 14-4: STARTING — PULLING AWAY

1. PULLING AWAY

Performance: You must accelerate smoothly from a stopped position. This test checks your ability to coordinate the use of the clutch and accelerator to smoothly put the vehicle into motion from a stopped position.

Situation: This performance will be checked at intersections:

- That require a complete stop (stop sign or flashing red light).

- Where the vehicle can rest on a level surface.

- Where the vehicle can proceed straight through the intersection.

Scoring: Grading of this performance takes place when the vehicle starts to move.

The performance is scored YES if it meets all of the following criteria:
1. Vehicle pulls away from the stop smoothly without too much bouncing or lurching.
2. Engine remains running.
3. Vehicle does not roll backwards.

Scored NO if:
1. Vehicle lurches or jerks away from the stop.
2. Engine dies.
3. Vehicle rolls backward.

2. UPSHIFTING

Performance: You must shift smoothly up through the gears after pulling away from the stop.

Situation: This performance should be checked on stretches of road that are about one-fourth to one-half mile long. The test zone should have only light traffic and must be on a straight and level stretch of roadway.

Scoring: Grading begins when the first shift after pulling away from the stop is made.

Performance is scored YES if all the following criteria are met:
1. Shifting is made smoothly up through all the gears.
2. Shifting is completed without hesitation and there is no coasting in neutral.
3. You do not miss or skip a gear causing the engine to lug.
4. Shift is completed smoothly without noticeable jerking or clashing of gears. Shift is made without having to force the shift lever or move it repeatedly to get it into gear.

Scored NO if:
1. You shift too late and over-rev the engine.
2. You shift too soon and lug the engine.
3. You cannot complete the shift and slow down too much, or stop before recovering.
4. The gears clash, and the shift lever is forced or moved repeatedly to put the transmission in gear.

NOTE: Lugging the engine means running the engine below the recommended operating range. The engine RPM is too low for the road speed.

Stopping

3. DOWNSHIFTING

Performance: You must be able to downshift smoothly. Downshifting measures your ability to read the tachometer, determine when to shift, coordinate the use of clutch, gear shift lever and gas pedal to shift down through the gears. All shifting is to be made in a smooth controlled manner while the proper engine speed (RPM) is maintained.

Situation: This performance is checked on the stretch of roadway prior to bringing the vehicle to a stop. The roadway is level and straight. A stop sign is located at the end of the test zone.

Scoring: A YES is scored if the performance meets all of the following criteria:
1. The transmission is shifted to the proper gear for vehicle road speed.
2. You shift smoothly without hesitation and with little grinding.
3. You do not lug or rev the engine too much.

Scored NO if
1. You are unable to downshift to a lower gear.
2. The vehicle lurches when the clutch is released.
3. The engine lugs or over-revs when the shift is completed.
4. You put the transmission in neutral and coast to a stop without downshifting.

4. BRAKING

Performance: You must regulate the brake pressure to bring the vehicle to a complete stop without overbraking or a hard slowdown.

Situation: This performance is checked in a zone with a stretch of straight roadway leading to an intersection with a stop sign or stop light.

Scoring: Scoring of the performance begins when the brake is applied and ends when the vehicle comes to a compete stop.

The performance is scored YES if all of these criteria are met:
1. You bring the vehicle to a smooth stop.
2. The vehicle comes to a complete stop.

Scored NO if:
1. The vehicle is over-braked and shudders to a stop.
2. The vehicle does not come to a complete stop.

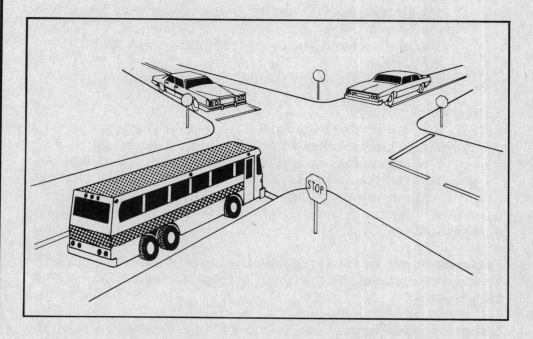

FIGURE 14-5: STOPPING POINT

5. STOPPING POINT

Performance: You must bring the vehicle to a complete stop at a designated point.

Situation: This performance will be checked in a zone with a stretch of straight roadway leading to an intersection where the vehicle must be brought to a complete stop.

Scoring: Scoring of this performance takes place after the vehicle has come to a complete stop. The examiner will observe the right front side of the test vehicle. The location of the front bumper is checked in relation to the stopping line (crosswalk, stop line or stop sign).

Scored YES if performance meets all of the criteria:
1. The vehicle comes to a complete stop.
2. The vehicle stops so that front bumper is within three feet of stop line, pedestrian crosswalk or stop sign, but not beyond it.

Scored NO if:
1. The front bumper extends past the stop line, crosswalk, or stop sign.
2. The front bumper stops more than three feet short of the stop line, crosswalk, or stop sign.

Driving Straight

6. MIRROR CHECKS

Performance: You must check the traffic behind your vehicle in the rear view mirrors on each side at least once every 10 seconds of normal travel.

Situation: This performance should be checked in a test zone which is a straight stretch of road one-eighth to one-fourth mile long.

Scoring: Grading this performance begins as the vehicle reaches the beginning of the test zone.

A YES is scored if you check both the left and right mirrors within 10 seconds after entering the test zone.

A NO is scored if you fail to look at both the left and right side rear view mirrors within the first 10 seconds after entering test zone.

7. SPEED

Performance: You must operate your vehicle within 10 mph of the posted speed limit without exceeding the limit when driving on a straight road. Exceeding the maximum safe speed is hazardous to yourself and others. Operating well below the legal or safe speed is a hindrance to traffic and is unsafe.

Situation: This test should be given in a test zone which is a straight stretch of road one-eighth to one-fourth mile long. The posted speed limit for the test zone should be at least 40 MPH.

Scoring: Grading of this performance begins after vehicle has entered the test zone and the first performance of the group (6- MIRROR CHECKS) has been scored.

YES is scored if performance meets all of the following criteria:
1. The speed does not fall below the posted limit by more than 10 MPH.
2. The speed does not exceed the posted limit.

NO is scored if:
1. The speed is more than 10 mph under posted limit.
2. The speed exceeds the posted limit.

8. LANE KEEPING

FIGURE 14-6: LANE KEEPING — STRAIGHT ROAD

Performance: You must keep vehicle within the existing travel lanes on a straight road. Lane keeping on a straight road is a good test of your hand-eye coordination. To maintain a straight path, you must focus well down the road; inexperienced drivers tend to fix their eyes right in front of the vehicle and wander back and forth.

Situation: This will be the same as the situation for performance checks 6 and 7 with one exception: All lanes should be clearly marked.

Scoring: After making mirror and speed checks, the examiner will watch lane keeping through the rest of the test zone.

YES is scored if the vehicle remains in the travel lane without crossing any lane markings.

NO is scored if the vehicle tires cross over lane markings.

Driving Around Curves

9. SPEED

Performance: You must adjust your speed to drive safely around a curve. Drivers who are new to a certain vehicle often misjudge the speed at which it can take a curve. The result is braking the vehicle in the curve. This, with the outward force of the curve, creates a danger.

At the other extreme, drivers who have poor vehicle handling skills may slow down too much. They do this to keep the vehicle in the lane while rounding the curve. This performance check prevents drivers from hiding their inability to handle a vehicle by driving at too low a speed.

Situation: This performance may be checked on any curve which has:

- Clearly marked lanes.

- No traffic signs, stop signs, or other factors that may control speed in the curve.

Scoring: Scoring begins when the vehicle enters the curve, continues through the curve, and ends when the vehicle reaches the straight stretch of roadway.

YES is scored if the performance meets all of the following criteria:
1. Speed does not drop more than 20 percent of the posted limit. For instance, if the speed limit is 40 mph, the speed should not drop over eight miles per hour (40 MPH x .20 = 8 MPH).
2. Speed does not exceed the posted limit.
3. You do not shift gears or brake through the curve.

NO is scored if:
1. The vehicle enters the curve at a speed more than 20 percent under the posted speed limit. (A speed of less than 32mph at the posted speed of 40 MPH).
2. The vehicle enters the curve at more than the posted speed limit.
3. You brake or shift gears while in the curve.
4. The examiner is pushed hard to either side of the vehicle by the outward force of the curve.

10. LANE KEEPING

Performance: You must keep the vehicle within the bounds of the lane markings. Because of "off-tracking" (the tendency for the rear wheels to follow a shorter path than the front wheels), the driver of a large vehicle must approach a curve from an outside position to keep the rear wheels from cutting across the sharp part of the curve. Failure to do this causes the rear of the vehicle to leave the road or creates a hazard for a vehicle in the next lane.

Situation: This performance is checked on a curve with lanes marked throughout the curve.

Scoring: Scoring begins where the roadway starts to curve and continues throughout curve.

YES is scored if the vehicle remains in the travel lane without crossing any lane markings.

NO is scored if any of the vehicle's tires cross over a lane marking at any point during the curve.

Lane Changing

11. MIRROR CHECKS

Performance: You must check the proper mirror to determine the presence of traffic before starting a lane change. The ability to maintain the vehicle's direction while looking in a mirror is a measure of operating skill.

Situation: This performance is checked on stretches of multi-lane roadway — at least two lanes traveling in each direction.

Scoring: Scoring begins before the lane change is started.

YES is scored if performance meets all these criteria:
1. You direct your eyes to the proper outside mirror before starting the lane change.
2. You keep the vehicle straight on course. The vehicle does not "weave" in the lane while you are checking the mirror.

NO is scored if:
1. You fail to check the proper mirror before starting a lane change.
2. The vehicle weaves in the lane while you are checking the mirror.

12. LANE POSITION

Performance: You must pause after starting a lane change, before crossing a lane line, in order to allow any unseen vehicles to get out of the way. To lessen the danger of collisions with unseen vehicles, you should pause briefly before starting the change. This lets the other drivers have time to react.

Situation: This situation will be the same as Performance 11.

Scoring: Grading of this performance begins when you start to change lanes and ends when the lane change is complete.

YES is scored if, after you give the signal to begin the lane change, you then pause before crossing the lane line into the next lane.

NO is scored if you turn sharply into the next lane.

13. CANCEL YOUR SIGNAL

Performance: You must cancel your turn signal after completing the lane change.

Scoring: Grading of the performance begins after the lane change has been completed.

YES is scored if you cancel the signal within three (3) seconds after entering the new lane.

NO is scored if you fail to cancel the signal within three (3) seconds after completing the lane change.

Turning

14. SPEED

Performance: You must drive at a safe speed prior to entering a turn. You must also complete the turn at a speed which is neither too fast nor too slow. What is an acceptable speed will depend upon the combined length of the vehicle and how sharp the turn is.

Situation: This performance will be checked on either left or right turns at intersections that do not require the vehicle to stop. This situation is most frequently found when turning from a major street or road into a secondary road.

Scoring: Grading begins as the vehicle reaches the intersection and ends when it enters the new travel lane.

YES is scored if the performance meets all of the following criteria:
1. Braking does not occur at any time during the turn.
2. The turn is completed without too much outward force.
3. The speed does not fall too low during the turn.

NO is scored if:
1. Brakes are applied during the turn.
2. The vehicle comes to a complete stop during the turn.
3. The turn is completed at too high or too low a speed.

15. POSITION — SINGLE LANE (RIGHT TURN)

Performance: You must position the vehicle close enough to the right side of the road to prevent being passed on the right when preparing for a tight right turn. Because of the vehicle's large turning radius, it is common for drivers to move to the left before they start the turn. Swinging to the left in order to create a wider turning radius can encourage an overtaking driver to try to pass on the right. This creates the risk of a collision.

Situation: This performance should be checked at intersections where you must make a sharp right turn. This means it is a turn that cannot be made entirely within lane boundaries.

Scoring: Grading of this performance covers only the vehicle's position before the turn starts. Grading begins when you approach the intersection and ends when the vehicle has reached the sharpest point of the turn.

YES is scored if the vehicle remains within six feet of the roadside (curb, shoulder, or parked vehicles) until the front of the vehicle has entered the new roadway.

NO is scored if at least some portion of the vehicle fails to remain within six feet of the roadside (curb, shoulder, or parked vehicle).

16. POSITION—MULTIPLE LANES

Performance: When you turn, you must use the outside lane if more than one lane is available.

When making a left turn at an intersection where there are two or more left-turn lanes, you must use the left-turn lane on the right — the lane that is farther from the left hand curb or side of the road. Only in this position can you observe vehicles in the next lane while you are completing the turn.

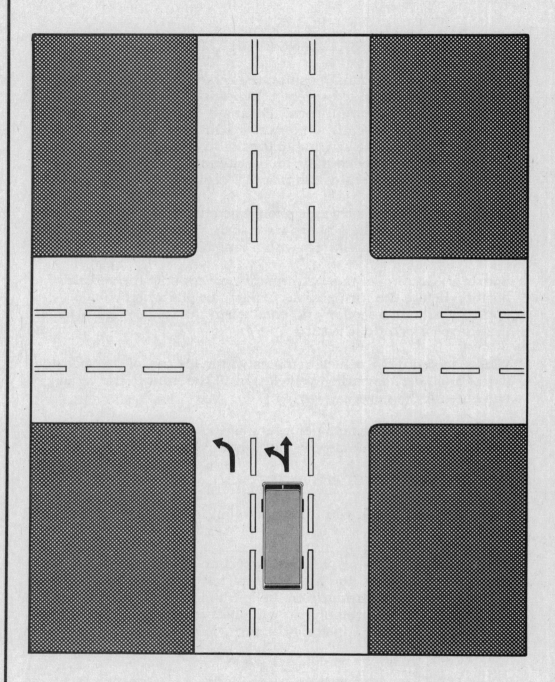

FIGURE 14-7: CHOICE OF LEFT TURN LANES

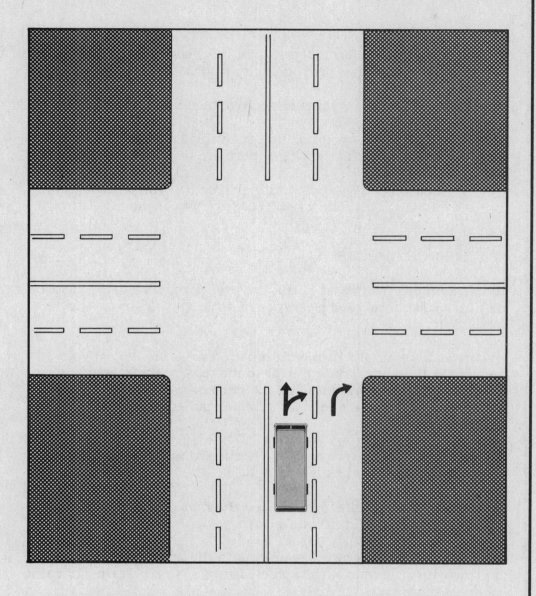

FIGURE 14-8: CHOICE OF RIGHT TURN LANES

When making a right turn where there are two or more right turn lanes, you must use the right turn lane on the far left.

Situation: This performance should be checked at intersections with two or more lanes for turning right or left.

Scoring: YES is scored if performance meets the appropriate criteria:
1. Right Turn: You position the vehicle in the outside lane — the far left lane when there are two or more right turn lanes.
2. Left Turn: You position the vehicle in the outside lane — the far right lane when there are two or more left turn lanes.

17. MIRROR CHECKS

Performance: You must check the proper mirror during right or left turns to check your clearance of other vehicles or roadside objects.

When making a right turn, you must observe the rear of your vehicle in the appropriate mirror to make sure there is enough clearance from such objects as the curb or parked cars. During a left turn, you must check for vehicles pulled up to the intersection.

Situation: This performance is checked at any intersection where you are required to turn left or right.

Scoring: Scoring takes place when the rear of the vehicle reaches the sharpest point (apex) of the turn.

YES is scored if you direct your eyes to the appropriate rearview mirror when the rear of the vehicle is about to reach the sharpest point of the turn.

NO is scored if you fail to check the mirror when the rear of the vehicle reaches the sharpest point of the turn.

18. LANE KEEPING

Performance: You must keep the rear of your vehicle within the lane. Failing to keep the rear end within the lane in a right turn can result in collisions with mailboxes, poles, and parked vehicles. During a left turn, it can result in collisions with the vehicles that have pulled up to the intersection from the left. In order to keep the rear wheels within the lane, you may have to swing into the far lane.

In making a right turn, it may be necessary to move into an opposing lane of traffic. This is acceptable and should not be scored NO as long as you yield to other vehicles.

Situation: This performance may be scored at any intersection allowing right-angle turns either to the left or right.

Scoring: Scoring of this performance begins when vehicle starts the turn and ends when trailer wheels clear the sharpest point of the turn.

Scored YES if performance meets the following:
1. Right Turn — right rear tires do not cross the lane line, touch the curb, or run off the pavement edge.
2. Left Turn — left rear tires obviously do not cut across the sharpest point of the turn.

Scored NO if:
1. Right Turn — right rear tires cross the lane line, touch the curb or run off the pavement edge.
2. Left Turn — You very obviously cut across the sharpest point of the turn.

19. CANCEL SIGNAL

Performance: You must cancel the directional signal after completing the turn. The signal must be canceled after the turn is completed and before you begin upshifting through the gears.

You may have wondered why this test does not call for signaling before the turn. Many drivers will remember to signal a turn. But, they frequently fail to cancel the signal properly. So, remember to signal before turning and then cancel your signal properly after the turn.

Situation: This performance is scored only upon completion of a turn at an intersection.

Scoring: Scoring of this performance begins after the turn is completed and ends three seconds after your vehicle has straightened out.

As soon as the rear of the vehicle has entered the new lane of travel, the examiner will look at your hand. The examiner will check to see if the signal is actually being canceled. If nothing happens at this time, the examiner will decide that you either 1) failed to signal in the first place; or 2) canceled the signal too early. Either of these will be considered an error.

Scored YES if the performance meets all of the following criteria:
1. You cancel the signal within three seconds after entering the new lane.
2. You do not cancel the signal while a portion of the vehicle is still turning.

Scored NO if:
1. You fail to cancel the signal within three seconds after entering the new lane;
2. You cancel the signal early — while any part of the vehicle is still turning.

20. UPSHIFTING

Performance: You must shift smoothly through the gears after entering the new path of travel.

Situation: This performance may be scored at any intersection where you are required to turn left or right.

Scoring: Scoring of this performance takes place after turn is completed.

Scored YES if performance meets all of the following:
1. The transmission is shifted smoothly up through gear pattern.
2. You shift without hesitation. You do not coast in neutral.
3. You do not miss or skip a gear so that it causes the engine to lug.
4. Shift is completed smoothly without noticeable jerking or clashing of gears and without having to force the shift lever or move it repeatedly to get it into gear.

Scored NO if one of the following occurs:
1. You shift too late and over-rev the engine.
2. You shift too soon and lug the engine.
3. You cannot complete the shift and slow down excessively or stop before recovering.

4. The gears clash, and the shift lever is forced or moved repeatedly to put transmission in gear.

No error is scored if traffic prevents you from shifting up through the gears.

Merging

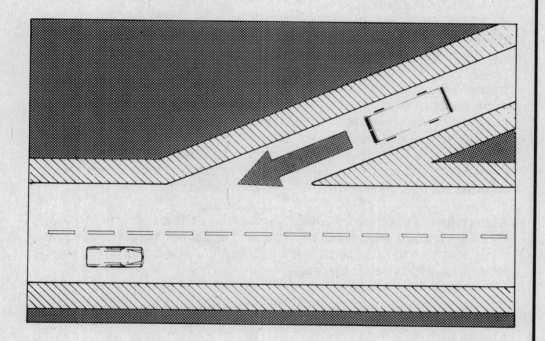

FIGURE 14-9: MERGING

21. SIGNALING

Performance: You must signal your intent to merge while you are on the entrance ramp leading to a freeway.

Situation: This performance is scored at the entrance to a freeway or highway where you must line up your vehicle with the roadway in order to see overtaking traffic in the mirror.

Scoring: Scoring of this performance begins after your vehicle enters the merge ramp.

Scored YES if you switch on the turn signal in the direction of your merge. The signal must be made after entering the acceleration lane and before entering the freeway or main roadway.

Scored NO if you fail to switch on the turn signal in the proper direction before entering the freeway or main roadway.

22. MIRROR CHECKS

Performance: You must position vehicle so that you can check the rear view mirror for traffic to the side of the vehicle.

In merging onto a main road, the driver of a heavy vehicle is dependent upon the mirrors as a means of observing traffic on the main road and locating a large enough gap in traffic. In order to be able to see the main travel lanes, the vehicle must be parallel to the roadway. The driver then must be able to shift his or her attention back and forth between the mirror and the road ahead in order to observe traffic and yet maintain the correct path.

Situation: This performance is assessed at the entrance to a freeway or road where the driver must align the vehicle with the road in order to be able to see in the mirror the traffic with which he or she will have to merge.

Scoring: Scoring of this performance begins as the vehicle enters the acceleration lane and ends when it starts movement to the new lane.

Scored YES if you check traffic through the appropriate mirror before entering the main roadway.

Scored NO if you fail to check the mirror before entering the main roadway.

23. SPEED

Performance: You must get as close to the highway speed as possible. You must use the acceleration lane to gain as much speed as possible.

Situation: This performance should be scored at the entrance to a freeway or road where you must align the vehicle with the road in order to be able to see overtaking traffic in the mirror.

Scoring: Scoring of this performance begins as vehicle enters the acceleration lane and ends when it enters the new travel lane on the road.

Scored YES if performance meets all of the following:
1. Vehicle is speeding up throughout the acceleration lane.
2. You do not slow or stop vehicle prior to entering the main road.

Scored NO if:
1. You slow down or bring the vehicle to a stop prior to entering the main road.
2. You fail to use as much of the acceleration lane as is necessary to gain speed.

Performance may not be scored if:
1. Stalled traffic on the roadway forces you to slow down or come to a stop in the acceleration lane.
2. There is no gap in traffic, and you merge before reaching the end of the acceleration lane.

24. CANCEL SIGNAL

Performance: You must cancel the directional signal after completing the merge.

Situation: The situation is the same as is found in Performances 21, 22, and 23.

Scoring: Scoring of this performance begins as soon as the rear of the vehicle has entered the new lane of travel.

Scored YES if you cancel the signal within three seconds after entering the new lane.

Scored NO if you do not cancel the signal within three seconds after entering the new lane.

Traffic Restrictions

25. LANE RESTRICTIONS

This check tests your ability to comply with lane usage rules. These rules are imposed by road signs, traffic signals, and lane markings.

Lane restrictions are important for safety. This performance check is an indirect test of skill. Test drivers who fail to comply with lane restrictions are often too busy controlling the vehicle to notice the restrictions. Because of this, inexperienced drivers tend to overlook these restrictions.

Performance: You are to comply with lane restrictions imposed by signs, signals, and markings. While most lane restrictions apply to all vehicles, there are some that apply only to heavy vehicles. These include special bus or truck lanes. Other examples are the lane controls which say:

- TRUCKS AND BUSES KEEP RIGHT

- LEFT LANE NO TRUCKS OR BUSES

There are also restrictions which apply to all vehicles, but with which drivers of heavy vehicles find it difficult to comply. An example of this is the zebra-striped area in a merge area. Big vehicles sometimes cross into this area as they merge onto a main road.

Situation: This performance is scored at locations where signs, signals, or markings are used to control lane use.

Scoring: Scoring of this performance begins at the point where a sign, signal, or marking specifies the start of the lane restriction. The scoring zone ends when the lane restriction ends.

Scored YES if you avoid operating your vehicle in the restricted area.

Scored NO if you clearly violate a lane restriction by using the wrong lane or driving across a solid roadway marking, zebra stripes, or other marking.

The performance should not be scored if:
1. The vehicle barely touches a lane line. This is not a test of lane keeping.
2. You are forced to drive over a portion of a lane marking because of vehicle length. For instance, a turning bay may not be large enough to handle the entire vehicle.
3. The presence of other vehicles prevents you from complying with the lane restrictions.

26. TRAVEL RESTRICTIONS

This check deals only with travel restrictions that apply uniquely to commercial motor vehicles. These travel restrictions may include bridge weight limits, underpass height clearance limits, and restricted roads ("NO COMMERCIAL VEHICLES"). Inexperienced commercial vehicle drivers tend to overlook these restrictions.

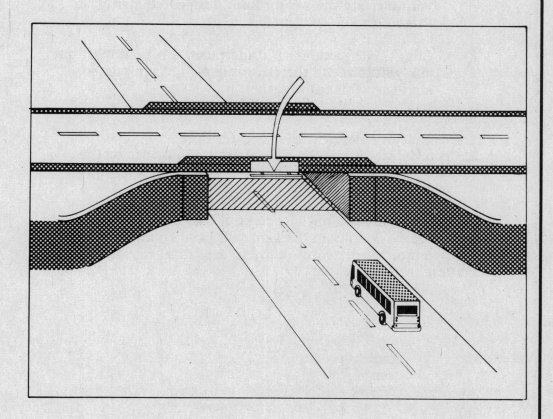

FIGURE 14-10: UNDERPASS CLEARANCE

Performance: You are to comply with travel restrictions that apply to commercial motor vehicles. These restrictions may be imposed by signs or roadway markings.

Situation: This performance is scored at locations where signs or markings are used to restrict commercial vehicle travel.

Scoring: Scoring of this performance begins at the point where a sign or marking indicates the start of the travel restriction. Scoring ends when the travel restriction is passed.

Scored YES if you meet all of the following requirements:
1. You avoid driving in a restricted area.
2. You know the weight limit for a bridge and the height clearance at an underpass.

    •   After passing over a bridge, the examiner may ask you to recite the weight limit if a posted sign gave this information.

    •   After driving under an underpass, the examiner may ask you to recite the clearance height if a posted sign gave this information.

Scored NO if:
1. You clearly violate a travel restriction.
2. You did not know the weight limit of a bridge or the clearance height of an overpass when this information was posted.

The performance should not be scored if the presence of other vehicles or traffic conditions prevent you from complying with the restriction or hinder your ability to see travel restriction information.

Blind Intersections

FIGURE 14-11: BLIND INTERSECTION

27. SEARCH

Performance: You must direct your attention toward the blind intersection as you approach it. You must be able to quickly detect and respond to any vehicle or pedestrian entering into view.

Situation: This performance is scored at intersections having these special features:

1. There is no traffic signal or sign to control the progress of your vehicle.
2. Vehicles on the cross street must yield the right of way to your vehicle.

3. The route requires you to drive straight across the intersection.
4. Your view of the intersection is blocked by buildings, trees, bushes, parked vehicles and other obstacles.

Scoring: This performance grades your ability to maintain awareness of highway and traffic surroundings while you drive. Many unskilled drivers are so busy controlling their vehicles that they do not notice potential hazards such as blind intersections.

Scoring of this performance begins before entering the intersection. Scoring ends as the vehicle enters the intersection.

Scored YES if you direct your attention to the intersection to detect any hazard entering into view.

Scored NO if you fail to look toward the blind intersection. You must look in both directions if your view of both directions is blocked.

28. SPEED

Performance: You must slow the vehicle before entering a blind intersection in order to be prepared to stop quickly if necessary.

Situation: The situation is the same as in blind intersection: SEARCH.

Scoring: Scoring of this performance begins before the vehicle enters the intersection and ends as it enters the intersection.

Scored YES if you slow the vehicle before the intersection.

Scored NO if you fail to reduce speed prior to entering the intersection.

Performance is not scored if you are forced to slow because of other traffic or hazards.

Driving Hills

FIGURE 14-12: HILL AHEAD

Although the following performances are all related to hills, it is
not likely your test route will have one location that meets the requirements for scoring each performance. Therefore, the performances may be scored at different locations along the test route.
In some instances, you may be asked to "make-believe" you are
on an upgrade or downgrade. In this case, you will probably be
asked to go through the motions and explain or demonstrate what
you would do.

29. STARTING UPHILL

Performance: You must accelerate the vehicle smoothly from a
complete stop. You may need to use extra engine power to handle
the vehicle's tendency to roll backwards. Big vehicles tend to roll
back because of their weight.

Situation: This performance is scored at intersections:

1. That require a complete stop.

2. Where the grade is steep enough to require you to keep the brakes applied to keep from rolling backwards.

3. Where the vehicle will go straight ahead after the stop.

4. Where all or a part of vehicle is on an incline.

Scoring: This performance is scored YES if the performance meets all of the following requirements:
1. The vehicle pulls away from the stop smoothly.
2. The engine remains running.
3. The vehicle does not roll backward.

Scored NO if:
1. The vehicle jerks forward.
2. The engine dies.
3. The vehicle rolls backward.

30. SHIFTING UPHILL

Performance: You must keep the engine speed within the normal operating range, avoiding lugging or over speeding the engine while driving on an upgrade.

Heavy vehicles must be shifted more often on upgrades. Since there is a tendency to lose speed quickly, shifts must be completed rapidly and smoothly. Failure to do so may result in a great loss of speed or having to stop.

Situation: This performance is scored on an upgrade which is long enough and steep enough to prevent driving uphill without downshifting. The road (test zone) should be straight and free of curves. This means that your speed control is solely in response to the upgrade.

Scoring: Scoring of this performance begins when the vehicle starts its upward path and ends when it reaches the top of the grade.

Scored YES if you operate the vehicle within the specified operating range (does not let the engine fall below or operate above the engine operating RPM level).

Scored NO if:
1. Engine lugs before downshifting.
2. Engine over-revs when downshifting.
3. You force the shift lever or have to move it several times to complete the downshift.
4. Gears clash when downshifting.

31. SPEED DOWNHILL

Performance: You must maintain a safe speed on downgrades. The purpose of this check is to measure your ability to control the speed of the vehicle on a long downgrade.

Situation: This performance should be scored on downgrades which are:

1. Steep enough to require you to apply continuous pressure to the brakes throughout the grade to control road speed. The test zone will be on a two or three percent grade.

2. Between one-fourth and one-half mile long.

The test zone should be:

- Straight so speed control is solely in response to the downward grade.

- Located in areas with a speed limit of 40 mph or above.

- Located where the speed of traffic is near the posted speed limit.

- In an area of light traffic so speed control is only in response to the grade.

Scoring: Scoring of this performance begins as the vehicle starts downhill. It ends when the entire vehicle levels off at the bottom of the grade.

Scored YES if the performance meets all of the following requirements:
1. The speed does not exceed the posted limit.
2. The speed does not drop more than 10 MPH below the posted limit.

Scored NO if:
1. The speed exceeds the posted limit.
2. The speed drops more than 10 MPH below the posted limit.

32. STOPPING UPHILL

You must bring your vehicle to a complete stop on an incline. You must maintain control of the vehicle and not allow it to roll back.

Situation: This performance is scored on a grade where the vehicle can be stopped and parked for a minute or two. The grade may be only a gentle slope, but one that will cause a roll back if the vehicle is not parked properly.

Scoring: Scoring of this performance depends on a complete stop without allowing the vehicle to roll back.

Scored YES if you stop and park on an incline without roll back.

Scored NO if the vehicle rolls backwards after being stopped and parked.

33. STOPPING DOWNHILL

Performance: You must bring the vehicle to a safe stop on a downgrade. You may also be asked to go through the motions of driving down a very long and steep hill and to explain how you would control the vehicle.

Situation: The situation is the same as in Performance 32. In addition, you may be asked to "make-believe" you are on a long and steep downgrade. The test zone may be a flat section of road with little or no traffic so you can explain how you would handle a long, steep downgrade.

Scoring: This performance may be scored in several ways because of the hazards of driving downhill and stopping on steep hills.

If the test is performed on a downhill stretch of roadway, YES is scored if you can stop and park without a noticeable roll back.

If test is simulated — you are asked to make-believe you are on a steep and long downhill grade — YES is scored if you can explain or demonstrate the proper actions to take in slowing, stopping, and parking a vehicle on a steep downgrade.

Scored NO if:
1. Your vehicle rolls backward while stopping and parking on a downhill stretch of roadway.
2. If a simulated downgrade is used and you cannot explain or demonstrate the proper actions to take in slowing, stopping, and parking a heavy vehicle on a long, steep downgrade.

Railway Crossings

This performance group may use any of three types of railways crossings. The best test situation is where there is:

1. A crossing controlled by signal lights and/or gates.

2. An uncontrolled crossing where no lights or gates are present.

These crossings may or may not be graded (raised tracks) crossings.

If neither of these crossings is available at the test area, you may be asked to demonstrate your railway crossing ability at a regular intersection. In this case, the examiner will ask you to pretend the intersection is a rail crossing.

Your state may have special laws governing buses at railway crossings. Many states require buses to make a complete stop and open the passenger door(s). What does your state require the driver to do at a railway crossing?

34. TRAIN CHECKS

Performance: You must check for the presence of trains at railway crossings. This calls for you to look left and right, roll down the window to listen, and open the door of the bus.

Situation: This performance is scored at any of three types of railway crossings: 1) controlled; 2) uncontrolled; or 3) simulated. A regular intersection may be used in place of an actual crossing.

The crossings should have enough sight distance so that the examiner can see if you make head movements (which indicate you are looking all about you) when you approach the crossing. As a driver who is being tested and graded, your head movements right and left may be the only way the examiner can tell if you are making a train check and search.

Scoring: Scoring of this performance begins during the approach to the crossing and ends before the crossing is reached.

Scored YES if all of the requirements are met:
1. You look left and right to check for trains before you reach the stop zone of the railway crossing. The stop zone is within 10 feet of the nearest tracks or at the bottom of the grade of a raised crossing.
2. Roll down a window to listen for trains.
3. Open the door of your vehicle to help you look and listen for trains. Some vehicles may be exempt from this requirement. What does your State require?

Scored NO if:
1. You fail to look left and right for the presence of trains before you reach the stop zone of a railway crossing.
2. You fail to roll down a window to listen for trains before you reach the stop zone of a railway crossing.

3. You fail to open the door of your vehicle to help you look and listen for trains. For some vehicles this requirement may not be scored.

35. STOPS

Performance: You must safely stop the vehicle at the proper point at a railway crossing. Your stop must be made at the location or point that is safest for the situation.

Situation: There are two situations that apply to this performance check:

1. When a train is actually approaching.

2. When a stop is mandatory — required by law. Some vehicles at some crossings may be exempt from this requirement. A stop may not be required at a streetcar crossing or railroad tracks used only for switching purposes within a business district or abandoned and spur line crossings marked by "abandoned" or "exempt" signs.

The Federal Motor Carrier Safety Act (FMCSR) states that all non-exempt commercial vehicles shall not cross a railroad track or tracks at grade unless the driver:

1. First stops the vehicle within 50 feet, and not closer than 15 feet to, the tracks.

2. Listens and looks in each direction along the tracks for an approaching train.

3. Makes sure that no train is approaching.

As a general rule, a bus or truck with hazardous goods must stop. The stop must be made not closer than 15 feet from the nearest rail. The driver may also be required to:

1. Open the window.

2. Open the door.

3. Put the parking brake on.

4. Shift into neutral gear.

For the purposes of a CDL Road Test, the test route may take you over railway crossings that may otherwise be exempt from a stop. Make sure you are clearly informed about the test procedure at railway crossings before you start the test drive.

Scoring: The performance is scored YES if all of these requirements are met:
1. You stop not closer than 15 feet from the nearest rail.
2. You open the window and door as required.
3. You put on the parking brake.
4. You shift into neutral gear.

You performance is scored NO if you fail to do any of the following things:
1. Come to a complete stop when you are within 15 feet of the nearest rail.
2. Open a window or door — if required — after the stop.
3. Shift into neutral gear after the stop.
4. Put your parking brake on after the stop.

36. CROSSING TRACKS

Performance: You must approach and cross tracks in a safe and proper manner. You do not cross tracks at a railway crossing until you are certain that no trains are coming.

When it is safe to do so, you may drive the vehicle across the tracks in a gear that permits the vehicle to complete the crossing without a change of gears. You must not shift gears while crossing the tracks.

Situation: The situation is the same as in Performances 34 and 35.

Scoring: The performance is scored YES if all these requirements are met:
1. You cross the tracks in the proper gear.
2. You do not change gears while you are on the tracks.
3. You do not stop or brake on the tracks.
4. You do not pass or make lane change on the tracks.

Scored NO if you do any of the following:
1. Cross the tracks in a gear that is not proper for the situation.
2. Change gears while you are on the tracks.
3. Stop or brake on the tracks.
4. Pass or make a lane change on the tracks.

This completes the listing of the 11 performance groups and their 36 performance checks.

Some road tests may include a General Driving group of performances. Here are some examples of what might be checked:

General Driving

USE OF CONTROLS

1.	Used clutch properly	YES	NO
2.	Used gears properly	YES	NO
3.	Used brakes properly	YES	NO
4.	Proper steering (both hands on wheel)	YES	NO
5.	Used auxiliary equipment properly	YES	NO

COURTESY

1.	Signaled and communicated properly	YES	NO
2.	Yielded right of way to pedestrians	YES	NO
3.	Yielded right of way to other vehicles when appropriate	YES	NO
4.	Maintained proper following distance	YES	NO

RULES OF THE ROAD

1.	Obeyed all traffic signs and signals	YES	NO
2.	Wore seat belt	YES	NO

These General Driving performances are usually scored after the test drive is completed. The scoring relies heavily on the examiner's opinion of your driving. It is for this reason that some road tests do not use this set of performance checks.

Summary

Now we will summarize the road test. Here is how it works:

1. The test is taken over a route that is planned in advance. As you drive, the examiner gives you directions. Follow the examiner's directions closely.

2. At certain locations along the test route the examiner will check your performance. For example, for a right turn, the examiner will score you on your:

    A. Speed.

    B. Position in the lane.

        1) Single lane street.
        2) Multiple lane street.

    C. Mirror checks

    D. Lane keeping

    E. Canceling signal

    F. Upshifting

So, if the test requires you to make four right turns, you will be scored on 24 performances (4 turns with 6 performance checks at each turn) during the right turn part of the test. You will probably need to make more than four right turns during the test drive. If your state requires four right turns you will be scored only at the four right turn locations picked for scoring. The same holds true for the other performance groups. Remember, the scoring zones are picked in advance.

Here is a list of the performance groups and the number of performance checks to be scored for each group:

	Number of Total Performance Group Checks	Performance Scoring Locations	Performances Scored
A. Starting	2	4	8
B. Stopping	3	4	12
C. Driving Straight	3	5	15
D. Driving Curves	2	4	8
E. Lane Changing	3	3	9
		Left Right	
F. Turning	6	4 4	48
G. Merging	4	2	8
H. Traffic Restrictions	2	2	4
I. Blind Intersections	2	2	4
J. Driving Hills	5	1	5
K. Railway Crossings	3	2	6
		Total	127

FIGURE 14-13: PERFORMANCE SCORING

The number of scoring locations may vary from state to state. They may vary among examination stations within a state. For instance, a state may test five right turns and two left turns instead of four of each. The roads surrounding a particular examination station may make it necessary to vary the number of scoring locations for a particular group. There may not be a railway crossing available. At any rate, there can be as many as 127 performances scored. This total may vary according to location. The number may vary because of time, weather, and any number of factors.

In most cases, a state using this type of road test will try not to let the number of scoring performances fall below 100 or exceed 130. Of course, this is up to the state. There are no national rules or requirements to follow on this matter. The same is true for the scoring method used, passing scores, and automatic failures.

One factor you can count on is that the test route will be long enough to provide all the traffic and road situations needed to grade your driving skill and ability.

3. For each driving error you make at a scoring location, points will be deducted. This is how it could work: You are given 100 points at the start of the test. One point is deducted for each driving error. A grade of 75 is needed to pass the test. In some scoring methods, more than one point may be deducted for a more serious error.

4. Before you take your road test, make sure you know:

- How you will be scored.

- What performances will be graded.

- What makes up the passing score.

- The grounds for immediate failure.

- The rules for repeating the test in case you fail.

REVIEW QUESTIONS

1. What is the purpose of the Road Test?

   _____

   _____

2. In your state, is the test taken over a route which has the scoring locations planned in advance? _____

   If so:

   A. How many right turns and left turns will be scored?

      _____

   B. Will your performance be graded on city business streets, at intersections, at railway crossings, on left and right curves, on rural roads, on freeways or expressways, and on hills?

      _____

      _____

      _____

3. What performance checks will you be graded on for these groups?

   • Starting _____

   • Stopping _____

   • Driving Straight _____

   • Driving Hills _____

   • Lane Changing _____

   • Turning _____

      _____

      _____

      _____

      _____

   • Merging _____

      _____

- Traffic Restrictions _____

  _____

- Blind Intersections _____

  _____

- Driving Hills _____

  _____

- Railway Crossings _____

  _____

4. Can you answer these questions about your State's CDL Road Test?

   - What performances will be graded?

     _____

     _____

   - How will your test performances be scored?

     _____

     _____

   - What will cause you to fail the test?

     _____

     _____

   - Can you retake or repeat the test if you fail? When?

     _____

     _____

5. In this chapter, the scoring rules for 36 road test performances are described. Do you know what makes up a "correct" and "incorrect" scoring performance for each of the 36? If not, you should review the scoring rules. They are found in the TEST SCORING section of this chapter. There is a good chance that your road test will be based on the same or similar rules.

PART FIVE
RESOURCE MATERIALS

Part Five is the reference portion of this guide. There are 14 sections of material. Each section provides information useful to the commercial vehicle driver. Some of the information is technical. The technical information is for reference rather than study purposes. Like other parts of this book, the contents of Part Five are meant not so much to be read but to be used as needed.

Section A: A Safe Driving Knowledge Test
This test covers the rules of the road and other information on safe driving all drivers should know. A section which explains each answer is included. It also provides general safe driving information.

Section B: Model Uniform Commercial Driver License Act
This "model" or example of a state's Commercial Driver's License Act will give you an idea of what this law may contain.

The example which appears here is an adapted version of a draft model law prepared by the Legal Services Committee of the American Association of Motor Vehicle Administrators for use by the various members of the Association.

Remember, this document is only a model — not a real law. It is intended only for use as an example of a CDL law.

Section C: U.S. Government Printing Office Bookstores
This listing provides the addresses of GPO bookstores across the country. You can obtain government documents such as the Federal Motor Carrier Safety Regulations frome these bookstores.

Section D: Written Examination — Federal Motor Carrier Safety Regulations
This 66-question test is designed to teach drivers about the federal rules and regulations that apply to them. The answers with references to the FMCSR are also included in this section.

The motor carrier is required to give the exam and be satisfied that the driver is familiar with the FMCSR. No grades are given. There are no pass-fail marks. The carrier must go over all questions that are answered incorrectly with the driver.

Section E: Federal Regulations Governing Commercial Motor Carriers and Drivers
This document lists and summarizes the various regulations which govern the operation of commercial motor vehicles (mainly those that operate between states).

Section F: Division Offices of the Office of Motor Carrier Safety
This state-by-state listing identifies the offices where information may be obtained about all federal regulations governing commercial motor vehicle operations.

Section G: Requirements for Commercial Vehicle Drivers
This listing of what the commercial motor vehicle driver may be required to know or do for either licensing or employment purposes.

Section H: Commercial Vehicle Cargo Classifications
These are the classes of commercial motor vehicle cargo as identified by the Federal Highway Administration.

Section I: Military Time
This chart will help you convert ordinary time into military time. The federal regulations require that military time be used when preparing accident reports.

Section J: Metric Conversion Chart
This metric conversion chart can help you convert weight and measures from one system to the other when needed.

Section K: Factors Contributing to Commercial Vehicle Accidents
This is a listing of the many factors which contribute to commercial vehicle accidents. It is similar to the one used by companies and official agencies in preparing accident reports and identifying causes or factors in accidents involving CMVs.

Section L: Lights and Reflectors
This appendix identifies the lights and reflectors which may be found on commercial motor vehicles.

Section M: Return of Out-of-State Licenses
This is a state-by-state listing of where to return your out-of-state driver's license if you have more than one. Federal rules require that you hold only one commercial driver's license. You must return all others under penalty of law. You may be fined up to $2,500 if you do not return them.

Section N: State Commercial Driver's License Offices
This is a state-by-state listing of who to contact for information about your state's commercial driver's license requirements.

Section A
Safe Driving Knowledge Test

A Safe Driving Knowledge Test checks your general knowledge of safe driving. This type of test is for all types of drivers. Whether you drive a car, motorcycle, truck, or bus, you should know the basics of safe driving. The test items which follow will give you a good idea of what you should know about safe driving in general.

As you take the test, you will notice that many of the questions are about driving a car. This should not distract you. Remember, in becoming a bus driver, it is assumed you are already licensed to drive an automobile. As a licensed driver, you must have a good general knowledge of safe driving. This test provides a review of your knowledge.

Directions

The test consists of questions you should be able to answer about safe driving. There is no time limit for the test. Some questions are multiple-choice. Several possible answers are given for each question. You are to circle the answer you think is best.

Example:

1. A red light means you are to:
    A. Continue driving.
    B. Stop.
    C. Slow down.
    D. Turn.

Some questions are completion items. You must provide the answers yourself. Long answers are not necessary. Just write what you think is most important.

Source

This test is from a report prepared by the Human Resources Research Organization (Alexandria, Virginia) for the U.S. Department of Transportation's National Highway Traffic Safety Administration. The report, DRIVER EDUCATION TASK ANALYSIS: INSTRUCTIONAL OBJECTIVES, is available from the National Technical Information Service (NTIS) under the same title, identified as DOT-HS 800 369 (HumRRO Technical Report 71-9), dated March, 1971.

Safe Driving Knowledge Test

1. In preventing injuries from collisions, the seat belt and shoulder harness in combination are:
   A. As effective as the seat belt alone.
   B. More effective than either alone.
   C. As effective as the shoulder harness alone.
   D. More helpful in reducing whiplash injuries rather than reducing other types of injuries.

2. Adjusting the sideview mirror so that the door handle and the tail of your car can be seen:
   A. Is particularly important in parallel parking.
   B. Provides a reference point for judging the distance of other cars.
   C. Will prevent you from seeing passing cars.
   D. Keeps you from seeing enough of the roadway.

3. Placing the car in neutral before you start the engine:
   A. Prevents lurching forward if the foot slips off the clutch pedal.
   B. Saves wear on the clutch.
   C. May cause the engine to race.
   D. May allow the car to roll backward.

4. When attempting to start a car, pumping the accelerator:
   A. Is a good idea because it gets plenty of gas to the carburetor.
   B. Has little effect on the ease of starting.
   C. May flood the engine.
   D. Helps prevent vapor lock

5. When the starter works but the engine will not start, any one of several problems may be the cause. Which one of the following problems is NOT the cause?
   A. A flooded engine
   B. A wet ignition system
   C. A frozen fuel line
   D. A poor connection at the battery cable

6. Once a manual shift car has been shifted into third gear:
   A. The left foot should remain on the clutch pedal for emergency reactions.
   B. The left foot should be rested against the brake pedal for possible emergency stopping.
   C. The left foot should be moved away from the clutch to avoid "riding" it.
   D. Speeds of under 40 mph should be avoided.

7. Pulling away quickly tends to:
   A. Save on gas consumption.
   B. Wear out the carburetor.
   C. Burn more gas than necessary.
   D. Reduce swaying.

8. When accelerating on snowy or slippery surfaces, smooth steady acceleration:
   A. Is not as important as it is on dry surfaces.
   B. Helps keep the rear wheels from spinning.
   C. Is best accomplished by starting in first gear in a manual shift car.
   D. Is no easier when using tires with snow treads.

9. Shifting gears while turning should be avoided because:
   A. Both hands should be kept on the steering wheel.
   B. The foot should be ready to break if necessary.
   C. The driver's attention is distracted.
   D. All of the above.

10. In general, the safest driving speed on the roadway is:
    A. 5 mph faster than the average vehicle.
    B. 5 mph slower than the average vehicle.
    C. The average speed of the other vehicles.
    D. A speed that more or less varies from the posted speed limit.

11. Before downshifting while driving at a relatively high speed, you should:
    A. Increase your speed slightly.
    B. Slow down.
    C. Check the oil pressure.
    D. Pump or repeatedly jab the brake pedal.

12. Which of the following is true of power brakes?
    A. They increase stopping distance.
    B. They decrease stopping distance.
    C. They do not change stopping distance.
    D. They give the driver a better feel of the pavement.

13. The best way to be sure that it is safe to back up is to:
    A. Look out the left side window.
    B. Look directly out the rear window.
    C. Look into the rearview mirror.
    D Blow the horn and wait a few seconds.

14. When backing up, the driver should:
    A. Rely entirely on mirrors to see behind him.
    B. Allow a greater stopping distance than when traveling forward at the same speed.
    C. Apply less pressure on the brake pedal when stopping because the brakes are more sensitive when the car is in reverse.
    D. Sound his horn before backing.

15. Which of the following situations would be least likely to produce a skid?
    A. Slowing down abruptly.
    B. Driving at high speeds on curves and turns.
    C. Accelerating rapidly.
    D. Pumping the brakes to slow down gradually.

16. The chief cause of accidents is:
    A. Drivers failing to continually watch for hazards.
    B. Drunken drivers.
    C. Use of drugs by drivers.
    D. Faulty vehicles.

17. Carbon monoxide from a faulty exhaust system:
    A. Can kill you.
    B. Is harmful but cannot kill.
    C. Is harmful to the vision only.
    D. Is not dangerous.

18. When you begin to get tired while driving, it is good idea to:
    A. Turn on the heater.
    B. Focus your eyes on the road directly in front of the car.
    C. Listen to lively music.
    D. Close the car windows.

19. Even a small amount of alcohol affects driving. A driver's judgment is affected by drinking alcohol in quantities as small as:
    A. 1 ounce of whiskey.
    B. 2 ounces of whiskey.
    C. 16 ounces of beer.
    D. 24 ounces of beer.

20. Rapid acceleration followed by sudden stops:
    A. Is not dangerous.
    B. Invites rear-end collisions.
    C. Does more harm to the car than anything else.
    D. Is a normal practice of expert drivers in stop-and-go situations.

21. Sudden strong wind gusts on highways:
    A. Generally affect only the movement of large vehicles.
    B. Cause only visual problems because of dust and dirt being blown about.
    C. Can move a car sideways into another lane.
    D. Do not affect the car's movement.

22. When approaching areas on freeways where other vehicles are entering, a driver can help the flow of traffic by:
    A. Slowing down.
    B. Moving to the middle or passing lane.
    C. Speeding up to get clear of the area.
    D. Adjusting his speed to equal the speed of the entering vehicles.

23. In this state, the legal separation distance you must maintain from an emergency vehicle is:
    A. 200 feet.
    B. 300 feet.
    C. 400 feet.
    D. 500 feet.

24. Motorcycles should be followed from a greater distance than automobiles to lessen the chances of a collision because:
    A. They can stop faster than four-wheeled vehicles.
    B. Motorcyclists tend to drive dangerously.
    C. Motorcyclists cannot drive dependably because of poor rear vision.
    D. Motorcycle brake lights are not as reliable as automobile brake lights.

25. If you are following a driver who is soon to leave an expressway, your greatest danger is that he will:
    A. Slow down on the roadway rather than the off-ramp.
    B. Turn into the off-ramp at the last minute.
    C. Leave the expressway at too great a speed.
    D. Fail to signal in time.

26. A broken line painted on the center of the highway means:
    A. You may pass or change lanes.
    B. Only drivers on the other side of the road may pass.
    C. You may not pass.
    D. Use extreme caution.

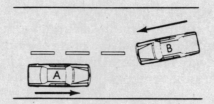

27. In the collision situation above, the best course of action for car A is to:
    A. Maintain course and hope that Car B returns to the proper lane.
    B. Pull off the road into the shrubbery at the right.
    C. Pull off the road onto the shoulder at the left.
    D. Hit the brakes and try to stop.

28. Braking hard can cause loss of steering control because it:
    A. May lock the front wheels.
    B. Forces you to concentrate less on steering.
    C. Can actually damage the steering mechanism when turning sharply.
    D. Places weight on the front tires, which causes them to buckle.

29. Vehicles are required to stop for a stopped school bus in your state:
    A. Except in an oncoming lane of a 4-lane highway.
    B. Only if children can be seen crossing the road.
    C. Only if a crossing guard signals for a stop.
    D. Whenever it has stopped to take on or discharge passengers.

30. Most pedestrians killed by automobiles were:
    A. Typically experienced drivers.
    B. Generally middle-aged men.
    C. Generally accident prone people.
    D. Not licensed drivers themselves.

31. A basic precaution to take in driving down long, steep grades is to:
    A. Keep your foot lightly on the brake at all times.
    B. Pump the brake occasionally.
    C. Keep the car in "drive" or third gear.
    D. Put the car in second gear or a lower driving range before starting down.

32. If, while going through an intersection, you decide that you are going in
    the wrong direction, you should:
    A. Make a U-turn if no traffic is present.
    B. Stop, back up, and turn in the direction you wish to travel.
    C. Use your turn signal and turn quickly.
    D. Continue through the intersection and drive around the block.

33. A traffic signal showing an "advanced green" means that:
    A. Oncoming traffic is stopping during the early period of the green signal.
    B. Oncoming traffic will get a green signal in advance of you.
    C. Oncoming traffic may proceed while you are stopped.
    D. You must proceed with caution when oncoming traffic begins to move.

34. On freeways, you should be particularly alert as you approach entrances where acceleration lanes are:
    A. Short and the freeway speed is slow.
    B. Long and the freeway speed is slow.
    C. Short and the freeway speed is high.
    D. Long and the freeway speed is high.

35. Downshifting:
    A. Slows the car down by reducing the pulling power of the engine.
    B. Slows the car down by increasing the pulling power of the engine.
    C. Causes the fan to turn at a lower speed and prevents the car from overheating.
    D. Has no effect on the rate of speed at which the fan turns.

36. Accelerating slightly through a curve:
    A. Is usually a dangerous practice.
    B. Reduces your chances of skidding if your original speed was slow enough.
    C. Helps speed up traffic.
    D. Is strictly for the race track.

37. If a curve turns out to be sharper than you expected, you should:
    A. Slow down by releasing the accelerator and lightly applying the brake if necessary.
    B. Accelerate slightly to reduce the chances of skidding.
    C. Steer to the "inside" of the curve.
    D. Steer to the "outside" of the curve.

38. Where should you expect to find the most slippery surfaces?
    A. On the crown of the road.
    B. Near curves.
    C. On hills.
    D. At intersections.

39. What procedure should you follow if you must drive through deep water?
    A. Slow down.
    B. Slow down and shift into a lower gear.
    C. Shift into a lower gear but try to maintain your original speed.
    D. Drive near the center of the roadway where the water is considerably more shallow due to the slant of the pavement.

40. Which area is likely to be the most slippery after a rainfall during freezing weather?
    A. The shoulders of the road.
    B. The roadway over a bridge or culvert.
    C. Roadways in sheltered areas.
    D. Areas paved with asphalt instead of concrete.

41. When stopping on wet pavement, the stopping distance allowance should be increased by:
    A. 25 percent (25%).
    B. 50 percent (50%).
    C. 200 percent (200%).
    D. 300 percent (300%).

42. If a wheel drops off the roadway onto the shoulder while you are driving at a normal highway speed, you should:
    A. Avoid braking if possible.
    B. Stop the car as abruptly as possible.
    C. Steer onto the roadway again as quickly as you can.
    D. Quickly drive completely off the roadway and stop as soon as possible.

43. While crossing railroad tracks, you should:
    A. Attempt to shift as you normally do.
    B. Downshift to increase your power.
    C. Accelerate to clear the tracks quickly.
    D. Avoid shifting gears.

44. When driving on a six-lane divided highway (three lanes each way), the driver should:
    A. Drive in the right-hand lane if he isn't preparing to turn off the roadway.
    B. Drive in the center lane(s) when driving slowly.
    C. Drive in the left lane only to pass.
    D. Do none of the above.

45. When there is standing water on the roadway, the best reason for avoiding driving through it at very high speeds is:
    A. The slippery roadway will increase stopping distance.
    B. Your tires will tend to ride on top of the water.
    C. Spray from other cars will make it hard to see.
    D. Spray may cause the engine to stop.

46. When driving on an ice- or snow-covered upgrade, you can prevent spinning your wheels by:
    A. Increasing your speed when you begin to climb.
    B. Shifting into a lower gear before starting up.
    C. Maintaining a constant pressure on the accelerator.
    D. Shifting into a lower gear and trying to maintain a constant speed.

47. If your car is stuck in heavy snow during a storm and cannot be moved, you should:
    A. Stay in the car with the engine running and the window open.
    B. Stay in the car with the engine running and the windows closed.
    C. Stay in the car with the engine off.
    D. Go look for help.

48. When his money misses the basket at the exact-change booth of a toll plaza, the driver should:
    A. Retrieve the money quickly and put it in the basket before proceeding.
    B. Not attempt to retrieve the money, but replace it.
    C. Continue to drive through in order not to delay the following vehicles.
    D. Wait until the attendant arrives.

49. Which of the following vehicles are frequently required to stop for a railroad crossing?
    A. Tank trucks carrying flammable materials
    B. School buses
    C. Passenger buses
    D. All of the above

50. When visibility is reduced, day or night, by heavy fog, rain, sleet, or snow, the driver should:
    A. Use parking lights rather than high or low beams since their color is easier for oncoming vehicles to see.
    B. Use low-beam headlights.
    C. Use high-beam headlights.
    D. Use four-way flashers.

51. To keep the engine cool when stopped in heavy traffic during a period of extreme heat, the driver should:
    A. Turn off the engine until traffic begins to move.
    B. Shift to neutral and let the engine idle.
    C. Shift to neutral and race the engine slightly.
    D. Turn the engine off occasionally.

52. When it is necessary for a disabled manual transmission vehicle to be moved a few feet to get it completely off the roadway, the driver should:
    A. Press the starter which will cause the car to move.
    B. Not press the starter because it will drain the battery quickly.
    C. Push the car off the roadway.
    D. Leave the car where it is and wait for a tow truck to arrive.

53. What proportion of the nation's highway deaths are caused by drivers who have been drinking alcoholic beverages?
    A. One-tenth (1/10)
    B. One-quarter (1/4)
    C. One-half (1/2)
    D. Two-thirds (2/3)

54. Which of the following substances reduces alcohol concentration in the blood by up to one-half?
    A. Coffee
    B. Any liquid
    C. Food, particularly carbohydrates
    D. Aspirin

55. About how many bottles of beer or one-ounce shots of whiskey can a 150-pound person drink in an hour before becoming intoxicated by most legal standards?
    A. One (1)
    B. Two (2)
    C. Five (5)
    D. Eight (8)

56. To offset the glare caused by oncoming blinding headlights, the driver should:
    A. Squint his eyes, keeping them on the center of his lane.
    B. Try to maintain normal eye position since the movement away will be dangerous.
    C. Focus eyes on the right side of the roadway beyond the oncoming vehicle.
    D. Look down if the road is straight, and lift eyes when oncoming vehicle has passed.

57. If the accelerator becomes stuck in the down position, the first thing you should do is:
    A. Reach down and try to pry it up with your hand.
    B. Try to pry it up with your foot.
    C. Apply the brakes and look for a safe place to leave the roadway.
    D. Turn the ignition off.

58. If your brakes fail while you are on the roadway, the first thing you should do is:
    A. Keep your foot on the brake and wait until you get brake action again.
    B. Shift into a lower gear.
    C. Leave the roadway.
    D. Pump your brakes a few times.

59. If power brakes fail due to loss of power, the driver should:
    A. Steer the car onto the road shoulder where it will stop as it loses speed.
    B. Not try to exert more pressure since it will not help.
    C. Exert more pressure on the pedal.
    D. Try pumping the brake pedal.

60. If your car is running low on fuel and there are no service facilities nearby, you should:
    A. Drive fast to reach a service station before the fuel runs out.
    B. Continue at your present speed until you reach a service station.
    C. Reduce speed to about 30 mph for maximum conservation of fuel.
    D. Stop the car and flag down another motorist for fuel.

61. Prescription drugs taken in combination with alcoholic beverages:
    A. Can cause trouble unless the drug was prescribed by a licensed physician.
    B. Will tend to have their effects cancelled by the effect of alcohol.
    C. Will cause trouble if you drink too much.
    D. Can produce extremely harmful effects.

62. The most important reason to have a vehicle's mechanical condition inspected periodically is:
    A. To spot a dangerous situation.
    B. To meet a state inspection requirement.
    C. To become better acquainted with the way the car works.
    D. To avoid breakdown on the road.

63. When is the best time to pull back into a lane after passing another car?
    A. When the other driver signals with his turn indicator
    B. When you can see the other car through your rear window
    C. When the other car's left headlight is visible in the rearview mirror
    D. When both of the other car's headlights are visible in the rearview mirror

64. When turning right into an angle parking lane, which points on your car are most likely to strike other cars?
   A. Left and right front fenders
   B. Right front fender and right rear door
   C. Left front fender and left rear door
   D. Left front fender and right rear door

65. When making a right turn from a busy street into a narrow side street you should:
   A. Almost come to a stop before beginning the turn.
   B. Slow down a little more than usual.
   C. Swing a little to the left before beginning your turn.
   D. Shift into first gear before beginning the turn.

66. Which of the following is most important in determining how fast you can drive in fog?
   A. How far you can see
   B. How quickly you can stop
   C. The amount of traffic
   D. Whether it is day or night

67. Why is it a good idea to slow down when the vehicle is being buffeted by cross winds?
   A. It reduces the impact in case of a collision.
   B. It helps you "feel" wind effects more quickly.
   C. It helps the car grip the road better.
   D. It keeps you from moving sideways as far.

68. What should you do in regard to your headlights when it begins to get dark?
   A. Avoid turning them on as long as you can see clearly; headlights may actually make it more difficult to see.
   B. Turn on your parking lights as soon as it begins to get dark.
   C. Turn on your low beams as soon as it begins to get dark.
   D. Turn on your high beams as soon as it begins to get dark.

69. If you come up behind a compact car at night, it will:
   A. Be more difficult to spot than a standard car.
   B. Look farther away than a standard car at the same distance.
   C. Look closer than a standard car at the same distance.
   D. Look larger than it really is.

70. Tinted contact lenses:
   A. Help screen out sunglare.
   B. Are better in general than sunglasses.
   C. Reduce the ability to see at night.
   D. Are not much different from untinted lenses.

71. What is the main reason that it is unsafe to pass a moving car on the right?
    A. It makes it hard to see traffic approaching from the left.
    B. It may distract the other driver.
    C. The other driver may suddenly move to the right.
    D. An oncoming driver planning to turn left cannot see you.

72. As car A prepares to pass and passes Car B, in which position is Car A in the greatest danger from Car B?
    A.   B.   C.   D.

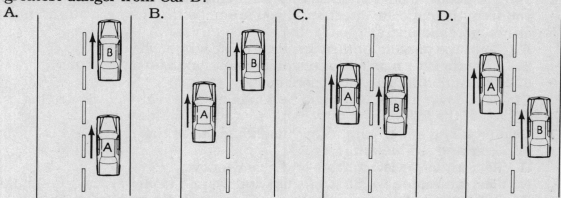

73. Looking to the sides of the road frequently:
    A. Is good because it helps you spot dangers.
    B. Is good because it is relaxing.
    C. Is bad because it takes your attention off the center of the road.
    D. Is bad because it is tiring.

74. Which of the following diagrams shows the best way to turn around using a driveway? Steps 1 and 3 are taken going forward. The heavy line (Step 2) indicates that the car is backing up.
    A.   B.   C.   D.

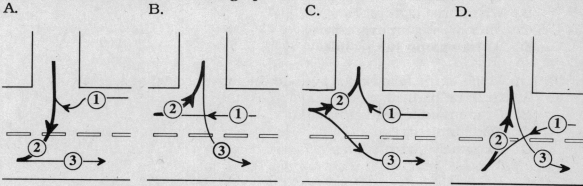

75. Under which of the following conditions should you sound your horn before passing another car?
    A. At night
    B. If the other car is signaling a right turn
    C. When the other car is coming up on a car ahead of it
    D. Under any condition

76. You are about to pass another car. Suddenly, you see a car approaching you from the opposite direction. If you are not sure whether you can make it or not, you should:
    A. Continue passing until you are sure one way or the other.
    B. Hesitate for a moment until you are sure one way or the other.
    C. Speed up a little to pass more quickly.
    D. Slow down immediately and pull in behind the car you were trying to pass.

77. Before pulling out to pass a car you should check the:
    A. Rear and sideview mirrors.
    B. Rear and sideview mirrors and side window.
    C. Rear and sideview mirrors, side window, and look over the left shoulder.
    D. Sideview mirror, rearview mirror, and then sideview mirror again.

78. If you have had too much to drink and want to drive, a few cups of strong black coffee:
    A. Do no good.
    B. Help you sober up a little sooner.
    C. Help you think a little more clearly for a short while.
    D. Keep you from passing out at the wheel.

79. When is the most important time to check your speedometer?
    A. When entering an expressway
    B. When driving at night
    C. After leaving an expressway
    D. When approaching a hill

80. On which of the following curves do the most accidents occur?
    A. Gradual banked curves
    B. Gradual unbanked curves
    C. Moderate curves
    D. Extremely sharp curves

81. As a general rule, if you are planning to make a turn at an intersection, the best time to signal your turn is:
    A. As soon as you have decided to make your turn.
    B. Whenever it will cause the least confusion.
    C. Approximately 100 feet from the intersection.
    D. When you begin to make the turn.

82. In general, people signal turns:
    A. Almost all the time.
    B. Anytime there is a car behind them.
    C. About half the time.
    D. Very rarely.

83. Which of the following diagrams shows the correct way to take a "Y" intersection?

    A. 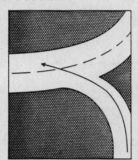   B. 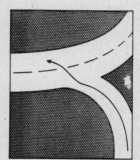   C.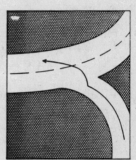

84. Draw a line connecting the sign with the correct description.

    (a)   1. Interstate highway system

    (b)   2. Stop

    (c)   3. Railroad crossing

    (d)   4. Yield

    (e)   5. Caution

85. You are stopped in a line of traffic headed uphill, waiting for the light to change. You should keep the car positioned by:
    A. Keeping your foot on the brake.
    B. Slipping the clutch.
    C. Putting the car in low gear.
    D. Idling in the "drive" position.

86. A road surface on a hot, rainy day is most slippery:
    A. Just after the first raindrops fall.
    B. During medium rain.
    C. During heavy rain.
    D. Immediately after the rain stops.

87. If a ball rolls out into the path of a car coming down the street, the driver should:
    A. Try to go around the ball.
    B. Stop his car immediately.
    C. Slow down.
    D. Continue at the same speed to avoid confusing other traffic..

88. Which way should the front wheels of a car be turned when parking downhill on a street?

    A. 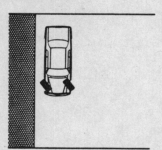   B. 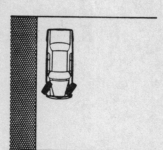   C.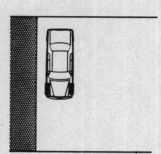

89. When stopped at an intersection waiting to turn left or cross oncoming traffic, you should:
    A. Avoid entering the intersection until oncoming traffic has stopped.
    B. Pull to the center of the intersection and stop with your wheels straight ahead.
    C. Pull to the center of the intersection and stop with your wheels turned to the left.
    D. Pull to the center of the intersection and turn the car slightly to the left.

All of the cars have arrived where they are in each digram at the same time. There are no traffic signs or lights. Circle the letter of the car that has the right-of-way in each diagram.

90.   91.   92.

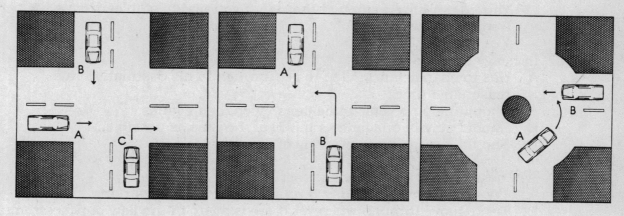

93. If a driver ahead of you extends his arm straight out, you can be fairly sure he is going to:
   A. Do something different.
   B. Turn left at the next intersection.
   C. Turn right at the next intersection.
   D. Slow down or stop.

94. Which way should the front wheels of a car be turned when parking uphill on a street with a curb?
   A. _____   B. _____   C. _____

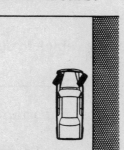   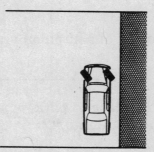   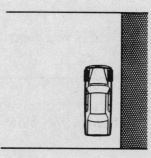

95. When you come to a stop sign:
     A. You should always come to a complete stop.
     B. You should come to a complete stop if traffic is present.
     C. A complete stop isn't necessary as long as you proceed slowly enough.
     D. You do not have to stop at the sign if you had to stop earlier as the cars in front of you stopped.

96. In heavy traffic, a driver:
     A. Has to change lanes often to get through to his destination in a reasonable time.
     B. Should help prevent traffic jams by changing lanes.
     C. Should stay in one lane as much of the time as possible.
     D. Should change lanes every so often.

97. When turning at a crowded intersection, you should:
     A. Try to move very carefully through the flow of pedestrians.
     B. Try to move through wherever there is a gap in the flow of pedestrians.
     C. Wait until there are no pedestrians actually in the intersection.
     D. Wait until there are no more pedestrians near the intersection.

98. What is wrong with driving more slowly than the traffic flow?

_____

99. What should you do if a tire blows out while you are driving?

_____

100. During a rapid temperature drop to below freezing after rainfall, brakes should be tested periodically because:

_____

_____

101. When you hear the sound of a siren on an emergency vehicle, you should:

_____

102. When you have found a place to park, what is the most important thing to do before you slow down to pull into it?

_____

103. Passing behind another car on a two- or three-lane road is dangerous because:

_____

_____

104. If you are stopped at a railroad crossing with more than one set of tracks, why should you wait at least ten seconds after the train has passed before you start driving across the tracks?

_____

_____

105. Why is it dangerous to drive with the window closed and the radio playing loudly?

_____

ANSWERS
SAFE DRIVING KNOWLEDGE TEST

This section provides the correct answers to questions in the Safe Driving Knowledge Test and explains why they are correct.

1. A seat belt and shoulder harness, in combination, are more effective than either alone. The seat belt restrains the lower part of the body while the shoulder harness prevents the upper part of the body from lurching forward and, in that way, keeps the chest from striking the steering column or the head from striking the windshield. Answer B is correct.

2. Adjusting the sideview mirror so that the door handle and tail of the car are visible provides a reference point to help you judge how far to your side another vehicle is. Side mirrors are often pushed out of position and you may, without knowing it, be looking at cars two lanes away rather than those coming alongside you. Answer B is correct.

3. Placing the gearshift in a neutral position helps to prevent the vehicle's lurching forward if your foot accidentally slips off the clutch pedal. While it does not happen often, some accidents have occurred when a driver's foot has slipped off the clutch pedal while the car was in gear. Answer A is correct.

4. Most cars do not require pumping the accelerator except on extremely cold days. Pumping the accelerator under normal conditions may well flood the engine. Answer C is correct.

5. A flooded engine, a wet ignition system, or frozen fuel line can keep the engine from starting when the starter worked. However, a poor connection at the battery cable does not even allow the starter to work; it is, therefore, the correct answer. Answer D is correct.

6. Leaving your left foot on the clutch pedal is too likely to result in "riding it" and thus wearing out the clutch plate. Resting the left foot against the brake pedal may cause the brake lights to go on and confuse drivers behind you. There is no reason why you cannot drive under 40 miles an hour in third gear. Answer C is correct.

7. Pulling away very quickly, so-called "jack-rabbit" start, burns much more gas than is necessary and increases gas consumption. Answer C is correct.

8. Sudden acceleration on a slippery surface will cause the wheels to spin and the tires to lose traction. Snow treads and dry surfaces provide more traction so the problem is not as great. Starting in first gear supplies more power to the rear wheels increasing the chances of slipping. Answer B is correct.

9. Answers A, B, and C are all good reasons to avoid shifting gears while turning a corner. Answer D is correct.

10. Studies have shown that you are least likely to get in an accident when you are driving at approximately the same speed as other cars on the roadway. Driving at a slower speed may seem safe, but it is not. Answer C is correct.

11. When you shift down, your engine will be forced to turn over faster. Driving at a slower speed may seem safe, but it is not. Answer A is correct.

12. Your stopping distance at any speed is dependent upon the friction between your tires and the pavement. While power brakes are easier to apply, they do not have any appreciable effect upon your stopping distance. Answer C is correct.

13. Looking directly out the rear window is the only way to get a good look at things that may be behind you when you back up. Answer B is correct.

14. Because of the way most brakes are constructed, they do not grab as well when the wheels are turning in reverse direction. Therefore, your stopping distance is greater when you are backing up. Answer B is correct.

15. Pumping your brakes helps to keep your wheels from locking and is, therefore, least likely to produce a skid. Answer D is correct.

16. While drinking, drugs, and unsafe vehicles cause a lot of accidents—especially severe accidents—most accidents occur because drivers are simply not paying attention. Answer A is correct.

17. Many people are killed each year from carbon monoxide that leaks into the automobile from a faulty exhaust system. Answer A is correct.

18. Turning on the heater, fixating on the road in front of you, or closing the windows are good ways to make yourself even more tired. Lively music will help keep you awake. However, do not play it so loudly that you cannot hear warning signals like sirens. Answer C is correct.

19. Any amount of alcohol will affect driving. One ounce of whiskey is the smallest amount listed, so Answer A is correct.

20. When you accelerate rapidly, the driver behind you is likely to do the same thing. Stopping suddenly almost invites him to run into you. In ordinary stop-and-go traffic, you can help "smooth out" the overall flow of traffic by accelerating and breaking gently. Answer B is correct.

21. Sudden strong wind gusts tend to push your vehicle sideways. If you are traveling at a high rate of speed, you can easily be moved into another lane before you can notice and react. Answer C is correct.

22. Moving to another lane will allow cars to enter the freeway without any disruption in the speed of traffic. Since the speed of other cars is hard to judge, attempting to adjust your speed to that of others is not a good idea. Answer B is correct.

23. This is just a memory item. If you do not know the answer, you should ask your teacher.

24. Most motorcycles can stop more quickly than automobiles, so you should maintain a greater following distance behind them. Answer A is correct.

25. Many drivers, when planning to leave an expressway, fail to maintain their speed until they reach the off-ramp. You should be prepared for the driver ahead to slow down upon nearing an exit. Answer A is correct.

26. A broken line in the center of a highway means that you may pass or change lanes if you wish. Answer A is correct.

27. The best course of action for Car A in this situation is to pull off the road and into the shrubbery. This way he or she risks only minor injury and damage. By maintaining course, he could escape a collision if the other driver altered his or her course; however, he is more likely to be killed or disabled for life. Attempting to reach the shoulder on the left will put him right in the path of Car B should Car B attempt to return to his own lane. Hitting the brakes will put the car in a skid and make it totally uncontrollable. Answer B is correct.

28. Braking hard will cause the front wheels to lock and the car will skid. Once this happens, they no longer guide the car. Answer A is correct.

29. While a school bus should have its warning lights on, you had better stop whenever a school bus is loading or discharging passengers. Most states allow you to pass if the bus is on the far side of a divided highway, but not any four lane highway. Answer D is correct.

30. Many pedestrians are not drivers and do not understand an automobile's limitations. Statistics show that these pedestrians are the most likely to be killed by an automobile. Answer D is correct.

31. The best way to maintain a slow speed on a long downgrade is by placing the car in second or first gear and allowing engine friction to hold you back. The brakes should not be applied for a sustained period. Answer D is correct.

32. If you change your mind in the middle of an intersection, you must keep going and use several turns around the block to get on the correct route. A U-turn, stopping, or turning quickly is likely to cause an accident. Remember, it was your mistake. Answer D is correct.

33. "Advanced green" means that you get the green light before oncoming traffic. After making sure that oncoming cars will remain stopped, you can go ahead with a left turn. However, you should watch oncoming cars closely so you can tell when they have gotten the green light. Answer A is correct.

34. A short acceleration lane makes it difficult for an entering car to build up sufficient speed when the speed on the freeway is high. If you are traveling on freeways, you should be particularly alert near short acceleration lanes. Answer C is correct.

35. Downshifting reduces the speed of the car but increases the pulling power of the engine. It also causes the fan to turn at a faster speed. Answer B is correct.

36. Accelerating slightly through a curve helps maintain rear wheel friction and reduces your chances of skidding, assuming you are driving slowly enough to be able to accelerate safely. Answer B is correct.

37. If a curve turns out to be sharper than you expected, you will have to slow down. This is best done by applying the brakes lightly so you will not lock your wheels and find yourself in a skid. If you are going too fast, accelerating will not help, nor will the way you steer. Answer A is correct.

38. Continued slowing down of cars near intersections tends to have a polishing effect on the road surface. Answer D is correct.

39. You must go through deep water slowly so as not to splash water over the ignition system. However, if you do not shift into a lower gear, you are likely to stall. Answer B is correct.

40. Since the earth is slow to respond to temperature changes, its surface will freeze more slowly than would a bridge or culvert. Answer B is correct.

41. On wet pavement, stopping distance is increased by about 50 percent (50%). Hard-packed snow, incidentally, increases stopping distance 200 percent (200%), while glare ice increases it 500 percent (500%)! Answer B is correct.

42. If one set of wheels suddenly drops off the roadway, you should avoid braking as this will tend to put the car in a skid. The correct procedure is to slow down gradually and turn back on the roadway only when you have reached a safe speed. Answer A is correct.

43. Since shifting gears can cause a car to stall, it should be avoided. Answer D is correct.

44. On a six-lane divided highway, you should drive in the left lane only when it is necessary in order to pass other cars. The more distance you can put between you and traffic coming the other way, the better. If a car suddenly comes across the center line or median, you want as much time to react as possible. Answer C is correct.

45. When the highway is covered with a thin layer of water, your tires will actually tend to ride on top of the water at very high speeds. This is called "hydroplaning," and it is almost like driving on ice. Answer B is correct.

46. When climbing up a slippery grade, you should maintain a constant pressure on the accelerator. Attempting to increase your speed or shifting to a lower gear will supply more power to the wheels and cause them to spin. Answer C is correct.

47. If your car is stuck in heavy snow during a storm, you want to keep the engine running both to keep you and the engine warm. However, remember to keep a window at least partially open to guard against carbon monoxide poisoning. Going off to look for help is a good way to freeze to death. Answer A is correct.

48. If you miss the exact change basket at the toll plaza, add some more change. After all, it was your "goof." Attendants are usually pretty busy, and driving through without paying is against the law. Leaving your car to scramble after the change is time consuming and dangerous. Answer B is correct.

49. Tank trucks, school buses, and passenger buses are frequently required to stop at railroad crossings. You had better be prepared to stop if you are approaching a railroad crossing behind one of them. Answer D is best.

50. The best way to let people see you is by using your headlights. However, keep them on low beam. High beams will not only blind oncoming cars, but in heavy fog or rain will reflect in your own eyes and make it difficult to see. Four way flashers are for emergency use only. Answer B is correct.

51. When stopped in heavy traffic, you want to keep water moving through your cooling system. The best way to do this is to shift into neutral and race the engine slightly. Answer C is correct.

52. If your car with a manual transmission won't start, you can move it a short distance by placing the car in first gear and pressing the starter. It's far better to do this than to try to push the car by hand or leave it in the roadway, both of which are dangerous. Answer A is correct.

53. Approximately one-half of the nation's highway deaths are caused by drivers who have been drinking. Alcohol is the number one cause of automobile fatalities. Answer C is correct.

54. A lot of food in your stomach, particularly carbohydrates, can reduce alcohol concentrations in the blood by up to one-half. Although eating will not keep you from becoming intoxicated, it is better than drinking on an empty stomach. Answer C is correct.

55. A 150-pound person could actually consume five bottles of beer or "shots" of whiskey before reaching the .10% level of blood alcohol concentration that is becoming the standard of intoxication in most states. Anyone who is found to have more than the legal standard is therefore a real menace. In fact, his chances of having an accident are more than five times what they would be if he were not drinking. Any more than one drink an hour is dangerous. Answer C is correct.

56. If you are blinded by headlight glare from an oncoming car, you should focus your eyes along the right side of the road. This minimizes the effects of the glare and allows you to see the edge of the roadway. Don't try to give the other driver "a dose of his own medicine." Your chances of having a head-on collision are even greater when the other driver can't see either. Answer C is correct.

57. If your accelerator becomes stuck in the down position, do not fool around — turn the ignition off. Once the engine is off, you can pry it up with your foot. Don't, for heaven's sake, try to reach it with your hand; it's too easy to lose control of the car. Also, remember to pull in at the nearest filling station and have them inspect your throttle linkage. Answer D is correct.

58. If your brakes fail suddenly, the first thing you should do is to pump them several times to try to build up pressure. Shifting to a lower gear will slow you down, but with bad brakes you want to stop. Leaving the roadway is a little drastic at this point. Answer D is correct.

59. Loss of power brakes is not rare. It often happens when a car stalls as you take the foot off the accelerator to slow down. However, the brakes will still work; it just takes a little more pressure on the pedal. Answer C is correct.

60. Your engine runs most efficiently and will give the longest mileage at about 30 miles per hour. It may be nerve wracking, but your chances of reaching a service station are better at this speed than a higher speed. Answer C is correct.

61. Many otherwise harmless prescription drugs can produce extremely harmful effects in combination with alcoholic beverages. Even a qualified physician may not know how a particular drug will mix with alcohol. It is best not to take any chances. Answer D is correct.

62. The reason for compulsory state inspection is to keep dangerous vehicles off the road. Having your car inspected and insisting that others do likewise is in your own best interest. Answer A is correct.

63. It is best to wait until you can see both headlights on the car that you have just passed before returning to the driving lane. Answer D is correct.

64. When you turn right into an angle parking lane, you will tend to start as far to the left as you can. This makes your left front fender a danger point. However, as you enter the parking lane, your car will be moving to the right, making your right rear door another danger area. Answer D is correct.

65. When pulling into a narrow side street, slow down a little more than you would at a normal intersection. However, since the car behind you will not expect you to turn at this point, even though you have signaled, you should not slow down any more than you have to, and certainly should not come to a stop. If you swing to the left, the driver behind you may think you're planning a left turn and try to pass you on the right. Answer B is correct.

66. In fog, you should drive no faster than you can see; that is, you should be driving slowly enough to stop before reaching any obstacle that suddenly appears in the roadway. Many accidents occur because the drivers assume there nothing in the roadway; they believe that if they can see the road, they are safe. Answer A is correct.

67. The faster you are driving, the more distance you will move sideways when a crosswind hits you. It's simple physics. By slowing down, you can recover before you cross into someone else's lane. Answer D is correct.

68. As it begins to get dark, you should turn on your headlights so the others can see you. They can see your headlights better than your parking lights. However, use your low beams; high beams can blind other drivers even in broad daylight. Answer C is correct.

69. At night, the only clue to your distance from the car ahead is how far apart the taillights look. Since the taillights on a compact car are closer together than those on a standard car, a compact car will look farther away than it really is. For this reason, you should slow down well before reaching a car ahead. Answer B is correct.

70. Tinted contact lenses can reduce the amount of light up to 20 percent (20%). This won't help very much with sunglare, but it can reduce your ability to see at night. It's wise not to use tinted contact lenses for night driving. Answer C is correct.

71. Drivers do not expect to be passed on the right and frequently will move into a right hand lane without signaling or looking. Answer C is correct.

72. Your greatest danger from the car you are passing comes as you move through his "blind spot," that is, in the "8 o'clock position" shown in answer B. At this point you cannot be seen through either the rear or side mirror, nor out of the corner of the eye. For this reason, it is wise not to stay in another driver's blind spot but move through it quickly. Answer B is correct.

73. Your eyes must scan the sides of the road continually if you are to spot the potential hazards before they appear directly in front of you. One of the biggest weaknesses of beginning drivers is their tendency to fix their eyes directly in front of them. Answer A is correct.

74. It is always dangerous to back into a highway from a driveway. The only way to avoid this is to back into the driveway from the highway. C shows the correct procedure. There is no point, however, in backing across two lanes of traffic as is shown in D.

75. To sound your horn when you pass another car is annoying and unnecessary. It should be saved for times when it is needed. One of these times is when the car you are intending to pass is coming up behind another car that he may be intending to pass. Answer C is correct.

76. If you are in doubt as to whether you can pass safely, do not try it! Your available passing distance is getting smaller all of the time you are trying to decide. If the situation was "chancy" to begin with, it will be more so by the time you make up your mind. Answer D is correct.

77. The only way to be sure of seeing another car in the lane next to you is to check both mirrors and the side window, and to look over your shoulder. Remember the "blind spot." Answer C is correct.

78. The idea that black coffee will sober you up is a myth. It will not help you at all. Answer A is correct.

79. After driving a long time at a high speed, as you would on an expressway, you tend to "adapt," that is, you think you are driving more slowly than you really are. Therefore, when you leave an expressway, it is very important to check your speedometer to make sure you are within the speed limit. Answer C is correct.

80. While extremely sharp curves may seem the most dangerous, drivers can see they are sharp and tend to slow down for them. Actually, moderate curves, because they don't look as sharp as they really are, are more dangerous. Answer C is correct.

81. The purpose of using your turn signal is to tell other drivers you are planning to turn at a particular place. You should, therefore, use it when they will best understand what you mean. If you plan to turn in a driveway beyond an intersection, you should not signal until you have passed the intersection; otherwise, other drivers may misunderstand. Answer B is correct.

82. Unfortunately, most people signal turns only about half the time. Do not assume another driver is not going to turn just because his turn signal isn't flashing. Answer C is correct.

83. You should take a "Y" intersection the same way you do any other intersection: that is, move into the correct lane as quickly as possible. In both A and B the driver spends too much time in the opposing lane. Answer C is correct.

84. The correct answers are A—4, B—3, C—1, D—5, E—2.

85. You should keep your foot on the brake any time you are stopped. Slipping the clutch or idling in "drive" will keep the car from sliding backward. However, they will not keep you from moving forward if you are struck from the rear. Answer A is correct.

86. On a hot day, oil in the pavement tends to come to the top. Just after the rain, the oil has run to the side of the road reducing the problem. Answer A is correct.

87. A ball rolling into the road is generally followed by a child, and not necessarily from the same direction as the ball. You should come to a complete stop until you've had a chance to check out the situation. Answer B is correct.

88. This one is easy! Only when the wheels are in the position shown in B will the car avoid rolling downhill if the brakes should fail to hold. Answer B is correct.

89. When you are stopped at an intersection waiting for a left turn, you should pull to the center of the intersection so that you can make the turn quickly when the time comes. However, you should keep your wheels pointed straight ahead so that if you are struck from behind you will not be pushed into oncoming traffic. Answer B is correct.

90. Car A legally has the right of way since Car B is coming from the left and Car C is preparing to turn. Notice that Car A would ordinarily pass in front of Car B anyway — that is why it is given the right of way. Answer A is correct.

91. Car A, since it is proceeding straight through the intersection, has the right-of-way over Car B. Answer A is correct.

92. Car A, already in the traffic circle, has the right-of-way over Car B entering in the traffic circle. This makes sense. If Car A were the one that had to stop, so much traffic would back up behind him that Car B could never get into the intersection. Answer A is correct.

93. A hand straight out indicates a left turn. Answer B is correct.

94. When you are parked on a hill where there is a curb, your wheels should be in the position shown in B. If the car starts to roll backward, the wheels will strike the curb. The position shown in A isn't bad. However, the car could get up enough speed before the rear wheels struck the curb to actually climb the curb. Position A would have been the correct answer had there been no curb. Answer B is correct.

95. You must always come to a complete stop at a stop sign. There are at least three good reasons for this rule: First, it is easier to detect cars approaching from the side if you are stopped. Second, if an approaching car is hidden by your doorpost, by stopping you give it a chance to come out where you can see it; Finally, if you do see traffic approaching, you can gauge its speed better if you are completely stopped. Answer A is correct.

96. Lane changes are always dangerous in heavy traffic and they do not accomplish very much. Drivers should stay in one lane as much as possible. Answer C is correct.

97. Whenever pedestrians are in the street they have the right-of-way. On the other hand, you will hold up traffic if you wait for the pedestrians that are not even near the intersection. Answer C is correct.

98. Driving more slowly than the traffic flow increases the chance of an accident. While you may feel safer, you run the risk of being struck from behind. The fact that you will not be legally responsible for the accident will not make a whiplash injury less painful.

99. The most important thing to remember if your tire blows is not to use your brakes. Using the brakes could cause your car to skid. Grab the steering wheel firmly and try to steer a straight course. Ease up on your accelerator and depress the brake only after you've slowed down.

100. Damp brake linings are particularly dangerous in freezing weather. You should test your brakes occasionally to make sure you have them when you need them.

101. When you hear the sound of a siren you should slow down, open the window so you can hear better, and look around to see if you can find its source. It is not necessary to pull over and stop unless you see that it is approaching you.

102. The first thing to do before you slow down to pull into a parking place is to signal the cars behind you. Following drivers have no idea what you are going to do unless you tell them. Many rear-end collisions are caused by drivers stopping, without warning, in order to park.

103. Passing behind another car on a two- or three-lane roadway is a risky business. The driver ahead of you may not complete the pass until an oncoming car is almost on top of you. Or, if he or she does complete the pass and return to the driving lane, he or she may not leave you enough room to get in behind. him. In addition, the oncoming car cannot help you out very much since he may not be able to see you until too late.

104. Many drivers are killed at railroad crossings each year because they started across the tracks as soon as a train passed and were struck by a train coming from the opposite direction. Never cross a railroad track unless you have clear vision in both directions. This is true even if there are signals — they don't always work.

105. It is difficult to hear sirens and other emergency signals with normal road and traffic noise. To have the radio playing loudly with the window closed makes it almost impossible. Cracking your window lets you hear sirens more easily.

Section B
A Model Uniform Commercial Driver License Act

This document is an example of what a state's commercial driver's license law may contain. This is an adapted version of a draft (not final) model law prepared by the Legal Services Committee of the American Association of Motor Vehicle Administrators. This document is only a model. It is not a real law. It is intended only for use as an example of a state CDL law. The actual name of the licensing authority in your state may be substituted for the words state licensing authority in this document.

Draft
Model Uniform
Commercial Driver License Act

Section 1. Short Title: This act may be cited as the Uniform Commercial Driver License Act.

Section 2. Statement of Intent and Purpose: The purpose of this Act is to implement the federal Commercial Motor Vehicle Safety Act of 1986 (CMVSA) (Title XII of Pub. Law 99-570) and reduce or prevent commercial motor vehicle accidents, fatalities and injuries by:
(a) Permitting commercial drivers to hold only one license.
(b) Disqualifying commercial drivers who have committed certain serious traffic violations or other specified offenses.
(c) Strengthening licensing and testing standards. This Act is a remedial law and shall be liberally construed to promote the public health, safety and welfare. To the extent that this Act conflicts with general driver licensing provisions, this Act prevails. Where this Act is silent, the general driver licensing provisions apply.

Section 3. Definitions: Notwithstanding any other provision of this code, the following definitions apply to this Act:
(a) Alcohol. *Alcohol* means:
   (1) Beer, ale, port, or stout, and other similar fermented beverages, including sake or similar products of any name or description containing one-half of one percentum or more of alcohol by volume, brewed or produced from malt, wholly or in part, or from any substitute thereof;
   (2) Wine of not less than one-half of one percentum of alcohol by volume; or
   (3) Distilled spirits which means that substance known as ethyl alcohol, ethanol, or spirits of wine in any form (including all dilutions and mixtures thereof from whatever source or by whatever process produced).

(b) Alcohol Concentration: *Alcohol concentration* means:
   (1) The number of grams of alcohol per 100 milliliters of blood; or
   (2) The number of grams of alcohol per 210 liters of breath; or
   (3) The number of grams of alcohol per 67 milliliters of urine.
(c) Commerce: *Commerce* means:
   (1) Trade, traffic, and transportation within the jurisdiction of the United States between a place in a state and a place outside of the state, including a place outside the United States; and
   (2) Trade, traffic, and transportation in the United States which affects any trade, traffic, and transportation in subparagraph (1).
(d) Commercial Driver License: *Commercial Driver License* (CDL) means a license issued to an individual in accordance with the requirements of this Act. This license authorizes the individual to drive a class of commercial motor vehicles.
(e) Commercial Driver License Information System: The *Commercial Driver License Information System (CDLIS)* is the information system established pursuant to the CMVSA to serve as a clearinghouse for information related to the licensing and identification of commercial motor vehicle drivers.
(f) Commercial Driver Instruction Permit: *Commercial Driver Instruction Permit* means a permit issued pursuant to Section 8 (d) of this Act.
(g) Commercial Motor Vehicle: *Commercial motor vehicle* means a motor vehicle designed or used to transport passengers or property:
   (1) If the vehicle has a gross vehicle weight rating of 26,001 or more pounds or such lesser rating as determined by federal regulation.
   (2) If the vehicle is designed to transport 16 or more passengers, including the driver.
   (3) If the vehicle is transporting hazardous materials and is required to be placarded in accordance with U.S. law.
(h) Controlled Substance: *Controlled substance* means any substance so classified under the Controlled Substances Act.
(i) Conviction: *Conviction* means the final judgment, or verdict, or a finding of guilty, a plea of guilty, or a forfeiture of bond or collateral upon a charge of a disqualifying offense, as a result of proceedings upon any violation of the requirements of the Act or an implied admission of guilt with implied consent laws.
(j) Disqualification: *Disqualification* means a prohibition against driving a commercial motor vehicle.
(k) Drive: *Drive* means to drive, operate, or be in physical control of a motor vehicle in any place open to the general public for purposes of vehicular traffic. For purposes of sections 12, 13, and 14 of this Act, *drive* includes operation or physical control of a motor vehicle anywhere in the state.
(l) Driver: *Driver* means any person who drives, operates, or is in physical control of a commercial motor vehicle, in any place open to the public for purposes of vehicular traffic, or who is required to hold a commercial driver license.

(m) Driver License: *Driver license* means a license issued by a state to an individual which authorizes the individual to drive a motor vehicle.

(n) Employer: *Employer* means any person, the United States, a state, or a political subdivision of a state who owns or leases a commercial motor vehicle or assigns a person to drive a commercial motor vehicle.

(o) Felony: *Felony* means any offense under state or federal law that is punishable by death or imprisonment for a term exceeding one year.

(p) Foreign Jurisdiction: *Foreign jurisdiction* means any jurisdiction outside of or not included in the United States.

(q) Gross Vehicle Weight Rating: *Gross vehicle weight rating (GVWR)* means the value specified by the manufacturer(s) as the maximum loaded weight of a single or combination (articulated) vehicle, or registered gross weight, whichever is greater. The GVWR of a combination (articulated) vehicle (commonly referred to as the *gross combination weight rating* or GCWR) is the GVWR of the power unit plus the GVWR of the towed unit or units.

(r) Hazardous Materials: *Hazardous materials* has the same meaning as that found in Section 103 of the Hazardous Materials Transportation Act.

(s) Motor Vehicle: *Motor vehicle* means a vehicle, machine, tractor, trailer, or semitrailer propelled or drawn by mechanical power which is used on highways; or any other vehicle required to be registered under the laws of this state, but does not include any vehicle, machine, tractor, trailer, or semitrailer operated exclusively on a rail.

(t) Non-Resident CDL: *Non-Resident CDL* means a commercial driver license issued by a state to an individual who resides in a foreign jurisdiction.

(u) Out of Service Order: *Out of Service Order* means a temporary prohibition against driving a commercial motor vehicle.

(v) Serious Traffic Violation: *Serious Traffic Violation* means:
   (1) Excessive speeding, as defined by the United States Secretary of Transportation by regulation.
   (2) Reckless driving, as defined under state or local law.
   (3) A violation of any state or local law relating to motor vehicle traffic control, other than a parking violation, arising in connection with an accident or collision resulting in death to any person.
   (4) Any other violation of a state or local law relating to motor vehicle traffic control, other than a parking violation, which the (state licensing authority) determines by regulation to be serious.

(w) State: *State* means a state of the United States or the District of Columbia.

(x) United States: *United States* means the fifty states and the District of Columbia.

NOTE: The definitions of *state* and *United States* are from the federal Act, and for that reason do not include territories such as Puerto Rico and Guam.

Section 4. Limitation on Number of Driver Licenses
   No person who drives a commercial motor vehicle may have more than one driver license.

Section 5. Notification Required by Driver
   (a) Notification of Convictions:
      (1) To State. Any driver of a commercial motor vehicle holding a driver license issued by this state, who is convicted of violating any state law or local ordinance relating to motor vehicle traffic control in any other state, other than parking violations, shall notify the state licensing authority in the manner specified by the state licensing authority within thirty days of the date of conviction.
      (2) To Employers. Any driver of a commercial motor vehicle holding a driver license issued by this state, who is convicted of violating any state law or local ordinance relating to motor vehicle traffic control in this or any other state, other than parking violations, must notify his or her employer in writing of the conviction within thirty days of the date of conviction.
   (b) Notification of Suspensions, Revocations and Cancellations: Each driver whose driver license is suspended, revoked, or canceled by any state, who loses the privilege to drive a commercial motor vehicle in any state for any period, or who is disqualified from driving a commercial motor vehicle for any period, must notify his or her employer of that fact before the end of the business day following the day the driver received notice of that fact.
   (c) Notification of Previous Employment: Each person who applies to be a commercial motor vehicle driver must provide the employer, at the time of the application, with the following information for the ten years preceding the date of the application:
      (1) A list of the names and addresses of the applicant's previous employers for which the applicant was a driver of a commercial vehicle;
      (2) The dates between which the applicant drove for each employer; and
      (3) The reason for leaving that employer. The applicant must certify that all information furnished is true and complete. An employer may require an applicant to provide additional information.

Section 6. Employer Responsibilities
   (a) Each employer must require the applicant to provide the information specified in Section 5 (c).
   (b) No employer may knowingly allow, permit, or authorize a driver to drive a commercial motor vehicle during any period:
      (1) In which the driver has a driver license suspended, revoked, or canceled by a state; has lost the privilege to drive a commercial motor vehicle.
      (2) In which the driver has more than one driver license.

Section 7. Commercial Driver License Required
   (a) Except when driving under a commercial driver instruction permit or a valid automobile or class "C" license and accompanied by the holder of a commercial driver license valid for the vehicle being driven, no person may drive a commercial motor vehicle unless the person holds a commercial driver license and applicable endorsements valid for the vehicle they are driving.
   (b) No person may drive a commercial motor vehicle while their driving privilege is suspended, revoked, or canceled, while subject to a disqualification, or in violation of an out-of-service order.

Section 8. Commercial Driver License Qualification Standards
   (a) Testing.
      (1) General — No person may be issued a commercial driver license unless that person is a resident of this state and has passed a knowledge and skill test which complies with minimum federal standards for driving a commercial motor vehicle, and has satisfied all other requirements of the CMVSA in addition to other requirements imposed by state law or federal regulation. The tests must be prescribed and conducted by the state licensing authority.
      (2) Third Party Testing — The state licensing authority may authorize a person, including an agency of this or another state, an employer, a private driver training facility, or other private institution, or a department, agency, or instrumentality of a local government, to administer the skills test specified by this Section, provided:
         (i) The test is the same which would otherwise be administered by the state.
         (ii) The third party has entered into an agreement with the state which complies with requirements of the federal standards.
   (b) Waiver of Skills Test — The state licensing authority may waive the skills test specified in this section for a commercial driver license applicant who meets the requirements of the federal standards.
       NOTE: A state need not provide for such a waiver unless it so desires. Such waivers may not, however, be more generous than those provided for in the federal rule, although such a waiver may be more restrictive.
   (c) Limitations on Issuance of License
       A Commercial Driver License, or Commercial Driver Instruction Permit, may not be issued to a person while the person is subject to a disqualification from driving a commercial motor vehicle, or while the person's driver license is suspended, revoked or canceled in any state; nor may a commercial driver license be issued to a person who has a commercial driver license issued by any other state unless the person first surrenders all such licenses, which must be returned to the issuing state(s) for cancellation.

(d) Commercial Driver Instruction Permit

    (1) A Commercial Driver Instruction Permit may be issued to an individual who holds a valid automobile or Class "C" driver license who has passed the vision and written tests required for an automobile Class "C" driver license.

    (2) The Commercial Driver Instruction Permit may not be issued for a period to exceed six months. Only one renewal or reissuance may be granted within a two-year period. The holder of a Commercial Driver Instruction Permit may drive a commercial motor vehicle on a highway only when accompanied by the holder of a commercial driver license, valid for the type of vehicle being driven who occupies the seat beside the individual for the purpose of giving instruction in driving the commercial motor vehicle.

NOTE: Since the federal rule establishing commercial driver testing and licensing standards does not mandate that states adopt a commercial driver instruction permit, this section is an option available to states wishing to do so.

Section 9. Non-Resident CDL

The state licensing authority may issue a Non-Resident CDL to a resident of a foreign jurisdiction if the United States Secretary of Transportation has determined that the commercial motor vehicle testing and licensing standards in the foreign jurisdiction do not meet the federal testing standards. The word "Non-Resident" must appear on the face of the Non-Resident CDL. An applicant must surrender any Non-Resident CDL issued by another state. Prior to issuing a Non-Resident CDL, the state licensing authority must establish the practical capability of revoking, suspending, canceling the Non-Resident CDL, and disqualifying that person using the same conditions as are applicable to the Commercial Driver License issued to a resident of this state.

Section 10. Application for Commercial Driver License

(a) The application for a Commercial Driver License or Commercial Driver Instruction Permit, must include the following:

    (1) The full name and current mailing and residential address of the person.

    (2) A physical description of the person including sex, height, weight, eye, and hair color.

    (3) Date of birth.

    (4) The applicant's Social Security number (unless the application is for a Non-Resident CDL).

    (5) The person's signature.

    (6) The person's color photograph.

    (7) Certifications including those required by 49 C.F.R. part 383.71 (a).

    (8) Any other information required by the state licensing authority.

    (9) A consent to release driving record information.

The application must be accompanied by an application fee of $(set by the state).

(b) When a licensee changes his or her name, mailing address, or residence, an application for a duplicate license must be made as provided for in the applicable state statute.

(c) No person who has been a resident of this state for 30 days may drive a commercial motor vehicle under the authority of a Commercial Driver License issued by another jurisdiction.

Section 11. Commercial Driver License

(a) Content of License

The commercial driver license must be marked "Commercial Driver License" or "CDL," and must be, to the maximum extent practicable, tamper proof. It must include, but not be limited to, the following information:

(1) The name and residential address of the person.

(2) The person's color photograph.

(3) A physical description of the person including sex, height, weight, eye and hair color.

(4) Date of birth.

(5) Except for Non-Resident CDL's, the person's social security number and any number or identifier deemed appropriate by the state licensing authority to reduce the possibility of drivers obtaining multiple licenses in violation of this Act.

(6) The person's signature.

(7) The class or type of commercial motor vehicle or vehicles which the person is authorized to drive, together with any endorsements or restrictions.

(8) The name of this state.

(9) The dates between which the license is valid.

(b) Classifications, Endorsements and Restrictions

Commercial driver licenses may be issued with the following classifications, endorsements, and restrictions: the holder of a valid Commercial Driver License may drive all vehicles in the class for which that license is issued, and all lesser classes of vehicles except motorcycles and vehicles which require endorsement, unless the proper endorsement appears on the license.

(1) Classifications

Class A — Any combination of vehicles with a Gross Vehicle Weight Rating (GVWR) of 26,001 pounds or more, provided the GVWR of the vehicle(s) being towed is in excess of 10,000 pounds.

Class B — Any single vehicle with a GVWR of 26,001 pounds or more, and any such vehicle towing a vehicle not in excess of 10,000 pounds.

Class C — Any single vehicle with a GVWR of less than 26,001 pounds or any such vehicle towing a vehicle with a GVWR not in excess of 10,000 pounds comprising:

(i) Vehicles designed to transport 16 or more passengers, including the driver.

(ii) Vehicles used in the transportation of hazardous materials which requires the vehicle to be placarded.

NOTE: States may include all other single vehicles in Class C or establish other classes or endorsements for light vehicles, including passenger vehicles and motorcycles.

(2) Endorsements and Restrictions

"H" — Authorizes the driver to drive a vehicle transporting hazardous materials.

"K" — Restricts the driver to vehicles not equipped with air brakes.

"T" — Authorizes driving double and triple trailers.

"P" — Authorizes driving vehicles carrying passengers.

"N" — Authorizes driving tank vehicles.

"X" — Represents a combination of hazardous materials and tank vehicle endorsements.

(c) Applicant Record Check

Before issuing a Commercial Driver License, the state licensing authority must obtain driving record information from the Commercial Driver License Information System, the National Driver Register, and each state in which the person has been licensed.

(d) Notification of License Issuance

Within ten days after issuing a Commercial Driver License, the state licensing authority must notify the Commercial Driver License Information System of that fact and provide all information required to ensure identification of the person who obtained the license.

(e) Expiration of License

The Commercial Driver License shall expire as set by existing state law.

(f) License Renewal Procedures

When applying for renewal of a Commercial Driver License, the applicant must complete the application form required by section 10(A), and provide updated information and required certifications. If the applicant wishes to retain a hazardous materials endorsement, the written test for a hazardous materials endorsement must be taken and passed.

Section 12. Disqualification and Cancellation

(a) Disqualification Offenses

Any person is disqualified from driving a commercial motor vehicle for a period of not less than one year if convicted of a first violation of:

(1) Driving a commercial motor vehicle while under the influence of alcohol or a controlled substance.

(2) Driving a commercial motor vehicle while the alcohol concentration of the driver's blood, breath (or other bodily substance) is 0.04 or more.

(3) Leaving the scene of an accident involving a commercial motor vehicle you are driving.

(4) Using a commercial motor vehicle while commiting a felony (as defined by this Act).

     (5)   Refusal by the driver to submit to a test to determine alcohol
concentration.

If any of the previously listed violations occurred while transporting a hazardous material requiring placards, the person is disqualified for a period of not less than three years.

(b)   A person is disqualified for life if convicted of two or more violations of any of the offenses specified in paragraph (a), or any combination of those offenses, arising from two or more separate incidents.

(c)   The state licensing authority may issue regulations establishing guidelines, including conditions, under which a disqualification for life for the reasons stated in paragraph (b) may be reduced to a period of not less than ten years. NOTE: This paragraph permits a state to implement any regulations which may be issued by the federal government to allow for such reduction of penalties.

(d)   A person is disqualified from driving a commercial motor vehicle for life if he or she uses a commercial motor vehicle in the commission of a felony involving the manufacture, distribution, or dispensing of a controlled substance or possession of such a substance with the intent to manufacture, distribute or dispense it.

(e)   A person is disqualified from driving a commercial motor vehicle for a period of not less than sixty days if convicted of two serious counts of traffic violations; or 120 days if convicted of three serious traffic violations (each in a separate incident), committed in a commercial motor vehicle during a three year period.

(f)   After suspending, revoking, or canceling a commercial driver license, the state licensing authority must update its records within ten days to reflect that action. After suspending, revoking, or canceling a nonresident commercial driver's privileges, the state licensing authority must notify the licensing authority of the state which issued the commercial driver license or commercial driver certificate within ten days.

Section 13. Commercial Drivers Prohibited From Operating a Vehicle with Any Alcohol in System

(a)   Not withstanding any other provision of this Code, a person may not drive, operate, or be in physical control of a commercial motor vehicle while having alcohol in his or her system.

(b)   A person who drives, operates, or is in physical control of a commercial motor vehicle while having alcohol in his or her system or who refuses to take a test to determine alcohol content as provided by Section 14 of this Act must be placed Out-of-Service for 24 hours.

Section 14. Implied Consent Requirements for Commercial Motor Vehicle Drivers

(a) A person who drives a commercial motor vehicle within this state is deemed to have given consent, subject to provisions of the state law establishing alcohol testing standards to take a test or tests of that person's blood, breath, or urine for the purpose of determining that person's blood alcohol concentration, or the presence of other drugs.

(b) A test or tests may be administered at the direction of a law enforcement officer who, after stopping or detaining the commercial motor vehicle driver, has probable cause to believe that driver was operating a commercial motor vehicle while having alcohol in his or her system.

(c) A person requested to submit to a test as provided in the previous subsection (a) must be warned by the law enforcement officer requesting the test that a refusal to submit to the test will result in that person being disqualified from operating a commercial motor vehicle under Section 12 of this Act.

(d) If the person refuses testing or submits to a test which discloses an alcohol concentration of 0.04 or more, the law enforcement officer must submit a sworn report to the state licensing authority certifying that the test was requested pursuant to Subsection (a) and that the person refused to submit to testing, or submitted to a test which disclosed an alcohol concentration of 0.04 or more.

(e) Upon receipt of the sworn report of a law enforcement officer submitted under Subsection (d), the state licensing authority must disqualify the driver from driving a commercial motor vehicle under section 12 of this Act.

Section 15. Notification of Traffic Convictions

Within ten days after receiving a report of the conviction of any nonresident holder of a commercial driver license for any violation of a state law or local ordinance relating to motor vehicle traffic control (other than parking violations) committed in a commercial motor vehicle, the state licensing authority must notify the driver licensing authority in the licensing state of the conviction.

Section 16. Driving Record Information to be Furnished

Notwithstanding any other provision of law to the contrary, the state licensing authority must furnish full information regarding the driving record of any person:

(a) To the driver license administrator of any other state, or Province or Territory of Canada requesting that information.

(b) To any employer or prospective employer upon request and payment of a fee of $(set by state).

(c) To insurers upon request and payment of a fee of $(set by state).

Section 17. Rulemaking Authority

The state licensing authority may adopt any rules and regulations necessary to carry out the provisions of this Act.

Section 18. Authority to Enter Agreements

The state licensing authority may enter into or make agreements, arrangements, or declarations to carry out the provisions of this Act.

Section 19. Reciprocity

Notwithstanding any law to the contrary, a person may drive a commercial motor vehicle if the person has a commercial driver license issued by any state in accordance with the minimum federal standards for the issuance of commercial motor vehicle driver licenses, if the person's license is not suspended, revoked, or canceled; and if the person is not disqualified from driving a commercial motor vehicle, or subject to an "Out-of-Service" order.

Section 20. Severability and Savings Clause

Section 21. Effective Date

Section C
U.S. Government Printing Office Bookstores

ALABAMA
9220-B Parkway East
Birmingham, AL 35206

CALIFORNIA
ARCO Plaza, C-Level
505 South Flower Street
Los Angeles, CA 90071

CALIFORNIA
Room 1023, Federal Building
450 Golden Gate Avenue
San Francisco, CA 94102

COLORADO
Room 117, Federal Building
1961 Stout Street
Denver, CO 80294

COLORADO
World Savings Building
720 North Main Street
Pueblo, CO 81003

FLORIDA
Room 158, Federal Building
400 West Bay Street
Jacksonville, FL 32202

GEORGIA
Room 100, Federal Building
275 Peachtree Street, NE
Atlanta, GA 30303

ILLINOIS
Room 1356, Federal Building
219 S. Dearborn Street
Chicago, IL 60604

MARYLAND
Retail Sales Outlet-Laurel
8660 Cherry Lane
Laurel, MD 20707

MASSACHUSETTS
Room G-25, Federal Building
Sudbury Street
Boston, MA 02203

MICHIGAN
Suite 160, Federal Building
477 Michigan Avenue
Detroit, MI 48226

MISSOURI
ROOM 144, Federal Building
601 East 12th Street
Kansas City, MO 64106

NEW YORK
Room 110, Federal Building
26 Federal Plaza
New York, NY 10278

OHIO
First Floor, Federal Building
1240 East Ninth Street
Cleveland, OH 44199

OHIO
Room 207, Federal Building
200 North High Street
Columbus, OH 43215

PENNSYLVANIA
Room 1214, Federal Building
660 Arch Street
Philadelphia, PA 19106

PENNSYLVANIA
Room 118, Federal Building
1000 Liberty Avenue
Pittsburgh, PA 15222

TEXAS
Room 1050, Federal Building
1100 Commerce Street
Dallas, TX 75242

TEXAS
9319 Gulf Freeway
Houston, TX 77017

WASHINGTON
Room 194, Federal Building
915 Second Avenue
Seattle, WA 88174

WASHINGTON D.C.
Main Bookstore
710 North Capitol Street, NW
Washington, DC 20310

WASHINGTON D.C.
Pentagon Bookstore
Main Concourse, South End
Room 2E172
Washington, DC 20230

WASHINGTON D.C.
Commerce Bookstore
14th & E Streets, NW
Room 1604, First Floor
Washington, DC 20230

WASHINGTON D.C.
State Bookstore
Room 2817, North Lobby
21st and C Streets, NW
Washington, DC 20520

WASHINGTON D.C.
HHS Bookstore
Room 1528, HHS North Building
330 Independence Avenue, SW
Washington, DC 20201

WASHINGTON D.C.
Farragut Bookstore
1717 H Street, NW
Washington, DC 20036

WISCONSIN
Room 190, Federal Building
517 E. Wisconsin Avenue
Milwaukee, WI 53202

Section D
Written Examination: Federal Motor Carrier Safety Regulations

APPLICANT _____ DATE _____

EXAMINER _____

Instructions

All of the questions contained herein are based on the United States Department of Transportation's Federal Motor Carrier Safety Regulations. Applicants for the position of commercial vehicle driver are required to take the examination.

Each question has four answers but only one is right. Your job is to read all of the answers and then to pick the one answer you believe is right. Circle the letter of the correct answer. Do not pick more than one answer for each question.

Here is a sample question to show you what is to be done:

The Federal Motor Carrier Safety Regulations were written for:
   A.   Vehicle makers.
   B.   Drivers only.
   C.   Carriers only.
   D.   Drivers and carriers.

The right answer is letter D, "Drivers and carriers," so you should circle answer D.

Finally, be sure to answer every question. Keep in mind that most of the regulations covered here apply to commercial bus and truck drivers and are different from what is required of passenger car drivers. Again, pick only one answer for each question. There is no time limit on the examination, but try to work as fast as you can.

1. §390.32 A motor carrier who is also a driver (owner-operator):
   A. Is not covered by the safety regulations.
   B. Must obey only those parts of the regulations which cover drivers.
   C. Must obey only those parts of the regulations which cover motor carriers.
   D. Must obey both the parts covering drivers and the parts covering motor carriers.

2. §391.11(b)(1) With only a few exceptions, the Federal Motor Carrier Safety Regulations say a driver must be:
   A. At least 18 years old.
   B. At least 19 years old.
   C. At least 20 years old.
   D. At least 21 years old.

3. §391.15(c)(2)(3) A driver cannot drive a motor vehicle:
   A. For one year after a first offense conviction for a felony involving a commercial motor vehicle operated by the driver.
   B. For one year after a first offense conviction for driving a commercial vehicle while under the influence of alcohol or narcotics.
   C. For one year after a first offense conviction for leaving the scene of an accident which resulted in personal injury or death.
   D. For one year after a first offense conviction for any of the above.

4. §391.21(b)(7)(8)(10) Every driver applicant must fill out an application form giving:
   A. A list of all vehicle accidents during the previous 3 years.
   B. A list of all motor vehicle violation convictions and bond forfeits (except for parking) during the previous three years.
   C. A list of names and addresses of all employers during the previous three years.
   D. All of the above.

5. §391.27(a)(b) At least once a year, a driver must fill out a form listing all motor vehicle violations (except parking) occurring during the previous 12 months. The driver must fill out the form:
   A. Even if there were no violations.
   B. Only if convicted.
   C. Only if convicted or had forfeited bond or collateral.
   D. Only if the carrier requires it.

6. §391.33(a)(2) If a driver applicant has a valid certificate showing successful completion of a driver's road test:
   A. The carrier must accept it.
   B. The carrier may still require the applicant to take a road test.
   C. The carrier cannot accept it.
   D. The carrier may request a road test waiver from the Bureau of Motor Carrier Safety.

7. §391.41(b)(5) A person with breathing problems which may affect safe driving:
   A. Cannot drive.
   B. Cannot drive unless the vehicle has an emergency oxygen supply.
   C. Cannot drive unless another driver is along.
   D. Cannot drive except on short runs.

8. §391.41(b)(7) Persons with arthritis, rheumatism, or any such condition which may affect safe driving:
   A. Cannot drive unless they are checked by a doctor before each trip.
   B. Cannot drive.
   C. Cannot drive unless they are free of pain.
   D. Cannot drive unless another driver is along.

9. §391.41(b)(8) Persons who have ever had epilepsy:
   A. Cannot drive unless another driver is along.
   B. Cannot drive.
   C. Cannot drive on long runs.
   D. Cannot drive without monthly medial examinations.

10. §391.41(b)(9)(12)(13) In order to be able to drive, a driver:
   A. Must not have any mental, nervous, or physical problem likely to affect safe driving.
   B. Must not use an amphetamine, narcotic, or any habit forming drug.
   C. Must not have a current alcoholism problem.
   D. Must not have or use any of the above.

11. §391.45(c) If a driver gets an injury or illness serious enough to affect the ability to perform duties, the driver:
   A. Must report it at the next scheduled physical.
   B. Cannot drive again.
   C. Must take another physical and be recertified before driving again.
   D. Must wait at least 1 month after recovery before driving again.

12. §392.2 A driver may not drive faster than posted speed limits:
   A. Unless the driver is sick and must complete the run quickly.
   B. At any time.
   C. Unless the driver is passing another vehicle.
   D. Unless the driver is late and must make a scheduled arrival.

13. §392.3 When a driver's physical condition requires the driver to stop driving while on a trip, but stopping would not be safe, the driver:
    A. Must stop anyway.
    B. May try to complete the trip, but as quickly as possible.
    C. May continue to drive to the home terminal.
    D. May continue to drive, but should stop at the nearest safe place.

14. §392.5(a)(1) A driver may not drink or be under the influence of any alcoholic beverage (regardless of alcoholic content):
    A. 4 hours before going on duty or driving.
    B. 6 hours before going on duty or driving.
    C. 8 hours before going on duty or driving.
    D. 12 hours before going on duty or driving.

15. §392.7 A driver must be satisfied that the service and parking brakes, tires, lights and reflectors, mirrors, couplings and other devices are in good working order:
    A. At the end of each trip.
    B. Before the vehicle may be driven.
    C. Only when the driver considers it necessary.
    D. According to schedules set by the carrier.

16. §392.8 The following must be in place and ready for use before the vehicle can be driven:
    A. At least one spare fuse or other overload protector of each type used on the vehicle.
    B. A tool kit containing a specified list of hand tools.
    C. At least one spare tire for every four wheels.
    D. A set of spark plugs.

17. §392.9(a)(3) If any part of the cargo or anything else blocks a driver's front or side views, arm or leg movements, or the driver's access to emergency equipment, the driver:
    A. Can drive the vehicle, but must report the problem at the end of the trip.
    B. Cannot drive the vehicle.
    C. Can drive the vehicle, but only at speeds under 40 miles per hour.
    D. Can drive the vehicle, but only on secondary roads.

18. §392.9(a) A driver who needs glasses to meet minimum visual requirements:
    A. Must drive only during daylight hours.
    B. Must always wear glasses when driving.
    C. Must always carry a spare pair of glasses.
    D. Must not drive a motor vehicle.

19. §392.9(b) A driver may drive with a hearing aid:
    A. If the driver always has it turned on while driving.
    B. If the driver always carries a spare power source for it.
    C. If the driver can meet the hearing requirements when the hearing aid is turned on.
    D. If all of the above requirements are met.

20. §392.10(a) A driver required to stop at a railroad crossing should bring the vehicle to a stop no closer to the tracks than:
    A. 5 feet.
    B. 10 feet.
    C. 15 feet.
    D. 20 feet.

21. §392.10(a) Shifting gears is not permitted:
    A. When traveling faster than 35 miles per hour.
    B. When moving across any bridge.
    C. When crossing railroad tracks.
    D. When traveling down a hill steeper than 10 degrees.

22. §392.13 A driver of a motor vehicle, not required to stop at drawbridges without signals, must:
    A. Drive at a rate of speed which will permit a stop before reaching the lip of the draw.
    B. Sound the horn before crossing.
    C. Proceed across without reducing speed.
    D. Slow down only if directed by an attendant.

23. §392.15(a) When turning a vehicle, a driver should begin flashing the turn signals:
    A. At least 50 feet before turning.
    B. At least 60 feet before turning.
    C. At least 75 feet before turning.
    D. At least 100 feet before turning.

24. §392.16 Which of the following is true?
    A. If a seat belt is installed in the vehicle, a driver must have it fastened before beginning to drive.
    B. A driver may or may not use the seatbelt, depending on the driver's judgement.
    C. Seat belts are not necessary on heavier vehicles.
    D. A driver must use the seatbelt only if required by the carrier.

25. §392.21 When a motor vehicle cannot be stopped off of the traveled part of the highway, the driver:
    A. Must keep driving.
    B. May stop, but shall get as far off of the traveled part of the highway as possible.
    C. May stop, but shall make sure the vehicle can be seen as far as possible to its front and rear.
    D. May stop if the driver has to, but should do both B and C above.

26. §392.22(b)(1) If a vehicle has a breakdown, the driver must place one emergency signal:
    A. 100 feet in front of the vehicle in the center of the lane it occupies.
    B. 100 feet in back of the vehicle in the center of the lane it occupies.
    C. 10 feet in front of and in back of the traffic side.
    D. At all of the above locations.

27. §392.22(b)(1)(i) If a vehicle has a breakdown on a poorly lit street or highway, the driver shall place on the traffic side:
    A. A reflective triangle.
    B. A lighted red electric lantern.
    C. A red reflector.
    D. Any one of the above.

28. §392.22(b)(2)(iii) No emergency signals are required for a vehicle with a breakdown if the street or highway lighting is bright enough so it can be seen at a distance of:
    A. 100 feet.
    B. 200 feet.
    C. 500 feet.
    D. 750 feet.

29. §392.22(b)(2)(v) If a vehicle has a breakdown and stops on a poorly lit divided or one lane highway, the driver must place one emergency signal:
    A. 200 feet in back of the vehicle in the center of the lane it occupies.
    B. 100 feet in back of the vehicle on the traffic side of the vehicle.
    C. 10 feet in back of the vehicle on the traffic side of the vehicle.
    D. At all of the above locations.

30. §392.25 Lighted flame-producing emergency signals, including fuses:
    A. May not be used with vehicles carrying class A or B explosives.
    B. May not be used with tank vehicles, loaded or empty, which are used to carry flammable liquids or gas.
    C. May not be used with any vehicle using compressed gas as a fuel.
    D. May not be used with any of the above.

31. §392.30(a) A driver is required to turn on vehicle lights:
    A. From one-half hour before sunset to one-half hour before sunrise.
    B. From one-half hour before sunset to sunrise.
    C. From one-half hour after sunset to one-half hour before sunrise.
    D. From sunset to one-half hour before sunrise.

32. §392.32(a)(b) When lights are required on the highway, the driver shall use the high beam:
    A. Except when within 500 feet of an on-coming vehicle or a vehicle the driver is following.
    B. Except when within 400 feet of an on-coming vehicle or a vehicle the driver is following.
    C. Except when within 200 feet of an on-coming vehicle or a vehicle the driver is following.
    D. Except when within 100 feet of an on-coming vehicle or a vehicle the driver is following.

33. §392.32(a) When lights are required, a driver may use lower beam lights:
    A. When fog, dust, or other such conditions exist.
    B. When approaching tunnels or bridges.
    C. When driving on one-way highways.
    D. When within 1,000 feet of business areas or where people live.

34. §392.40 Every driver involved in an accident must follow the safety regulation procedures whenever an injury or death is involved or if:
    A. The accident is caused by the driver and property damage of over $2,000.00 results.
    B. Property damage of over $2,000.00 results, no matter who is at fault.
    C. Property damage of over $100.00 results.
    D. Property damage of any kind results.

35. §392.41 If a driver strikes a parked vehicle, the driver should first:
    A. Stop and call the local police.
    B. Stop and call the carrier.
    C. Stop and try to find the driver or owner of the parked vehicle.
    D. Stop and estimate the damages.

36. §392.42 When a driver receives notice of license or permit revocation, suspension or other withdrawal action, the driver must:
    A. Notify the carrier within 72 hours.
    B. Notify the carrier within one week.
    C. Notify the carrier before the end of the next business day.
    D. Take no action since the carrier will get a notice.

37. §392.61 Except in emergencies, no driver shall allow a vehicle to be driven by any other person:
    A. Except by those the driver knows are capable.
    B. Except on roads with little or no traffic.
    C. Except by those allowed by the carrier to do it.
    D. Unless the driver goes along with the person driving.

38. § 392.64 A person may ride inside a vehicle's closed body or trailer:
    A. Only on short runs.
    B. Only if there is an easy way to get out from the inside.
    C. Only if the inside of the body or trailer is lighted.
    D. Only if there is no cargo in it.

39. §392.66 If carbon monoxide is inside a vehicle or if a mechanical problem may produce a carbon monoxide danger, the vehicle:
    A. May be sent out and driven so long as the windows are left open.
    B. May not be sent out or driven.
    C. May be sent out and driven only if the carrier decides the vehicle has to be used.
    D. May be sent out and driven on short runs.

40. §392.68 No motor vehicle shall be operated out of gear:
    A. Except when fuel must be saved.
    B. Except on hills which are less than 20 degrees.
    C. Except when it is necessary for stopping or shifting gears.
    D. Except when the vehicle's speed is under 25 miles per hour.

41. §393.1(a) Under the Federal Motor Carrier Safety Regulations, no vehicle may be driven:
    A. Until a list of all missing or defective equipment has been prepared and given to the carrier.
    B. Until all equipment has been inspected and replacements for defective parts have been ordered.
    C. Unless all missing equipment is to replaced no later than the end of the vehicle's next run.
    D. Until it meets all of the equipment requirements of the regulations.

42. §393 Minimum requirements for lighting, reflecting and electrical equipment and devices on buses and trucks:
    A. Are set by the vehicle makers.
    B. Are set by the National Safety Council.
    C. Are specified in the safety regulations.
    D. Are set by the trucking associations.

43. §393.18(a)(b) Every motor vehicle which has a load sticking over its sides must be specifically marked with flags and lamps. Additional flags and lamps must be added if the load or tailgate sticks out beyond the rear of the vehicle by more than:
    A. 2 feet.
    B. 4 feet.
    C. 6 feet.
    D. 8 feet.

44. §393.41(a) No matter what its load, every vehicle shall have a parking brake system which will hold it:
    A. On any grade on which it is operated which is free from ice and snow.
    B. On all grades under 15 degrees which are free from ice and snow.
    C. On all grades under 20 degrees which are free from ice and snow.
    D. On all grades under 25 degrees which are free from ice and snow.

45. §393.77(b)(6) A portable heater may not be used in a vehicle cab:
    A. Unless the heater is secured.
    B. Unless the heater is of the electric filament type.
    C. At any time.
    D. Wihout approval from the carrier.

46. §395.3(a) A driver is not generally allowed to drive for more than:
    A. 6 hours following 8 straight hours off-duty.
    B. 8 hours following 8 straight hours off-duty.
    C. 10 hours following 8 straight hours off-duty.
    D. 12 hours following 8 straight hours off-duty.

47. §395.3(a) Most drivers of large vehicles are not allowed to drive:
    A. After they have been on duty for 16 hours.
    B. After they have been on duty for 15 hours.
    C. After they have been on duty for 14 hours.
    D. After they have been on duty for 12 hours.

48. §395.3(b) Generally, a driver may not be on duty:
    A. For more than 40 hours in 7 straight days.
    B. For more than 50 hours in 7 straight days.
    C. For more than 60 hours in 7 straight days.
    D. For more than 70 hours in 7 straight days.

49. §395.7 When a driver is riding in a vehicle but is not driving, and has no other responsibility, such time shall be counted as:
   A. On-duty time.
   B. On-duty time unless the driver is allowed 8 straight hours off-duty upon arrival at the destination.
   C. On-duty time unless the driver is allowed 6 straight hours off-duty upon arrival at the destination.
   D. On-duty time unless the driver is allowed 4 straight hours off-duty upon arrival at the destination.

50. §395.8(f)(1) Every driver must prepare an original and one copy of the driver's record of duty status which must be kept current by updating it:
   A. Every time a change of duty is made.
   B. Every 24 hours.
   C. Every 8 hours.
   D. At the end of each trip.

51. §395.8(f)(2) Except for the name and main address of the carrier, all entries relating to the driver's record of duty status:
   A. Must be printed in ink or typed.
   B. Must be made by the carrier dispatcher.
   C. Must be made in front of a witness.
   D. Must be in the driver's handwriting.

52. §395.8(d)(12)(14)(15) & (h)(2) Which of the following is not required to be put in a driver's record of duty status?
   A. Time spent in a sleeper berth.
   B. Total hours in each duty status.
   C. Origin and destination.
   D. The name and make of the vehicle.

53. §395.11 If an emergency delays a run which could normally have been completed within hours of service limits, the driver:
   A. Must still stop driving when the hours of service limit is reached.
   B. May drive for 1 extra hour.
   C. May drive for 2 extra hours.
   D. May finish the run without being in violation.

54. §395.13 A driver declared "Out of Service:"
   A. Must take a road test before driving again.
   B. Must wait 72 hours before driving again.
   C. Must appeal to the Director of the Bureau of Motor Carrier Safety to drive again.
   D. Can drive again only after hours of service requirements are met.

WRITTEN EXAMINATION: FEDERAL MOTOR CARRIER REGULATIONS

55. §396.7 If a vehicle on a trip is in a condition likely to cause an accident or breakdown:
    A. The driver should report it at the end of the run so repairs can be made.
    B. The driver should drive at lower speeds for the rest of the run.
    C. The driver should stop immediately unless going on to the nearest repair shop is safer than stopping.
    D. The driver should change the route in order to get away from heavily traveled roads.

56. §396.9(c) If authorized federal inspectors find a vehicle which is likely to cause an accident or breakdown:
    A. It will be reported to the carrier for repair as soon as the vehicle is not scheduled.
    B. It will be reported to the carrier for repair at the end of the trip.
    C. It will be marked with an "Out of Service Vehicle" sticker and not driven until repairs are made.
    D. The driver will be held responsible and declared "Out of Service."

57. §396.9(c)(4) If the driver personally makes repairs on an "Out of Service" vehicle: (EDITOR'S NOTE: Question is inapplicable because regulation was deleted.)
    A. The work must be approved by a mechanic.
    B. The driver must complete and sign a "Certification of Repairman" form.
    C. The work must be approved by a supervisor.
    D. The work must be approved by a federal inspector.

58. §397.3 Department of Transportation regulations covering driving and parking of vehicles containing hazardous materials:
    A. Replace state and local laws.
    B. Prevent states and cities from having their own laws.
    C. Must be obeyed even if the state or local laws are less strict or disagree.
    D. Should not be obeyed if state or local laws disagree.

59. §397.5(c) A vehicle which contains hazardous materials other than Class A or Class B explosives must be attended at all times:
    A. By the driver.
    B. By the driver except when involved in other driver duties.
    C. By the driver or a person chosen by the driver.
    D. By the driver or a police officer.

60. §397.5(d)(1) A vehicle containing Class A or Class B explosives or other hazardous materials on a trip is "attended:"
    A. When the person in charge is anywhere within 100 feet of the vehicle.
    B. As long as the driver can see the vehicle from 200 feet away.
    C. When the person in charge is within 100 feet and has a clear view of the vehicle.
    D. When the person in charge is resting in the berth.

61. §397.7(a)(3) Except for short periods when operations make it necessary, trucks carrying Class A or Class B explosives cannot be parked any closer to bridges, tunnels, buildings, or crowds of people than:
    A. 50 feet.
    B. 100 feet.
    C. 200 feet.
    D. 300 feet.

62. §397.13(a) Smoking or carrying a lighted cigarette, cigar, or pipe near a vehicle which contains explosives or oxidizing or flammable materials is not allowed:
    A. Except in the closed vehicle of the cab.
    B. Except when the vehicle is moving.
    C. Except at a distance of 25 feet or more from the vehicle.
    D. Except when approved by the carrier.

63. §397.15(b) When a vehicle containing hazardous materials is being fueled:
    A. No person may remain in the cab.
    B. A person must be in control of the fueling process at the point where the fuel tank is filled.
    C. The area within 50 feet of the vehicle must be cleared.
    D. The person who controls the fueling process must wear special clothes.

64. §397.17(a) If a vehicle carrying hazardous materials is equipped with dual tires on any axle, the driver must examine the tires:
    A. At all fueling stops only.
    B. Only at the end of each day or tour of duty.
    C. At the beginning of each trip and each time the vehicle is parked.
    D. At the beginning of each trip only.

65. §397.17(c) If a driver of a vehicle carrying hazardous materials finds a tire which is overheated, the driver must:
    A. Wait for the overheated tire to cool before going on.
    B. Remove and replace the overheated tire, store it on the vehicle, and drive on.
    C. Remove the tire, place it a safe distance from the vehicle, and do not drive the vehicle until the cause of the overheating is fixed.
    D. Drive slowly to the nearest repair shop and have the cause of the overheating fixed.

66. §177.823(a) When required, specific hazardous materials markings or signs must be placed:
    A. Wherever they can be seen clearly.
    B. On the sides and rear of the vehicle.
    C. On the front, rear, and sides of the vehicle.
    D. On the front and rear bumpers of the vehicle.

Scoring Key for Written Examination

SECTION	ANSWER	SECTION	ANSWER
(1) 390.32	D	(34) 392.40	D
(2) 391.11(b)(1)	D	(35) 392.41	C
(3) 391.15(c)(2)(3)	D	(36) 392.42	D
(4) 391.21(b)(7)(8)(10)	D	(37) 392.61	C
(5) 391.27(a)(b)	A	(38) 392.64	B
(6) 391.33(a)(2)	B	(39) 392.66	C
(7) 391.41(b)(5)	A	(40) 392.68	C
(8) 391.41(b)(7)	B	(41) 393.1(a)	D
(9) 391.41(b)(8)	B	(42) 393	C
(10) 391.41(b)(9)(12)(13)	D	(43) 393.18(a)(b)	B
(11) 391.45(c)	C	(44) 393.41(a)	A
(12) 392.2	B	(45) 393.77(b)(6)	C
(13) 392.3	D	(46) 395.3(a)	C
(14) 392.5 (a)(1)	A	(47) 395.3(a)	B
(15) 392.7	B	(48) 395.3(b)	C
(16) 392.8	A	(49) 395.7	B
(17) 392.9(a)(3)	B	(50) 395.8(f)(1)	A
(18) 392.9(a)	B	(51) 395.8(f)(2)	D
(19) 392.9(b)	D	(52) 395.8(d)(12)(14)(15) & (h)(2)	D
(20) 392.10(a)	C	(53) 395.11	D
(21) 392.10(a)	C	(54) 395.13	D
(22) 392.13	A	(55) 396.7	C
(23) 392.15(a)	D	(56) 396.9(c)	C
(24) 392.16	A	(57) 396.9(c)(4)	B
(25) 392.21	D	(58) 397.3	C
(26) 392.22(b)(1)	D	(59) 397.5(c)	B
(27) 392.22(b)(1)(i)	D	(60) 397.5(d)(1)	C
(28) 392.22(b)(2)(iii)	C	(61) 397.7(a)(3)	D
(29) 392.22(b)(2)(v)	D	(62) 397.13(a)	C
(30) 392.25	D	(63) 397.15(b)	B
(31) 392.30 (a)	C	(64) 397.17(a)	C
(32) 392.32(a)(b)	A	(65) 397.17(c)	C
(33) 392.32(a)	A	(66) 177.823(a)	C

Section E
Federal Regulations Governing
Commercial Motor Carriers and Drivers

Summary of DOT Motor Carrier Safety Regulations
in Title 49 of the Code of Federal Regulations

Part 325: Compliance with Interstate Motor Carrier Noise Emission Standards: Establishes procedures for inspection, surveillance, and measurement of motor vehicles to determine compliance with noise emission standards.

Part 350: Commercial Motor Carrier Safety Assistance Program: Establishes guidelines for the development and implementation of state programs for the enforcement of federal motor carrier safety regulations. Conditions, objectives, and funding of the program are also detailed.

Part 383: Commercial Driver's License Standards; Requirements and Penalties: Requires that drivers have a single commercial motor vehicles driver's license, and that drivers provide employers with information about previous employment and previous violations and suspensions. Also prohibits an employer from allowing a person with a suspended license to operate a commercial motor vehicle and sets penalties for violations.

Part 385: Safety Ratings: Prescribes procedures for issuing motor carrier ratings of satisfactory, unsatisfactory, or conditional. Also lists the factors to be considered in determining a safety rating and sets procedures for notification and review.

Part 386: Rules of Practice for Motor Carrier Safety and Hazardous Materials Proceedings: Authorizes the Associate Administrator for Motor Carriers of the Federal Highway Administration (FHWA) to determine whether a motor carrier or person subject to the jurisdiction of FHWA has failed to comply with motor carrier safety regulations. Also authorizes the Associate Administrator to compel compliance, issue a civil penalty, or both.

Part 387: Minimum Levels of Financial Responsibility for Motor Carriers: Establishes minimum level of financial responsibility required of motor carriers and mandates that motor carriers must have proof of insurance and authorization from the Interstate Commerce Commission (ICC) to operate.

Part 388: Cooperative Agreements With States: Authorizes any state to enforce FHWA safety regulations and establishes terms of eligibility, cancellation, exchange of information, and requests for assistance.

Part 389: Rulemaking Procedures — Federal Motor Carrier Safety Regulations: Establishes rulemaking procedures that apply to the issuance, amendment, and revocation of Federal Motor Carrier Safety Regulations.

Part 390: Federal Motor Carrier Regulations, General: Establishes definitions and applicability of regulations. (For a list of exemptions, see Table E-1.)

Part 391: Qualifications of Drivers: Establishes minimum qualifications for motor carrier drivers (i.e., to qualify to drive a commercial motor vehicle, Part 391 states that a person must be at least 21 years old, have a currently valid commercial motor vehicle operator's permit, have prepared and furnished the motor carrier that employs him or her with a list of violations, have successfully completed and been issued a certificate of driver's road test or an equivalent.) In addition, part 391 establishes minimum duties of motor carriers with respect to the qualifications of their drivers.

Part 392: Driving Motor Vehicles: Establishes driving practices in cases of railway grade crossings, drawbridges, and hazardous driving conditions. Also sets regulations for use of lighted lamps and reflectors, accidents and license revocation, emergency signals, fueling precautions, and specifies prohibited practices.

Part 393: Parts and Accessories Necessary for Safe Operation: Establishes requirements for motor carriers including lighting devices, reflectors, and electrical equipment, brakes, glazing and window construction, fuel systems, coupling devices and towing methods, miscellaneous parts and accessories, emergency equipment, and protection against shifting or falling cargo.

Part 394: Notification and Reporting of Accidents: Defines reportable accidents and establishes duties of motor carriers to make reports and keep records of accidents that occur during their operations.

Part 395: Hours of Service Drivers: Establishes hours-of-service regulations for drivers, restricting driving periods of more than 10 hours after 8 consecutive hours off duty, for any period after having been on duty for 15 hours after 8 consecutive hours off duty, or more than 60 hours in any consecutive 7 days. Regulations are also set for recording driver duty status.

Part 396: Inspection, Repair, and Maintenance: Establishes requirements for the inspections, repair, and maintenance of commercial motor vehicles.

Part 397: Transportation of Hazardous Materials; Driving and Parking Rules: Establishes requirements for transportation of hazardous materials including special parking, route, tire, and smoking regulations.

Part 398: Transportation of Migrant Workers: Establishes regulations governing the transportation of migrant workers for more than 75 miles when crossing the boundary of another state, a U.S. territory, or another country.

Part 399: Employee Safety and Health Standards: Establishes step, handhold, and deck requirements that apply to drivers of trucks and truck-tractors, having a high profile cab-over-engine configuration for entrance, exit, and back of cab access manufactured on or after September 1, 1982.

Source: Office of Technology Assessment.

Table E-1: Regulatory Exemptions to Title 49 of the Code of Federal Regulations

Vehicle/Driver type	391[a]	392	393	394	395	396	397
Vehicles owned, operated, and regulated by federal, state, or local governments	X	X	X	X	X	X	X
Private carrier of passengers (i.e. school buses)	X	X	X	X	X	X	X
Intracity operations[b]	X	X	X	—	—	X	X
Lightweight mail trucks[c]	X	X	X	X	X	X	—
Farm custom operations[d]	X	—	—	—	—	—	—
Certain farm vehicle drivers[e]	X	—	—	—	—	—	—
Farm-to-market operations[f]	—	—	—	X	—	—	—
Apiarian industries[g]	X	—	—	—	—	—	—
Drivers traveling beyond a commercial zone, transporting cargo other than explosives or other dangerous articles	—	—	—	—	—	—	X

KEY:

X = exemption from requirement.

[a] Drivers in the following categories are exempt from portions of Part 391: drivers regularly employed before Jan. 1, 1971; intermittent or occasional drivers; drivers furnished by other motor carriers; drivers of articulated farm vehicles; intrastate drivers of vehicles transporting combustible liquid; and drivers operating in the State of Hawaii. The Department of Transportation has ended this exemption effective Nov. 15, 1988.

[b] This exemption applies to vehicles or drivers wholly within a municipality or commercial zone, unless transporting hazardous materials that require a placard and weigh 2,500 pounds or more in the case of one dangerous article, or 5,000 pounds or more in the case of more than one dangerous article. The exemption does not apply to drivers in the State of Hawaii. The Department of Transportation ended this exemption effective Nov. 15, 1988.

[c] This exemption applies to motor carriers that have a gross vehicle weight of 10,000 pounds or less and are used exclusively to transport mail under contract with the U.S. Postal Service

[d] This exemption applies to drivers who operate motor vehicles controlled and operated by a person engaged in custom harvesting. If the vehicle is used to transport farm machinery or supplies to or from a farm for custom harvesting operations, or used to transport custom-harvested crops to storage or market.

[e] This exemption to farm vehicle drivers, except those driving articulated motor vehicles with gross vehicle weights, including loads, of more than 10,000 pounds.

[f] This exemption applies to drivers of vehicles controlled and operated by a farmer who, as a private carrier, is using the vehicle to transport agricultural products from his or her farm, or to transport farm machinery, farm supplies, or both to his farm. Drivers transporting hazardous materials that require a placard are not exempt.

[g] This exemption applies to drivers operating motor vehicles controlled and operated by a beekeeper engaged in the seasonal transportation of bees.

Source: Office of Technology Assessment, based on 49 CFR 390.33.

Section F
Division Offices of the Office of Motor Carrier Safety

In addition to the Federal Motor Carrier Safety Regulations, the Office of Motor Carrier Safety maintains Division Offices in the following cities throughout the United States. The staff of the Federal Highway Administration and the Office of Motor Carrier Safety in these offices is always ready to answer questions and to help those who are interested in improved commercial vehicle safety.

ALABAMA
Office of Motor Vehicle Safety
Federal Highway Administration
441 High Street
Montgomery, AL 36104

ALASKA
Office of Motor Carrier Safety
Federal Highway Administration
701 C Street
Box 14, AAL-700
Anchorage, AK 99513

ARIZONA
Office of Motor Vehicle Safety
Federal Highway Administration
234 N. Central Avenue, Suite 201
Phoenix, AZ 85102

ARKANSAS
Office of Motor Vehicle Safety
Federal Highway Administration
3128 Federal Building
700 W. Capitol Avenue
Little Rock, AR 72201

CALIFORNIA
Office of Motor Vehicle Safety
Federal Highway Administration
111 N. La Brea Avenue, Suite 407
Inglewood, CA 90301

Office of Motor Carrier Safety
Federal Highway Administration
Federal Building, Room 236
801 I Street
P.O. Box 1915
Sacramento, CA 95809-1915

Office of Motor Carrier Safety
Federal Highway Administration
211 Main Street, Room 1108
San Francisco, CA 94105

COLORADO
Office of Motor Carrier Safety
Federal Highway Administration
555 Zang Street, Room 250
Denver, CO 80228

CONNECTICUT
Office of Motor Carrier Safety
Federal Highway Administration
1 Hartford Square West-South Building
Hartford, CT 06106

DELAWARE
Office of Motor Carrier Safety
Federal Highway Administration
Federal Office Building, 2nd Floor
300 S. New Street, Room 2101
Dover, DE 19901

FLORIDA
Office of Motor Carrier Safety
Federal Highway Administration
400 West Bay Street, Federal Building
P.O. Box 35012
Jacksonville, FL 32202

Office of Motor Carrier Safety
Federal Highway Administration
227 N. Bronough Street, Room 2015
Tallahassee, FL 32302

GEORGIA
Office of Motor Carrier Safety
Federal Highway Administration
1720 W Peachtree Road, NW, Room 300 ·
Atlanta, GA 30309

HAWAII
Office of Motor Carrier Safety
Federal Highway Administration
Prince Jonah Kuhio Kalanianaole
   Building, Suite 4119
300 Ala Moana Boulevard
P.O. Box 50206
Honolulu, HI 96850

IDAHO
Office of Motor Carrier Safety
Federal Highway Administration
3010 W. State Street
Boise, ID 83703

ILLINOIS
Office of Motor Carrier Safety
Federal Highway Administration
7th Floor
320 W. Washington Street
Springfield, IL 62701

Office of Motor Carrier Safety
Federal Highway Administration
18209 Dixie Highway
Homewood, Illinois 60430

INDIANA
Office of Motor Carrier Safety
Federal Highway Administration
Minton-Capehart Federal Building
575 N. Pennsylvania Street, Room 254
Indianapolis, IN 46204

IOWA
Office of Motor Carrier Safety
Federal Highway Administration
105 6th Street
P.O. Box 627
Ames, IA 50010

KANSAS
Office of Motor Carrier Safety
Federal Highway Administration
Frank Carlson Federal Building &
   U.S. Courthouse
444 SE Quincy, Room 240
Topeka, KS 66683

KENTUCKY
Office of Motor Carrier Safety
Federal Highway Administration
Federal Building & U.S. Courthouse
330 W. Broadway
P.O. Box 536
Frankfort, KY 46602

LOUISIANA
Office of Motor Carrier Safety
Federal Highway Administration
239 Federal Building
750 Florida Street
P.O. Box 3929
Baton Rouge, LA 70821

MAINE
Office of Motor Carrier Safety
Federal Highway Administration
Federal Building & U.S. Post Office
Room 614, 40 Western Avenue
Augusta, ME 04330

Office of Motor Carrier Safety
Federal Highway Administration
Post Office Building, Room 217
Houlton, ME 04730

MARYLAND
Office of Motor Carrier Safety
Federal Highway Administration
Federal Building, Room 1615
31 Hopkins Plaza
Baltimore, MD 21201

Office of Motor Carrier Safety
Federal Highway Administration
Rotunda, Suite 222
711 W. 40th Street
Baltimore, MD 21211

MASSACHUSETTS
Office of Motor Vehicle Safety
Federal Highway Administration
Transportation Systems Center
55 Broadway, 10th Floor
Cambridge, MA 02142

MICHIGAN
Office of Motor Carrier Safety
Federal Highway Administration
Federal Building, Room 211
315 W. Allegan Street
P.O. Box 10147
Lansing, MI 48901

MINNESOTA
Office of Motor Carrier Safety
Federal Highway Administration
Metro Square Building, Suite 490
7th & Robert Streets
St. Paul, MN 55101

MISSISSIPPI
Office of Motor Carrier Safety
Federal Highway Administration
666 North Street, Suite 105
Jackson, MS 39202

MISSOURI
Office of Motor Carrier Safety
Federal Highway Administration
209 Adams Street
P.O. Box 1787
Jefferson City, MO 65101

Office of Motor Carrier Safety
Federal Highway Administration
6301 Rockhill Road
P.O. Box 19715
Kansas City, MO 64141

MONTANA
Office of Motor Carrier Safety
Federal Highway Administration
301 S. Park Street
Drawer 10056
Helena, MT 59601

NEBRASKA
Office of Motor Carrier Safety
Federal Highway Administration
100 Centennial Mall North
Lincoln, NE 68508

NEVADA
Office of Motor Carrier Safety
Federal Highway Administration
1535 Hot Springs Road, Suite 100
Carson City, NV 89701-0602

NEW HAMPSHIRE
Office of Motor Carrier Safety
Federal Highway Administration
Federal Building, Room 219
55 Pleasant Street
Concord, NH 03301

NEW JERSEY
Office of Motor Carrier Safety
Federal Highway Administration
25 Scotch Road, 2nd Floor
Trenton, NJ 08628

NEW MEXICO
Office of Motor Carrier Safety
Federal Highway Administration
2930 Yale Boulevard, SE, Room 113
Albuquerque, NM 87106

NEW YORK
Office of Motor Carrier Safety
Federal Highway Administration
Leo O'Brien Federal Building, 9th Floor
Albany, NY 12207

Office of Motor Carrier Safety
Federal Highway Administration
909B Federal Office Building
111 W. Huron Street
Buffalo, NY 14202

Office of Motor Carrier Safety
Federal Highway Administration
Jacob K. Javits Federal Building,
Room 507
26 Federal Plaza
New York, NY 10278

Office of Motor Carrier Safety
Federal Highway Administration
James M. Hanley U.S. Court House
Federal Building, Room 527
P.O. Box 7065
Syracuse, NY 13260
(315) 423-5464

NORTH CAROLINA
Office of Motor Carrier Safety
Federal Highway Administration
Mart Office Building, Room DD 507
800 Briar Creek Road
Charlotte, NC 28205

Office of Motor Carrier Safety
Federal Highway Administration
Federal Building, Room 420-D
P.O. Box 26806
Raleigh, NC 27611

NORTH DAKOTA
Office of Motor Carrier Safety
Federal Highway Administration
New Federal Office Building
3rd & Rosser Avenue
P.O. Box 1755
Bismarck, ND 58501

OHIO
Office of Motor Carrier Safety
Federal Highway Administration
200 N. High Street, Room 328
Columbus, OH 43215

OKLAHOMA
Office of Motor Carrier Safety
Federal Highway Administration
454 Federal Building
200 NW 5th Street
Oklahoma City, OK 73102

OREGON
Office of Motor Carrier Safety
Federal Highway Administration
Mohawk Building, Room 312
708 SW 3rd Avenue
Portland, OR 97204

Office of Motor Carrier Safety
Federal Highway Administration
The Equitable Center, Suite 100
530 Center Street, NE
Salem, OR 97301

PENNSYLVANIA
Office of Motor Carrier Safety
Federal Highway Administration
Federal Office Building
228 Walnut Street
P.O. Box 1086
Harrisburg, PA 17108

Office of Motor Carrier Safety
Federal Highway Administration
Federal Building, Room 121
1000 Liberty Avenue
Pittsburgh, PA 15222

Office of Motor Carrier Safety
Federal Highway Administration
Room 171
841 Chestnut Street
Philadelphia, PA 19107

Office of Motor Carrier Safety
Federal Highway Administration
U.S. Court House and Federal Building,
Room 340
Scranton, PA 18503

RHODE ISLAND
Office of Motor Carrier Safety
Federal Highway Administration
380 Westminster Hall, Fifth Floor
Providence, RI 02903

SOUTH CAROLINA
Office of Motor Carrier Safety
Federal Highway Administration
1835 Assembly Street, Suite 758
Columbia, SC 29201

SOUTH DAKOTA
Office of Motor Carrier Safety
Federal Highway Administration
Federal Office Building
225 S. Pierre Street
P.O. Box 700
Pierre, SD 57501

TENNESSEE
Office of Motor Carrier Safety
Federal Highway Administration
Federal Building & U.S. Court House
801 Broadway, Room A 926
Nashville, TN 37203

Office of Motor Carrier Safety
Federal Highway Administration
33 Old Hickory Boulevard, Room 310
Jackson, TN 38301

Office of Motor Carrier Safety
Federal Highway Administration
111 Northshore Building
Room 605A
P.O. Box 177
Knoxville, TN 37919

TEXAS
Office of Motor Carrier Safety
Federal Highway Administration
826 Federal Office Building
300 E. 8th Street
Austin, TX 78701

Office of Motor Carrier Safety
Federal Highway Administration
A423 Federal Building
727 E. Durango
San Antonio, TX 78206

Office of Motor Carrier Safety
Federal Highway Administration
2320 LaBranch, Room 2119
Houston, TX 77004

Office of Motor Carrier Safety
Federal Highway Administration
1205 Texas Street, Room 614
P.O. Box 1767
Lubbock, TX 79408

Office of Motor Carrier Safety
Federal Highway Administration
8A00 Federal Building
819 Taylor Street
Fort Worth, TX 76102

Office of Motor Carrier Safety
Federal Highway Administration
14 C 32 Federal Building
1100 Commerce
Dallas, TX 75242

UTAH
Office of Motor Carrier Safety
Federal Highway Administration
2420 Federal Building
Box 11563
Salt Lake City, UT 84147

VERMONT
Office of Motor Carrier Safety
Federal Highway Administration
Federal Building, Room 216
87 State Street
P.O. Box 568
Montpelier, VT 05602

VIRGINIA
Office of Motor Carrier Safety
Federal Highway Administration
10-502 Federal Building
P.O. Box 10045
400 N. 8th Street
Richmond, VA 23240

Motor Carrier Safety Investigators
Poff Federal Building, Room 720
310 Franklin Road, SW
P.O. Box 121
Roanoke, VA 24002

WASHINGTON
Office of Motor Carrier Safety
Federal Highway Administration
Evergreen Plaza, Suite 501
711 S. Capitol Way
Olympia, WA 98501

WEST VIRGINIA
Office of Motor Carrier Safety
Federal Highway Administration
550 Eagan Street, Suite 309
Charleston, WV 25301

WISCONSIN
Office of Motor Carrier Safety
Federal Highway Administration
4502 Vernon Boulevard
Madison, WI 53705-4095

WYOMING
Office of Motor Carrier Safety
Federal Highway Administration
1916 Evans Avenue
P.O. Box 1127
Cheyenne, WY 82001

Section G
Requirements for Commercial Vehicle Drivers

Knowledge, Skill and Performance Testing

The safe and proper operation of heavy commercial motor vehicles — particularly combination vehicles — is a very demanding and specialized task. Long stopping distances, restricted maneuverability, possibility of brake fade on steep hills, cargo shifting, and danger of jackknifing are only a few of the problems that drivers of heavy commercial vehicles must face constantly, but which drivers of automobiles and other vehicles experience rarely, if at all. Safe and proper heavy commercial motor vehicle driving requires special characteristics of the driver such as:

- Patience in sharing the road with drivers of other vehicles.

- Understanding the handling properties of heavy vehicles and cargos.

- The ability to operate the vehicle properly in all types of weather, road, and loading conditions.

- Knowledge of the correct procedures to use in special applications such as the pre-trip inspection, loading, and unloading.

- The ability to recognize hazardous vehicle conditions and dangerous traffic events and situations.

- Maturity of attitude toward risk taking.

- Knowledge of the requirements of federal regulations, state laws, company policy, and recordkeeping.

- A desire to pursue and upgrade his or her professional competence.

- The ability to drive defensively to compensate for the relative unwieldiness of their vehicles.

- Good health — free from ailments or drug influence that might impair driving performance: Adequate rest and nourishment.

- An attitude that reflects courtesy, respect for the rules of the road, and an appreciation of the responsibility that comes with the job.

Clearly, some of the attributes listed above are currently beyond the objective knowledge, skill and performance testing that is conducted by State Driver Licensing Administrators. However, there are certain areas involving safe operation of heavy commercial motor vehicles for which objective knowledge, skill and performance can and should be measured. They are as follows:

- Pre-trip inspection
- Coupling and uncoupling
- Cargo loading
- Controlling the vehicle
      Accelerating
      Steering
      Shifting gears
      Braking
- Operating on the road
      Observing
      Managing space
      Communicating
      Managing speed
- Emergencies
      Traffic emergencies
      Vehicle emergencies
      Skids
- Handling and reporting accidents
- Fatigue
- Federal and state regulations
- State traffic laws
- Physical requirements

As previously stated, there are specific knowledges, skills and performances relating to each of the above areas of heavy commercial motor vehicle operation. The following sections list a sampling of the knowledge, skill, and performance that should be tested by State Driver Licensing Administrators.

Knowledge

A driver must know:

1. The major components of the vehicle.
2. The name, location, and function of each of the primary controls, including those required for steering, accelerating, shifting, braking, and parking.

3. The name, location, and function of each of the secondary controls, including those required for control of lights, signals, windshield wipers and washers, interior climate, engine starting and shutdown, suspension, and coupling.
4. The name, location, function, and the acceptable reading range of the various instruments required to monitor vehicle and engine speed as well as the status of fuel, oil, cooling, exhaust, and electrical systems.
5. A systematic procedure to assure a complete pre-trip inspection.
6. The effect of undiscovered malfunctions upon safety, effectiveness, and economy.
7. The importance of correcting malfunctions quickly.
8. Federal, state, and other regulations governing inspection, including special regulations for hazardous cargo.
9. Procedures for post-trip inspection.
10. The relationship of the wheel base length, articulation, and number of axles to the path of a turn.
11. The proper position from which to begin a turn and how to set up and execute a turn and how to recover from it.
12. Shifting procedures.
13. Common shifting errors and their consequences.
14. The procedures for backing and parking.
15. The procedures for proper coupling and uncoupling.
16. The hazards of attempting to operate a commercial vehicle when the driver is not familiar with it.
17. The proper adjustments of the various types of mirrors.
18. The relationship between speed and sight distance.
19. Search patterns appropriate for straight driving, changing speed or direction, and entering or crossing traffic.
20. When to actuate the turn signals in order to provide adequate warning without creating confusion.
21. State traffic laws for turn signals.
22. The importance of signaling to prevent accidents.
23. The relationship of speed to stopping distance, hydroplaning, crash severity, ability to maneuver, and fuel economy.
24. The effect on the maximum safe speed of the vehicle weight, center of gravity, loss of stability, available sight distance, and road surface conditions.
25. State regulations concerning following distances by commercial vehicles, lane use, changing lanes, and passing other vehicles.
26. The importance of maintaining maximum separation from other vehicles to ensure the room to maneuver in response to errors of other drivers.
27. The effect of the level of illumination on the ability to see under nighttime conditions.
28. State laws covering the use of headlights and auxiliary lights.
29. The symptoms and dangers of fatigue in relationship to night driving.

30. The general factors affecting night vision including interior illumination and sunglasses.
31. The effects of rain, snow, and ice upon the ability to maneuver and stop the vehicle.
32. The causes of and procedures for avoiding skidding and jackknifing during adverse weather.
33. The effect of ice, snow, water, mud, and debris on the operation of the brakes.
34. Procedures for hot weather driving.
35. The effect of vehicle weight and speed upon braking and shifting ability on long downgrades.
36. The use and meaning of percent of grade signs.
37. The activities of other road users that provide clues to potential danger, including head and body movement, vehicle movement, and conflict situations.
38. That in an impending head-on collision, it is generally safer to leave the roadway than to strike another vehicle.
39. The procedures for handling brake failure and blowouts.
40. The causes of skidding.
41. The location, function, operation, and common failures of the following vehicle components:

    • Frames, suspension, and axles
    • Engines
    • Fuel systems
    • Air intake and exhaust systems
    • Lubrication systems
    • Cooling systems
    • Electrical systems
    • Drive trains
    • Brake systems
    • Wheels, bearings, rims, and tires
    • Steering systems
    • Coupling systems

42. The procedures for performing inspections and authorized maintenance and repairs.
43. The importance of periodic inspection and repair to longevity of parts, safety, economy of operation, and prevention of enroute breakdowns.
44. The inspection, repair, and maintenance requirements of the Federal Motor Carrier Safety Regulations.
45. The symptoms of improper operation as indicated by the instruments, vehicle operation characteristics, sights, sound, feel, and smell.
46. The procedures for securing cargo.
47. The categories of hazardous materials, the need for specialized training to handle hazardous materials, the use of the placard, and other paperwork requirements.

48. Federal and state regulations for the weight limits and distrubution of cargo and how to load it.
49. The consequences of improper loading and unloading, overloading, and improper weight distribution of cargo.
50. The driver's responsibilities for ensuring that the paperwork is properly filled out.
51. All the requirements of Part 395 of the FMCSR covering Hours of Service.
52. How to comply with the Hours of Service Regulations.
53. State laws and company requirements dealing with stopping and rendering assistance at the scene of an accident.
54. The federal and state requirements for protecting the scene of an accident and the procedures for doing so.
55. The federal, state, insurance company, and employer requirements for accident reporting.
56. The types of fire extinguishers appropriate for each class of fire.
57. The effects of alcohol, drugs, poor diet, fatigue, poor vision, hearing, and general health upon safe operation of a CMV.
58. The federal and state regulations governing physical requirements.
59. The types of vehicles, cargo, and routes requiring special permits.
60. The state and local law restrictions on vehicle size and weight.

Skills and Performances

The mere possession of information is not enough to insure that drivers have mastered the skills and performances necessary to operate a heavy commercial motor vehicle safely on the public highways. Therefore, the State Driver License Administrators must conduct in-vehicle tests — using the type of vehicle which the operator will be driving — to insure that the driver can meet the skill and performance requirements. The following is a sample listing of the skill and performance requirements that must be evaluated and met by drivers of heavy commercial motor vehicles:

1. The ability to identify each of the vehicular driving controls and monitoring devices (gauges, alarms, lights, etc.) required to operate the vehicle safely and efficiently.

2. The ability to inspect and determine the condition of critical vehicle components, including instruments and controls; engine and drive train; chassis and suspension; steering system; braking system; coupling system; emergency equipment; and cargo securement device(s).

3. The ability to perform pre-trip inspections in a regular, systematic sequence that is accurate, uniform, and timely.

4. The ability to perform enroute inspections by checking the mirrors for signs of trouble; monitoring instruments and looking, listening and feeling for indications of malfunctions; making periodic roadside inspections of critical components; and meeting the enroute requirements for transporting dangerous cargo.

5. The ability to perform post-trip inspections by making accurate notes of actual and suspected component abnormalities or malfunctions.

6. The ability to check the trailer coupling.

7. The ability to start, warm up, and shut down the engine according to the manufacturer's specifications.

8. The ability to put the vehicle in motion and accelerate smoothly, forward and backward.

9. The ability to bring the vehicle to a smooth stop.

10. The ability to back the vehicle in a straight line.

11. The ability to position the vehicle for a turn and negotiate turns of different distances and sharpness.

12. The ability to shift up and down through all the gears of all major types of convetional transmissions, including auxiliary transmissions and multispeed axles.

13. The ability to double clutch and time shift for a smooth and fuel efficient performance.

14. The ability to select the proper gear for speed and highway conditions.

15. The ability to parallel park.

16. The ability to park in a jackknife position.

17. Get out of vehicle and check to the rear before backing.

18. Use mirrors to check path and clearances while backing.

19. Be able to scan both sides of the road using quick glances to observe roadside activity and the behavior of adjacent vehicles.

20. Be able to maintain a visual pattern that involves frequent checking of all mirrors for hazards, particularly before changing speed and direction.

21. Be able to frequently check instrument panel.

22. Be able to monitor overtaking traffic and be aware of vehicles in the rear and side blind spots.

23. Signal the intention to change position before pulling onto or off of the road or changing lanes.

24. Cancel turn signals after trailer is around the corner and straightened out.

25. Flash brake lights to warn following drivers that the vehicle is slowing or stopping.

26. Adjust speed to the configuration and condition of the roadway; weather and visibility conditions; traffic conditions; and vehicle, cargo and driver conditions.

27. Obey the legal speed limit.

28. Select a lane offering the best mobility and least traffic interruption in accordance with the law.

29. Assure a safe gap before changing lanes, passing other vehicles, or crossing or entering traffic.

30. Position the vehicle correctly when initiating and completing a turn in order to prevent other vehicles from passing on the wrong side and to minimize encroachment on other lanes.

31. Maintain a following distance appropriate to traffic, road surface, visibility, and vehicle weight.

32. Be able to adjust the operation of the vehicle to adverse weather conditions. This includes speed selection, braking, direction changes, and following distance. You will need to be able to maintain control and avoid skidding.

33. Use the right lane or special vehicle lane going up mountain grades.

34. Place the transmission in an appropriate gear for engine braking before starting down the grade.

35. Use proper braking techniques and maintain proper engine braking before starting down grades.

36. Be able to identify road conditions and road users that are a potential threat to the safety of the commercial vehicle driver.

37. Be able to bring the vehicle to a stop in the shortest possible distance while maintaining directional control on a dry surface.

38. Be able to identify vehicle systems or components that are functioning properly, are in imminent danger of failing, or functioning improperly.

39. Be able to describe the symptoms of improper operation completely and accurately to testing personnel.

40. Be courteous to other drivers by avoiding unnecessary use of the horn, not blocking driveways and entrances, and pulling to the side of the road (when necessary) to allow faster vehicles to pass.

Section H
Commercial Vehicle Cargo Classifications

A. General freight
B. Household goods
C. Metal: sheets, coils, rolls
D. Motor vehicles
E. Driveaway/towaway
F. Logs, poles, beams, lumber
G. Building materials
H. Mobile homes
I. Machinery, large objects
J. Produce, fruit, seafood
K. Liquid or gas in cargo tanks
L. Intermodal containers
M. Passengers
N. Oilfield equipment or service
O. Livestock
P. Grain, feed, hay
Q. Coal, coke
R. Suspended meat
S. New furniture or fixtures
T. U.S. mail
U. Chemicals
V. Commodities in dry bulk
W. Non-refrigerated foods
X. Beverages
Y. Paper products
Z. Other

Source: Federal Highway Administration

Section I
Military Time

The FMCSR requires that military time be used when preparing accident reports. Ordinary time may be converted to military time as shown on the chart.

Ordinary Time	Military Time
1 a.m.	0100
2 a.m.	0200
3 a.m.	0300
4 a.m.	0400
5 a.m.	0500
6 a.m.	0600
7 a.m.	0700
8 a.m.	0800
9 a.m.	0900
10 a.m.	1000
11 a.m.	1100
Noon	1200
1 p.m.	1300
2 p.m.	1400
3.p.m.	1500
4 p.m.	1600
5 p.m.	1700
6 p.m.	1800
7 p.m.	1900
8 p.m.	2000
9 p.m.	2100
10 p.m.	2200
11 p.m.	2300
Midnight	2400

Section J
Metric Conversion Chart

In some cases, laws and regulations describe weights and measurements in the metric system. The metric conversion chart below will help you convert weights and measures from one system to the other.

Conversion Chart

1 millimeter	0.0394 inch
1 centimeter	0.3937 inch
1 meter	39.3708 inches
1 kilometer	1093.63 yards
1 inch	25.4 millimeters
1 foot	0.3048 meter
1 yard	0.9144 meter
1 mile	1.6093 kilometers
1 international nautical mile	1.852 kilometers
1 square centimeter	0.155 square inch
1 square meter	1.196 square yards
1 acre	119.6 square yards
1 hectare	2.471 acres
1 square inch	6.452 square centimeters
1 square foot	9.290 square decimeters
1 square yard	0.836 square meter
1 acre	0.405 hectare
1 square mile	259 hectares
1 milligram	0.015 grain
1 gram	15.432 grains
1 kilogram	2.2046 lb
1 metric ton	1.1 tons
1 grain	0.0648 gram
1 ounce	28.350 grams
1 pound	0.4536 kilogram
1 hundredweight	45.359 kilograms
1 ton	909.2 kilograms
1 ton	0.907 metric ton

Section K
Factors Contributing to Commercial Vehicle Accidents

A. Commercial Driver Contributing Factors

1. Sick
2. Alcohol
3. Drugs (illegal)
4. Drugs/medicine (legal)
5. Dozing
6. Known medical condition
7. Inattentive
8. Careless/erratic driving
9. Reckless (wild)
10. Vehicle unattended — engine running
11. Vehicle unattended in road
12. Prohibited stopping
13. Prohibited parking
14. Overloaded
15. Improperly loaded
16. Load improperly secured
17. Failure to dim lights
18. Failure to turn on headlights
19. Improper turn signal
20. Following too closely
21. Improper lane change
22. Improper entry/exit
23. Starting/backing improperly
24. Improper passing
25. Failure to yield right of way
26. Failure to obey traffic control sign
27. Failure to obey traffic control signal
28. Failure to obey officer
29. Failure to obey signal control
30. Driving too fast
31. Making improper turn
32. Driving wrong way
33. Getting in or out of vehicle
34. Failure to clean window
35. Failure to clean lights
36. Failure to keep brakes in proper condition
37. Failure to keep vehicle in proper condition
38. Failure to allow for pedestrian
39. Failure to allow for bicyclist
40. Failure to allow for the error of the other driver
41. Failure to allow for adverse environmental conditions or oil on the road
42. Failure to anticipate animals in the roadway
43. Failure to allow for spray or splash
44. Failure to anticipate debris or other objects in the road
45. Failure to anticipate holes or ruts in roadway
46. Failure to allow for accidents, congestion, construction, unexpected traffic disruptions
47. Failure to maintain control
48. Failure to allow for highway curves
49. Losing control from other accident
50. Failure to secure vehicle
51. Failure to ensure clearance

B. Commercial Vehicle Contributing Factors

1. Headlights not operable
2. Headlights not adjusted properly
3. Headlights obstructed
4. Turn signals not operative
5. Turn signal not visible
6. Brake lights not operative
7. Brake lights not visible
8. Other lights not operative
9. Speedometer not operative
10. Warning lights or instruments not operative
11. Tires — blow out
12. Tires — excessive wear
13. Tires — improperly mounted
14. Brakes not properly adjusted or excessive wear
15. Brake system failure
16. Trailer brakes inadequate
17. Trailer brakes not properly adjusted
18. Trailer brakes system failure
19. Vehicle stopped by system failure
20. Vehicle forced to stop — out of fuel
21. Failure of trailer hitch or fifth wheel
22. Trailer/tractor steering failure
23. Trailer suspension/structural failure
24. Seatbelt not operative or not in use
25. Window or mirror broken
26. Windshield wiper not operative
27. Horn not operable
28. Fire
29. Hydraulic line burst
30. Fuel pump/line leak
31. Engine failure
32. Exhaust leak
33. Product hose rupture
34. Truck/trailer axle broken
35. Wheel bearing failure
36. Throttle spring broken

C. Highway System Contributing Factors

1. Inadequate warning of exit or lane narrowing
2. Inadequate warning of construction
3. Construction created condition
4. Inadequate warning of accident
5. Roadway obstructed by accident
6. Inadequate warning of congestion (no sign)
7. Inadequate warning of low bridge
8. Game on road
9. Fallen rocks
10. Inadequate or obscure pavement marking
11. Road washed out
12. Surface under water
13. Bumps, potholes, broken pavement
14. Roadway unpaved, not graded
15. Object in road
16. Inadequate curve banking
17. Soft shoulder
18. Gravel road
19. Traffic signal inoperative
20. Low hanging wire
21. Culvert collapsed
22. Low tree branch
23. Sign broken loose

D. Other Driver Contributing Factors

1. Sick
2. Alcohol
3. Drugs (Illegal)
4. Drugs or medicine (legal)
5. Dozing
6. Known medical condition
7. Inattentive
8. Careless/erratic driving
9. Reckless (wild) driving
10. Vehicle unattended — engine running
11. Vehicle unattended in road
12. Prohibited stopping
13. Prohibited parking
14. Overloaded
15. Improperly loaded
16. Load improperly secured
17. Failure to dim lights
18. Failure to turn on headlights
19. Improper turn signal
20. Following too closely
21. Improper lane change
22. Improper entry/exit
23. Starting/backing improperly
24. Improper passing
25. Failure to yield right of way
26. Failure to obey traffic control sign
27. Failure to obey traffic control signal
28. Failure to obey officer
29. Failure to obey signal control
30. Driving too fast
31. Making improper turn
32. Driving wrong way
33. Getting in or out vehicle
34. Failure to clean window
35. Failure to clean lights
36. Failure to keep brakes in proper condition
37. Failure to keep vehicle in proper condition
38. Failure to allow for pedestrian
39. Failure to allow for bicyclist
40. Failure to allow for the error of other drivers
41. Failure to allow for adverse environmental conditions or oil on the road
42. Failure to anticipate animals in the roadway
43. Failure to allow for spray or splash
44. Failure to anticipate debris or other objects in the road
45. Failure to anticipate holes or ruts in roadway
46. Failure to allow for accidents, congestion, construction, unexpected traffic disruptions
47. Failure to maintain control
48. Failure to allow for highway curves
49. Losing control from other accident
50. Failure to secure vehicle
51. Failure to ensure clearance
52. Tires — blowout

E. Owner Contributing Factors

1. Inadequate maintenance of vehicle
2. Failure to observe or enforce load limit
3. Inadequate screening of driver
4. Failure to observe or enforce Hours in Service rules

F. Environmental Contributing Factors

1. Vision obscured by sand
2. Vision obscured by bright sunlight or glare
3. Vision obscured by vegetation
4. Vehicle control impaired by wind
5. Vehicle control impaired by rain, snow, sleet, hail on road
6. Vision obscured by spray
7. Brakes impaired by cold

G. Miscellaneous Contributing Factors

1. Vehicle on shoulder
2. Vandalism
3. Pedestrian error
4. Bicyclist error
5. Preventability not determined

Section L
Lights and Reflectors

This section defines the lights and reflectors found on commercial vehicles. The various kinds of lights and reflectors are illustrated for your use. The numbers found on the illustration are explained in the *legend*. This information is from FMSCR section 393.11.

Definitions

Clearance Lamp	A lamp used on the front and rear of a motor vehicle to indicate its overall width and height
Hazard Warning Signals	Lamps that flash simultaneously to the front and rear, on both sides of a commercial motor vehicle, to indicate to an approaching driver the presence of a vehicular hazard
Head Lamps	Lamps used to provide general illumination ahead of a motor vehicle
Identification Lamps	Lamps used to identify certain types of commercial vehicles
Lamp	A device used to produce artificial light
License Plate Lamp	A lamp used to illuminate the license plate on the rear of a motor vehicle
Reflex Reflector	A device on a vehicle which is used to warn an approaching driver of a vehicular hazard by reflecting lights from the lamps on the approaching vehicle
Side Marker Lamps	Lamps used on each side of a trailer to indicate its overall length
Stop Lamps	Lamps near the rear of a motor vehicle which indicate that the service brake system is engaged

Tail Lamps

Lamps used to designate the rear of a motor vehicle

Turn Signals

Lamps used to indicate a change in direction. They emit a flashing light on the side of the motor vehicle toward which a turn will be made.

Legend		
Number	Device	Color
1	Head lamps (2) optional (4)	White
2	Side marker lamps front (2)	Amber
3	Side reflectors front (2)	Amber
4	Turn signal lamps front (2)	Amber
4a	Turn signal lamps front (2) (optional location)	Amber
5	Identification lamps front (3)	Amber
5a	Identification lamps front (3) (optional location)	Amber
6	Clearance lamps front (2)	Amber
7	Side marker lamps rear (2)	Red
8	Side reflectors rear (2)	Red

Number	Device	Color
9	Identification lamps rear	Red
10	Clearance lamps rear (2)	Red
11	Reflectors rear (2)	Red
12	Stop lamps rear (2)	Red
13	License plate lamp rear (1)	White
14	Backup lamp rear (1)	White

15	Side marker lamps —
	Intermediate
	    side (2) if vehicle
	    is 30 feet or more
	    in length
		Amber

16	Side reflectors —
	Intermediate
	    side (2) if vehicle
	    is 30 feet or more
	    in length
		Amber

17	Turn signal lamps rear (2)	Amber or Red
18	Tail lamps rear (2)	Red

Large Bus

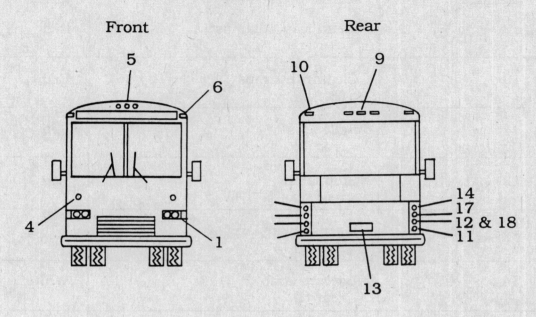

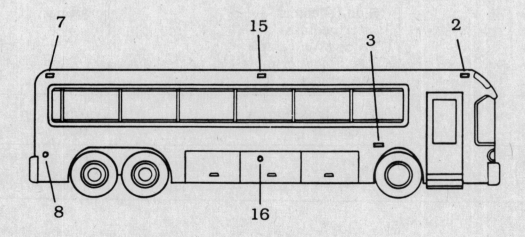

FIGURE L-1: LIGHTS AND REFLECTORS

Section M
Return of Out-of-State Licenses

Commercial vehicle operators are allowed to hold only one commercial driver's license. This license must be from the state of the operator's residence. All other licenses should be mailed back to the state that issued them so that records can be cleared. Here are the addresses for the return of out-of-state licenses.

Alabama Department of Public Safety
Montgomery, AL 36130

Alaska Division of Motor Vehicles
Juneau, AK 99802

Arizona Motor Vehicle Division
Phoenix, AZ 85007

Arkansas Office of Driver Services
Little Rock, AR 72203

California Department of Motor Vehicles
Sacramento, CA 95818

Colorado Motor Vehicle Division
Denver, CO 80204

Connecticut Department of
  Motor Vehicles
Wethersfield, CT 06109

Delaware Division of Motor Vehicles
Dover, DE 19903

District of Columbia Bureau of Motor
  Vehicle Services
Washington, DC 20001

Florida Division of Driver Licenses
Neil Kirkman Building
Tallahassee, FL 32399-0575

Georgia State Patrol
Atlanta, GA 30316

Hawaii Motor Vehicle Safety Office
Honolulu, HI 96813

Idaho Motor Vehicle Bureau
Boise, ID 83731-0034

Illinois Driver Services Department
Springfield, IL 62723

Indiana Bureau of Motor Vehicles
Indianapolis, IN 46204

Iowa Office of Driver Services
Des Moines, IA 50319

Kansas Division of Vehicles
Topeka, KS 66626

Kentucky Department of Vehicle
  Regulation
Frankfort, KY 40622

Louisiana Office of Motor Vehicles
Baton Rouge, LA 70806

Maine Motor Vehicle Division
Augusta, ME 04333

Maryland Motor Vehicle Administration
Glen Burnie, MD 21062

Massachusetts Registry of Motor Vehicles
Boston, MA 02114

Michigan Department of State
Lansing, MI 48918

Minnesota Driver & Vehicle Service
Division
St. Paul, MN 55155

Mississippi Highway Safety Patrol
Jackson, MS 39216

Missouri Division of Motor Vehicle &
Drivers Licensing
Jefferson City, MO 65105

Montana Motor Vehicles Division
Helena, MT 59620

Nebraska Department of Motor Vehicles
Lincoln, NE 68509

Nevada Department of Motor Vehicles
Carson City, NV 89711

New Hampshire Division of Motor
Vehicles
Concord, NH 03305

New Jersey Division of Motor Vehicles
Trenton, NJ 08666

New Mexico Motor Vehicle Division
Santa Fe, NM 85703

New York Department of Motor Vehicles
Albany, NY 12228

North Carolina Division of Motor Vehicles
Raleigh, NC 27697

North Dakota Drivers License Division
Bismarck, ND 58505

Ohio Bureau of Motor Vehicles
Columbus, OH 43233

Oklahoma Department of Public Safety
Oklahoma City, OK 73136

Oregon Motor Vehicles Division
Salem, OR 97314

Pennsylvania Department of
Transportation
Harrisburg, PA 17120

Rhode Island Division of Motor Vehicles
Providence, RI 02903

South Carolina Motor Vehicle Division
Columbia, SC 29216

South Dakota Division of Motor Vehicles
Pierre, SD 57501-2080

Tennessee Department of Safety
Nashville, TN 37219

Texas Department of Public Safety
Austin, TX 78752

Utah Driver License Division
Salt Lake City, UT 84119

Vermont Department of Motor Vehicles
Montpelier, VT 05603-0001

Virginia Department of Motor Vehicles
Richmond, VA 23269

Washington Department of Licensing
Olympia, WA 98504

West Virginia Department of Motor
Vehicles
Charleston, WV 25317

Wisconsin Division of Motor Vehicles
Madison, WI 53702

Wyoming Field Services Division
Cheyenne, WY 82002

Source: Federal Highway Administration

Section N
State Commercial Driver's License Offices

For more information about your state's commercial driver's license program, you can contact the offices below.   Address your inquiries to the CDL COORDINATOR:

ALABAMA
Department of Public Safety
P.O. Box 1471
Montgomery, AL 36192

ALASKA
Division of Motor Vehicles
Post Box 20
450 Whittier Street
Juneau, AK 99802

ARIZONA
Motor Vehicle Division
P.O. Box 2100
Phoenix, AZ 85001

ARKANSAS
Office of Driver Services
P.O. Box 1272
Little Rock, AR 72203

CALIFORNIA
Department of Motor Vehicles
P.O. Box 932328
Sacramento, CA 95818

COLORADO
Motor Vehicle Division
516 Acoma Street
Denver, CO 80204-5195

CONNECTICUT
Department of Motor Vehicles
60 State Street
Wethersfield, CT 06109-1896

DELAWARE
Division of Motor Vehicles
P.O. Box 698
Dover, DE 19903

DISTRICT OF COLUMBIA
Bureau of Motor Vehicle Services
301 "C" Street, NW
Washington, DC 20001

FLORIDA
Department of Highway Safety
   & Motor Vehicles
Division of Driver Licenses
Room A403, Neil Kirkman Building
2900 Appalachee Parkway
Tallahassee, FL 32301

GEORGIA
Georgia State Patrol
P.O. Box 1456
Atlanta, GA 30371

HAWAII
Motor Vehicle Safety Office
79 S. Nimitz Highway
Honolulu, HI 96813

IDAHO
Transportation Department
P.O. Box 7129
3311 West State
Boise, ID 83703-1129

ILLINOIS
Driver Services Department
2701 S. Dirksen Parkway
Springfield, IL 62723

INDIANA
Bureau of Motor Vehicles
100 North Senate Avenue
Indianapolis, IN 46204

IOWA
Office of Driver Services
Lucas State Office Building
Des Moines, IA 50319

KANSAS
Division of Motor Vehicles
State Office Building
Topeka, KS 66626-0001

KENTUCKY
Kentucky State Police
919 Versailles Road
Frankfort, KY 40601

LOUISIANA
Office of Motor Vehicles
P.O. Box 64886
Baton Rouge, LA 70896

MAINE
Motor Vehicle Division
Child Street, Station 29
Augusta, ME 04333

MARYLAND
Motor Vehicle Administration
6601 Ritchie Highway
Glen Burnie, MD 21062

MASSACHUSETTS
Registry of Motor Vehicles
100 Nashua Street
Boston, MA 02114

MICHIGAN
Department of State
Office of Traffic Safety
7064 Crowner Drive
Lansing, MI 48018

MINNESOTA
Driver & Vehicle Services Division
161 Transportation Building
St. Paul, MN 55155

MISSISSIPPI
Highway Safety Patrol
P.O. Box 958
Jackson, MS 39205

MISSOURI
Division of Motor Vehicle
  Driver Licensing
P.O. Box 629
Jefferson City, MO 65105

MONTANA
Division of Motor Vehicles
303 N. Roberts
Helena, MT 59620

NEBRASKA
Driver Services Division
301 Centennial Mall S.
P.O. Box 94789
Lincoln, NE 68509

NEVADA
Department of Motor Vehicles
555 Wright Way
Carson City, NV 89711

NEW HAMPSHIRE
Department of Motor Vehicles
James H. Hays Safety Building,
Concord, NH 03305

NEW JERSEY
Division of Motor Vehicles
25 South Montgomery Street
Trenton, NJ 08666

NEW MEXICO
Motor Vehicle Division
P.O. Box 1028
Santa Fe, NM 87504-1028

NEW YORK
Department of Motor Vehicles
Empire State Plaza
Albany, NY 12228

NORTH CAROLINA
Division of Motor Vehicles
1100 New Bern Avenue
Raleigh, NC 27697

NORTH DAKOTA
Driver's License & Traffic Safety
  Division
600 E Boulevard Avenue
Bismark, ND 58505-0700

OHIO
Department of Highway Safety
240 Parsons Avenue
Columbus, OH 43266-0563

OKLAHOMA
Department of Public Safety
P.O. Box 11415
Oklahoma City, OK 73136

OREGON
Department of Transportation
1905 Lana Avenue, NE
Salem, OR 97314

PENNSYLVANIA
Bureau of Driver Licensing
Transportation & Safety Building
Harrisburg, PA 17120

RHODE ISLAND
Division of Motor Vehicles
State Office Building, Rm 100
Providence, RI 02903

SOUTH CAROLINA
Dept. of Highways and Public
  Transportation
P.O. Box 1498
Columbia, SC 29216-0025

SOUTH DAKOTA
Department of Revenue
118 W. Capitol Avenue
Pierre, SD 57501-2080

TENNESSEE
Department of Safety
1150 Foster Avenue
Nashville, TN 37210

TEXAS
Department of Public Safety
5805 N. Lamar Boulevard
Box 4087
Austin, TX 78773-0001

UTAH
Driver License Division
4501 South 2700 West
Salt Lake City, UT 84119

VERMONT
Department of Motor Vehicles
120 State Street
State Office Building
Montpelier, VT 05603-0001

VIRGINIA
Department of Motor Vehicles
P.O. Box 27412
Richmond, VA 23269

WASHINGTON
Department of Licensing
Olympia, WA 98504

WEST VIRGINIA
West Virginia State Police
725 Jefferson Road
South Charleston, WV 25309

WISCONSIN
Bureau of Driver Licensing
P.O. Box 7917
Madison, WI 53707

WYOMING
Wyoming Department of Revenue and Tax
122 W. 25th Street
Herschler Building
Cheyenne, WY 82002-0110

Index